The New World of Dreams

THE
NEW WORLD
OF DREAMS

Ralph L. Woods and
Herbert B. Greenhouse

EDITORS

MACMILLAN PUBLISHING CO., INC.

NEW YORK

Macmillan Publishing Co., Inc.
866 Third Avenue, New York, N.Y. 10022
Collier-Macmillan Canada Ltd.

Library of Congress Cataloging in Publication Data

Woods, Ralph Louis, 1904-   comp.
    The new world of dreams.

    Bibliography: p.
    1. Dreams—Collected works. I. Greenhouse,
Herbert B., joint comp. II. Title.
BF1078.W65 1974   153.6'3'08   73-16903
ISBN 0-02-631540-8

Second Printing 1974
Printed in the United States of America

Acknowledgments

The editors and the publisher gratefully acknowledge the courtesy and cooperation of the following publishers, agents, and copyright owners in granting
permission to use selections from the works mentioned below:

Joseph Adelson, from his "Creativity and the Dream," *Merrill-Palmer
Quarterly*, vol. 6, Fall 1959.

George Allen & Unwin Ltd., from Wilhelm Stekel's *The Interpretation of
Dreams*, translated by Eden and Cedar Paul; from Alfred Adler's *What Life
Should Mean to You*.

Kenneth Z. Altshuler, from his "A Survey of Dreams in the Aged," (coauthored with Martin Barad and Alvin I. Goldfarb), *Archives of General
Psychiatry*, vol. 8 (1), 1963.

American Anthropological Association, reproduced from *American Anthropologist*, vol. 54 (4), 1952. Excerpts from "The Manifest Content of
Dreams: A Challenge to Social Science" by Dorothy Eggan.

American Association for the Advancement of Science, for "Incidence of
Color in Immediately Recalled Dreams" by E. Khan et al., *Science*, vol. 137,
pp. 1054–1055, Table 1, 28 September 1962, copyright 1962 by the American
Association for the Advancement of Science; "Sleep Stage Characteristics of
Long and Short Sleepers" by W. B. Webb, and H. W. Agnew, Jr., *Science*,
vol. 168, pp. 146–147, Table 1, Fig. 1, 3 April 1970, copyright 1970 by the
American Association for the Advancement of Science; "The Effect of Dream
Deprivation" by W. Dement, *Science*, vol. 131, pp. 1705–1707, 10 June 1960,
copyright 1960 by the American Association for the Advancement of Science;
"Ontogenetic Development of the Human Sleep-Dream Cycle" by Howard P.
Roffwarg et al., *Science*, vol. 152, pp. 604–619, Diagram, 29 April, copyright
1966 by the American Association for the Advancement of Science.

American Medical Association, from "A Survey of Dreams in the Aged"
by Kenneth Z. Altshuler, Martin Barad, and Alvin I. Goldfarb, *Archives of
General Psychiatry*, vol. 8 (1), 1963, copyright 1963 by the American Medical
Association; "Posthypnotically Suggested Dreams and the Sleep Cycle" by
Johann Martin Stoyva, *Archives of General Psychiatry*, vol. 12, March 1965,
copyright 1965 by the American Medical Association.

American Psychiatric Association, from "Subliminal and Supraliminal Influences on Dreams" by Charles Fisher, Ph.D., *American Journal of Psychiatry*,
vol. 116, May 1960, copyright 1960 by the American Psychiatric Association;
"Psychiatric Observations on Congenital and Acquired Deafness: Symbolic
and Perceptual Processes in Dreams" by Jack H. Mendelson, Leonard Siger,
and Philip Solomon, *American Journal of Psychiatry*, vol. 116, April 1960,
copyright 1960 by the American Psychiatric Association.

Bailliere, Tindall, & Cassell Ltd., from Carl G. Jung's *Collected Papers on
Analytical Psychology*, 2d ed., 1917, translated by Dr. C. E. Long.

Basic Books, Inc., from Chapters 3, 4, 5, 6, and 7 of *The Interpretation of*

Dreams by Sigmund Freud, translated and edited by James Strachey, published by Basic Books, Inc., Publishers, N. Y.

Bodley Head Ltd., England, from *The Dream World* by R. L. Megroz, 1939.

Clarendon Press, from *Religion and Art in Ashanti* by R. S. Rattray, © 1927 by Oxford University Press.

Collins Publishers, England, from *Memories, Dreams, Reflections* by Carl G. Jung, translated by Richard and Clara Winston, 1961.

William Dement, from his "The Relation of Eye Movements, Body Motility, and External Stimuli to Dream Content" (co-authored with Edward A. Wolpert), *The Journal of Experimental Psychology*, vol. 55, No. 6, June 1958; "The Relation of Eye Movements During Sleep to Dream Activity: An Objective Method for the Study of Dreaming" (co-authored with Nathaniel Kleitman), *The Journal of Experimental Psychology*, vol. 53, No. 5, 1957; "The Effect of Dream Deprivation," *Science*, vol. 131, June 10, 1960; "Ontogenetic Development of the Human Sleep-Dream Cycle (co-authored with Howard P. Roffwarg and Joseph N. Muzio), *Science*, vol. 152, Diagram, April 29, 1966.

Dodd Mead & Co., from Carl G. Jung's *Collected Papers on Analytical Psychology*, translated by Dr C E. Long.

Downe Publishing, Inc., from "Where Do Nightmares Come From?" by Bruno Bettelheim, *Ladies Home Journal*, February 1969, © 1969 Downe Publishing, Inc.

E. P. Dutton & Co., Inc., from *The Dream World* by R. L. Megroz, published by E. P. Dutton & Co., Inc., and used with their permission.

Elsevier Publishing Co., from *Sleeping and Waking* by Ian Oswald, copyright 1962.

Faber & Faber, Ltd, England, from *An Experiment in Time* by J. W. Dunne, 1927.

Charles Fisher, from his "Subliminal and Supraliminal Influences on Dreams," *American Journal of Psychiatry*, vol. 116, May 1960; "An Experimental Approach to Dream Psychology Through the Use of Hypnosis" (coauthored with Leslie H. Farber), *The Psychoanalytic Quarterly*, vol. 12, 1943; "Incidence of Color in Immediately Recalled Dreams" (coauthored with Edwin Kahn, Joseph Barmack, and William Dement), *Science*, vol. 137, Table 1, September 28, 1962.

David Foulkes, for his "Theories of Dream Formation and Recent Studies of Dream Consciousness," *Psychological Bulletin*, vol. 62, No. 4, October 1964.

W. H. Freeman & Co., from "Science and the Citizen," *Scientific American*, May 1969, copyright © 1969 by Scientific American, Inc. All rights reserved.

Erika Fromm, from her "Formation and Evaluation of Hypotheses in Dream Interpretation" (coauthored with Thomas M. French), *Journal of Psychology*, vol. 54, 1962.

General Learning Corporation, from *The Psychology of Dreaming* by Robert L. Van de Castle, copyright © 1971 by General Learning Corporation.

Sanford J. Greenburger Associates, Inc., for the estate of Alfred Adler, from his *What Life Should Mean to You*, copyright © 1931, 1958 by Kurt A. Adler.

Calvin S. Hall, from his *The Meaning of Dreams*, Harper & Row, 1953; "A Ubiquitous Sex Difference in Dreams" (coauthored with Bill Domhoff), *Journal of Abnormal and Social Psychology*, vol. 66, no. 3, 1963.

Hamish Hamilton, Ltd., England, from *Lucid Dreams* by Celia Green, copyright © 1968, Institute of Psychophysical Research (Hamish Hamilton Ltd., London).

Harvard University Press and Loeb Classical Library, from *Geography of Strabo*, vol. 6, translated by H. A. Jones, Cambridge, Mass., 1929.

Holt, Rinehart, & Winston, Inc., from *The Integration of Personality* by Carl G. Jung, translated by S. M. Dell, copyright 1939 © 1967 by Holt, Rinehart, & Winston, Inc.

Hutchinson Publishing Group Ltd., England, from *The Analysis of Dreams* by Medard Boss, edition of Rider and Co., 1957.

Journal of Humanistic Psychology, from "Dreams and Human Potential" by Stanley Krippner and William Hughes, *Journal of Humanistic Psychology*, vol. 10, No. 1, Spring 1970.

Journal Press, from "Formation and Evaluation of Hypotheses in Dream Interpretation" by Erika Fromm and Thomas M. French, *Journal of Psychology*, 54, 1962, copyright 1962 by The Journal Press.

David Ballin Klein, for "The Experimental Production of Dreams Through Hypnosis," a University of Texas Bulletin, March 1930.

Stanley Krippner, from "Dreams and Human Potential" (coauthored with William Hughes), *Journal of Humanistic Psychology*, vol. 10, No. 1, Spring 1970; "An Investigation of Dream Content among Male Pre-operative Transsexuals" (coauthored with Richard Davidson and Geraldine Lenz) and "A Second Investigation of Dream Content During Pregnancy" (coauthored with Norman Posner, William Pomerance, and Stuart Fischer), papers published by the Association for the Psychophysiological Study of Sleep, First International Congress, Bruges, Belgium, 1971.

Rolf Krojanker, M.D., from his "Training of the Unconscious by Hypnodramatic Re-enactment of Dreams," *Group Psychotherapy*, vol. 15 (2), 1962.

Little, Brown & Co., from *Nightmares and Human Conflict* by John E. Mack, copyright 1970.

Liveright Publishing Corp., from *The Handbook of Dream Analysis* by Emil A. Gutheil, copyright © 1951 by Liveright Publishing Corporation; *The Interpretation of Dreams* by Wilhelm Stekel, copyright ® 1970 by Liveright Publishing Corporation.

Longmans Group Ltd., England, from *Children's Dreams* by Charles W. Kimmins, 1920.

Sandor Lorand, M.D., for his "Dream Interpretation in the Talmud," *International Journal of Psychoanalysis*, vol. 38, 1957.

John E. Mack, from his *Nightmares and Human Conflict*, Little, Brown & Co., 1970.

Macmillan Publishing Co., Inc., from *Dream Telepathy* by Montague Ullman, Stanley Krippner, and Alan Vaughan, copyright © 1973 by Montague Ullman, Stanley Krippner, and Alan Vaughan; *An Experiment in Time* by J. W. Dunne, copyright 1938 by Macmillan Publishing Co., Inc.

Jack H. Mendelson, M.D., from his "Psychiatric Observations on Congenital and Acquired Deafness: Symbolic and Perceptual Processes in Dreams" (coauthored with Leonard Siger and Philip Solomon), *American Journal of Psychiatry*, vol. 116, April 1960.

Merrill-Palmer Institute, from "Creativity and the Dream," by Joseph Adelson, *Merrill-Palmer Quarterly*, vol. 6, Fall 1959.

Natural History, for "The Evolution of Sleep" by Truett Allison and Henry Van Twyver, reprinted from *Natural History* magazine, February 1970. Copyright © The American Museum of Natural History, 1970.

New Yorker, from "A Third State of Existence" by Calvin Trillin, *New Yorker*, 18 September 1965. Copyright © 1965 by the *New Yorker* Magazine, Inc.

Ian Oswald, from his *Sleeping and Waking*, Elsevier Publishing Co., 1962.

Psychoanalytic Review, for "Hermaphroditic Dreams" by Isador H. Coriat, reprinted from *Psychoanalytic Review*, vol. 4, 1917, through the courtesy of the Editors and the Publisher, National Psychological Association for Psychoanalysis, New York, N. Y.

Psychology Today, for "The Dreams of Freud and Jung" by Calvin S. Hall and Bill Domhoff, reprinted from *Psychology Today*, June 1968. Copyright © Communications/Research/Machines, Inc.

Quadrangle Books, from *The Third Reich of Dreams* by Charlotte Beradt, copyright 1968 by Quadrangle Books.

Random House, Inc., from *Memories, Dreams, Reflections*, by Carl G. Jung, recorded and edited by Aniela Jaffe, translated by Richard and Clara Winston. Copyright © 1961, 1962, 1963 by Random House, Inc. Reprinted by permission of the publisher, Pantheon Books, a Division of Random House, Inc.

Rider & Co., from "The Pineal Doorway—A Record of Research" by Oliver Fox, *Occult Review*, vol. 31, No. 4, April 1920.

Routledge & Kegan Paul Ltd., from *Egyptian Magic* by E. A. Wallis-Budge; *Sex and Repression in Savage Society* by Bronislaw Malinowski, 1927.

Paul Sacerdote, from his *Induced Dreams*, Vantage Press, 1967, copyright 1967 by Paul Sacerdote, M.D.

Charles Scribner's Sons, from *The Psychology of Sleep* by David Foulkes, reprinted by permission of Charles Scribner's Sons. Copyright © 1966 David Foulkes.

Howard Shevrin, from "The Measurement of Preconscious Perception in Dreams and Images: An Investigation of the Poetzl Phenomenon" (coauthored with Lester Luborsky), *Journal of Abnormal and Social Psychology*, vol. 56, No. 2, March 1958.

Society for Psychical Research, London, England, from "Subconscious Reasoning" by William Romaine Newbold, *Proceedings*, S.P.R., vol. 12, 1896.

Walter A. Stewart, M.D., from his "Comments on the Manifest Content of Certain Types of Unusual Dreams," *Psychoanalytic Quarterly*, vol. 36 (3), 1967.

Johann Martin Stoyva, from his "Posthypnotically Suggested Dreams and the Sleep Cycle," *Archives of General Psychiatry*, vol. 12, March 1965.

University of California Press, from "Parapsychological Dream Studies" by Martin Ebon and "Logical and Philosophical Problems of the Dream" by Roger Caillois, originally published in *The Dream and Human Societies* by the University of California Press, 1966. Reprinted by permission of the Regents of the University of California.

Robert L. Van de Castle, from his *The Psychology of Dreaming*, General Learning Corporation, 1971.

A. P. Watt & Son, England, and Faber & Faber Ltd. for the Estate of J. W. Dunne, from *An Experiment in Time* by J. W. Dunne, 1927.

W. B. Webb, from his "Sleep Stage Characteristics of Long and Short Sleepers" (coauthored with H. W. Agnew, Jr.), *Science*, vol. 168, Table 1, Fig. 1, 3 April 1970.

Carolyn Winget, for her "A Comparison of the Dreams of Homosexual and Non-homosexual Males" (coauthored with Ronald A. Farrell), First International Congress, the Association for the Psychophysiological Study of Sleep, Bruges, Belgium, 1971.

Table of Contents

xi

PART II

DREAM THEORIES THROUGHOUT THE WORLD 107

Introduction to Part II   HERBERT GREENHOUSE   109

PART III
THE NEW WORLD OF DREAM RESEARCH 269

Introduction

TWO DATES ARE of paramount importance in the history of dreams: 1900 and 1952. In 1900 Sigmund Freud published *The Interpretation of Dreams*, which for more than seventy years has been a source book for psychiatrists, social scientists, and dream researchers. Freud put the study of dreams on a scientific basis by showing that they were a mirror of the unconscious mind and played a dynamic role in the psychological life of the dreamer. Before Freud, psychologists, philosophers, theologians, and even primitive peoples had had intimations that dreams were self-revealing, but Freud made the most comprehensive analysis of dreams up to that time and stressed the importance of the "latent" or hidden content of th dream.

Then, in 1952, two researchers at the University of Chicago, Eugene Aserinsky and Nathaniel Kleitman, made the astonishing discovery that when a sleeper dreams, his eyes move back and forth spasmodically as though he were watching something. By attaching electrodes to the sleeper's forehead near his eyes, the researchers could observe on a polygraph when the rapid eye movements, known as REMS, began. At these times, when the sleeper was awakened, he would usually report that he had been dreaming. Since 1952 hundreds of experiments have uncovered many new facts about sleep and dreams, which are discussed in the articles and research papers in Part III of this book. The main fact disclosed was that everyone dreams every night and has from four to six dream periods at fairly regular intervals, with the first dream taking place about ninety minutes after sleep begins and lasting from five to ten minutes, and the following dream periods becoming progressively longer.

Thus dreaming has been established as both a psychological and a biological phenomenon. In our dreams, the psychiatrists tell us, we balance our emotional accounts by acting out our repressed desires, mostly in symbolic form (Freud); we review our problems and experiment with solutions (Hadfield); we reveal our conflicts to ourselves (Stekel); we continue the lifestyle of our waking life (Adler); or we strive to return to wholeness by tapping the unconscious sources of knowledge available to all dreamers (Jung). But no matter what the content or motivation of our dreams, we must dream every night in a prescribed cycle because a biological rhythm of sleeping and dreaming starts from birth—and perhaps from the fetus stage—and continues throughout life. If we are deprived of our dreams, we suffer psychological and possibly physical damage.

Within the framework of these two discoveries about dreams—and outside it—there is room for endless theorizing about the nature of dreaming. In *The World of Dreams* (New York, Random House, 1947), editor Ralph Woods states that "most people are endlessly fascinated by dreams but few of us know much, if anything, about the many expert studies, ingenious scientific experiments, philosophical speculations, theological conclusions, and psychological theories concerned not only with why we dream, but why we experience various kinds of dreams and what they mean." Thus *The World of Dreams* was born, an anthology that explored dreams and dream theory from Pharaoh to Freud and well into the present century, a book that has proved of inestimable value to dream researchers such as Calvin Hall, Robert Van de Castle, Morton Kelsey, and others interested as professionals and laymen in the study of dreams.

The present volume, *The New World of Dreams*, has streamlined Woods's anthology, retaining pertinent selections from the earlier book and adding important new material from recent years. The most significant addition, of course, has been in the field of experimental research that followed the discovery of the REMS, and a complete section has been devoted to the fascinating work in the dream laboratories of 1952–1974.

The New World of Dreams, like its predecessor *The World of Dreams*, looks at the dream from every point of view. What have philosophers as well as psychologists and dream researchers thought about dreams and what they mean? What have writers and poets said about dreams? Physiologists, sociologists, anthropologists, theologians, medical doctors? Ordinary people with extraordinary dreams? How important were (and are) dreams in primitive societies, in ancient civilizations such as India and Persia, in the Old and New Testaments?

And what of the dream itself? Dreams do not have to be interpreted to be enjoyed for their own sake. Dreams have endless variety and drama. Dreams, like plays and motion pictures, occur in settings that may be full of color, indoors or outdoors. Dreams have characters, action, conflict, love and hate, all the essentials of a story. Medard Boss, a psychiatrist, believes that the dream should be explored without preconceived theories because it may be as real to the dreamer as his waking life, perhaps even more real. This is an old point of view, taken very seriously in ancient times and especially in primitive cultures, where dreams are not separated from life but are an integral part of living.

In order to examine the many facets of the dream, *The New World of Dreams* is divided into three parts: (1) "The World of Dreams and Dreamers," (2) "Dream Theories throughout the World," and (3) "The New World of Dream Research." Part I concentrates on the *manifest* content of dreams, the way the dream appears to us without its hidden motivation (*latent* content). We ask who does the dreaming—men, women, children, the elderly, college students, the sexually aberrant—and what do they dream about. We look at the theme of each dream—the military dream, the political dream, the musical dream, the telepathic dream, and so on.

Part II explores the theories of dreams for the last two thousand and more years and in various parts of the world. There were primitive societies, past and present, which believed that the dreamer wanders in spirit among the dead and the living, seeking advice for his daily behavior. There was the belief that the dreamer sees into the future. There was, and still is, the spate of dream books that give simple formulas for understanding the dream. There was the conviction during most of the nineteenth century that dreams were merely the result of eating the wrong food the night before or were caused by outside stimuli during sleep. Then came Freud and his contemporaries with a new in-depth look at dreams, along with theorists who studied the fringe area of dreaming: sleepwalking, narcolepsy, nightmares, etc., as well as the effect of drugs and hypnotic trances on dreams.

Part III covers the experimental period from 1952 to 1974, and describes the procedure in dream laboratories and the new body of facts learned about dreams and how they substantiate or refute the theories of the past. There are articles on such topics as color in dreams, the effect of hypnosis on nighttime dreaming, what happens when people are prevented from sleeping and dreaming, how stimuli before and during dreams are incorporated into the action of the dream, and how the dreams of the same night are dramatically related.

The New World of Dreams gives more space than *The World of Dreams* to the paranormal experience because the study of psychic phenomena has made giant strides since 1947 and has been accepted as a scientific discipline. Many of the paranormal dreams described in Part I, such as the Aberfan coal slide tragedy and the "Dream of a Severed Head" were investigated by researchers who were scientifically oriented. Of special importance are the experiments in dream telepathy at the Division of Parapsychology and Psychophysics of Maimonides Medical Center in Brooklyn, New York.

The editors of the present work feel that interest in dreams, stimulated by the new discoveries, is now at a peak. We believe that the book has equal appeal to professionals in the dream field and to intelligent laymen who are fascinated by the mystery of dreams and wish to have a more comprehensive understanding of them.

The New World of Dreams

PART I

THE WORLD OF DREAMS AND DREAMERS

Introduction to Part I

HERBERT GREENHOUSE

WHAT DO PEOPLE *dream about?*

Calvin S. Hall, director of the Institute of Dream Research, collected more than ten thousand dreams and analyzed them in terms of their characters, the interactions between the dream characters, the emotions of the dreamer, the locale or setting of each dream, and the color content of the dream. How many persons appear in the average dream? How many males and females? How many times does the dream take place in an indoor or outdoor setting, on the top floor or in the basement of a house? How often does the dreamer ride in an automobile, a plane, or a train? How active or passive is the dreamer? Does he sit, walk, run, fly, or glide in his dream? Is he happy or sad? Does he feel friendly or hostile to the other characters in his dream?

Who are the people that dream?

What do men dream about? Women and children? Old people? The blind and deaf? How passive or aggressive are men and women in their dreams? How do the dreams of lesbians and homosexuals differ from those of other men and women? How do creative persons differ in their dreams from the unimaginative? What do pregnant women dream about? Do the dreams of black people differ from those of whites? Married from single?

What is the theme of a dream?

Dreams reveal the preoccupation of the dreamer with his work or profession, his hobbies and goals, and the political, social, and environmental milieu in which he lives. A citizen of Hitler's Germany dreams that the Gestapo can read her thoughts. The Carthaginian general Hannibal dreams

3

that he must conquer Rome. The composer Tartini dreams that the devil plays the violin for him. Writer Robert Louis Stevenson dreams that "little people" perform on the stage of his mind and give him plots for books. There are paradoxical dreams in which we are transformed into something else, as Chuang Tzŭ was when he dreamed he was a butterfly. We have paranormal dreams in which we see the future or contact the minds of other dreamers. We have "lucid" dreams when we know we are dreaming.

"The World of Dreams and Dreamers" explores the dream for its own sake, in all its variety of characters, settings, actions; its range and color; its themes; its reflections of the dreamer himself in terms of age, sex, marital status, race, etc. There is less attempt to analyze the dream on a deeper level than is done later in the book, although many of the articles in this section are written by dream researchers who are quite capable of doing so. The emphasis is on the manifest content of the dream, the materials of the dream itself.

A. WHAT PEOPLE DREAM AB

What We Dream About

CALVIN S. HALL

DREAM SETTINGS

A DREAM LIKE A PLAY nearly always has a setting. The setting may be one that is strange and unfamiliar to the dreamer, or it may be one that he recognizes in a vague and uncertain way without feeling quite at home in it. Other settings are taken from the dreamer's everyday life and appear in his dreams as faithful and realistic reproductions of familiar scenes. In a few dreams, about five in every hundred, the dreamer is not aware of the setting; in others, there is little else save scenery, as in the following dream of a young man.

I was standing on a cliff near the edge. As I look down I see huge blocks of stone and the sea pounding against them and churning itself into white, foamy and sparkling particles. As I gaze out calmly across the blue water, I can see the setting sun sink like a blazing ball of fire and it creates a golden path across the waters to my feet. The sky is light blue and very light on the horizon. Yet at the same time I feel as though there is a bright noonday sun shining down on me. I am standing on grass and it feels like a thick carpet beneath my feet, very soft and comforting. On the whole, the water is very blue and sometimes almost black or a deep purple violet.

In this pretty dream, there is no action, no people other than the dreamer, no strong emotion—just scenery.

In about fifteen out of every hundred dreams the dreamer is in a conveyance, the most frequent kind being an automobile and to a lesser degree, airplanes, boats and streetcars. The significance of conveyance settings is that the dreamer is going somewhere, he is on the move, he is in motion. Movement represents such ideas as ambition, progress and achievement, breaking family ties, fleeing from something or dying. Automobiles, trains, boats and airplanes are instruments of power, and as such can stand for the vital energy of one's impulses, particularly the sex impulse. We use the language of conveyances when we speak of the "transports of love." In days gone by, the horse was a favorite embodiment of sexual energy in dreams, but the automobile and airplane have been displacing it as a symbol of virility in recent years.

Whether the dreamer is driving an automobile, steering a ship or piloting an airplane or whether he is merely a passenger in a conveyance signifies something about the dreamer's conception of himself. As a passenger, who is transported somewhere and who has little to say about the route, the destination, or the way in which the vehicle is being driven, the dreamer is playing the part of a passive person who is dependent upon others. As the driver, he expresses a self-image of independence and mastery. An example of a dream which contains both of these conceptions is the following one reported by a young woman.

I dreamed that my father and I were in an old Chevrolet. I was driving but I could not seem to make the car go up a very steep hill, so my father took the wheel.

This dreamer is attempting to view herself as a person of independence but as the going gets rough she reverts to a role of dependence upon her father.

The manner in which the driver controls the car may also be revealing. If the driver loses control of it, hits another vehicle or pedestrian, goes over a cliff, breaks through the guard rail of a bridge, crashes a red light or plunges down a steep hill, this means that he sees himself being overwhelmed by uncontrollable impulses. If he avoids having an accident by a display of skill, this means that he has brought the impulse under control.

A setting closely allied to conveyances is one in which the dreamer is on or walking along a street or road. About ten out of every hundred dreams have this type of setting. They do not appear to have the significance that conveyance dreams do, except for those in which the dreamer is crossing a bridge. This is rather an elegant symbol of a transition in one's life, a passing from youth to adulthood, from middle age to old age, or from life to death.

Dreamers spend quite a bit of their time in recreational settings, at dances and parties, on the beach and in swimming, watching sports events, and visiting amusement parks. These settings are frankly sensual in character, involving as they do pleasure and fun. About one out of every ten dreams is of this type. In contrast, places where people work—such as offices, factories, and stores—rarely appear in dreams, which implies that dreams are oriented more toward pleasure than work.

Houses or rooms in houses are by far the most popular type of dream locale. One out of every three dreams occurs in a dwelling, although usually it is not the dreamer's own house.

Among the specific places in a house where dreams occur, the living room is the most popular, followed by bedroom, kitchen, stairway, basement, bathroom, dining room and hall in that order. The particular room chosen may have a special symbolic significance. A basement for example, is a place where *base* deeds are committed or represents *base* unconscious impulses. . . .

DREAM CHARACTERS

A dream also has a cast. First, there is the dreamer himself. His role may be a minor one, hardly more than that of a spectator, or he may be the hero of the piece. In about fifteen out of every hundred dreams, the dreamer is the sole character. In the other eighty-five dreams, there are, on the average, two characters in addition to the dreamer. Although a trio of dream actors is typical, there is a good deal of variation. Some dreams may be as thickly populated as an elaborate extravaganza.

Who are these persons of the dream and why do they come into our dreams? We have made an actual count of dream characters, classified as to age, sex and relationship to the dreamer. These are our findings based upon the analysis of thousands of dreams.

Members of the dreamer's family constitute a fairly high percentage of dream characters. For younger dreamers, those in their late teens and early twenties, mother and father are dreamed about more often than any other family members, while among middle-aged dreamers the dreamer's mate and his children play important roles. Why should we dream about our family? We believe that the people who enter our dreams are ones with whom we are emotionally involved. The emotion may be one of love, fear or anger, or a mixture of these feelings. For young people who are not married and who do not have children, the most significant members of the family and the ones with whom they are emotionally involved are their parents. Young people are trying to break family ties and assert their independence yet they are apprehensive about leaving the security of home for the hazards of the world. Moreover, they often feel guilty about deserting their parents. On the other hand, older dreamers, having resolved these particular conflicts, find themselves involved with their husbands or wives and with their children. It is rather ironical that while children are dreaming about parents, parents are dreaming about children, and while husbands are dreaming about wives, wives are dreaming about husbands. It might be said that if a person wants to know who is dreaming about him, he will find the answer by consulting his own dreams. The people in his dreams are likely to be those who are dreaming about him.

Friends and acquaintances constitute another large class of dream characters. As might be expected, these characters are mostly of the same age as the dreamer. It is interesting that men dream more often about male friends and acquaints than they do about females, while women dream about equally of both sexes. This is really a large and significant difference. Why should it be true? We believe that the same explanation used to account for the differences among family members holds here. For men, relations with other men are more unsettled than relations with women. Women, on the other hand, have about an equal amount of emotional conflict with members of both sexes.

About four out of every ten characters in our dreams are strangers. Strangers represent the unknown, the ambiguous and the uncertain. Strangeness both frightens and fascinates. Sometimes a stranger in our dreams stands for an alien part of our own personality which we are reluctant to acknowledge as belonging to us. Sometimes a stranger personifies an aspect of an individual we know. For example, a woman dreams about being attacked by an unfamiliar man. The man may personify one of the conceptions she has of her boy friend, brother, husband or father, a conception that he is to be feared because she imagines he wants to harm her. She may not be aware of this conception, but it comes out in her dream nevertheless.

We rarely dream about prominent people, people we read about in the paper, hear over the radio or see in the movies. This fits in with our contention that dreams have very little to do with the world of current events. For all of our apparent concern about the world of public affairs, this concern does not go very deep nor it is emotionally relevant for us.

It should be remembered that the dreamer is the author of his dream and that it is he and he alone who determines who shall be invited into his dream. He invites those people for whom he has mixed feelings of affection and antagonism. They are people about whom he has divergent conceptions and with whom he has not achieved a stable relationship. They are the focal points of unresolved tension. When the tension abates, the appearance of the person in one's dreams diminishes, when the tension increases his entrances are more numerous. Those people toward whom the dreamer feels both love and hate or fear and hate occupy the center of the dream stage. Putting it in another way it can be said that we do not dream about people with whom we have achieved a stable and satisfying relationship. A husband and wife, for example, will not dream about one another if they have unmixed feelings of affection for each other. Nor will a person dream about someone toward whom he feels neutral.

You may ask, "What about those people who come into our dreams and who mean very little to us in waking life? Why did I dream about the butcher the other night, and a casual acquaintance whom I haven't seen or thought about for years the night before? Surely I am not emotionally involved with these people." These people come into our dreams because they stand for some significant aspect of our life or because they represent a feature of a person with whom we are involved, or because they are associated with some past conflict that is reasserting itself in our present life or because they symbolize some trait within ourselves. The corner butcher may represent an aggressive tendency in ourselves or someone else and the casual acquaintance of years ago may have some connection with a revived tension of the past. . . .

DREAM ACTIONS

What does a dreamer do in his dreams? An analysis of hundreds of dreams gives the following answer. The largest class of actions performed by the dreamer is that of movement, which includes all changes in location whether by riding, walking, running, jumping, climbing or falling. One out of every three recognized activities is of this type. Apparently sleep permits greater freedom of movement to the dreamer. Contrary to popular expectations, however, falling, floating and flying under one's own power do not often occur. Customarily the dreamer moves from place to place by conventional means. His excursions are usually limited to his home environment; rarely does he travel in foreign lands or strange places.

Passive activities such as talking, sitting, standing, watching, looking and seeing are very common in dreams, accounting for one-quarter of all activities. In fact, what strikes one most about dreams is the absence of strenuous activities. The dreamer does things which do not require a great deal of effort. Such commonplace waking pursuits as working, buying, and selling are virtually non-existent in dreams. Even drinking and eating occur very infrequently.

Manual and bodily activities, although not frequently represented in dreams, show considerable diversification, yet even here many of the common chores of waking life are omitted. Typing, sewing, ironing, working with tools, repairing something and a host of other daily pursuits are not found in the hundreds of dreams studied. Cooking, cleaning house, making beds and washing dishes are the only domestic activities found, and each of these occurs but once. Bathing, washing and grooming are also very infrequent. In contrast, swimming, dancing and playing games occur with greater frequency. The lesson to be learned from this analysis is that in our dreams we rarely engage in the routine duties of life. When we are being energetic, it is in the service of pleasure. The world of dreams does not duplicate the workaday world.

Women are more passive in their dreams than are men. If we divide dream activities into the two classes of *passive* which includes looking, sitting, talking, standing and the like, and *active* which includes running, driving a car, swimming, dancing, playing ball and similar actions, then women have far fewer of the active ones in their dreams as compared with men. Taking only the most strenuous activities performed by men and women in their dreams, the men's list includes unloading heavy steel rails, digging for ore, working on a boiler, scaling the side of a building, fist fighting and rowing a boat, while the women's list includes moving beds, mixing batter, sweeping stairs, sorting out flowers, taking clothes from a line and carrying dishes. It is obvious from these two lists that the activities of men require a greater expenditure of energy than those performed by women. Although dreams reveal that women are more passive than men they do not tell us the reason for this difference. It may be because women are physically weaker than men or it may be because women think of themselves as being more passive and phlegmatic. Men whether by nature or by self-conception appear to have an active orientation while women appear to have a passive one. . . .

DREAM EMOTIONS

Some dreams are such delightful fantasies that it is disappointing to wake up and find it was only a dream, while others are such terrifying nightmares that it is a relief to discover that they really did not happen. Between the two extremes of fantasy and nightmare there are many degrees of pleasure and displeasure. Some dreams contain both feelings; others appear to be without any emotional color at all.

Unpleasant dreams are more numerous than pleasant ones, and as one gets older the proportion of unpleasant dreams increases.

If dreams are classified according to the particular emotion experienced by the dreamer fear is more common than anger and sadness is more common than happiness. The unpleasant emotions of fear, anger and sadness are twice as frequent as the pleasant emotions of joy and happiness. Dreaming on the whole is not a pleasurable pastime.

When individual dreams series are analyzed, wide differences in the proportion of pleasant dreams are found. In some series only one or two dreams are pleasant, and in others, pleasant dreams predominate. James, for instance, reported that ten of his sixteen dreams were enjoyable. The subject matter of these ten dreams are making love to a girl in two dreams, playing softball, being admitted to medical school, wishing good luck to a candidate for public office, buying magazines in a drugstore, being home from the Army, being back in the Army with his friends, organizing a sabotage campaign against the Germans and leading a revolt against the Army.

James gets pleasure from a variety of activities—social, athletic, sexual and aggressive. His energy discharges itself easily and smoothly, nor does one find in his dreams that quality of impulsiveness which seems to be the mark of an inhibited person. His impulses flow within channels defined by fairly conventional standards. James does not feel anxious when he revolts against authority, as he does in one dream, or when he makes love to a girl, as he does in several, because he does not have a rigid, demanding conscience. James is one of those rare individuals who is able to express his impulses without feeling guilty. In waking life he is a sanguine, exuberant young man. He likes to play baseball, had a good time in the Army, finds people interesting, enjoys girls and thinks his parents are wonderful. He says that his mind is untroubled and that the future looks bright. He is the sort of person who likes to drink a glass of milk and eat a piece of cake before going to bed. His chief worries are making satisfactory grades in college, gaining admission to medical school, and supporting a wife. He admits that he is lazy. James' dreams convey an impression of a happy-go-lucky, uninhibited youth, which in truth, he is.

Happy dreams do not necessarily reflect a happy disposition. Our next dreamer, Jane, has a number of dreams that are very pleasing because in all of them she is achieving success. She is loudly applauded for making a brilliant speech, acclaimed for her skill as a dressmaker, envied by other girls for her popularity with boys, gratified by her success as a schoolteacher and pleased by her expert performance as an ice skater. Her need for attention is so great that in two dreams she has her family killed off for the sole purpose of attracting sympathy to herself. Actually, Jane is a retiring girl who has marked feelings of inferiority and a sense of her own worthlessness. Jane's unpleasant dreams, although they are in the minority, more nearly represent the true state of affairs. In one dream she is apprehensive because she thinks she is going to be asked to sing and she knows she cannot sing, and in another she is elected beauty queen but is unable to get to the center of the stage before another person is chosen. Jane is really an unhappy person who tries to compensate during sleep for her waking unhappiness by imagining that she is a successful, outstanding and admired person. Her pleasant dreams are more like daydreams with their conquering-hero theme than they are like nocturnal ones.

When we compare Jane's dreams with those of James, an important psychological difference is noted. Jane's happy dreams conform to a single type—they are all success stories—whereas James' pleasurable dreams display a great deal of variation. Jane concentrates all of her energy on achieving a single goal, while James deploys his energy in various directions. Furthermore, and this is the crucial difference, Jane compensates in her dreams for what she wants but does not have during waking life while James lives out his impulses in a regulated way just as he does when he is awake. Jane is an *autistic* person, that is, she gratifies her wishes in a fanciful unrealistic fashion. By comparison, James is *realistic*. He is on friendly terms with his needs, recognizes them for what they are, and proceeds to gratify them in a lifelike manner. His dreams are not improbable and magical as Jane's are, but rather convey an impression of verisimilitude. . . .

In this chapter we have made a quick survey of what normal people dream about. We have seen that each of the four major components of a dream helps us to understand the personal significance of dreams. Settings, characters, actions and emotions are visible projections of what is on the dreamer's mind. They are vehicles of thought bearing messages from the innermost realm of the mind.

B. THE PEOPLE WHO DREAM

The Difference between Men and Women Dreamers

CALVIN HALL and BILL DOMHOFF

In 3874 DREAM NARRATIVES collected from 1399 male dreamers, 5811 characters, exclusive of the dreamer, could be identified as to sex. Of these 5811 characters, 3695 are males and 2116 are females. The percentage of male characters is 64.

In 3065 dream narratives collected from 1418 female dreamers, 5342 characters, exclusive of the dreamer, could be identified as to sex. Of these 5342 characters, 2782 are males and 2560 are females. The percentage of male characters is 52.

The foregoing figures were obtained by pooling data from 11 separate investigations. The results for these 11 studies are presented in Table 1. The consistency among the percentages for the various populations is striking.

In addition to the principal fact established by these 11 investigations, namely, that in male dreams there are more male characters than female characters, and in female dreams there are nearly as many females as males, other conclusions may be drawn. These are:

1. The sex difference holds throughout the age range from 2 to 80 (Groups 1 through 6).

2. The sex difference is found for dream series as well as for collections of individual dreams (Group 7 compared with Groups 1-6).

3. The same or approximately the same percentage of male characters is found for neurotic males as for normal males (Group 8 compared with Groups 1-6).

4. The same result is found for two long dream series of two males as for collections of individual dreams (Groups 9 and 10 compared with Groups 1-6).

5. Approximately the same percentage of male characters is found for a young adult Negro epileptic man and a middle-aged white man (Group 9 compared with Group 10).

TABLE 1

MALE AND FEMALE CHARACTERS IN DREAMS

Description of population	Number of dreamers		Number of dreams		Percentage of male characters	
	MALE	FEMALE	MALE	FEMALE	MALE	FEMALE
1. College students	78	80	841	978	64	52
2. College students	199	499	357	670	63	51
3. College students	225	225	658	662	61	54
4. College students	200	200	200	200	60	53
5. Adults (ages 30–80)	281	281	281	281	66	52
6. Children (ages 2 through 12)	119	133	217	274	69	49
7. College students: average percentage of male characters obtained from individual dream series	30	34	543	629	68	55
8. Neurotic patients	15		400		64	
9. Epileptic Negro patient (age 25)	1		340		64	
10. White adult (age 37–52)	1		300		65	
11. College students	280		280		65	
All groups, except Group 7, combined	1399	1418	3874	3065	64	52

That this differential proportion of male and female characters in dreams may be a universal phenomenon is suggested by evidence from the dreams of two widely separated ethnic groups, the Hopi of southwest United States and the Yir Yoront of Cape York, Australia. The Hopi dreams were collected by Dorothy Eggan during the years 1939–1942, and the Yir Yoront dreams by R. L. Sharp during 1933–1935. We are indebted to Dorothy Eggan and David Schneider for providing us with these collections.

The Hopi collection consists of the dreams of four adult males and three adult females. A character analysis of each dream series was made and results are presented in Table 2. (See "The Culture Shapes the Dream," page 120.)

Although the percentage of male characters in the dreams of Hopi males is considerably higher than any of the groups in Table 1, the percentage for Hopi females is about the same as for white females.

The Yir Yoront dreams were collected from 43 men and 8 women. The men contributed 139 dreams; one man contributed 14, one 11, and the rest 1–5 each. The 8 women contributed 10 dreams. An analysis was made only for the men's dreams (see Table 3).

TABLE 2

MALE AND FEMALE CHARACTERS IN HOPI DREAMS

Group	Age	Number of dreams	Number of male characters	Number of female characters	Percentage of male characters
Males					
1	60	24	49	5	91
2	38	18	36	11	77
3	36	10	10	4	71
4	36	6	6	3	67
Total		58	101	23	81
Females					
1	60	18	11	14	44
2	28	60	56	60	48
3	36	18	21	20	51
Total		96	88	94	48

TABLE 3

MALE AND FEMALE CHARACTERS IN YIR YORONT
MALE DREAMS

Number of dreamers	Number of dreams	Number of male characters	Number of female characters	Percentage of male characters
43	139	181	67	73

The percentage of male characters is higher than it is for the white male groups and lower than the Hopi males.

In spite of the differences between these two ethnic groups and the white samples, the fact remains that Hopi and Yir Yoront males dream more of males than they do of females, and Hopi females dream of males and females with equal frequency. . . .

DISCUSSION

What is the explanation for this ubiquitous sex difference? Why do men dream more about other men whereas women dream about men and women with almost equal frequency?

Virtually all of the current dream theories with which the writers are familiar stress the principle that dreams are primarily concerned with the preoccupations, anxieties, conflicts, and unsatisfied wishes of the dreamer. We dream during the night as we think during the day about our unresolved problems.

If this is the case, then our findings suggest that the unresolved problems of males center more around their relationships with men than with women, and those of females are focused upon their relationships with both sexes about equally.

We have some evidence which supports this hypothesis. An analysis of aggressive interactions between the dreamer and male and female dream characters shows that male dreamers have a higher proportion of aggressions with other males whereas female dreamers divide their aggressions about equally between male and female characters. These data are reported by Hall and Domhoff (1962). A comparable analysis for friendly interactions revealed that male dreamers have a higher proportion of friendly encounters with females than with male characters, whereas female dreamers have about an equal proportion of friendly interactions with male and female characters. These data are reported by Hall and Domhoff (1962).

If it is assumed that aggression is a sign of conflict and that friendliness is not, then the foregoing data support the hypothesis that men dream more about men because male-male relationships produce more conflict than male-female relationships, and that women dream about males and females with almost the same frequency because their relationships with both sexes are equally conflictual.

Are Girls More Aggressive Than Boys in Their Dreams?

HERBERT GREENHOUSE

Most studies comparing men and women dreamers show that females are usually more passive and males more aggressive in their dreams. This fits the popular concept of male aggression and female passivity. Is it the result of biological differences or is it culturally determined? Some recent dream studies indicate that women may be just as aggressive as men and often more so in response to what happens in their environment.

Paul R. Robbins and Roland H. Tanck of George Washington University obtained dream reports from two groups of women college students ("Community Violence and Aggression in Dreams: An Observation," *Perceptual and Motor Skills*, vol. 29, pp. 41–42, 1969). One of the groups reported their dreams when life was quiescent in their community environment, the other during a period of civil disorder. The researchers assumed that the dreams of the latter group would show more violence and aggression. To their surprise they found that the reverse was true and concluded that "a very strong outside stimulus for aggression served to depress or inhibit aggressive tendencies in dream content."

Since both groups of girls measured about the same amount of aggression in personality testing, it would seem that environmental factors play a large role in the aggressiveness of both men and women. This point of view was supported by a recent thesis on the amount of aggression in the dreams of high school students (John Joseph Buckley, Ph.D., "The Dreams of Young Adults—A Sociological Analysis of Eleven Hundred and Thirty-three Dreams of Black and White Students," Wayne State University, 1970, *Dissertations Abstracts International*, vol. 31 (7a) January 1971). Several paragraphs are quoted here:

"This research is a study of the statistical differences in aggression expressed in the dreams of students of five metropolitan Detroit high schools. The student population was subjected to controls according to race, sex, social class, and other social variables. . . .

"A content analysis for aggression was made on the 1133 dreams contributed by 260 students. The dreams ranged from one to sixteen. Aggression in the study was defined and measured by two content analysis scales developed by Calvin S. Hall and Robert Van de Castle. . . .

"As predicted in the study, the lower-class students were found to have expressed a significantly greater amount of aggression in their dreams than middle-class students. . . .

"Contrary to prediction girls were found significantly more aggressive than boys. Lower-class girls expressed more aggression in their dreams than boys of both classes and also middle-class girls. . . . The difference in aggressive content in the dreams of the two sexes was felt to reflect that girls can be as aggressive or more aggressive than boys when they are permitted to be so with impunity."

The Dreams of Creative College Girls

JOSEPH ADELSON

[The following experiment explores the correlation between creativity in the classroom and creativity in dreams.]

The dreams for the study were collected from a group of 30 college girls who had enrolled for a course in creative writing. During the period of the research they were asked each morning if they had dreamed the night before. If they had, their accounts were transcribed as nearly verbatim as possible. The girl was then questioned about the dream, asked to clarify its obscure or personal parts, to identify the dream figures, to report what experiences she was reminded of, and so on. At the end of the semester, the instructor of the course chose the ten least and most imaginative students. The criterion was not craft or literary skill, but literary inventiveness, originality in choice of theme and treatment. We used no more than 10 dreams from any subject, and we included only those subjects who had reported at least four dreams. The final sample consisted of eight girls rated high on imaginativeness, who had a total of 52 dreams, and seven uninventive subjects, with 46 dreams. With such a small number of subjects, this study cannot be considered more than exploratory. But the results are so striking and so consistent in trend that it seems worthwhile to report them now, if only to indicate the empirical promise of this topic.

We coded the dreams on a realism-unrealism scale, using several separate categories—action, time, space, and transition. We also gave a global rating of the degree of realism of each dream. Since these separate ratings show similar trends, I will report only the results of the global analysis. We used three categories here: a dream was rated "one" if the sequence of events narrated was logically or physically impossible—a simple example of this might be a dream of someone walking on air. A rating of "two" was given if the dream's events were improbable or unusual, but logically or physically possible. And a rating of "three" was given to those dreams whose action was plausible, realistic and commonplace.

We find that the groups differ most markedly in the proportion of their absurd and prelogical dreams. The non-creative group has a somewhat higher frequency of commonplace and of improbable dreams. But in category "one" we find 42% of the creative group's dreams, and only 15% for the non-creative. Six out of eight creative girls report at least two bizarre dreams, and this is true of only two of the seven non-creative girls.

These differences in the dreams' form-quality are given somewhat more meaning when we look at the dreams directly, through an analysis of their content. For example, we find that our non-inventive dreamers are very much tied to the local and familiar, to the here and now. Consider the scene of the dream. Where does its action take place? In the dreams of creative subjects, anywhere—in Paris, in a mosque, or in the jungles of Africa; 13% of their dreams take place in a foreign or exotic setting, while this occurs in only one of the 46 non-creative dreams. We also discover that one-third of the non-creative dreams are located in the sleeper's immediate milieu, in this case, the college they were attending; we find this in only 14% of the inventive dreams. A similar constriction in range is evident for the category of dream population: in one of every five inventive dreams there is an alien or exotic dream figure—a king and queen, for example, or a Roman soldier. We have this happen but once in the 46 non-inventive dreams.

How does the dreamer represent herself? Here we discover another example of the non-inventive subject's commitment to objective reality. She finds it hard to disown or to transform her present identity; with only two exceptions the non-creative dreams picture the self contemporaneously, the dreamer as she is now, in her current role and status. The inventive dreamer frequently—23% of the time—accomplishes a transformation of role, sometimes a radical one, but more often a prospective one, dreaming herself into an expected or longed-for status, as a wife or mother, as an actress or artist, and so on. The inventive girl also exercises her power to transform identity on other figures of the dream, though she does so somewhat less frequently; she turns a friend into a dentist, her mother into her employee. There is not a single transformation of this kind in the non-creative sample.

I used the word "power" just now, and I feel it is a good term for the quality we are describing. The inventive girl's dreaming shows an energy of construction which contrasts sharply with the sluggishness, the insipidity of invention in the dreams of the non-creative. One gets a most vivid sense of this difference in reading the dreams through, one set of protocols simple and stereotyped in design, the other complex, dense, and richly textured. It is a hard difference to measure directly, but one of our findings may give you some idea of it. We find that the inventive subjects create a proliferation of settings within a single dream; we see a continual transformation of scene, a fluid, or sometimes jerky shifting of locale. The preponderance of inventive dreams contain more than one scene, and some contain seven or more; their median number of settings per dream is three. On the other hand, the majority of non-inventive dreams—70%—take place against a single background, and none of these dreams has more than three settings.

Another difference which is hard to state in simple quantitative terms concerns the descriptive texture of the dream. In the dreams of the noninventive we find a flat, almost skeletal perception of actuality; persons and things exist as noun categories—Mary is Mary, a house is a house—without metaphoric or even adjectival enrichment. Some of our data may offer you a sense of their constriction. The inventive subjects describe things by color about twice as often as do the non-inventive. The only major use of color-naming by the non-creative group is in regard to clothing, and if we exclude clothing for both groups, we find that the inventive dreams contain three and one-half times more color-references. The insensitivity of the non-creative subject is most apparent where the dream population is concerned. We find that these girls refer to the physical or psychological qualities of dream personages more than three times less frequently than do the inventives.

There are many other differences which the content analysis revealed, but of these I would like to choose three which seem especially illuminating. First, the comic. Ernst Kris has taught us to recognize the essential similarity between creativity and the comic. He writes "of persons to whom the comic in general is unknown; they fear the regression in all comic pleasure, they lack the faculty of 'letting themselves go.'" This self-same ability to let go, to suspend, momentarily, a commitment to the givens of reality, is a quality which differentiates inventive and non-inventive persons. We tabulated the presence of the comic in these dreams, defining this very generally—any reference to humor in any of its manifestations. We find that it is present in 17% of the creative dreams, but is never found in the dreams of the non-creative.

There is another finding which, I feel, carries some implication. We discovered that in 20% of the inventive dreams the dreamer, at one point or another, does not participate in the action of the dream, but represents herself as detached from it, observing it. The non-inventive dreamer is always—there is not a single exception—immersed in the events of the dream. How shall we understand this difference? I suppose that to stand apart from reality is a necessary first condition for transforming it imaginatively; to re-create our sense of circumstance we must first be able to have a detached consciousness of it, to know it, reflect on it, judge it. This modality, detachment, seems also to be related to the defense mechanism of isolation, which we have some reason to believe is commonly used by creative individuals. Finally, and I hope this will not sound merely facile, it appears that the emphasis on observation in these dreams may represent a transformation of voyeuristic drives; it is my strong impression that both voyeuristic and exhibitionistic motives are highly developed among our creative subjects; speaking generally, these may be among the central motives which inform the creative enterprise.

By now you may have come to suspect that the two groups of dreamers are drawn from very different populations. This is both so and not so. From a crudely demographic point of view we had an extremely homogeneous sample, almost all of them the daughters of prosperous business and professional men. Very likely the two groups differ somewhat, but not profoundly, in intelligence. However, when we consider their goals, attitudes, values, interests, experiences, we find we are dealing with entirely different social and personality types. There are a good many indications of this in the dreams, and I want to discuss just one of these, the expression of sexuality.

I remind you that our subjects were between 18 and 21 and unmarried —an extremely nubile group, therefore; so it is not surprising to find that their dreams are suffused with expressions of sexuality, direct, allusive, and covert. When the theme of sexuality appears in the non-inventive dreams it is only alluded to, or handled with some degree of delicacy. "There is a boy in my room," one dreamer reports, "but I am only talking to him." Another non-creative subject tells a dream in which she wants to spite her fiance, and so is considering sleeping with another young man; she then adds, "Thank God I don't remember if I slept with him or not." More frequently, however, we find that these dreams treat sexuality in a more or less classically symbolic fashion: there is a vaguely ominous man who threatens to do something vaguely dreadful to the dreamer; while she is sleeping two friends throw a black and red snake into the dreamer's room; someone is rummaging around in the dreamer's chest of drawers. There is a constant preoccupation, when sex is the theme, with being caught or found out. The non-creative girl represents herself in these dreams as sexually passive, vulnerable to and endangered by the aggressive sexuality of men.

The creative girls are likely to present a more active, open, and indeed flamboyant sexuality. In a number of cases, for example, the dreamer is having sexual intercourse while other people are looking on. Sexual activity takes place in a variety of not quite conventional settings, in one instance the kitchen floor of the dreamer's grandmother's house. Now it is quite likely that the relative sexual freedom of these dreams corresponds to the actual sexual experience of their dreamers; the information from our inquiry suggests this in any case. But I suspect that we ought not to take this seeming freedom at its face value. We may rightly suppose that in their dreams, as well as in real life, heterosexuality is being used to ward off pregenital sexuality. In several dreams we find suggestions that homosexual and other pregenital impulses lie just behind the heterosexuality; at times they break through and we see an emergence of perverse sexuality. This tactic, the bringing to awareness of one conflict-system to ward off a deeper and more formidable one, is a style of defense commonly used by creatively gifted individuals.

The differences in the representation of sexuality reflect a more general set of differences, in the social and psychological orientations of our two groups. The non-creative girls have conventional interests and goals—clothing, dating, marriage are the major manifest themes of their dreams—and an extremely stereotyped way of organizing and locating themselves in reality. They achieve what seems to be a fairly successful adaptation to their life circumstances, and do so through a thoroughgoing use of repressions and reaction-formations. What we see here is, of course, a particular type of character formation, one which seems to be nearly ubiquitous in middleclass American society; the ego purchases a freedom from inner discomfort by accepting severe restrictions on its cognitive functioning. The ego's vigilance extends inwardly against the primary process and outwardly toward the real world; this study has suggested how deeply the ego's vigilance can reach, to the very core of unconsciousness, dream sleep.

The Dreams of Pregnant Women*

STANLEY KRIPPNER, NORMAN POSNER, WILLIAM POMERANCE, and STUART FISCHER

An initial study of the dreams of pregnant women disclosed several significant differences in their dream content when compared to dreams from a normative female group. An additional study was done, with special attention paid to social class differences.

A total of 100 dreams was contributed by the 15 subjects in the study. All dreams were scored by using the Hall-Van de Castle method of content analysis. For the total sample, it was found that the pregnancy dreams demonstrated, at statistically significant levels, an increase in emotional sensitivity but a decrease in concern with both success and failure. An inspection of specific dreams revealed a number of pregnancy-related concerns: appointment with physicians, physical clumsiness, reduced locomotion, reduced sexual attractiveness, and appearance of the newborn baby. Several additional differences appeared when the middle-income group was compared to the normative group and when the lower-income group was compared to the normative (nonpregnant) group upon whose dreams Hall and Van de Castle based their norms.

The middle-income women demonstrated in their dreams a statistically significant increase in passivity during pregnancy, an increased expression of friendliness, an increased mention of architectural detail, and an increase in the number of people occurring in the dream. There were significant decreases in the number of physical activities and in the initiation of both social activities and friendly interactions. The lower-income group showed none of these differences: their dreams differed less from those of nonpregnant women than did the dreams of the middle-income group. In conclusion this study indicated that the process of dreaming is basically healthy for the sample studied. Further, pregnancy is a time of "turning inward"; there is less external activity of both a locomotor and a social type. Emotional sensitivity is increased—but about such pregnancy-related concerns as sexual attractiveness rather than concern with success and failure.

It is hoped that future studies of this type will eventually assist the obstetrician in using dreams to check on the course of the women's emotional reaction to pregnancy.

* This abstract was prepared for the First International Congress of the Association for the Psychophysiological Study of Sleep, Bruges, Belgium, 1971. Conclusions to be drawn should be tentative until results of further studies in progress are released.

Women's Sexual Dreams in Ancient Egypt*

RAYMOND DE BECKER

If a woman kisses her husband, she will have trouble;

If a horse couples with her, she will be violent with her husband;

If an ass couples with her, she will be punished for a great fault;

If a he-goat couples with her, she will die promptly;

If a ram couples with her, Pharaoh will be full of kindness to her;

If a Syrian couples with her, she will weep, for she will let a slave "couple with her";

If she gives birth to a cat, she will have many children;

If she gives birth to a dog, she will have a boy;

If she gives birth to an ass, she will have an idiot child;

If she gives birth to a crocodile, she will have many children.

Sex Roles Switched in Dreams

CALVIN S. HALL

Dreams offer a splendid opportunity to observe the bisexual conflict and the various ways in which a person tries to handle it. Occasionally we find dreams in which an actual sex reversal has taken place, as in the following dream of a young man.

I dreamed that I was lying in bed with white and red strips of cloth over me. Across my breasts the white strip stuck up as if I had female breasts. When I stood up the strips resolved themselves into a dress, and I did have breasts.

We happen to know from his other dreams and from additional sources of information that this lad has a strong bisexual conflict. He enjoys both homosexual and heterosexual outlets and is a curious mixture of feminine

* From a papyrus in the Cairo Museum.

and masculine traits with passivity and self-love being his strongest features. At times he frankly admits that he would like to be a girl, and in this dream his wish is fulfilled. The white and red strips probably symbolize his conceptions of femininity and masculinity.

An example of sex reversal in women is seen in the next dream.

The main point of the dream is that there was a reversal of sexes. All of my girl friends were dressed as men and played the role of men while the men played the role of women.

This dream has the added feature of turning men into women as well as women into men, which suggests that not only does the dreamer want to be a man but also that she would like to get revenge on the dominant male by transforming him into the weaker sex.

A Lesbian Dreams

CALVIN S. HALL

Another way by which a person can defend himself against a shameful idea is to attribute the idea to another person and then have that person try to persuade the dreamer to do something which he wanted to do all along. The defending person can excuse himself by saying, "I couldn't help myself because he made me do it." This is the strategy employed by a young woman in the following dream.

I dreamed that a sorority sister of mine saw me in a movie theater and started to chase me throughout the theater. She was trying to seduce me and I did everything possible to avert her. I went up to several of my friends and told them that she was a homosexual. They refused to believe me and to help me get away from her. I started to leave the theater and she was sitting in the lobby reading a book. She did not see me walk out so I managed to get away from her.

The sorority sister personifies the dreamer's homosexuality, from which she tries to and finally does escape.

Homosexual Dreams

CAROLYN WINGET and RONALD A. FARRELL

As part of a broader social-psychological study of how the homosexual experiences culture conflict, rejection, and movement toward the homosexual stereotype, questions on dreams were included in a questionnaire distributed to a homophile organization, a personal rights organization, homosexual bars and social clubs, and through individual contacts. A recent dream was present in 76 of the 148 returned protocols. These and 56 dreams from a non-homosexual male sample were assigned code numbers and typed on individual cards. The randomized dreams were then coded blindly using selected Whitman, Hall-Van de Castle, and Gottschalk-Gleser scales. In brief the content analysis revealed the following:

Dream Variable	Non-homosexual Males N = 56		Homosexual Males N = 76		X^2	p
	N	%	N	%		
Sexual Interaction	0	0	31	41	27.63	.001
Homosexual Themes	11	20	37	49	10.53	.025
Heterosexual Themes	11	20	14	18	.00	n. s.
Anxiety	33	59	31	41	3.55	n. s.
Hostility Outwards	27	48	20	26	3.08	n. s.
Friendly Interaction	5	9	12	16	.81	n. s.
Characters	34	61	58	76	3.01	n. s.
Setting: In	6	11	26	34 ⎫		
Out	21	38	11	15 ⎬	14.39	.001
None or?	29	51	39	51 ⎭		

Variable present in dreams of:

These data tend to support an earlier finding of Bieber et al. (1962) with regard to the lack of exclusive interest in males in the dream life of homosexuals. In a number of respects, however, the dream content of homosexuals appears to resemble that of females: the increased presence of characters, the significantly higher indoor settings, lowered aggressive-hostile content, and a higher incidence of friendly interactions. In spite of sampling difficulties and problems in generalizability, these findings are incipient steps toward improving our insights into the self-views, preoccupations, and "psychic self-regulation" of the homosexual.

The Dreams of Transsexuals*

STANLEY KRIPPNER, RICHARD DAVIDSON, and GERALDINE LENZ

A total of 105 dreams was collected from the 37 male pre-operative transsexual Ss in this study. All Ss were patients of Dr. Harry Benjamin and were personally interviewed in his New York office. After a S volunteered for the study, he was given notebooks and was instructed to keep a "dream diary" for several weeks.

Once collected, the dreams were scored according to the Hall-Van de Castle system and were compared with the 500 normative male dreams as well as the 500 normative female dreams utilized by Hall and Van de Castle.

Statistically significant differences were obtained in 51 of the Hall-Van de Castle categories. In 24 of the cases, the transsexual dreams differed from the normative male dreams. In 27 instances, the transsexual dreams differed from the normative female dreams. In several of these comparisons, the transsexual dreams differed from both normative groups.

The pre-operative male transsexuals in this study dreamed more frequently about hospitals and other institutional buildings than did both the males and females in the normative groups. The torso region of the body (i.e., chest, abdomen, hips) was mentioned more frequently by transsexuals in their dream reports than by either the males or females in the normative groups. Sex organs were mentioned more often by the transsexuals than by normative females (but not normative males). Transsexual dreams included more frequent mentions of clothing than dreams of normative males or females, especially in regard to such details as accessories, buttons, and underwear. There were significantly less dreams of assault and murder among transsexuals than among normative males. In almost every category measuring friendly social interactions, transsexuals surpassed both normative groups. They dream about sexual intercourse more often than normative females but at about the same frequency as normative males; typically, these dream reports pictured the male pre-operative transsexual as a female during intercourse.

* This abstract was prepared for the First International Congress of the Association for the Psychophysiological Study of Sleep, Bruges, Belgium, 1971. Conclusions to be drawn should be tentative until results of further studies in progress are released.

Hermaphroditic Dreams

ISADOR H. CORIAT, M.D.

Our psychoanalytic investigations have demonstrated that the best evidence of bisexuality in human beings is furnished by the dreams of conscious or unconscious homosexuality. Such dreams, which I have termed hermaphroditic dreams, are essentially bisexual in their blurrings or blendings, a sort of dream condensation, in either a symbolical or literal form. . . .

Because the infantile is the source of the unconscious, the appearance of hermaphroditic dreams may be interpreted as the infantile type of thinking occurring in the adult mind. These types of dreams, therefore, refer to those primitive mental processes which are so characteristic of the child mentality. Hence this hermaphroditism is emphasized in certain peoples, such as the bearded Venus of Cyprus or the bearded Isis in ancient Egypt or in a more symbolic form in the Cretan snake goddess. Dreams originate from the past in every sense, and not only are reflections of the childhood of man, but likewise of the childhood of the world.

It is stated by Freud that the adult sexual constitution is really formed from the original bisexuality of the infantile life. Such types of hermaphroditic dreams furnish the best evidence of the bisexual nature of man. They have been found particularly to occur in the psychoanalysis of homosexual individuals and have a decided prognostic value as showing the median point of the swing of the pendulum from homo to heterosexuality, a sort of neutral sexual image due to a fusion or a condensation of the bisexual tendency of the unconscious. In a previous contribution, the prognostic value of these hermaphroditic dreams was emphasized in the following terms, as indicating the progress of the psychoanalysis of a case of homosexuality.

"Homosexual individuals are troubled with dreams which are either literally homosexual or certain elements of a disguised Œdipus complex. If the psychoanalytic treatment is successful the literal homosexual and Œdipus dreams gradually disappear and are replaced by dreams that are neutrally sexual; finally as the treatment successfully proceeds, the dream life becomes distinctly heterosexual. Thus the dreams of homosexual individuals not only furnish the material for reaching the unconscious mechanism of the homosexuality, but are of decided prognostic value" (from "The Psychogenesis of Homosexuality," by Coriat, *New York Medical Journal*, March 22, 1913).

In cases where unconscious homosexuality may occur, as in certain paranoiac states in the compulsion or anxiety neuroses, the same types of dreams have been found. Sometimes the dreams are literal, sometimes symbolized. . . .

In a case of a compulsion neurosis, with a strong repressed homosexual tendency, the following dream occurred during a period of the rapid subsidence of the compulsive thinking.

Dream: He seemed to enter a dance hall where there were a number of boys and girls. The latter, although dressed in female costumes, yet had full beards on their faces. He remained there only a short while and then descended some stairs to a sort of basement pool-room, where there were a number of rather tough-looking young men. He remained there only a short time and then fearful that he might come to some harm, he said to himself, "This is no place for me," and started to climb the stairs. The stairs seemed then to be very rickety, particularly the last three or four stairs, which seemed about to fall down. Then he appealed to a young man, who seemed to be the proprietor of the establishment, to help him up, which he did.

Analysis: This dream was instigated by a bearded woman whom he had seen at an amusement resort some weeks previously. The hermaphroditic nature of the bearded girls in the dream is of significance as showing the progress of the psychoneurosis toward cure. This particular dream picture bears a striking resemblance to the bearded Venus in female attire occurring in Cyprus as noted by Dr. Frazer in his *Adonis, Attis and Osiris*, where the bearded goddess was worshipped in this double form, a proof of the strong relationship between dream-work and myth-making. This work of both condensation and displacement is the same for both dreams and myths. . . .

The entire dream is a symbolical expression of the subject's struggle with the unconscious homosexuality. The descent into the basement (the subject's unconscious) where only men were present, represents a desire to return to his homosexuality, while the ascent of the staircase, with all its difficulties and being finally helped up the last few stairs, symbolizes the saving effect of the psychoanalysis. Thus the descending of the stairs is a symbolic representation of a sexual (homosexual act) and the climbing up stairs represents the hermaphroditic tendency of the unconscious at this particular stage in the treatment of the neurosis. The girls with the beards represent the neutral point of his sexual struggle as an hermaphroditic symbol, before he again reverted to his unconscious homosexuality and when he was again saved from it by the psychoanalyst. Therefore, in this dream, the hermaphroditic figures through a sort of condensation and displacement symbolize the neutral point of preparation for getting well.

The Dreams of City Blacks:
Castration Anxiety

HERBERT GREENHOUSE

Three dream researchers from the University of Cincinnati did a profile of 300 residents of Cincinnati, Ohio (Milton Kramer, M. D.; Roy M. Whitman, M. D.; and Carolyn Winget, M.A., "A Survey Approach to Normative Dream Content: Sex, Age, Marital Status, Race, and Educational Differences," *Psychophysiology*, September 1970). Among their findings was that older persons dream more about death, while younger ones show more guilt in their dreams. The "been marrieds" have more death anxiety and premonition dreams than single persons or those presently married. Blacks reveal more castration anxiety and penis envy, but overall there were not as many differences between the races as had been expected.

The Dreams of Children
CHARLES W. KIMMINS

ANALYSIS OF DREAMS OF CHILDREN OF FIVE, SIX AND SEVEN YEARS OF AGE

1. *Fulfilled Wishes*—Dreams of this nature consisted very largely in the return of father, brother or near relations from the war, more particularly in the girls' dreams. Prospective dreams of Christmas with Santa Claus and his presents figured very largely, especially with the five-year-old children, reaching in fact 15 per cent of the total dream elements at this age.

2. *Fears*—With very young children the fear dream is very prominent. In this investigation, no less than 25 per cent were of this nature, consisting chiefly of the dread of objectionable men. At seven years of age children, both boys and girls, dream more about burglars than at any other age. The fear dream of animals is, curiously enough, far more common among the boys than the girls...

The Influence of the Cinema is felt very little in the girls' dreams, but in the boys', especially at the age of seven, it is an important factor.

Fairy-Story Dreams are very common with girls, but are rarely experienced by boys.

Normal Domestic Occurrences appear frequently in the material of the girls' dreams, but only occasionally in those of the boys'. . . .

At five years of age the child is the center of the dream, and is rarely a passive observer. . . . There are many incongruities which will be seen by the following dreams:

A burglar came into my house and stole Mother's money. He stuck a knife into me, and I dreamt that he had shot another boy after he had killed me.

I dreamt that a robber came to our house and broke the cups. (This boy had broken a cup and concealed the matter from his mother. This is an interesting case of repressed material at an early age.)

Someone came and took our white baby and left a black one.

After the visit of the King and Queen to Peckham, a girl of five dreamt that "A lady was sitting on my bed, and the King and Queen were under the bed eating bread and butter, and a lot of ladies with them."

At the age of five the experiences of conscious life carry over into the unconscious. The child mixes up the dreaming with the waking element.

At the age of seven, there is a great advance. The family relationship is fully realized, and members of the family group take part in the dream. The child is not so much the central figure. At this age, he recognizes the dream phenomenon as a thing apart. There is less confusion between the dreaming and waking experience, and the record of the dream becomes much more valuable.

A few examples of the dreams of children of this age will illustrate this:

The sun and moon were on the floor in my room, so that I could not walk about, so I went to heaven where all the lights were up, and there were many colors.

I dreamt a dustman put me in a box and took me in a cart, and brought me back to the wrong bed, but when I woke up, I was in the right bed.

I dreamt there were burglars in the room and they lit the fire and sat in a chair, and got green curtains by the door. There were flowers in the next-door garden; the two burglars took them and they gave me two stamps and a sheet of paper. . . .

The dreams appear to vary with the temperament and health of the child.

Children in poor districts dream far more about toys than those in the well-to-do.

There appears to be no connection of dreaming with intelligence, though this appears later. Dull children dream quite as much as bright children. . . .

The death element comes into the dreams of delicate, neurotic children, but rarely into those of healthy, normal children. . . .

Young children sometimes imagine that they take other forms; *e.g.*:

A nervous boy of five, whose father was a baker, had two dreams of this character:

(a) I was in a loaf of bread, and a German cut me into little bits, and saw me; I went under the gas pipes.

(b) I was in a kettle, and I drank up all the water. Mother could not find me; I went under the gas pipes. . . .

ANALYSIS OF DREAM ELEMENTS OF BOYS AND GIRLS IN THE NORMAL ELEMENTARY SCHOOLS (EIGHT TO FOURTEEN YEARS OF AGE)

Fear Dreams—Boys have more fear dreams (19 per cent) than girls (16 per cent). The most marked difference is in the fear of burglars and robbers, which appear twice as often in the boys' as in girls' dreams. Girls dream rather more of strange men and women than boys, but the difference is not marked. It is the old man who is the terror of the dreaming boy and the girl. He is responsible in both cases for about half of the fear dreams. The fear of animals is practically the same in both sexes, and is the cause of about 20 per cent of fear dreams. The larger animals, *e.g.*, lions, tigers and bulls predominate in boys', and dogs, rats, mice and snakes in girls' dreams. The ghost has practically disappeared from the child's dream, but occurs occasionally when the fairy story dream begins to wane. It is more common in boys' than in girls' dreams. . . .

Love Sentiment—Anything in the nature of sentiment between members of the opposite sex is very rarely found in the dreams of children from eight to fourteen years of age, but is more common in girls' than in boys' dreams. . . .

SOME DREAM ACCOUNTS

A Boy of Eight:

I cannot tell you my dream last night, but I can tell you my other dream the night before. I dreamt that I was going to be washed. And then I was being put in the bath to be washed. After I was washed I was wrung out in the mangle. Then I was hung on the line. I was hanging on the line when it started to rain. My mother took me in and ironed me. The iron was hot. And then I woke up.

A Girl of Eight:

Last night I dreamt that I was in fairyland, and that I had beautiful little fairies to wait upon me. One day, a little fairy said to me, "Would you like to come into the woods with us?" and so I said "Yes." So we went into the woods, and we saw lots of rabbits running about.

Presently the fairies thought it was time to go home, so we went home and had tea. For tea we had ice cakes and cream. Then we went out and had some moonbeam slides like all fairies like to do. Soon after we went home to bed. Now our beds were not made of iron, they were made of moss with rose petals for pillows and fern leaves for a cover. Just as I was going to sleep, I awoke.

A Girl of Thirteen:

I dreamt that I was sitting by the fire wishing to be with my aunt, when I heard a noise like somebody patting the window. I went forward and opened it and into the room a little white mouse jumped. After giving it some milk it seemed to grow bigger and when it had grown as big as Beal, my kitten, he said to me, "Every egg that you have eaten has made you a bigger criminal." At this I was very astonished and said, "Why?" "Because you have eaten a great number of chickens." "They are very little use," I answered and with this I went out of the room.

The following is a particularly interesting dream, or rather series of three dreams, which were dreamt in the same night by a girl of twelve years of age. In each part the kinaesthetic element (flying) predominates. The rapid transition from one type of experience to another is very striking and assumes rather the form of a continuous nightmare than a normal dream. For convenience I divide it into three sections.

First Section—At the beginning I found myself in the house next door, with a lot of horrid men running after me, and when they caught me they said they were going to kill me, so I was put out between two lions and in ten minutes a huge wave was coming up the road and it came over me. Then I heard some clapping and I had just finished singing a song before all the school.

Second Section—I was in my own bedroom and there was a lion under my bed and in the cupboard was a terrible ghost. I heard him walking about and then he came out and I was on a bicycle riding round the bed with the ghost after me. All at once I jumped out of the window with a great scream, then I woke up and found myself on the floor.

Third Section—I went to sleep again and dreamt that Mother and Father had turned into cabbages and I was getting them ready for dinner, but just as I was putting them into the saucepan they turned into people again, and asked me if I liked the airplane which we were in, and then I found myself in a Handley-Page. I was driving it when all of a sudden it vanished and I was swimming in the sea. When I woke up I was sitting up in bed, and it was morning so I did not dream any more that night.

Girls of twelve and thirteen dream much more about religion, and there were several interesting dreams of heaven. . . .

One girl after describing the scene adds: "Much information was given to us (girl and friend) by a nice gentleman, who, I presume, was a cherub. In appearance he strongly reminded me of our school caretaker." Another, after describing the kindness of the angels to herself and her friend, concludes: "We had tea with them and they afterwards kindly assisted us in washing-up."

Dreams of Deaf and Blind Children

The deaf child can draw upon a rich field of visual experience which, in their fantastic combinations, give such a wealth of interest to the dream, whereas these experiences are wanting in the dream of the child who has been blind from birth.

The percentage of clearly defined wish-fulfilments in both types of child corresponds closely to that of normal children, but the wishes are of a different nature. Concerts, parties and domestic experience bulk largely in the dreams of the blind child, and there is not that variety which corresponds to the much fuller life of the deaf child. In the latter, visits of the town child to the country form, especially among older children, a very important item, whereas in the former, there are practically no references to such experiences. The railway journey, the change of scene, and even the seaside have no message for the blind child.

The fears of the deaf and blind are somewhat in excess of those of normal children. In both the fear of animals is greater than among ordinary children. . . .

Deaf girls dream much of personal adornment, which is entirely lacking in dreams of blind girls.

Many blind children claim to see in their dreams. A girl of fourteen says, "I can always see in my dreams. I have never yet had a dream without seeing quite plainly." But the dreams recorded are generally of an uneventful nature dealing with domestic incidents in which the vision takes no part. There are many auditory dreams and a few taste dreams. . . .

Deaf children state that in their dreams they hear clearly and, as has been pointed out, the accounts of their dreams contain more definite conversations than those of any other type of child. . . .

There is no evidence whatever in the dreams analyzed that a blind child from birth sees as a dreamer, but there is abundant evidence that those who have recently become blind see clearly. The age of becoming blind appears to be the deciding factor. Jastrow and Heerman investigated this point fully. Their researches point to the conclusion:

That a child who becomes blind before the age of five never sees in his dreams.

That when total blindness occurs between the age of five and seven, much depends on the mental development of the child as to whether he sees in dreams in after-life or not. . . .

That all dreamers becoming blind after the age of seven see in dreams even after an interval of twenty or thirty years.

[1920]

The Dreams of a Blind and Deaf Lady

HELEN KELLER

The likeness between my waking state and the sleeping one is still marked. In both states I see, but not with my eyes. I hear, but not with my ears. I speak, and am spoken to, without the sound of a voice. I am moved to pleasure by visions of ineffable beauty which I have never beheld in the physical world. Once in a dream I held in my hand a pearl. I have no memory-vision of a real pearl. The one I saw in my dream must, therefore, have been a creation of my imagination. It was a smooth, exquisitely molded crystal. As I gazed into its shimmering deeps, my soul was flooded with an ecstasy of tenderness, I was filled with wonder, as one who should for the first time look into the cool, sweet heart of a rose. My pearl was dew and fire, the velvety green of moss, the soft whiteness of lilies, and the distilled hues and sweetness of a thousand roses. It seemed to me the soul of beauty was dissolved in its crystal bosom. This beauteous vision strengthens my conviction that the world which the mind builds up out of countless subtle experiences and suggestions is fairer than the world of the senses. The splendor of the sunset my friends gaze at across the purple hills is wonderful; but the sunset of the inner visions brings pure delight because it is the worshipful blending of all the beauty that we have known and desired.

I believe I am more fortunate in my dreams than most people; for as I think back over my dreams, the pleasant ones seem to predominate, although we naturally recall most vividly and tell most eagerly the grotesque and fantastic adventures in Slumberland. . . . It is true that my dreams have uses as many and sweet as those of adversity. All my yearning for the strange, the weird, the ghostlike is gratified in dreams. They carry me out of the accustomed and commonplace. In a flash, in the winking of an eye, they snatch the burden from my shoulders, the trivial task from my hand, and the pain and disappointment from my heart, and I behold the lovely face of my dream. It dances round me with merry measure, and darts hither and thither in happy abandon. Sudden, sweet fancies spring forth from any nook and corner, and delightful surprises meet me at every turn. A happy dream is more precious than gold or rubies.

I like to think that in dreams we catch glimpses of a life larger than our own. We see it as a little child, or as a savage who visits a civilized nation. Thoughts are imparted to us far above our ordinary thinking. Feelings nobler and wiser than any we have known thrill us between heartbeats. For one fleeting night a princelier nature captures us and we become as great as our aspirations.

Dreams of the Aged

KENNETH Z. ALTSHULER, M.D.;
MARTIN BARAD, M.D.; and ALVIN I. GOLDFARB, M.D.

Volunteers over age 65 were obtained in a New York City day center for the aged with a daily active membership of 150 persons. Anyone who offered a recent dream was interviewed weekly over a period of 2 months for the collection of further dream material. The 9 men and 16 women who participated in this study were all on their own in the community, in the sense that they maintained their living quarters without supervision. Able to travel freely and actively take part in the club's many programs, they considered themselves to be in good health, although each had some minor complaints and limitations. They reflected a variety of national, religious, and socioeconomic backgrounds within the framework of western culture. The age range was 65 to 86, with the median age of 69, considerably lower than that of the institutionalized group (median age 80 years).

A complete mental status examination was done in the initial interview, allowing for an impression of character diagnosis and the presence and degree of chronic brain syndrome, before the first dream was obtained. From a psychiatric point of view the subjects were classifiable as obsessional, hysterical (expressive), or passive dependent persons, except for one who was schizophrenic. All were making an adequate adjustment in the community, although 7 of the participants showed very mild depressive phenomena. Four persons clearly had chronic brain syndrome of mild degree, and in a number of other cases chronic brain syndrome was suspected on the brief evaluation.

About half of the 25 participants contributed material weekly, the others less regularly, for a total of 93 dreams during the survey period. Each person was asked what he thought his dream meant and why he felt he had it; whether he had been in the dream or only observing it; whether it was in color; whether it was flat or conveyed a sense of dimension and depth; whether his age in the dream was his present one, or younger or older. Spontaneous associations were also recorded and the physician asked about the person's general health and any specific problems. Aside from these considerations, the psychiatrist collecting the dreams was essentially a passive participant, and no therapeutic actions were undertaken.

RESULTS AND COMMENT

Many of the dreams reported seemed to have direct reference to concern about lost resources for coping with problems. There was no other clearly defined single category; the remainder were "miscellaneous."

A. *Dreams of Lost Resources.*—Several of the day center members presented dreams very similar to those of the institutionalized aged. The major theme was that of lost resources with or without clear indication of a wish for restoration of powers. Characteristically, the content of these dreams included wandering in a strange place, being lost or unable to find a way or choose a road, looking for help, being left behind, or losing something familiar. Sometimes the loss appeared to be projected, and it was the environment that changed in the course of a dream from the familiar to something threatening, strange, or uncontrollable. The affect in these dreams was rarely panic or frank fear. Rather, there was an uncomfortable vague sense of apprehension, uneasy confusion, helpless uncertainty, or strangeness. In some of the dreams the problem presented was successfully handled, and the unpleasant emotional tinge was dissipated.

A few of the dreams may serve as illustrations:

Dream of Being Lost: Dream 1. (Female, age 73): I lost my way traveling. I had to ask many strangers where to go. I'm not sure I got where I was going.

Dream of Loss of Control with Projection and Subsequent Anxiety: Dream 2. (Male, age 76): I go on the subway or elevator. At first it's okay. Then people look odd, like crazy people in a mental institution. It's uncomfortable and I want to get out.

Dream of Vulnerability to Harm from Others: Dream 3. (Male, age 66): I'm back with the Bolsheviks, without anything to show who I was. It looks like I'm going to be arrested and won't get free.

Dream of Loss in Protective Setting: Dream 4. (Female, age 86): I'm in my friend's house, but with bigger rooms, and I lost my coat. I keep finding my coat and losing it.

Dream of Finding Protective Feeding Parents: Dream 5. (Female, age 68): I was walking alone in endless space. Suddenly I saw my mother and father. They looked well and we talked. It seemed we were going out for dinner.

As shown in the last example, the hoped-for solution is usually cast in terms of receiving food, soothing physical closeness, or contact and comfort, often with actual or symbolic representation of a parent. In successive dreams such ideas of magical restoration frequently imply that, as in the institutionalized aged, the dream-collecting doctor is the source of help.

Dream of Being Helped by a Man: Dream 6. (Female, age 69, seen for second time): I'm in a hotel but I lost my room and don't know where to go. Then I was led to a small new "comfy" room by a man.

Dream in Which the Desire for Protection Is Sexualized: Dream 7. (Female, age 70, after 3 interviews): It's very embarrassing for a woman my age but I had a sexy dream with a rich young man who was very nice and who was going to "keep" me.

B. *The Miscellaneous Group of Dreams.*—The theme of loss and repair was not the major component in the dreams of another distinct group of persons. Their dreams were more richly elaborated, detailed, and varied. The dreamer often saw himself as active in pursuit of a goal, in contrast to the oral themes of wishful passivity coupled with bewilderment so frequently represented in the dreams of loss, weakness, or aloneness. Moreover, these dreams could be more easily referred to both neutral and disturbing specific events of the day, and appeared to be in intimate connection to problems in living. The dreamers were usually relatively self-sufficient persons deeply engaged in living and running their lives. The serial dreams from the group also showed less obvious evidence of incorporation of the psychiatrist into the dream content.

C. DREAM THEMES

Political Dreams in Hitler's Germany

CHARLOTTE BERADT

[A DREAM IN 1933 *by a thirty-year-old woman*]: "I was sitting in a box at the opera, dressed in a new gown, and with my hair beautifully done. It was a huge opera house with many, many tiers, and I was enjoying considerable admiration. They were presenting my favorite opera, *The Magic Flute*. When it came to the line 'That is the devil certainly,' a squad of policemen came stomping in and marched directly up to me. A machine had registered the fact that I had thought of Hitler on hearing the word 'devil.' I imploringly searched the festive crowd for some sign of help, but they all just sat there staring straight ahead, silent and expressionless, not one showing even pity. The old gentleman in an adjoining box looked kind and distinguished, but when I tried to catch his eye, he spat at me. . . ."

[*The dream of a woman milliner in 1933*]: "I dreamt I was talking in my sleep and to be on the safe side was speaking Russian (which I don't know, and anyway I never talk in my sleep) *so I'd not even understand myself* and so no one else could understand me in case I said anything about the government, for that, of course, is not permitted and must be reported. . . ."

[*A young man's dream*]: "I dreamt that I no longer dream about anything but rectangles, triangles, and octagons, all of which somehow look like Christmas cookies—you see, it was forbidden to dream. . . ."

[*A commentary by Bruno Bettelheim*]: "It is interesting to compare these dreams of persons who are threatened but have not yet suffered real extremity, with those dreamt, for example, by prisoners in concen-

38

tration camps. The concentration camp prisoner hardly ever dreamt about the dangers that stalked him nor about persecution by the Nazis. Short of his naked existence he had no further reason to fear what might happen to him. It had already happened. . . . Most of their [the prisoners'] dreams were of the good times they had had or were going to have—reassuring themselves that the nightmare of the camps was not permanent."

A Dream of Gladstone and Disraeli

EDWARD MAITLAND

February 1, 1881. In the early morning of the past night, being, I believe, asleep, I found myself in a vast building which I presently recognised as Westminster Hall. And as I stood on the steps which lead up to one of the law courts, which are on the right-hand side from the entrance, I observed in the centre of the hall a statue on a pedestal, both of which seemed to be of a light-grey stone; and remembering that I had never seen any statue there before, I looked at it with curiosity to see who it could be that had been deemed worthy of being thus commemorated in so distinguished a place. But before my glance had reached the face, it was arrested by the sight of two large labels depending from the waist, and bearing in graven characters, one the word *Judas*, and the other *Pilate*. Then continuing my glance upwards, with enhanced curiosity to see who it could be that was thus strangely labelled, and in a place the last conceivable for a practical joke, I found it was the living image of the Premier, Mr. Gladstone, being more like him than even the original. The labels were so hung as to be visible also from the steps at the upper end of the hall, towards which the statue faced . . . then my attention was drawn to the upper end of the hall. Here I noticed that the flight of steps which stretch across it had assumed the aspect of a stage; and upon that stage there presently stepped, coming as from behind the scenes to the right, the figure of Lord Beaconsfield. He wore his peer's dress, coronet, vest, knee-breeches, silk stockings, buckled shoes, all except the robes; and thus attired, looked tall beyond his actual height and very gaunt. His face as he entered bore a look of wistful expectation, and he gazed about as if anticipating some gratifying surprise, of the precise nature of which he was unaware.

Another moment and he had caught sight of the effigy of his hated rival, and advancing to the extreme verge of the stage, bent forward over it, the better to inspect it and read the inscriptions; having done which, he stepped back and drew himself up to his full height, and then stalked up and down the stage almost on tiptoe, his countenance radiant with glee and wearing an expression of triumph beyond description sardonic and malignant. Then advancing to the front again, he pointed with both arms outstretched to the utmost towards the statue, and in a stage-whisper startlingly loud, distinct, and intense, exclaimed several times over, "Pilate! Judas! Both! Both! Judas! Pilate! Both! Both!" fairly pirouetting up and down the stage in an ecstasy of delight. Presently his attention was attracted by something at the opposite end of the hall; and, following his glance, I saw the door open and the form of Mr. Gladstone himself enter and take up a position about midway between it and his statue, facing the latter, the back of which was towards him. He wore a court or some similar official costume, and the attitude he struck reminded me of the painting which represents Napoleon Buonaparte standing on the heights of St. Helena, absorbed in contemplation; for the arms were crossed over the chest, the face was down-turned, and the eyes glanced upwards from beneath the brows at his effigy.

Meanwhile Lord Beaconsfield had quitted his position on the stage, and gliding swiftly and noiselessly as a meteor across the hall, without touching the ground, took his stand close by Mr. Gladstone, and commenced circling and almost dancing around him; and then, pointing alternately to him and to his image, he exclaimed over and over again, with redoubled glee and bitterness of mockery, "Judas! Pilate! You! You! Traitor! Executioner! You! You! Both! Both! You! You!" And this he continued to do without ceasing so long as the vision lasted.

But neither by look, by gesture, nor by word did Mr. Gladstone betray the smallest consciousness of his tormentor's presence, but kept his eyes steadfastly fixed on his effigy, absorbed in contemplating with anguish and remorse unspeakable his own spiritual self and history. For as he gazed and brooded his whole form writhed and his face blanched as with an extremity of agony at the contrast he now recognised as subsisting between that which he had it in him to have been and to have done, had he but followed his better nature and higher impulses, and that which he had actually been and actually done. No spectacle could be imagined more painful than this one of a lapsed soul undergoing the awful penance of the consciousness of having turned his back upon its true ideal . . . and enduring the while the taunts of the fiend who, as his evil genius, had lured him to his ruin. Nevertheless, it was clearly impressed upon me, as I looked, that his very ability thus to suffer was a demonstration of his salvability; while, as for the other, he was an ingrained mocker, and as such was as clearly past praying for. In both cases that which I beheld was the very essence of the men, their own innermost spiritual selves, unveiled and undimmed by any material covering, so marvellously vivid were their portraitures as thus presented to my spiritual eyes.

The Military Dream

HERBERT GREENHOUSE

Generals and politicians who lead their countries during wars often dream of victory or defeat in battle. The ancient Romans fought many times with their most hated foe, Carthage, whose great hero was Hannibal. One night in a dream Hannibal was visited by a comely young man who said he was a messenger from heaven, sent to tell Hannibal he must invade Italy. In the dream there was an enormous serpent which destroyed everything in sight while lightning flashed from an angry sky. The dream visitor told Hannibal that this was the fate of Rome if Hannibal went to war with his enemy. Encouraged by his dream, Hannibal invaded Rome and devastated the city.

Xerxes, the leader of Persia in the first part of the fifth century B.C., was another general who went to war because of a dream, but he would have been better off if he had stayed home. Xerxes, debating whether to invade Greece, was visited in a dream by a tall man who criticized him for not carrying through his invasion plans. The next night the dream visitor came again and warned that if Xerxes did not invade Greece, he would lose his power and greatness. Worried, Xerxes consulted his uncle Artabanus, who had advised against the invasion, and asked him to sleep in the royal bed to see if the visitor would return. Artabanus dressed himself in Xerxes' clothes and slept in the king's bed.

The tall man came again that night in Artabanus's dream and threatened to gouge out the old man's eyes if he continued to advise against the invasion. Artabanus woke up yelling and ran to Xerxes, now convinced that the orders to invade had come from God. Whereupon Xerxes, who had the largest and most formidable army in the world in 480 B.C., invaded the city states of Greece and lost the war when he was soundly defeated at the naval battle of Salamis.

Alexander the Great had his share of dreams, and one of them led directly to military victory. The city of Tyre had stubbornly held out for seven months against the onslaughts of his vast army. One night he dreamed that a satyr was playing nearby, but everytime he tried to grab it, it skillfully eluded him. Finally, in the dream, he persuaded the satyr to surrender. Alexander's dream interpreters cleverly divided the word "satyr" into two parts—*sa Tyros*—meaning "Tyre is yours." Thus encouraged, Alexander stormed the city and forced it to surrender.

Three Paradoxical Dreams
1. A Dream Dilemma
CHUANG TZŬ

Translated by H. A. Giles

Once upon a time, I, Chuang Tzŭ, dreamt I was a butterfly, fluttering hither and thither, to all intents and purposes a butterfly. I was conscious only of following my fancies as a butterfly, and was unconscious of my individuality as a man. Suddenly I awaked, and there I lay, myself again. Now I do not know whether I was a man dreaming I was a butterfly, or whether I am now a butterfly dreaming I am a man. Between a man and a butterfly there is necessarily a barrier. The transition is called metempsychosis.

2. C. G. Jung and the Yogi*
CARL G. JUNG, M.D.

In one dream, which I had in October 1958, I caught sight from my house of two lens-shaped metallically gleaming disks, which hurtled in a narrow arc over the house and down to the lake. They were two UFOs (Unidentified Flying Objects). Then another body came flying directly toward me. It was a perfectly circular lens, like the objective of a telescope. At a distance of four or five hundred yards it stood still for a moment, and then flew off. Immediately afterward, another came speeding through the air: a lens with a metallic extension which led to a box—a magic lantern. At a distance of sixty or seventy yards it stood still in the air, pointing straight at me. I awoke with a feeling of astonishment. Still half in the dream, the thought passed through my head: "We always think that the UFOs are projections of ours. Now it turns out that we are their projections. I am projected by the magic lantern as C. G. Jung. But who manipulates the apparatus?"

* From *Memories, Dreams, Reflections*.

I had dreamed once before of the problem of the self and the ego. In that earlier dream I was on a hiking trip. I was walking along a little road through a hilly landscape; the sun was shining and I had a wide view in all directions. Then I came to a small wayside chapel. The door was ajar, and I went in. To my surprise there was no image of the Virgin on the altar, and no crucifix either, but only a wonderful flower arrangement. But then I saw that on the floor in front of the altar, facing me, sat a yogi—in lotus posture, in deep meditation. When I looked at him more closely, I realized that he had my face. I started in profound fright, and awoke with the thought: "Aha, so he is the one who is meditating me. He has a dream, and I am it." I knew that when he awakened, I would no longer be.

3. The Doctor Becomes the Poet

SILAS WEIR MITCHELL, M.D.

On January 29, 1905 Dr. Silas Weir Mitchell wrote Howard Pyle, American artist, in part as follows:

"I once dreamed of an author—only once. It was while in Rome. I stood besides Keats's grave at night; I knew that he was standing beside me. He said, 'I am you and you are I.' I said 'Impossible.' 'Oh,' he replied, 'all things are possible in sleep,' and then I was alone. I recall for you this queer experience, and thank you for the delightful remembrance."

Two Musical Dreams
1. A Handelian Concert

SAMUEL BUTLER

I found myself going off into a doze, and thought the burnished man from the furnace came up and sat beside me, and laid his hand upon my shoulder. Then I saw the green slopes that rise all round the lake were much higher than I had thought; they went up thousands of feet, and there were pine forests upon them, while two large glaciers came down in streams that ended in a precipice of ice, falling sheer into the lake. The edges of the mountains against the sky were rugged and full of clefts, through which I saw thick clouds of dust being blown by the wind as though from the other side of the mountains.

And as I looked, I saw that this was not dust, but people coming in crowds from the other side, but so small as to be visible at first only as dust. And the people became musicians, and the mountainous amphitheatre a huge orchestra, and the glaciers were two noble armies of womensingers in white robes, ranged tier upon tier behind each other, and the pines became orchestral players, while the thick dust-like cloud of chorussingers kept pouring in through the clefts in the precipices in inconceivable numbers. When I turned my telescope upon them I saw they were crowded up to the extreme edge of the mountains, so that I could see underneath the soles of their boots as their legs dangled in the air. In the midst of all, a precipice that rose from out of the glaciers shaped itself suddenly into an organ, and there was one whose face I well knew sitting at the keyboard, smiling and pluming himself like a bird as he thundered forth a giant fugue by way of overture. I heard the great pedal notes of the bass stalk majestically up and down, like the rays of the Aurora that go about upon the face of the heavens in Labrador. Then presently the people rose and sang the chorus "Venus laughing from the skies"; but ere the sound had died away, I awoke.

2. *Lucifer Plays the Violin*

HERBERT GREENHOUSE

The devil has appeared in dreams in many roles, but the first indication that he was a superb musician in addition to his other talents came in a dream of the eighteenth-century composer Giuseppe Tartini. Tartini dreamed one night that he had made a deal with Lucifer, who promised aid and comfort whenever the composer needed him. Now on a friendly basis with the Lord of the Lower Regions, Tartini handed his guest a violin and asked him to play.

The Evil One then played a melody "so singularly beautiful, and executed with such taste and precision, that it surpassed all that he had ever heard or conceived in his life." Tartini woke up, stumbled over to his violin case, removed the instrument, and tried to play what he had heard in his dream. All he could remember, however, was a repeated trill, but he used it later as the theme for his best work, "The Devil's Trill."

A Theater Dream

THOMAS HOOD

I had a dismal dream once . . . which originated in the failure of my first, and last, attempt as a dramatic writer. Many of my readers, if I were to name the piece in question, would remember its signal condemnation. As soon as the *Tragedy of my Tragedy* was completed, I got into a coach and rode home. My nerves were quivering with shame and mortification. I tried to compose myself over *Paradise Lost*, but it failed to soothe me. I flung myself into bed, and at length slept; but the disaster of the night still haunted my dreams; I was again in the accursed theatre, but with a difference. It was a compound of the Drury Lane Building and Pandemonium. There were the old shining green pillars, on either side of the stage, but, above, a sublimer dome than ever overhung mortal playhouse. The wonted familiars were in keeping of the fore-spoken seats, but the first companies they admitted were new and strange to the place. The first and second tiers,

"With dreadful faces throng'd, and fiery arms,"

showed like those purgatorial circles sung of by the ancient Florentine. Satan was in the stage-box. The pit, dismally associated with its bottomless namesake, was peopled with fiends. Mehu scowled from the critics' seat. Belial, flushed with wine, led on with shout and catcall the uproar of the one shilling infernals. My hair stood upright with dread and horror; I had an appalling sense that more than my dramatic welfare was at stake:—that it was to be not a purely literary ordeal. An alarming figure, sometimes a newspaper reporter, sometimes a devil, so prevaricating are the communications of sleep, was sitting, with his notebook, at my side. My play began. As it proceeded, sounds indescribable arose from the infernal auditory, increasing till the end of the first act. The familiar cry of "Chuse any oranges!" was then intermingled with the murmuring of demons. The tumult grew with the progress of the play. The last act passed in dumb show, the horned monsters bellowing, throughout, like the wild bulls of

Bashan. Prongs and flesh-hooks showered upon the stage. Mrs. Siddons— the human nature thus jumbling with the diabolical—was struck by a brim- stone ball. Her lofty brother, robed in imperial purple, came forward to- wards the orchestra, to remonstrate, and was received like the Arch-devil in the poem:

> "He hears
> On all sides, from innumerable tongues,
> A dismal universal hiss, the sound
> Of public scorn."

He bowed to the sense of the house, and withdrew. My doom was sealed; the recording devil noted down my sentence. A suffocating vapour, now smelling of sulphur, and now of gas, issued from the unquenchable stage lamps. The flames of the Catalonian Castle, burning in the back scene, in compliance with the catastrophe of the piece, blazed up with horrible import. My flesh crept all over me. I thought of the everlasting torments, and at the next moment, of the morrow's paragraphs, I shrunk at once from the comments of the *Morning Post*, and the hot marl of Malebolge. The sins of authorship had confounded themselves, inextricably, with the mortal sins of the law. I could not disentangle my own from my play's perdition. I was damned; but whether spiritually or dramatically the twilight intelligence of a dream was not clear enough to determine.

A Medical Dream

ANONYMOUS

Galen's three dreams—the third more worthy of being called a miracle, was, when being twice admonished in his sleep, to cut the artery that lies between the fore finger and the thumb, and doing it accordingly, he was afreed from a continual daily pain with which he was afflicted in that part, where the liver is joined to the midriff; and this he has testified at the end of his book of Venesection. 'Tis certainly a very great example, when a man so great as he was in the medicinal art, put so much confidence in a dream as to try experiments upon himself; where he was to run the risque of his life, in his very own art. I cannot help but admire his probity in the next place, that where he might have arrogated the merit of the invention to himself, and placed it wholly to the account of the subtilty, and pene- tration of his own genius, he attributed it to God, to whom it was due.

Creative Dreams of Writers and Scholars
1. A Scholar's Translation Dream

WILLIAM ROMAINE NEWBOLD

During the winter of 1882–3 Dr. Herman V. Hilprecht, Professor of Assyrian in the University of Pennsylvania, was working with Professor Friedrich Delitzsch and was preparing to publish, as his dissertation, a text, transliteration and translation of a stone of Nebuchadnezzar I, with notes. He accepted at that time the explanation given by Professor Delitzsch of the name Nebuchadnezzar—Nabû-kudûrru-usur—"Nebo protect my mason's pad, or mortar board," *i.e.*, "my work as a builder." One night after working late, he went to bed about two o'clock in the morning. After a somewhat restless sleep, he awoke with his mind full of the thought that the name should be translated "Nebo protect my boundary." He had a dim consciousness of having been working at his table in a dream, but he could never recall the details of the process by which he arrived at this con-clusion. Reflecting upon it when awake, however, he at once saw that *kudûrru*, "boundary," could be derived from the verb *kadâru*, to enclose. Shortly afterwards he published this translation in his dissertation, and it has since been universally adopted.

I quote this experience, in itself of a familiar type, on account of its interest when viewed with the more curious dream next to be related. I was told of the latter shortly after it happened, and here translate an account written in German by Professor Hilprecht, August 8, 1893, before the more complete confirmation was received.

"One Saturday evening about the middle of March, 1893, I had been wearying myself, as I had done so often in the weeks preceding, in the vain attempt to decipher two small fragments of agate which were sup-posed to belong to the finger rings of some Babylonian. The labor was much increased by the fact that the fragments presented remnants only of characters and lines, that dozens of similar small fragments had been found in the ruins of the temple of Bel at Nippur with which nothing could be done, that in this case, furthermore, I had never had the originals before me, but only a hasty sketch made by one of the members of the expedition sent by the University of Pennsylvania to Babylonia. I could not say more than the fragments, taking into consideration the place in which they were found and the peculiar characteristics of the cuneiform characters pre-served upon them, sprang from the Cassite period of Babylonian history

(Ca. 1700–1140 B.C.); moreover, as the first character of the third line of the first fragment seemed to be KU, I ascribed this fragment, with an interrogation point, to King Kurigalzu, while I placed the other fragment, as unclassifiable, with other Cassite fragments upon a page of my book where I published the unclassifiable fragments. The proofs already lay before me, but I was far from satisfied. The whole problem passed yet again through my mind that March evening before I placed my mark of approval upon the last correction in the book. Even then I had come to no conclusion. About midnight, weary and exhausted, I went to bed and was soon in deep sleep. Then I dreamed the following remarkable dream:

"A tall, thin priest of the old pre-Christian Nippur, about forty years of age and clad in a simple abba, led me to the treasure chamber of the temple, on its southeast side. He went with me into a small, low-ceiled room without windows, in which there was a large wooden chest, while scraps of agate and lapis lazuli lay scattered on the floor. Here he addressed me as follows: 'The two fragments which you have published separately on pages 22 and 26, belong together, are not finger rings and their history is as follows: King Kurigalzu (Ca. 1300 B.C.) once sent to the temple of Bel, among other articles of agate and lapis lazuli, an inscribed votive cylinder of agate. Then we priests suddenly received the command to make for the statue of the god Ninib a pair of earrings of agate. We were in great dismay, since there was no agate as raw material at hand. In order to execute the command there was nothing for us to do but cut the votive cylinder into three parts, thus making three rings, each of which contained a portion of the original inscription. The first two rings served as earrings for the statue of the god; the two fragments which have given you so much trouble are portions of them. If you will put the two together you will have confirmation of my words. But the third ring you have not found in the course of your excavations and you never will find it.' With this the priest disappeared. I woke at once and immediately told my wife the dream that I might not forget it. Next morning—Sunday—I examined the fragments once more in the light of these disclosures, and to my astonishment found all the details of the dream precisely verified in so far as the means of verification were in my hands. The original inscription on the votive cylinder reads: 'To the god Ninib, son of Bel, his lord, has Kurigalzu, pontifex of Bel, presented this.'

The problem was thus at last solved . . .

H. V. Hilprecht."

Upon the priest's statement that the fragments were those of a votive cylinder, Professor Hilprecht makes the following comment:

"There are not many of these votive cylinders. I had seen, all told, up to that evening, not more than two. They very much resemble the so-called seal cylinders, but usually have no pictorial representation upon them, and the inscription is not reversed, not being intended for use in sealing, but is written as it is read." . . .

At the time Professor told me of this curious dream, which was a few weeks after its occurrence, there remained a serious difficulty which he was not able to explain. According to the memoranda in our possession, the fragments were of different colors, and therefore could have scarcely belonged to the same object. The original fragments were in Constantinople, and it was with no little interest that I awaited Professor Hilprecht's return from the trip which he made thither in the summer of 1893. I translate again his own account of what he then ascertained.

"In August, 1893, I was sent by the Committee on the Babylonian Expedition to Constantinople, to catalogue and study the objects got from Nippur and preserved there in the Imperial Museum. It was to me a matter of the greatest interest to see for myself the objects which, according to my dream, belonged together, in order to satisfy myself that they had both originally been parts of the same votive cylinder. Halil Bey, the director of the Museum, to whom I told my dream, and of whom I asked permission to see the objects, was so interested in the matter, that he at once opened the case of the Babylonian section, and requested me to search. Father Scheil, an Assyriologist from Paris, who had examined and arranged the articles excavated by us before me, had not recognized the fact that these fragments belonged together, and consequently I found one fragment in one case, and the other in a case far away from it. As soon as I found the fragments and put them together, the truth of the dream was demonstrated *ad oculos*—they had, in fact, once belonged to one and the same votive cylinder. As it had originally been of finely veined agate, the stonecutter's saw had accidentally divided the object in such a way that the whitish vein of the stone appeared only upon the one fragment and the larger gray surface upon the other. Thus I was able to explain Dr. Peters' discordant descriptions of the two fragments.—November 10, 1895."

Professor Hilprecht is unable to say what language the old priest used in addressing him. He is quite certain that it was not Assyrian, and thinks it was either English or German.

There are two especial points of interest in this case, the character of the information conveyed, and the dramatic form in which it was put. The apparently novel points of information given were:

1. That the fragments belonged together.
2. That they were fragments of a votive cylinder.
3. That the cylinder was presented by King Kurigalzu.
4. That is was dedicated to Ninib.
5. That it had been made into a pair of earrings.
6. That the "treasure chamber" was located upon the southeast side of the temple.

A careful analysis reveals the fact that not one of these items was beyond the reaches of the processes of associative reasoning which Professor Hilprecht daily employs. Among the possible associative consequents of the writing upon the one fragment, some of the associative consequents of the writing on the other were sub-consciously involved; the attraction of these identical elements brings the separate pieces into mental juxtaposition, precisely as the pieces of a "dissected map" find one another in thought. In waking life the dissimilarity in color inhibited any tendency on the part of the associative process to bring them together, but in sleep this difference of color seems to have been forgotten—there being no mention made of it—and the assimilation took place. The second point is more curious, but is not inexplicable. For as soon as the fragments were brought into juxtaposition mentally, enough of the inscription became legible to suggest the original character of the object. This is true also of the third and fourth points. The source of the fifth is not so clear. Upon examining the originals, Professor Hilprecht felt convinced from the size of the hole still to be seen through the fragments that they could not have been used as finger-rings and that they had been used as earrings, but the written description which he had before him at the time of his dream did not bring these points to view. Still, such earrings are by no means uncommon objects. Such a supposition might well have occurred to Professor Hilprecht in his waking state and, in view of the lack of positive confirmation, it would be rash to ascribe it to any supernormal power. The last point is most interesting. When he told me this story, Professor Hilprecht remembered that he had heard from Dr. John J. Peters, before he had the dream, of the discovery of a room in which were remnants of a wooden box, while the floor was strewn with fragments of agate and lapis lazuli. The walls, of course, and ceiling have long since perished. The location, however, of the room he did not know, and suggested I should write to Dr. Peters and find out whether it was correctly given in his dream, and whether Dr. Peters had told him of it. Dr. Peters replied that the location given was correct, but, he adds, he told Professor Hilprecht all these facts as long ago as 1891, and thinks he provided him with a drawing of the room's relation to the temple. Of this Professor Hilprecht had no recollection. He thinks it probable that Dr. Peters told him orally of the location of the room, but feels sure that if any plan was given him it would now be found among his papers. This is a point of no importance, however. We certainly cannot regard the location as ascertained by supernormal mean. . . .

Undoubtedly the old priest's statements were attained by normal processes of associative reasoning which Professor Hilprecht has now forgotten, and upon them, as upon a logical core, the dream imagery has been superimposed, thus producing a time-hallucination.

2. The "Little People" in an Author's Dreams

ROBERT LOUIS STEVENSON

The past is all of one texture—whether feigned or suffered—whether acted out in three dimensions, or only witnessed in that small theatre of the brain which we keep brightly lighted all night long, after the jets are down, and darkness and sleep reign undisturbed in the remainder of the body. There is no distinction on the face of our experiences; one is vivid indeed, and one dull, and one pleasant, and another agonizing to remember; but which of them is what we call true, and which a dream, there is not one hair to prove. The past stands on a precarious footing; another straw split in the field of metaphysic, and behold us robbed of it. . . . Not an hour, not a mood, not a glance of the eye, can we revoke; it is all gone, past conjuring. And yet conceive us robbed of it, conceive that little thread of memory that we trail behind us broken at the pocket's edge; and in what naked nullity should we be left! for we only guide ourselves, and only know ourselves, by these air-painted pictures of the past.

Upon these grounds, there are some among us who claimed to have lived longer and more richly than their neighbors; when they lay asleep they claim they were still active; and among the treasures of memory that all men review for their amusement, these count in no second place the harvests of their dreams. There is one of this kind whom I have in my eye, and whose case is perhaps unusual enough to be described. He was from a child an ardent and uncomfortable dreamer. When he had a touch of fever at night, and the room swelled and shrank, and his clothes, hanging on a nail, now loomed up instant to the bigness of a church, and now drew away into a horror of infinite distance and infinite littleness, the poor soul was very well aware of what must follow, and struggled hard against the approaches of that slumber which was the beginning of sorrows. But his struggles were in vain; sooner or later the night-hag would have him by the throat, and pluck him, strangling and screaming, from his sleep. His dreams were at times commonplace enough, at times very strange; at times they were almost formless. He would be haunted, for instance, by nothing more definite than a certain hue of brown, which he did not mind in the least while he was awake, but feared and loathed while he was dreaming; at times, again, they took on every detail of circumstance, as when once he supposed he must swallow the populous world, and awoke screaming with horror of the thought. . . .

These were extremely poor experiences, on the whole; and at that time of life my dreamer would have very willingly parted with his power of dreams. But presently, in the course of his growth, the cries and physical contortions passed away, seemingly forever; his visions were still for the most part miserable, but they were more constantly supported; and he would awake with no more extreme symptom than a flying heart, a freezing scalp, cold sweats, and the speechless midnight fear. His dreams, too, as befitted a mind better stocked with particulars, became more circumstantial, and had more the air and continuity of life. The look of the world beginning to take hold on his attention, scenery came to play a part in his sleeping as well as in his waking thoughts, so that he would take long, uneventful journeys and see strange towns and beautiful places as he lay in bed. And, what is more significant, an odd taste that he had for the Georgian costume and for stories laid in that period of English history, began to rule the features of his dreams; so that he masqueraded there in a three-cornered hat, and was much engaged with the Jacobite conspiracy between the hour for bed and that for breakfast. About the same time, he began to read in his dreams—tales, for the most part, and for the most part after the manner of G. P. R. James, but so incredibly more vivid and moving than any printed book, that he has ever since been malcontent with literature.

And then, while he was yet a student, there came to him a dream-adventure which he has no anxiety to repeat; he began, that is to say, to dream in sequence and thus to lead a double life—one of the day, one of the night —one that he had every reason to believe was the true one, another that he had no means of proving to be false. I should have said he studied, or was by way of studying, at Edinburgh College, which (it may be supposed) was how I came to know him. Well, in his dream life, he passed a long day in the surgical theatre, his heart in his mouth, his teeth on edge, seeing monstrous malformations and the abhorred dexterity of surgeons. In a heavy, rainy, foggy evening he came forth into the South Bridge, turned up the High Street, and entered the door of a tall *land*, at the top of which he supposed himself to lodge. All night long, in his wet clothes, he climbed the stairs, stair after stair in endless series, and at every second flight a flaring lamp with a reflector. All night long, he brushed by single persons passing downwards—beggarly women of the street, great, weary, muddy laborers, poor scarecrows of men, pale parodies of women—but all drowsy and weary like himself, and all single, and all brushing against him as they passed. In the end, out of a northern window, he would see day beginning to whiten over the Firth, give up the ascent, turn to descend, and in a breath be back again upon the streets, in his wet clothes, haggard dawn trudging to another day of monstrosities and operations. Time went quicker in the life of dreams, some seven hours (as near as he can guess) to one; and it went, besides, more intensely, so that the gloom of these fancied experiences clouded the day, and he had not shaken off their shadow ere it was time to lie down and to renew them. I cannot tell how long it was that he endured this discipline; but it was long enough to leave a great black blot upon his memory, long enough to send him, trembling for his reason, to the doors of a certain doctor; whereupon with a single draught he was restored to the common lot of man.

The poor gentleman has since been troubled by nothing of the sort; indeed, his nights were for some while like other men's, now blank, now checkered with dreams, and these sometimes charming, sometimes appalling, but except for an occasional vividness, of no extraordinary kind. I will just note one of these occasions, ere I pass on to what makes my dreamer truly interesting. It seemed to him that he was in the first floor of a rough hill-farm. The room showed some poor efforts at gentility, a carpet on the floor, a piano, I think, against the wall; but, for all these refinements, there was no mistaking he was in a moorland place, among hillside people, and set in miles of heather. He looked down from the window upon a bare farmyard, that seemed to have been long disused. A great, uneasy stillness lay upon the world. There was no sign of the farm-folk or of any livestock, save for an old brown, curly dog of the retriever breed, who sat close in against the wall of the house and seemed to be dozing. Something about this dog disquieted the dreamer; it was quite a nameless feeling, for the beast looked right enough—indeed, he was so old and dull and dusty and broken down, that he should rather have awakened pity; and yet the conviction came and grew upon the dreamer that this was no proper dog at all, but something hellish. A great many dozing summer flies hummed about the yard; and presently the dog thrust forth his paw, caught a fly in his open palm, carried it to his mouth like an ape, and looking suddenly up at the dreamer in the window, winked to him with one eye. The dream went on, it matters not how it went; it was a good dream as dreams go; but there was nothing in the sequel worthy of that devilish brown dog. And the point of interest for me lies partly in that very fact; that having found so singular an incident, my imperfect dreamer should prove unable to carry the tale to a fit end and fall back on indescribable noises and indiscriminate horrors. It would be different now; he knows his business better!

For, to approach the last point: This honest fellow had long been in the custom of setting himself to sleep with tales, and so had his father before him; but these were irresponsible inventions, told for the teller's pleasure, with no eye to the crass public or the thwart reviewer; tales where a thread might be dropped, or one adventure quitted for another, on fancy's least suggestion. So that the little people who manage man's internal theatre had not as yet received a very rigorous training; and played upon their stage like children who should have slipped into the house and found it empty, rather than like drilled actors performing a set piece to a huge hall of faces. But presently my dreamer began to turn his former amusement of story-telling to (what is called) account; by which I mean that he began to write and sell his tales. Here he was, and here were the little people who did that part of his business, in quite new conditions. The stories must now be trimmed and pared and set upon all fours, they must run from a beginning to an end and fit (after a manner) with the laws of life; the pleasure, in one word, had become a business; and that not only for the dreamer, but for the little people of his theatre. These understood the change as well as he. When he lay down to prepare himself for sleep, he no longer sought amusement, but printable and profitable tales; and after he had dozed off in his box seat, his little people continued their evolutions with the same mercantile signs. All other forms of dream deserted him but two; he still occasionally reads the most delightful books, he still visits at times the most delightful places; and it is perhaps worthy of note that to these same places, and to one in particular, he returns at intervals of months and years, finding new field-paths, visiting new neighbors, beholding that happy valley under new effects of noon and dawn and sunset. But all the rest of the family of visions is quite lost to him; the common, mangled versions of yesterday's affairs, the raw-head-and-bloody-bones nightmare, rumored to be the child of toasted cheese—these and their like are gone; and, for the most part, whether awake or asleep, he is simply occupied—he or his little people—in consciously making stories for the market. This dreamer (like many other persons) has encountered some trifling vicissitudes of fortune. When the bank begins to send letters and the butcher to linger at the back gate, he sets to belaboring his brain after a story, for that is his readiest money-winner; and, behold! at once the little people begin to bestir them-selves in the same quest, and labor all night long, and all night long set before him truncheons of tales upon their lighted theatre. No fear of his being frightened now; the flying heart and the frozen scalp are things bygone; applause, growing applause, growing interest, growing exultation in his own cleverness (for he takes all the credit), and at last a jubilant leap to wakefulness, with the cry, "I have it, that'll do!" upon his lips: with such and similar emotions he sits at these nocturnal dramas, with such outbreaks, like Claudius in the play, he scatters the performance in the midst. Often enough the waking is a disappointment: he has been too deep asleep, as I explain the thing; drowsiness has gained his little people, they have gone stumbling and maundering through their parts; and the play, to the awakened mind, is seen to be a tissue of absurdities. And yet how often have these sleepless Brownies done him honest service, and given him, as he sat idly taking his pleasure in the boxes, better tales than he could fashion for himself. . . .

The more I think of it, the more I am moved to press upon the world my question: Who are the Little People? They are near connections of the dreamer's, beyond doubt; they share in his financial worries and have an eye to the bankbook; they share plainly in his training; they have plainly learned like him to build the scheme of a considerable story in progressive order; only I think they have more talent; and one thing is beyond doubt, they can tell him a story piece by piece, like a serial, and keep him all the while in ignorance of where they aim. Who are they, then? and who is the dreamer?

Well, as regards the dreamer, I can answer that, for he is no less a person than myself—as I might have told you from the beginning, only that the critics murmur over my consistent egotism—and as I am positively forced to tell you now, or I could advance but little farther with my story. And for the Little People, what shall I say they are but just my Brownies, God bless them! who do one-half my work for me while I am fast asleep, and in all human likelihood, do the rest for me as well, when I am wide awake and fondly suppose I do it myself. That part which is done while I am sleeping is the Brownies' part beyond contention; but that which is done when I am up and about is by no means necessarily mine, since all goes to show the Brownies have a hand in it even then. Here is a doubt that much concerns my conscience. For myself—what I call I, my conscience ego, the denizen of the pineal gland unless he has changed his residence since Descartes, the man with the conscience and the variable bank account, the man with the hat and the boots, and the privilege of voting and not carrying the candidate at the general elections—I am sometimes tempted to suppose he is no storyteller at all, but a creature as matter of fact as any cheesemonger or any cheese, and a realist bemired up to the ears in actuality; so that, by that account, the whole of my published fiction should be the single-handed product of some Brownie, some Familiar, some unseen collaborator, whom I keep locked in a back garret, while I get all the praise and he but a share (which I cannot prevent him getting) of the pudding. I am an excellent adviser, something like Molière's servant; I will pull back and cut down; and I dress the whole in the best words and sentences that I can find and make; I hold the pen, too; and I do the sitting at the table, which is about the worst of it; and when all is done, I make up the manuscript and pay for the registration; so that, on the whole, I have some claim to share, though not so largely as I do, in the profits of our common enterprise.

I can give but an instance or so of what part is done sleeping and what part awake, and leave the reader to share what laurels there are, at his own nod, between myself and my collaborators; and to do this I will first take a book that a number of persons have been polite enough to read, the *Strange Case of Dr. Jekyll and Mr. Hyde.* I had long been trying to write a story on this subject, to find a body, a vehicle, for that strong sense of man's double being which must at times come in upon and overwhelm the mind of every thinking creature. I had even written one, *The Travelling Com-*

panion, which was returned by an editor on the plea that it was a work of genius and indecent, and which I burned the other day on the ground that it was not a work of genius, and that *Jekyll* had supplanted it. Then came one of those financial fluctuations which (with an elegant modesty) I have hitherto referred to in the third person. For two days I went about racking my brains for a plot of any sort; and on the second night I dreamed the scene at the window, and a scene afterwards split in two, in which Hyde, pursued for some crime, took the powder and underwent the change in the presence of his pursuers. All the rest was made awake, and consciously, although I think I can trace in much of it the manner of my Brownies. The meaning of the tale is therefore mine, and had long pre-existed in my garden of Adonis, and tried one body after another in vain; indeed, I do most of the morality, worse luck! and my Brownies have not a rudiment of what we call a conscience. Mine, too, is the setting, mine the characters. All that was given me was the matter of three scenes, and the central idea of a voluntary change becoming involuntary. Will it be thought ungenerous, after I have been so liberally ladling out praise to my unseen collaborators, if I here toss them over, bound hand and foot, into the arena of the critics? For the business of the powders, which so many have censured, is, I am relieved to say, not mine at all but the Brownies'. Of another tale, in case the reader should have glanced at it, I may say a word: the not very defensible story of *Olalla.* Here the court, the mother, the mother's niche, Olalla, Olalla's chamber, the meetings on the stair, the broken window, the ugly scene of the bite, were all given me in bulk and detail as I have tried to write them; to this I added only the external scenery (for in my dream I never was beyond the court), the portrait, the characters of Felipe and the priest, the moral, such as it is, and the last pages, such as, alas! they are. And I may even say that in this case the moral itself was given me; for it arose immediately on a comparison of the mother and the daughter, and from the hideous trick of atavism in the first. Sometimes a parabolic sense is still more undeniably present in a dream; sometimes I cannot but suppose my Brownies have been aping Bunyan, and yet in no case with what would possibly be called a moral in a tract; never with the ethical narrowness; conveying hints instead of life's larger limitations and that sort of sense which we seem to perceive in the arabesque of time and space.

For the most part, it will be seen, my Brownies are somewhat fantastic, like their stories hot and hot, full of passion and the picturesque, alive with animating incident; and they have no prejudice against the supernatural. But the other day they gave me a surprise, entertaining me with a love story, a little April comedy, which I ought certainly to hand over to the author of *A Chance Acquaintance,* for he could write it as it should be written, and I am sure (although I mean to try) that I cannot. But who would have supposed that a Brownie of mine should invent a tale for Mr. Howells?

3. How Coleridge Wrote "Kubla Khan"

SAMUEL TAYLOR COLERIDGE

The following fragment is here published at the request of a poet of great and deserved celebrity [Byron] and, as far as the author's own opinions are concerned, rather as a psychological curiosity, than on the ground of any supposed poetic merits.

In the summer of the year 1797 the author, then in ill health, had retired to a lonely farmhouse between Porlock and Linton, on the Exmoor confines of Somerset and Devonshire. In consequence of a slight indisposition, an anodyne had been prescribed, from the effects of which he fell asleep in his chair at the moment that he was reading the following sentence, or words of the same substance, in "Purchas's Pilgrimage": "Here the Khan Kubla commanded a palace to be built, and a stately garden thereunto. And thus ten miles of fertile ground were inclosed with a wall." The author continued for about three hours in a profound sleep, at least of the external senses, during which time he had the most vivid confidence, that he could not have composed less than from two to three hundred lines; if that indeed can be called composition in which all the images rose up before him as things, with a parallel production of the correspondent expressions, without any sensation or consciousness of effort. On awaking he appeared to himself to have a distinct recollection of the whole, and taking his pen, ink and paper, instantly and eagerly wrote down the lines that are here preserved. At this moment he was unfortunately called out by a person on business from Porlock, and detained by him above an hour, and on his return to his room, found, to his no small surprise and mortification, that though he still retained some vague and dim recollection of the general purport of the vision, yet, with the exception of some eight or ten scattered lines and images, all the rest had passed away like the images on the surface of a stream into which a stone has been cast, but, alas! without the after restoration of the latter!

> Then all the charm
> Is broken—all that phantom-world so fair
> Vanishes, and a thousand circlets spread,
> And each mis-shapes the other. Stay awhile,
> Poor youth! who scarcely dar'st lift up thine eyes—
> The stream will soon renew its smoothness, soon
> The visions will return! and lo, he stays
> And soon the fragments dim of lovely forms

Come trembling back, unite, and now once more
The pool becomes a mirror.   S. T. C.

KUBLA KHAN

In Xanadu did Kubla Khan
A stately pleasure-dome decree:
Where Alph, the sacred river, ran
Through caverns measureless to man
    Down to a sunless sea.
So twice five miles of fertile ground
With walls and towers were girdled round:
And there were gardens bright with sinuous rills,
Where blossomed many an incense-bearing tree;
And here were forests ancient as the hills,
Enfolding sunny spots of greenery.

But oh! that deep romantic chasm which slanted
Down the green hill athwart a cedarn cover!
A savage place! as holy and enchanted
As e'er beneath a waning moon was haunted
By woman wailing for her demon-lover!
And from this chasm, with ceaseless turmoil seething,
As if this earth in fast thick pants were breathing,
A mighty fountain momently was forced:
Amid whose swift half-intermitted burst
Huge fragments vaulted like rebounding hail,
Or chaffy grain beneath the thresher's flail:
And 'mid these dancing rocks at once and ever
It flung up momently the sacred river.
Five miles meandering with a mazy motion
Through wood and dale the sacred river ran,
Then reached the caverns measureless to man,
And sank in tumult to a lifeless ocean:
And 'mid this tumult Kubla heard from far
Ancestral voices prophesying war!
    The shadow of the dome of pleasure
    Floated midway on the waves;
    Where was heard the mingled measure
    From the fountain and the caves.
It was a miracle of rare device,
A sunny pleasure-dome with caves of ice!
    A damsel with a dulcimer
    In a vision once I saw:
    It was an Abyssinian maid,
    And on her dulcimer she played,
    Singing on Mount Abora.
    Could I revive within me

Her symphony and song,
To such a deep delight 'twould win me,
That with music loud and long,
I would build that dome in air.
That sunny dome! those caves of ice!
And all who heard should see them there,
And all should cry, Beware! Beware!
His flashing eyes, his floating hair!
Weave a circle round him thrice,
And close your eyes with holy dread,
For he on honey-dew hath fed,
And drunk the milk of Paradise.

4. The Dreams of the English Opium-Eater

THOMAS DE QUINCEY

O just, subtle, and all-conquering opium! that, to the hearts of rich and poor alike, for the wounds that will never heal, and for the pangs of grief that "tempt the spirit to rebel," bringest an assuaging balm—eloquent opium! that with thy potent rhetoric stealest away the purposes of wrath, pleadest effectually for relenting pity, and through one night's heavenly sleep callest back to the guilty man the visions of his infancy, and hands washed pure from blood—O just and righteous opium! that to the chancery of dream summonest, for the triumphs of despairing innocence, false witnesses, and confoundest perjury, and dost reverse the sentences of un-righteous judges—thou buildest upon the bosom of darkness, out of the fantastic imagery of the brain, cities and temples, beyond the art of Phidias and Praxiteles, beyond the splendors of Babylon and Hekatómpylos; and from "the anarchy of dreaming sleep," callest into the sunny light the faces of long-buried beauties, and the blessed household countenances, cleansed from the "dishonors of the grave." Thou only givest these gifts to man; and thou hast the keys of Paradise, O just, subtle, and mighty opium!

But from this I now pass to what is the main subject of these latter *Confessions*—the history and journal of what took place in my dreams; for these were the immediate and proximate cause of shadowy terrors that settled and brooded over my whole waking life.

The first notice I had of any important change going on in this part of my physical economy was from the re-awaking of a state of eye oftentimes incident to childhood. I know not whether my reader is aware that many children have a power of painting, as it were, upon the darkness all sorts of phantoms; in some that power is simply a mechanic affection of the eye; others have a voluntary or semi-voluntary power to dismiss or summon such phantoms; or, as a child once said to me, when I questioned him on the matter, "I can tell them to go, and they go; but sometimes they come when I don't tell them to come." He had by one-half as unlimited a command over apparitions as a Roman centurion over his soldiers. In the middle of 1817 this faculty became increasingly distressing to me: at night, when I lay awake in bed, vast processions moved along continually in mournful pomp; friezes of never-ending stories, that to my feelings were as sad and solemn as stories drawn from times before Œdipus or Priam, before Tyre, before Memphis. And, concurrently with this, a corresponding change took place in my dreams; a theatre seemed suddenly opened and lighted up within my brain, which presented nightly spectacles of more than earthly splendor. And the four following facts may be mentioned, as noticeable at this time:

1. That, as the creative state of the eye increased, a sympathy seemed to arise between the waking and the dreaming states of the brain in one point—that whatsoever I happened to call up and to trace by a voluntary act upon the darkness was very apt to transfer itself to my dreams; and at length I feared to exercise this faculty; for, as Midas turned all things to gold that yet baffled his hopes and defrauded his human desires, so whatsoever things capable of being visually represented I did but think of in the darkness immediately shaped themselves into phantoms for the eye; and, by a process apparently no less inevitable, when thus once traced in faint and visionary colors, like writings in sympathetic ink, they were drawn out, by the fierce chemistry of my dreams, into insufferable splendor that fretted my heart.

2. This and all other changes in my dreams were accompanied by deep-seated anxiety and funereal melancholy, such as are wholly incommunicable by words. I seemed every night to descend—not metaphorically, but literally to descend—into chasms and sunless abysses, depths below depths, from which it seemed hopeless that I could ever re-ascend. Nor did I, by waking, feel that I *had* re-ascended. Why should I dwell upon this? For indeed the state of gloom which attended these gorgeous spectacles, amounting at last to utter darkness, as of some suicidal despondency, cannot be approached by words.

3. The sense of space, and in the end the sense of time, were both powerfully affected. Buildings, landscapes, etc. were exhibited in proportions so vast as the bodily eye is not fitted to receive. Space swelled, and was amplified to an extent of unutterable and self-repeating infinity. This

disturbed me very much less than the vast expansion of time. Sometimes I seemed to have lived for seventy or a hundred years in one night; nay, sometimes had feelings representative of a duration far beyond the limits of any human experience.

4. The minutest incidents of childhood, or forgotten scenes of later years, were often revived. I could not be said to recollect them; for, if I had been told of them waking, I should not have been able to acknowledge them as parts of my past experience. But, placed as they were before me in dreams like intuitions, and clothed in all their evanescent circumstances and accompanying feelings, I *recognized* them instantaneously. I was once told by a near relative of mine that, having in her childhood fallen into a river, and being on the verge of death but for the assistance which reached her at the last critical moment, she saw in a moment her whole life, arrayed before her as in a mirror, not successively, but simultaneously; and she had a faculty developed as suddenly for comprehending the whole and every part. This, from some opium experiences, I can believe; I have, indeed, seen the same thing asserted twice in modern books, and accompanied by a remark which probably is true—*viz.*, that the dread book of account which the Scriptures speak of is, in fact, the mind itself of each individual. Of this, at least, I feel assured, that there is no such thing as ultimate *forgetting*; traces once impressed upon the memory are indestructible; a thousand accidents may and will interpose a veil between our present consciousness and the secret inscriptions on the mind. Accidents of the same sort will also rend away this veil. But alike, whether veiled or unveiled, the inscription remains forever; just as the stars seem to withdraw before the common light of day, whereas, in fact, we all know that it is the light which is drawn over them as a veil, and that they are waiting to be revealed whenever the obscuring daylight itself shall have withdrawn.

Having noticed these four facts as memorably distinguishing my dreams from those of health, I shall now cite a few illustrative cases; and shall then cite such others as I remember, in any order that may give them most effect as pictures to the reader. . . .

Many years ago, when I was looking over Piranesi's *Antiquities of Rome*, Coleridge, then standing by, described to me a set of plates from that artist, called his "Dreams," and which recorded the scenery of his own visions during the delirium of a fever. Some of these (I describe only from memory of Coleridge's account) represented vast Gothic halls; on the floor of which stood mighty engines and machinery, wheels, cables, catapults, etc., expressive of enormous power put forth, or resistance overcome. Creeping along the sides of the walls, you perceived a staircase; and upon this, groping his way upwards, was Piranesi himself. Follow the stairs a little farther, and you perceive them reaching an abrupt termination, without any balustrade, and allowing no steps onward to him who should reach the extremity, except into the depths below. Whatever is to become of poor Piranesi, at least you suppose that his labors must now in some way terminate. But raise your eyes, and behold a second flight of stairs still higher, on which again Piranesi is perceived, by this time standing on the very brink of the abyss. Once again elevate your eye, and a still more aerial flight of stairs is descried; and there, again, is the delirious Piranesi, busy on his aspiring labors; and so on, until the unfinished stairs and the hopeless Piranesi both are lost in the upper gloom of the hall. With the same power of endless growth and self-reproduction did my architecture proceed in dreams. In the early stage of the malady, the splendors of my dreams were indeed chiefly architectural; and I beheld such pomp of cities and palaces as never yet was beheld by the waking eye, unless in clouds. . . .

To my architecture succeeded dreams of lakes and silvery expanses of water; these haunted me so much that I feared lest some dropsical state or tendency of the brain might thus be making itself (to use a metaphysical word) *objective*, and that the sentient organ might be projecting itself as its own object. For two months I suffered greatly in my head—a part of my bodily structure which had hitherto been so clear from all touch or taint of weakness (physically, I mean) that I used to say of it, as the last Lord Orford said of his stomach, that it seemed likely to survive the rest of my person. Till now I had never felt a headache even, or any the slightest pain, except rheumatic pains caused by my own folly.

The waters gradually changed their character—from translucent lakes, shining like mirrors, they became seas and oceans. And now came a tremendous change, which, unfolding itself slowly like a scroll, through many months, promised an abiding torment; and, in fact, it never left me, though recurring more or less intermittingly. Hitherto the human face had often mixed in my dreams, but not despotically, nor with any special power of tormenting. But now that affection which I have called the tyranny of the human face began to unfold itself. Perhaps some part of my London life (the searching for Ann amongst fluctuating crowds) might be answerable for this. Be that as it may, now it was that upon the rocking waters of the ocean the human face began to reveal itself; the sea appeared paved with innumerable faces, upturned to the heavens; faces, imploring, wrathful, despairing; faces that surged upwards by thousands, by myriads, by generations; infinite was my agitation; my mind tossed, as it seemed, upon the billowy ocean, and weltered upon the weltering waves.

May, 1818. The Malay has been a fearful enemy for months. Every night, through his means, I have been transported into Asiatic scenery. I know not whether others share in my feelings on this point; but I have often thought that, if I were compelled to forego England, and to live in China, among Chinese manners and modes of life and scenery, I should go mad. The causes of my horror lie deep, and some of them must be common to others. . . . In China, over and above what it has in common with the rest of Southern Asia, I am terrified by the modes of life, by the manners, by the barrier of utter abhorrence placed between myself and them, by counter-sympathies deeper than I can analyze. I could sooner live with lunatics, with vermin, with crocodiles or snakes. All this, and much more than I can say, the reader must enter into before he can comprehend the unimaginable horror which these dreams of oriental imagery and mythological tortures impressed upon me. Under the connecting feeling of tropical heat and vertical sunlight, I brought together all creatures, birds, beasts, reptiles, all trees and plants, usages and appearances, that are found in all tropical regions, and assembled them together in China or Hindustan. From kindred feelings, I soon brought Egypt and her gods under the same law. I was stared at, hooted at, grinned at, chattered at, by monkeys, by paroqueets, by cockatoos. I ran into pagodas, and was fixed for centuries at the summit, or in secret rooms; I was the idol; I was the priest; I was worshipped; I was sacrificed. I fled from the wrath of Brama through all the forests of Asia; Vishnu hated me; Siva lay in wait for me. I came suddenly upon Isis and Osiris: I had done a deed, they said, which the ibis and the crocodile trembled at. Thousands of years I lived and was buried in stone coffins, with mummies and sphinxes, in narrow chambers at the heart of eternal pyramids. I was kissed, with cancerous kisses, by crocodiles, and was laid, confounded with all unutterable abortions, amongst reeds and Nilótic mud.

Some slight abstraction I thus attempt of my oriental dreams, which filled me always with such amazement at the monstrous scenery that horror seemed absorbed for a while in sheer astonishment. Sooner or later came a reflux of feeling that swallowed up the astonishment, and left me, not so much in terror, as in hatred and abomination of what I saw. Over every form, and threat, and punishment, and dim sightless incarceration, brooded a killing sense of eternity and infinity. . . .

Then suddenly would come a dream of far different character—a tumultuous dream—commencing with a music such as now I often heard in my sleep—music of preparation and of awakening suspense. The undulations of fast-gathering tumults were like the opening of the Coronation Anthem, and, like *that*, gave the feeling of a multitudinous movement, of infinite cavalcades filing off, and the tread of innumerable armies. The morning was come of a mighty day—a day of crisis and of ultimate hope for human nature, then suffering mysterious eclipse, and laboring in some dread extremity. Somewhere, but I knew not where—somehow, but I knew not how—by some beings, but I knew not by whom—a battle, a strife, an agony, was traveling through all its stages—was evolving itself, like the catastrophe of some mighty drama, with which my sympathy was the more insupportable from deepening confusion as to its local scene, its cause, its nature, and its undecipherable issue. I (as is usual in dreams where, of necessity, we make ourselves central to every movement) had the power, and yet had not the power, to decide it. I had the power, if I could raise myself to will it; and yet again had not the power, for the weight of twenty Atlantics was upon me, or the oppression of inexpiable guilt. "Deeper than ever plummet sounded," I lay inactive. Then, like a chorus, the passion deepened. Some greater interest was at stake, some mightier cause, than ever yet the sword had pleaded, or trumpet had proclaimed. Then came sudden alarms; hurryings to and fro; trepidations of innumerable fugitives, I knew not whether from the good cause or the bad; darkness and lights; tempest and human faces; and at last, with the sense that all was lost, female forms, and the features that were worth all the world to me; and but a moment allowed—and clasped hands, with heartbreaking partings, and then—everlasting farewells! and with a sight such as the caves of hell sighed when the incestuous mother uttered the abhorred name of Death, the sound was reverberated—everlasting farewells! and again, and yet again reverberated—everlasting farewells!

And I awoke in struggles, and cried aloud, "I will sleep no more!"

One memorial of my former condition nevertheless remains; my dreams are not calm; the dread swell and agitation of the storm have not wholly subsided; the legions that encamped in them are drawing off, but not departed; my sleep is still tumultuous; and, like the gates of Paradise to our first parents when looking back from afar, it is still (in the tremendous line of Milton):

> With dreadful faces thronged and fiery arms.

The Dreams of Jet Pilots and Astronauts*

Jet pilots are invariably cool when facing a crisis but the possibility of peril is always on their mind.

A study showed that even their dreams are filled with themes that involve meeting difficult situations and mastering them.

Having been there in their dreams, they are less fearful when the

* *New York Post* News Item, May 18, 1970.

actual event occurs. This may explain the calmness of Apollo 13 astronauts, all experienced jet pilots, when their spaceship oxygen tank exploded last month.

The study presented today at the American Psychiatric Assn. meeting here by Dr. Robert F. Reinhardt, chief of psychiatry at the U.S. Naval Aerospace Medical Institute, Pensacola, Fla., showed 84 per cent of the 104 pilots never had a personal injury and only 3 per cent gave a history of more than one accident.

D. PARANORMAL DREAMS

Parapsychological Dream Studies

MARTIN EBON

MODERN PARAPSYCHOLOGY has its origins in ancient and primitive occult beliefs and practices, just as the modern sciences are indebted to the alchemists, just as medicine, specifically, acknowledges the allegedly magical or miraculous healing powers of saints and witch doctors. Parapsychology has remained close to traditions of the supernatural which remain as a strong but mostly unacknowledged residue within our own materialistic society. It has tried to apply up-to-date scientific methods to verify, record, and analyze phenomena that do not seem to fit into the pattern of known scientific laws.

Modern parapsychology, just because it has as its subject matter what may be termed the supernatural, paranormal, magical, or pseudomagical, is intent upon applying the most rigid standards of documentation, experimental control, and statistical evaluation available to current scientific research. Aside from criticism that it entertains and requests from nonparapsychologists, parapsychology generally is much concerned with self-criticism and subsequent refinement of its own methodology. This very tendency toward high standards of evidence and experimentation may, however, endanger the delicate fiber of the phenomena that modern parapsychology seeks to record, study, and, if possible, repeat.

Parapsychological dream studies cannot be entirely separated from the general mass of research in parapsychology or, as it has often been called, psychical research. Parapsychology owes a heavy debt to British researchers active during the second half of the nineteenth century. Often they were men of distinction in such diverse areas as public affairs, literature, the-

66

ology, and the sciences. Their original research, undertaken through the London Society for Psychical Research, received its main stimulus from a desire to study the possibility of the survival of the human personality after bodily death. The leading researchers of the British Society hoped to apply new methods of documentation to the ancient concept of man's immortality in order to achieve a union of science and faith.

Much material of varied quality, but of undoubted originality and sincerity, emerged from these studies. As a by-product, so to speak, other areas of more or less "occult" phenomena were made the subject of investigations. There thus exists, accumulated during the past eight decades, a considerable body of data concerning dreams in categories such as these:

1. the dream as omen, as a more or less supernatural indication of certain critical events, present or future;

2. the dream as part of initiatory rituals, notably those of shamanism;

3. a telepathic or precognitive quality of the dream, which has been the subject of current research;

4. other areas in which the dream plays a major or minor part linking it with the magical, supernormal, metaphysical, or extrasensory.

It is specifically in the third category that modern parapsychologists seek to apply various scientific criteria to the dream. They are aware, of course, that these very criteria are continuously undergoing tests concerning their general validity and their applicability to the phenomena with which they are concerned. In dream studies, as in various other parapsychological research areas, the relative values of qualitative and quantitative studies are constantly being tested and examined.

The dilemma of parapsychological dream studies, and, indeed, of virtually all other parapsychological studies, centers on the problem of capturing, so to speak, highly elusive (and presumably subjective) phenomena with the still rather limited scientific tools at hand. By its very nature, the parapsychological phenomenon depends on a constellation of factors that are exceedingly difficult to anticipate or control, and virtually impossible to adapt to laboratory conditions. Indeed, the verification of these phenomena often proves so difficult that I am tempted, at the cost of sounding flippant, to use a somewhat primitive parable to illustrate this point.

The parapsychological researcher all too frequently faces a situation that resembles the hunt for a mythical animal, whose presence has long been "known," and which has just been reported, once again, by a rather excited (and therefore, of course, not entirely trustworthy) witness. Let us assume that a boy has just come into a remote, forest-ringed Asian village, shouting that he has positively seen the famed and fabled purple tiger. This animal, for our purposes, might be a telepathic or precognitive dream. Naturally, the villagers are much excited: at last, they feel, the elusive beast may be encircled, hunted down, trapped, and finally exhibited to prove to all doubters that it does, indeed, exist.

Teams of skilled hunters are assembled, wielding special traps perfected in their trade; statisticians bearing computers, as if they were lighted torches; anthropologists, equipped with data of similar cases; psychologists, loaded down with Rorschach, Thematic Apperception, and Rosenzweig test materials; physicists with delicate instruments and charts; theologians, bearing the wisdom and doubt of the ages; even psychopharmacologists, with the more esoteric products of Swiss pharmaceutical firms; and physiologists with highly specialized electroencephalographic equipment. Thus, with drumbeating and shouting, a ring is completed, and everyone is in high spirits, temporarily convinced that this time, surely, the purple tiger will be trapped, caged, and suitably exhibited before learned societies. The hunting party at last converges upon the center of the forest. But, behold, their precious prey has, once again, vanished.

To finish the parable appropriately, the assembled scientists have little more to show for their pursuit than more or less painful scratches on their academic reputation, and possibly the makings of a learned paper, "Some Preliminary Observations on the Trapping of Alleged Purple Tigers"; plus a great deal of controversy as to whether it might not be more significant, statistically, to trap several purple tigers instead of only one inconclusive specimen.

And that, essentially, is the dilemma of the parapsychological researcher who seeks to observe and verify such phenomena as telepathic or precognitive dreams, or who endeavors to develop experiments and perfect methods of evaluation. The very attempt to "trap" the phenomenon, to measure or verify it, may destroy it, may "scare it away." Indeed, the high emotional content of most "paranormal" dreams, the deep involvement of the dreamer, tend to make scientific appraisal extraordinarily difficult.

Telepathy and Dreams

EDMUND GURNEY, F. W. H. MYERS, and FRANK PODMORE

The department of dreams, where inward ideas, images dominate unchecked, is also one which covers so large a period of human existence as to make it *a priori* probable that a considerable number of "transferred impressions" (supposing such things to exist) would fall within it. . . .

Dreams have this peculiarity; they are distinct affections of the senses, which yet, in reflecting on them, we rarely or never confound with objective facts; waking hallucinations, on the other hand—spectral illusions or ghostly visitants—are often so confounded. The sleeping experiences are marked off from external reality in the minds of all of us by the very fact that we wake from them; our change of condition makes their vanishing seem natural; and thus looked back on, they will often seem to have been mere vague representations; *i.e.*, something *less* than affections of the senses. The waking experiences cannot be woke from; their vanishing seems unconnected with the percipient and therefore *un*natural; and thus looked back on, they will often seem to have been independent realities; *i.e.*, something *more* than affections of the senses. . . .

Before proceeding further, it will be well to examine with some care the *general evidential value* of dreams, in relation to a theory of transferred impressions. The field may seem a fair one enough, as long as we keep to general expectations; if telepathy is a reality, here is a probable scene of telepathic events. But what opportunities does it afford for confirming these expectations by accurate and convincing evidence? This is a question which may rapidly convert our hopes into doubts.

The first objection to dreams, as evidence for transferred impressions of distant conditions or events, is this—that dreams being often somewhat dim and shapeless things, subsequent knowledge of the conditions or events may easily have the effect of giving body and definiteness to the recollection of a dream. When the actual facts are learnt, a faint amount of resemblance may often suggest a past dream, and set the mind on the track of trying accurately to recall it. This very act involves a search for details, for something tangible and distinct; and the real features and definite incidents which are now present in the mind, in close association with some general scene or fact which actually figured in the dream, will be apt to be unconsciously *read back* into the dream. They make part of the original, of which the mind conceives the dream to have been a picture; and the picture, when evoked in memory, will only too probably include details drawn from the original. After we have once realized the matter in its full distinctions, it becomes almost impossible to recall with due *in*distinctness the distant and shadowy suggestion of it. Dreams in this way resemble objects seen in the dusk; which begin by puzzling the eye, but which, when once we know or think we know what they are, seem quite unmistakable and even full of familiar detail. For our purposes, therefore, it is of prime importance that the dream shall be told in detail to someone on whose memory we can rely; or, better still, written down, or in some way acted on, at the time, and before the confirmation arrives. Nearly all the evidence to be brought forward has, at any rate, this mark of accuracy.

But there is a more general and sweeping objection. Millions of people are dreaming every night; and in dreams, if anywhere, the range of possibilities seems infinite; can any positive conclusion be drawn from such a chaos of meaningless and fragmentary impressions? Must we not admit the force of the obvious *a priori* argument that among the countless multitudes of dreams, one here and there is likely to correspond in time with an actual occurrence resembling the one dreamed of; and that when a dream thus "comes true," unscientific minds are sure to note and store up the fact as something extraordinary, without taking the trouble to reflect whether such incidents occur oftener than pure chance would allow? Can the chances be at all estimated? Are any valid means at hand for distinguishing between a transferred impression and a lucky coincidence? What degree of exactitude of date and circumstance must be reached before we consider even a striking correspondence as worth attention? And what proportion of striking correspondence are we to demand before we consider that the hypothesis of chance is strained in accounting for them?

In the first place it must be noted that there has, so far, been a complete lack of the statistics which alone could form the basis for an answer to these questions. It has never been known with any certainty what proportion of people habitually dream; what proportion of dreams are remembered at all, in what proportion of these remembered dreams the memory is evanescent, and in what proportion it is profound and durable. This latter point may be specially hard to establish satisfactorily in a particular case, as it is affected by the question whether a person's attention is habitually directed to his dreams, and also by the question whether he has happened to recount a particular dream to others, and so stamp it on his memory. By making inquiries on a large scale, however, a considerable approximation to certainty may be attained on these and various other points of importance. A good deal has been done in this way during the last three years; and though I cannot say that the results are such as would allow us to base a theory of telepathy upon the facts of dreams alone, I think that they do much to diminish the *a priori* plausibility of the theory of chance, as a sufficient explanation of all cases of marked correspondence between a dream and an external event. . . .

An exceedingly small proportion of dreams are remembered with distinctness several hours after waking. Even of the dreams which dwell in the memory, an exceedingly small proportion produce any appreciable amount of distress or excitement. And of these more impressive dreams, an exceedingly small proportion prove their intensity by being in any way acted on. . . . The rapid repetition of a distinct dream two or three times on the same night . . . seems to be a comparatively rare occurrence. The dreams to be cited in this book will nearly all, I think, be distinguishable by one or another of those tests of exceptional intensity. And in proportion as the dreams which coincide with the events dreamed of are thus found to be in some other way exceptional—in proportion as the class to which they belong is found to form a small and sparse minority among the swarming multitude of unmarked dreams—in that proportion does it clearly become unreasonable to argue that the coincidences are sufficiently accounted for by the laws of chances. The argument which might seem ineffective so long as we had the whole multitude of dreams to range over—that multitude seeming sufficient to give the law of chance ample scope—assumes quite a different aspect when we find ourselves limited to the comparatively small group of *intense* dreams.

Before we can give weight to a dream-coincidence as pointing to anything beyond the operation of chance, we should inquire whether the event dreamed of is distinct, unexpected, and unusual. If it combines all three characteristics in a high degree, its evidential value may be very considerable; in proportion as the degree falls short, or the combination fails, the evidential value sinks; and none of the characteristics taken alone, even though present in a high degree, would lead us to include a dream in the present collection. Thus the dream content must be neither a vague impression of calamity nor of happiness; nor a catastrophe on which the sleeper's mind is already fixed; nor some such ordinary event as has frequently occurred in waking experience. It may, indeed, be not the less significant for being trivial; but in that case it must be of a bizarre and unlikely kind. Then again, amount of detail, and the number of connected events, are of immense importance, as each subsequently verified detail tells with ever-mounting strength against the hypothesis of accidental coincidence. Once more, dream content must be considered to some extent in relation to the dream-habits of the particular dreamer. Before estimating the value of the fact that a person has dreamt of the sudden death of a friend on the night when the death took place, we should have to ascertain that that person is not in the habit of dreaming of distressing or horrible events. In respect of these points the instances to be cited here are the sifted survival of many less definite coincidences in which the popular imagination would find a marvel. And in the case of this residue, where we have complete fulfilment of some of the above conditions, over and above the close proximity in time or (it may be) absolute synchronism, of the event and the dream, the questions as to causal connection between the two is, at any rate, not to be swept out of court by a mere general appeal to the doctrine of chances.

But there is a further point in the content of the dreams that correspond with real events—true dreams, as we may for brevity call them—which cannot but strike the attention as soon as we begin to examine actual specimens. It is that, among true dreams, by very far the largest class is the class where the truth is *death*—i.e., where the event dreamt of as happening to another is of that most restricted kind which can only happen once in each individual's experience. Out of the 149 coincident dreams which are included in this book [*Phantasms of the Living*]—as at least clearly finding in telepathy, if it exists, their most natural explanation—no less than 79 have represented or suggested death. . . .

Among considerations so complex and data so uncertain, it is not easy to sum up a view in very precise terms; but our general position has been made sufficiently clear by my statement that we should not, with our present evidence, have undertaken to make out a case for telepathy on the ground of dreams alone. The question whether a case could be completely made out on that ground, though it may be worth debating, seems incapable of final settlement, until a very large section of the population takes to keeping a daily record of their dream-experiences. A much larger number of examples is needed for which, even taken in isolation, a high evidential rank could be claimed—whether from the amount of detail in the coincidence or from some exceptional features. . . . But meanwhile an argument of a quite different sort can be imported from the department of evidence on which we mainly rely—the evidence of telepathic impressions of distant events received in the waking state. The probabilities of some real causal connection between event and impression in the *less* conclusive cases cannot be fairly weighed without regard to the existence of the *more conclusive*; and that dreams form, on the whole, the less evidentially conclusive class can be no ground for tabooing them, unless we can assign special reasons why sleep should be a condition adverse to telepathic influence. In the conception of telepathy which it is hoped that the reader will by degrees come to share, no such reasons appear; while the resemblances to the transition-cases, already referred to, make it practically impossible to reject in the one class an explanation which we admit in the other. . . .

In surveying a large number of cases where a dream has corresponded in time with the real occurrence of the event or events which it represented, in such a way as strongly to suggest that it had its source in a telepathic influence, we find that they at once fall into distinct classes. In the first class, the agent is in a normal state, or is himself also dreaming; the external event here is simply the occurrence to the agent of a particular thought or dream; and the percipient's impression is concerned simply with the content of that thought or dream, not with the agent himself. In all other classes the agent is in some condition or situation which is more or less abnormal; and the percipient has an impression of the agent as in this situation, but an impression which may take various forms. Not infrequently the central fact is dreamt of merely as a fact—as something the dreamer hears of, or becomes aware of, as having occurred, without himself in any way coming into contact with it. In another class of cases, he perceives the principal actor in the matter dreamt of—the dying person, if death is the occasion—in such a manner as to suggest the actual catastrophe; this suggestion being often connected with some special imaging or symbolism. And in yet another class, he seems himself transported into the actual scene—to be an actual spectator of the event. . . .

One marked group of cases is the simultaneous occurrence of the same dream to two persons. Such an occurrence would not be likely to be heard

of except when the two dreamers were nearly related or liv
house; indeed, unless the correspondence were extraordir
detailed, it is only the fact of the dreamers belonging to
stricted circle that could justify one in attaching the slig
to it. In a wider circle, coincidences of the sort might obviously happ..,
perhaps often do happen, by pure accident. But relationship or habitual
propinquity involves, of course, the chance that some item of joint waking
experience has been the independent source of both dreams; and no case
would be admissible where any recent cause of this sort could be traced.

[1886]

Psychic Phenomena in Dreams

F. W. H. MYERS

We have now to consider whether we can detect in sleep any manifestation of *supernormal* faculty—any experience which seems to suggest that
man is a cosmical spirit as well as a terrestrial organism, and is in some
way in relation with a spiritual as well as with a material world. It will
seem, in this view, to be natural that this commerce with a spiritual environment should be more perceptible in sleep than in waking. The dogma
which my point of view thus renders probable is perhaps, as a mere
matter of history, the dogma of all dogmas which has been most universally
believed by mankind.

Quod semper, quod ubique, quod ab omnibus—For how many narrow
theological propositions have we not heard this proud claim—that they
have been believed everywhere, and by everybody, and in every age?
Yet what can approach the antiquity, the ubiquity, the unanimity of man's
belief in the wanderings of the spirit in dream? In the Stone Age, the
sceptic would have been rash indeed who ventured to contradict it. And
though I grant that this "palaeolithic psychology" has gone out of fashion
for the last few centuries, I do not think that (in view of the telaesthetic
evidence now collected) we can any longer dismiss as a mere *bizarrerie*
of dream-imagery the constant recurrence of the idea of visiting in sleep
some distant scene, with the acquisition thereby of new facts not otherwise
accessible.

Starting, then, not from savage authority, but from the evidential
scrutiny of modern facts, we shall find, I think, that there are coincidences
of dream with truth which neither pure chance nor any subconscious
mentation of an ordinary kind will adequately explain. We shall find that

re is a perception of concealed material objects or of distant scenes and also a perception of a communion with the thoughts and emotions of other minds. Both these phenomena have been noted sporadically in many ages and countries, and were observed with serious attention especially by the early French mesmerists. The first group of phenomena was called *clairvoyance* or *lucidité*, and the second *communication de pensées*, or in English, *thought-transference*. These terms are scarcely comprehensive enough to satisfy a more systematic study. The distant perception is not *optical*, nor is it confined even to the apparent sense of sight alone. It extends to all the senses, and includes also impressions hardly referable to any special sense. Similarly the communication between distant persons is not a transference of thought alone, but of emotion, of motor impulses, and of many impressions not easy to define. I ventured in 1882 to suggest the wider term *telaesthesia*, sensation at a distance, and *telepathy*, fellow-feeling at a distance, and shall use these words in the present work. But I am far from assuming that these terms correspond with definite and clearly separated groups of phenomena, or comprise the whole field of supernormal faculty. On the contrary, I think it probable that the facts of the metetherial world are far more complex than the facts of the material world; and the ways in which spirits perceive and communicate, apart from fleshly organisms, are subtler and more varied than any perception or communication which we know.

I have hinted above at another line of demarcation which the dreamer's own sensations suggest—the distinction between active psychical excursion or invasion and the passive reception of psychical invasion from without. But even here, as was also hinted, a clear line of division is hard to draw. For whether we are dealing with dream-perceptions of distant material scenes, or of distant living persons, or of discarnate spirits, it is often impossible for the dreamer himself to say either from what point he is himself observing, or where the scene of the vision is laid.

[1903]

Dreams of Future Events

J. W. DUNNE

As a rule, on nine mornings out of ten, I have no recollection of having dreamed at all. That, however, did not greatly trouble me. Many people, I knew, were genuinely convinced they never dreamed; but, from experiments I made, I was satisfied that "dreamless sleep" is an illusion of memory. What happens is that one forgets the dreams at the very instant of waking. I myself have remembered, some days later, a dream which occurred when I was under an anaesthetic, although, during the intervening interval, I had believed myself to have been, at the time, in a state of complete unconsciousness.

My starting-point, then, was a belief in the possibility of recalling a fraction of the lost dreams of these apparently blank nights of mine. Now, according to the new hypothesis, that fraction could contain images of both past and future events. *It was probable that the majority of such images would not be distinct and separate, but, on the contrary, so blended and intermingled that the components would not be distinguishable as belonging to any special waking event.* But just as one can, occasionally, clearly identify one part of such a blend of images as relating to a particular past event so should one be able, on occasion, to identify an element in the blend as pertaining to a particular future occurrence. The point was (and this is an important point) that one must not ever expect to come upon a complete idea or scene which related *wholly* to the future. . . .

The dream, if recalled, would preferably be written down, so as to make the remainder of the experiment a matter of comparison between two hard, material facts—the record and the waking event. And, to facilitate subsequent analysis of the dream-images, these would best be described with as much detail as possible. A short record, full of detail, would be of more value than a long one drafted in vaguer terms.

But there was an even more cogent reason why amplitude of detail would be essential. A long dream contains a great many images, and a long day a great many impressions. By the ordinary laws of chance some of these would be bound to fit, if the experiment were sufficiently extended. Hence corroborative detail would have to be the crucial test. For example, the dream of a pile of coins on a book, followed next day by the observation of a pile of coins in such a position, would be of the class of coincidence which would be bound to occur in any case. What would be required would be something more in the nature of a pile of *sixpences upsetting* off a *red* book, followed by such a waking experience. (The rest of the scene of such a dream—the table and the room and the cause of the mishap—would probably be entirely different; but that would not matter.) The point was that nothing should be accepted as relating clearly to the future which did not contain the elements of what a racing man would call a "double event."

The next thing to be considered was the necessity of a time limit. Obviously, even a dream of a pile of sixpences upsetting off a red book would be likely to be matched by a similar waking experience, if one allowed oneself the whole of one's life in which to look for the matching. A bank clerk might even find fulfilment in a fortnight. I decided that two days should be the accepted limit; *but that this might be extended in ratio to the oddity and unusualness of the incident.* That would be a matter of judgment. . . .

Since, then, the possibility of satisfactory identification would depend mainly upon unusualness in the incident, the worst time to choose for the experiment would be the period when one was leading a dull life with each day exactly like the last. But in such circumstances a visit to the theatre or to a cinema might well prove a useful auxiliary to the experiment. (That, I may say now, is an invaluable tip.) Also, one might expect to get dreams of novels one was going to read. (I may add here that one does, as a matter of fact, get some of one's best results that way.) *But, speaking generally, it would be best to select nights preceding a journey or some other expected break in the monotony of circumstances.*

Another factor would be evidently the *number* of the results achieved. Satisfaction might be obtained either from the previous dreaming of a single, very unusual incident; *or equally well from the previous dreaming of several fairly unusual events, any one of which results, had it been the only one, might justly have been attributed to rather exceptional coincidence.* . . .

The foregoing describes the conditions I laid down for the test, and also the nature of the difficulties I was prepared to encounter. And encounter these I did in abundance. But there were two which I did not foresee.

The dreaming mind is a master-hand at tacking false interpretations onto everything it perceives. For this reason, the record of the dream should describe as separate facts, (a) the actual appearance of what is seen, and (b) the interpretation given to that appearance. . . .

The second difficulty is one which demands careful attention. For it was here, at last, that I found the thing I had been looking for—the reason why this curious feature in the character of temporal experience has managed, through all these centuries, to escape universal observation.

The waking mind refuses point-blank to accept the association between the dream and the subsequent event. For it, this association is the *wrong way round*, and no sooner does it make itself perceived than it is instantly rejected. The intellectual revolt is automatic and extremely powerful. Even when confronted with the indisputable evidence of the written record, one jumps at any excuse to avoid recognition. One excuse which is nearly always seized is the dissimilarity of the adjacent parts of the scene, or the fact that there are parts in the "integration" which do *not* fit the incident; matters which do not, of course, in the least affect the fact that there are parts of the scene or integration which *do* fit with the required degree of exactitude.

The result is that, on reading over the record on the succeeding day (or two days), *one is apt to read straight on through the very thing one is looking for, without even noticing its connection with the waking incident.* The reading should therefore be done slowly, with frequent pauses for consideration and for comparison with the day's events. In the cases of nearly all the results I am going to relate, the connection was, at first, only half glimpsed, *was then immediately rejected*, and was finally accepted only on account of the accumulating weight of the previously unnoticed points of corroborative detail.

The dodge for recalling the forgotten dreams is quite simple. A notebook and pencil is kept under the pillow, and *immediately* on waking, before you even open your eyes, you set yourself to remembering the rapidly vanishing dream. As a rule, a single incident is all that you can recall, and this appears so dim and small and isolated that you doubt the value of noting it down. Do not, however, attempt to remember anything more, but *fix your attention on that single incident, and try to remember its details.* Like a flash, a large section of the dream in which that incident occurred comes back. What is more important, however, is that, with that section, there usually comes into view an isolated incident from a previous dream. Get hold of as many of these isolated incidents as you can, neglecting temporarily the rest of the dreams of which they formed part. Then jot down these incidents in your notebook as shortly as possible; a word or two for each should suffice.

Now take incident number one. Concentrate upon it until you have recovered part of the dream story associated therewith, and write down the briefest possible outline of that story. Do the same in turn with the other incidents you have noted. Finally, take the abbreviated record thus made and write it out in full. Note *details*, as many as possible. *Be specially careful to do this wherever the incident is one which, if it were to happen in real life, would seem unusual; for it is in connection with events of this kind that your evidence is most likely to be obtained.*

Until you have completed your record, do not allow yourself to think of anything else.

Do not attempt merely to remember. Write the dream down. Waking in the middle of the night, I have several times carefully memorized my preceding dreams. But, no matter how certain I have been that those memories were firmly fixed, I have never found one shred of them remaining in the morning. Even dreams which I have memorized just before getting up, and rememorized while dressing, have nearly always vanished by the end of breakfast.

It will be impossible, of course, for you to write down *all* the details. To describe the appearance of a single dream-character completely would keep you busy for ten minutes. But write down the general detail, and *all uncommon detail.* Memorize the remainder by reading through your final record and attentively revisualizing each picture described therein;

so that, should one of these unwritten details subsequently prove important, you can be satisfied that you are not then recalling it for the first time.

If, on waking, you are convinced that you have not dreamed at all, and cannot recall a single detail, stop trying to recollect the dream, and concentrate, instead, on remembering what you were *thinking* when you first awoke. On recalling that thought, you will find that it was consequent on the dream, and this dream will immediately begin to return.

Read your records over from their beginning at the end of each day of the experiment. . . .

In the experiments to be narrated it was found, to begin with, that the great bulk of the dreams exhibited *no* resemblances to any chronologically definite incident of waking life—past or future. This was entirely contrary to the popular supposition. The very small residue consisted of resemblances to incidents which were distinctly past only or distinctly future only; but these resemblances were mostly too slight to be evidential. However, a closer study of some of these apparently trivial coincidences would bring to light, *previously unnoticed corroborative details* which rendered the dream evidential of retrospection or of precognition. Thus, though all dreams were clearly related to waking life as a whole, it would be extremely difficult for anyone to prove, by actual experiment, whether they related to the past or the future or both. Evidence, in either direction, was about equally rare.

But that evidence was not equally difficult to notice. Attention would be arrested at once by the most trivial resemblances to the past, while passing over similar resemblances to the future with scarcely a pause. And the reason was obvious. In the case of a resemblance to the past, a *causal connection* is presupposed; so that the feeble character of the resemblance is ignored, and the dream record is regarded as meriting further examination. But in the case of a resemblance to the future, the degree of resemblance is the *only* evidence of a causal connection hostile to common sense, so that the judgment demands a far higher degree of resemblance before it will regard the incident as *worth considering.* Now, this would not matter, if the resemblances of dreams to waking events leapt to the eye all complete, with every detail in full view and readily estimable at its proper value. *But that, practically, never happens.* The resemblance dawns on one piecemeal; one very trivial similarity is noticed first, and, *if* the judgment is arrested by this, the dream is re-read and the corroborative details come slowly and singly to light. And, for the reasons already given, this all-important, first, feeble resemblance is promptly—almost unconsciously —dismissed as too far-fetched to merit further consideration, *if it relates to the future.*

Supposing, now, that a man of that time [the end of the last century] had experienced a series of dreams similar to those narrated in the earlier part of this book; he would have discovered something flatly opposed to the conventional view of Time. And that view was sacrosanct; the whole supposedly unassailable picture of physics bore witness to its accuracy. In these circumstances, our hypothetical dreamer would have been compelled to take refuge in Mysticism. He would have had to accept the existence of two disconnected worlds, the one rational, the other irrational.

But by 1917 the situation had changed entirely. The one thing that I did *not* need to worry about was the classical theory of Time. That, already, was in the melting-pot. Modern science had put it there—and was wondering what to do next.

Now, the probabilities that the whole series of dreams already described had been due to pure coincidence were so excessively minute that, *taking into account the partial collapse of the classical theory of Time*, I was bound to postulate precognition as a working hypothesis. Then, as a disciple of science, I must assume, pending absolute proof to the contrary, that precognition was scientifically possible, *i.e.*, that the nature of Time allowed the observer a four-dimensional outlook on the universe. That was eminently reasonable; for, if modern science insisted upon the reality of its four-dimensional "space-time," it could not dispute that observers in that world must be similarly four-dimensional. But that would involve that everyone possessed precognitive faculties. Unfortunately, it did not follow that he would employ them. It was possible to enumerate many personal factors which might make retrospection more attractive to the dreamer. And here was the difficulty. To establish my case I should have to overcome the objections of those who would urge, *as a matter of common knowledge*, that dreams which offer a resemblance to the future strong enough to arouse a suspicion of precognition were *not* vouchsafed to the multitude, but were, on the contrary, the prerogative of a few rare individuals.

I should like the reader to be quite clear about the nature of this obstacle. In science, one uses the word "effect" when one wishes to consider a phenomenon apart from any presumptions as to its possible cause. The strong "effects" to which I have just referred might or might not be due to coincidence, but that was not the difficulty. The objection which I should have to meet was not that the strong "effects" were inconclusive evidence of precognition; it was the far more formidable assertion that only an abnormal few could observe any such effects at all!

Now, if I were right, and there remained a still unsuspected logical fallacy in our notions of Time, that fallacy would prove, of course, self-evident—once it was discovered. Moreover, the discovery could hardly fail to affect every branch of science and to reap its quota of confirmation from each. The inexact evidence of dreams could provide no part of the essential basis of a serious scientific theory, and to attempt to make it such would be the worst possible policy. But I could not *ignore* that evidence. My opponents would be able to point out that the existence of universal faculties for dream precognition was a necessary *corollary* of my proposition, and they would demand to know why it was that not one person in a thousand utilized these supposed opportunities. "The evidence of dreams," they would say, "is extremely relevant to your theory. And that evidence is flatly against you."

In these circumstances, it seemed inadvisable to expend further energy upon the extremely difficult Time problem until I had satisfied myself that the striking effects in question were far more widely distributed *among individuals* than the popular view supposed. . . .

I trust I have it clear that the object of the projected experiments was to see whether the evidence of dreams in general was really for or against the theory that the faculty of precognition, if it existed, was a normal characteristic of man's general relation to Time. I hoped, in other words, to be able to turn the tables upon objectors of the classes cited above, and to show that effects suggesting precognition were observed by far too many people to allow us to entertain the supposition that these persons differed from their fellows in some supernormal fashion. . . .

We have to recognize that there are *no* limits to the possibilities of coincidence; consequently, evidence of precognition is of a purely statistical character—a matter of balancing probabilities. We are not dealing with an exact science, but with a method which approximates steadily toward exact science as the probabilities grow higher.

Now, the chances against a series of effects being coincidences depend upon two factors, *viz.*,

(1) The oddity of the individual effects.

(2) The frequency of their occurrence. . . .

The account of the following experiments, once again, is not scientific evidence, nor is it intended to be regarded as such. It is evidence for me, and part of my excuse for publication; but it is not, of course, evidence for the reader. . . .

Personally, I found this image-hunting a fascinating and even exciting business. But it was a new kind of sport, and I made every possible blunder open to a raw beginner. Not only did I delay the attempt to recall the dream until I had been awake for half a minute or more; but I also failed to appreciate sufficiently the importance of detail in the written accounts. Incidents which should have been described in fifty words were described in three. The result was that, although the dreams yielded much that was suggestive of future experience, I could find little that was *identifiable* as belonging to either half of Time. There was one fully described image, the original of which was seen four years later; but that was outside the prescribed limits of the test. It was not, in fact, until the eleventh day that I got the clear, conclusive result I had expected.

On the afternoon of that day I was out shooting over some rough country. I was a little uncertain regarding the boundaries covered by the permission I had obtained, and presently found myself on land where, I realized, I might have no right to be. As I crossed this, I heard two men shouting at me from different directions. They seemed, moreover, to be urging on a furiously barking dog. I made tracks for the nearest gate in the boundary wall, trying to look as if unaware of anything unusual. The shouting and barking came near and nearer. I walked a trifle faster, and managed to slip through the gate before the pursuers came into view. Altogether a most unpleasant episode for a sensitive individual, and one quite likely to make him dream thereof.

On reading over my records that evening, I, at first, noticed nothing; and was just going to close the book, when my eye caught, written more faintly, right at the end:

> Hunted by two men and a dog.

And the amazing thing about it was that I had completely forgotten having had any such dream. I could not even recall having written it down.

There was nothing identifiable on the twelfth day; but the thirteenth gave another excellent result.

During the day I read a novel in which one of the characters hid in a large secret loft in the roof of an old house. Later on in the story he had to fly from the house, and escaped from the loft by way of a chimney.

The previous night's dream was about a large, mysterious, secret loft, which I discovered and explored with great interest. A little later in the dream it became advisable for me to escape from the house, and I decided to do this by way of the loft. . . .

The net result of the experiment was that in the course of a fortnight I had been able to identify two conclusive instances of the "effect," and six, which, though not conclusive when regarded singly, could scarcely be attributed to coincidence when their number was taken into account. But the most important point was this: Not one of those instances would ever have been observed at all, had not the dreams been memorized and written down, and the records reinspected after the waking events.

So far, then, the theory that the effect was merely a normal characteristic of man's general relationship to Time—but one so constituted as to elude casual observation—had been partly borne out by experiment. But, on that theory, the effect in question should be just as experimentally observable to everyone else as it was to myself. This meant I must persuade another person to make a similar trial.

A young woman, whom I will call Miss B., good-naturedly agreed to undertake the task. I selected her mainly because she was an extremely normal individual, who had never had any sort of "psychical" experience, and who (this was the great thing) believed that she practically never dreamed at all. Indeed, she assured me that it would be useless for her to experiment, as she had only some six or seven dreams in the whole course of her life. . . .

The morning after the first night she came to me and told me that it was quite hopeless. She had tried to remember her dreams the very instant she woke; but there had been nothing to remember. So I told her not to bother about looking for memories of dreams, but to endeavour instead to recollect what she had been *thinking* at the moment of waking, and, after she had got that, to try to recall *why* she had been thinking it. That worked, as I had known it would; and on each of the next six mornings she was able to remember that she had had one short dream.

Counting the experiment as starting from the first dream, she obtained, on the sixth day, the following result.

Waiting at Plymouth Station for a train, she walked up to one end of a platform and came upon a five-or-six-barred gate leading on to a road. As she reached the gate a man passed on the other side, driving three brown cows. He was holding a stick out over the cows in peculiar fashion—as if it were a fishing-rod.

In the dream she walked up a path she knew, and found, to her great surprise, that it ended in a five-or-six-barred gate which had no business to be there. The gate was just like the one at the station, and, as she reached it, the man and the three brown cows passed on the other side, exactly as in the waking experience, the man holding out the stick fishing-rod fashion over the cows, and the whole group being arranged just like the group she saw.

The dream occurred the morning before the waking experience.

The blending of the "past" image of the path with the "future" image of the gate provided an excellent specimen of integration.*

I then asked my cousin, Miss C., to try. She was positive she had never had any experience of this kind, and was sure that, as a general rule, she dreamed very little. She proved excellent at recovering the lost dreams, and good at noting detail. But at first she was very weak at perceiving connections, even with past events. She could not, for example, understand how a dream of walking on roofs could be connected with the experience of climbing about the roof of a bungalow with me on the previous day, though she had not been on a roof of any sort for years. She obtained, however, on the eighth day, the following first-class result:

Immediately upon her arrival at a certain country hotel she was told of a curious person staying there whom all the guests suspected, having made up their minds that she was a German. (This was during the last stages of

---

* Miss B. had only one dream resembling a distinctive waking incident of the past within the preceding fortnight, and this dream she failed to spot until I pointed it out to her.

the war.) Shortly afterwards she met this person—for the first time—in the hotel grounds. These are rather uncommon. They extend a long way, contain numbers of large, rare trees, and would certainly be taken for public gardens by anyone who did not know that they belonged to the hotel. The supposed German was dressed in a black skirt with a black-and-white-striped blouse, and had her hair scraped back in a "bun" on the top of her head.

My cousin's dream was that a German woman, dressed in a black skirt, with a black-and-white-striped blouse, and having her hair scraped back in a "bun" on the top of her head, met her in a public garden. My cousin suspected her of being a spy.

The dream occurred about two days before the event. (The record is undated, but was in my hands when the confirmatory event took place.)

She had already had one almost, but not quite, conclusive result earlier in the experiment—a dream connected with some news in a letter she subsequently received from a friend.

[1927]

Abraham Lincoln Dreams
of His Assassination

WARD HILL LAMON

Mr. Lincoln had his Patmos, his "kinship with the shades," and this is, perhaps, the strangest feature of his character....

From early youth he seemed conscious of a high mission. Long before his admission to the bar, or his entrance into politics, he believed that he was destined to rise to a great height; that from a lofty station to which he should be called he would be able to confer lasting benefits on his fellow man. He believed also that from a lofty station he should fall. It was a vision of grandeur and of gloom which was confirmed in his mind by the dreams of his childhood, of his youthful days, and of his maturer years. The plain people with whom his life was spent, and with whom he was in cordial sympathy, believed also in the marvelous as reflected in presentiments and dreams....

The most startling incident in the life of Mr. Lincoln was a dream he had only a few days before his assassination. To him it was a thing of deadly import, and certainly no vision was ever fashioned more exactly like a dread reality. Coupled with other dreams . . . there was something about it so amazingly real, so true to the actual tragedy which occurred soon after, that more than mortal strength and wisdom would have been required to let it pass without a shudder or a pang. After worrying over it for some days Mr. Lincoln seemed no longer able to keep the secret. I give it as nearly in his own words as I can, from notes which I made immediately after its recital. There were only two or three persons present. The President was in a melancholy, meditative mood, and had been silent for some time. Mrs. Lincoln, who was present, rallied him on his solemn visage and want of spirit. This seemed to arouse him, and without seeming to notice her sally, he said, in slow and measured tones:

"It seems strange how much there is in the Bible about dreams. There are, I think, some sixteen chapters in the Old Testament and four or five in the New in which dreams are mentioned; and there are many other passages scattered throughout the book which refer to vision. If we believe the Bible, we must accept the fact that in the old days God and His angels came to men in their sleep and made themselves known in dreams. Nowadays dreams are regarded as very foolish, and are seldom told, except by old women and by young men and maidens in love."

Mrs. Lincoln here remarked: "Why, you look dreadfully solemn: do you believe in dreams?"

"I can't say that I do," returned Mr. Lincoln: "but I had one the other night which has haunted me ever since. After it occurred, the first time I opened the Bible, strange as it may appear, it was at the twenty-eight chapter of Genesis, which relates the wonderful dream Jacob had. I turned to other passages, and seemed to encounter a dream or vision wherever I looked. I kept on turning the leaves of the old book, and everywhere my eyes fell upon passages recording matters strongly in keeping with my own thoughts, supernatural visitations, dreams, visions, etc. . . ."

He now looked so serious and disturbed that Mrs. Lincoln exclaimed: "You frighten me! What is the matter?"

"I am afraid," said Mr. Lincoln, observing the effect his words had upon his wife, "that I have done wrong to mention the subject at all; but somehow the thing has got possession of me, and like Banquo's ghost, it will not down."

This only inflamed Mrs. Lincoln's curiosity the more, and while bravely disclaiming any belief in dreams, she strongly urged him to tell the dream which seemed to have such a hold upon him, being seconded in this by another listener. Mr. Lincoln hesitated, but at length commenced very deliberately, his brow overcast with a shade of melancholy.

"About ten days ago," said he, "I retired very late. I had been up waiting for important dispatches from the front. I could not have been long in bed when I fell into a slumber, for I was weary. I soon began to dream.

There seemed to be a deathlike stillness about me. Then I heard subdued sobs, as if a number of people were weeping. I thought I left my bed and wandered downstairs. There the silence was broken by the same pitiful sobbing, but the mourners were invisible. I went from room to room; no living person was in sight, but the same mournful sounds of distress met me as I passed along. It was light in all the rooms; every object was familiar to me; but where were all the people who were grieving as if their hearts would break? I was puzzled and alarmed. What could be the meaning of all this? Determined to find the cause of a state of things so mysterious and so shocking, I kept on until I arrived at the East Room, which I entered. There I met with a sickening surprise. Before me was a catafalque, on which rested a corpse wrapped in funeral vestments. Around it were stationed soldiers who were acting as guards; and there was a throng of people, some gazing mournfully upon the corpse, whose face was covered, others weeping pitifully. 'Who is dead in the White House?' I demanded of one of the soldiers. 'The President,' was his answer; 'he was killed by an assassin!' Then came a loud burst of grief from the crowd, which awoke me from my dreams. I slept no more that night, and although it was only a dream, I have been strongly annoyed by it ever since."

"That is horrid!" said Mrs. Lincoln. "I wish you had not told it. I am glad I don't believe in dreams, or I should be in terror from this time forth."

"Well," responded Mr. Lincoln thoughtfully, "it was only a dream, Mary. Let us say no more about it, and try to forget it."

Once the President alluded to this terrible dream with some show of playful humor. "Hill," said he, "your apprehension of harm to me from some hidden enemy is downright foolishness. For a long time you have been trying to keep somebody—the Lord knows who—from killing me. Don't you see how it will turn out? In this dream it was not me, but some other fellow, that was killed. It seems that this ghostly assassin tried his hand on someone else. And this reminds me of an old farmer in Illinois whose family were made sick by eating greens. Some poisonous herb had got into the mess, and members of the family were in danger of dying. There was a half-witted boy in the family called Jake; and always afterwards when they had greens the old man would say 'Let's try 'em on Jake. If he stands 'em, we're all right.' Just so with me. As long as this imaginary assassin continues to exercise himself on others I can stand it." He then became serious and said, "Well, let it go. I think the Lord in His own good time and way will work this out all right. God knows what is best."

These words he spoke with a sigh, and rather in a tone of soliloquy, as if hardly noticing my presence. . . .

Concerning presentiment and dreams Mr. Lincoln had a philosophy of his own, which, strange as it may appear, was in perfect harmony with his character in all other respects. He was no dabbler in divination, astrology, horoscopy, prophecy, ghostly lore, or witcheries of any sort. With Goethe, he held that "Nature cannot but do right eternally." Dreams, presentiments, in his judgment, are not of supernatural origin; that is, they proceed in natural order, their essence being preternatural, but not *above* Nature. The moving power of dreams and visions of an extraordinary nature he ascribed, as did the Patriarchs of old, to the Almighty Intelligence that governs the universe, their processes conforming strictly to natural laws. "Nature," said he, "is the workmanship of the Almighty; and we form but links in the general chain of intellectual and material life."

"I Dreamed I Went to School, and There Was No School There"

HERBERT GREENHOUSE

On October 21, 1966, a half million tons of coal slag slid down a mountain overlooking the village of Aberfan, Wales, and killed 144 persons, 28 adults and 116 children. Later investigations by three newspapers revealed that nearly 200 persons had had premonitions of the disaster, coming in dreams, visions, and feelings of discomfort and distress before the day of the tragedy.

One of the 200 was nine-year-old Eryl Mai Jones, who lived in Aberfan and attended the Pantglas Junior School, which stood at the base of the mountain. Two weeks before the disaster the child had told her mother, "Mummy, I'm not afraid to die, because I shall be there with Peter and June." Peter and June were her classmates at school. On Thursday, October 20, she woke up and said, "Mummy, let me tell you about my dream last night. I dreamed I went to school and there was no school there. Something black had come down all over it."

Many of the premonitions came in dreams. A telephone operator dreamed the night before of a screaming child in a telephone booth and another child walking toward the dreamer, followed by a "black, billowing mass." Others dreamed of "something black . . . deep blackness . . . hundreds of black horses thundering down a hillside dragging hearses." A week before the disaster an amateur artist had an irresistible urge to sketch his feelings of impending doom on paper. He drew a human head against an ominous black background.

A man living in Kent began to have a feeling several days before: "On Friday something terrible connected with death is going to happen." He was depressed for the rest of the week and when he came into his office on Friday, he told a fellow employee, "Today is the day it is going to happen." On the same morning a secretary in an aircraft plant had a sudden premonition that "something terrible" was just about to happen. In her mind's eye she saw "a black mountain moving and children buried under it."

Minutes later the coal slag, which for years had been dumped by the British government on top of the mountain, began to rumble, then roared down over the village, crushing houses and cottages, and demolishing two schools, one of them the Pantglas Junior School. One of the children killed was Eryl Mai Jones. Three days later a mass funeral was held, and the dead children were buried in a common grave. Eryl Mai was buried between her classmates, Peter and June.

The Murder That Triggered World War I

HERBERT GREENHOUSE

One night in 1912 there was a gathering at the home of Archduchess Isabella of Austria. A medium was present who was known as Madame Sylvia. After going into a mild trance, Madame Sylvia suddenly turned to the Archduchess and said, "Your Royal Highness, I beseech you to soften your antipathy toward Archduke Franz Ferdinand and his wife. We must be kind to them; in two years they are fated to die from the same bullet."

Two years later, on June 28, 1914, Monseigneur Joseph de Lanyi, Bishop of Grosswarden, had a terrifying dream, in which he saw a letter bordered in black lying on his desk. The letter bore the arms of Archduke Franz Ferdinand, who had at one time been his pupil. In the dream the Bishop opened the letter and saw a strange drama being enacted. The Archduke was sitting in an auto with his wife, while a crowd milled around outside. A man stepped out of the crowd and fired two bullets into the car.

Superimposed on this scene were the words of the letter: "Your Eminence, dear Dr. Lanyi, my wife and I have been victims of a political crime at Sarajevo. We commend ourselves to your prayers. Sarajevo. June 28, 1914. 4 A.M."

The Bishop woke up trembling, looked at his clock and saw that it was 4:30 A.M. He got up immediately and wrote down the details of his dream, which he dispatched in a letter to his brother, Professor Edouard de Lanyi.

Later that morning, about ten hours after the Bishop's dream, Archduke Ferdinand and his wife were murdered at Sarajevo as they sat in an automobile. Two bullets were fired, one of them fatally wounding the royal couple.

Did Bishop de Lanyi get a psychic message from the Archduke, who subconsciously knew that he would be killed? Or was the dream a projection of the Bishop's own clairvoyant knowledge of what was to happen ten hours later? How did Madame Sylvia know two years earlier that the Archduke and his wife would be assassinated—and by the same bullet? Did the bullet "know" what its course would be?

The time sequence of this psychic melodrama staggers the mind. The Archduke wrote in the dream (if it was actually the mind of the Archduke that transmitted the psychic letter) that he had already been murdered, yet he meticulously recorded the time of the message as 4 A.M., ten hours before the actual killing. Do time and space exist as we know them or are they distortions of a reality we cannot clearly glimpse because of our physical and mental limitations?

Dream of a Severed Head

HERBERT GREENHOUSE

Walter Franklin Prince was one of America's leading psychical researchers. He was also a psychic himself and had many premonitions of future events. When he felt that a dream contained a valid premonition, he wrote it down and had his account witnessed by two other persons.

His "hands" dream is one of the most celebrated in the literature of psychic events. During the night of November 27–28, 1917, Prince dreamed that a blond woman in her early thirties, slender and pretty, brought an order to him for her own death by beheading. As the light went out in the dream, she took one of his hands, and he sensed that the execution was taking place.

When Prince woke up, he recorded the details of the dream in his diary and told his wife about it. Then he visited the offices of the American

Society for Psychical Research in New York City and gave the account of his dream to an officer of the ASPR. He wrote: "I felt one *hand* (of mine) on the hair of the head, which was loose and severed from the body, and felt the moisture of blood." The fingers of his other hand had been "caught in her teeth, and the mouth opened and shut several times as the teeth refastened on my *hand*, and I was filled with the horror of the thought of a severed but living head."

The following morning, the 29th of November, Prince went to church with his wife, and on the way home saw this headline in the afternoon newspaper: HEAD SEVERED BY TRAIN AS WOMAN ENDS HER LIFE.

A woman by the name of Hand had placed her head on a track of the Long Island Railroad, directly in front of a train coming out of the station. She was decapitated. She had left a note in her handbag stating that her head would continue to live after it had been severed from her body.

The accident happened at 11:15 P.M. on Wednesday night, less than twenty-four hours after Prince's dream. Mrs. Hand was thirty-one years old, was slender and pretty and had golden brown hair. The dream corresponded in other ways with the real event: the dramatization of the "hand" (the woman's name); the fact that she "ordered" her own death; death by decapitation; death occurring "in the dark"; the belief of Mrs. Hand that her head would continue to live, as it did in the dream. Two other significant details are that the suicide took place a short distance (six miles) from Dr. Prince's home and within twenty-four hours of the dream.

The dream of the severed head was Dr. Prince's second premonitory dream in which a train was involved. It is possible that trains held a certain fascination for Prince. In any event, the severed head dream is one of the most remarkable death-portent dreams on record, especially because of the careful steps taken to make the dream known before the event.

Dream of the Guillotine

HERBERT GREENHOUSE

One of the most famous of all dreams was the guillotine dream of Alfred Maury, a psychologist of the mid-nineteenth century. In this dream Maury was living in France during the French Revolution and was tried and convicted by a tribunal. He was then taken to the guillotine and beheaded.

At the exact moment that the blade descended, a piece of the wooden molding from the canopy of Maury's bed fell on his neck and woke him up.

At the time of Maury's dream (1840), it was believed that even dreams with many events, appearing subjectively to take quite a while to unfold, might actually consume only a few seconds. If that were true, the molding itself may have instigated the events of the dream when it made contact with Maury's neck. Thus what seemed to last several hours may have taken place in seconds.

Dream laboratory research since 1952 (see Part III) has conclusively proved, however, that dreams take just about as long in time as dreamers believe they do. It would therefore have been unlikely that the many events of Maury's dream could have flashed through his dreaming mind in so short a time.

What, then, is the explanation? One theory is that Maury was already dreaming about the Revolution when the molding fell, and the physical event produced the beheading in the dream. The odds against a coincidence of this kind are very great. There is another possibility—it may have been a precognitive dream. If in his subliminal mind Maury knew that the molding would fall, he may then have accommodated his dream to the event that was coming, and in the precise way that dreamers have, timed the fall of the blade to the exact moment that the molding fell.

A Clairvoyant Dream of the Past

HERBERT GREENHOUSE

To gain knowledge of a past event by psychically reliving it is called retrocognition. This knowledge may come in the form of a vision in which characters appear in a past setting and replay a drama from that period. Many persons living in towns where Civil War battles were fought claim that they often see ghosts of the soldiers reenacting these battles. Sometimes, even more dramatically, the psychic will find himself actually a part of the scene, as if he had been taken back through time. Two young Englishwomen had such an experience in 1901, when they were vacationing in France. They found themselves at the court of Louis XVI, observed persons dressed in the costume of that period, and even saw Marie Antoinette as if she were alive.

Dreams often give us such scenes from the past, although the dreamer may not understand their significance. In his paper "Social Influences in Zulu Dreaming" (*Journal of Social Psychology*, 1958, vol. 47, pp. 265–283), S. G. Lee tells of his investigations of dreams in Zululand. One dream was of particular interest:

. . . I found that dreams of "graves" were reported by a few women. I asked for a description of these "graves," and was told that they were made of four flat stones, making a rectangular box, with another stone as a lid. At the time this description struck me as most peculiar, as it bore no relation at all to traditional Zulu burial methods. It was only later that I realized that I had been given a perfect description of a burial kist, common in Neolithic Europe. Dream graves, then, among the Zulu, can differ from the ones used by the people since times immemorial. Whether we have here a genuine museum piece of an archetype or not is beyond all useful conjectures, though the occurrence seems very difficult to explain in terms of cultural diffusion.

It is quite possible that this is an archetypal dream (see "An Archetypal Dream, page 201), but it may also be classed as retrocognitive. What is difficult to explain is why not one but several Zulu women, far removed in time and space from Neolithic Europe, should dream of such burial kists, but it seems evident that one or more of them had the psychic experience known as retrocognition.

A Dream of Astral Travel

OLIVER FOX

Eighteen years ago, when I was a student at a technical college, a dream impelled me to start my research. I dreamed simply that I was standing outside my home. Looking down, I discovered that the paving stones had mysteriously changed their position—the long sides were now parallel to the curb instead of perpendicular to it. Then the solution flashed upon me: though that glorious summer morning seemed as real as real could be, I was *dreaming!* Instantly the vividness of life increased a hundredfold. Never had sea and sky and trees shone with such glorious beauty; even the commonplace houses seemed alive and mystically beautiful. Never had I felt so absolutely well, so clear-brained, so divinely powerful. Verily the world had become my oyster. The sensation was exquisite beyond words; but it lasted only a few moments, and I awoke. As I was to learn later, my mental control had been overwhelmed by my emotions; so the tiresome body asserted its claim and pulled me back. And now I had a (for me) wonderful new idea; was it possible to regain at will the glory of the dream? Could I *prolong* my dreams?

It sounds simple; but in practice I found it one of the most difficult things imaginable. A hundred times would I pass the most glaring incongruities, and then at last some inconsistency would tell me that I was dreaming; and always this knowledge brought the change I have described. I found that I was then able to do little tricks at will, levitate, pass through seemingly solid walls, mold matter into new forms, etc., but in these early experiments I could stay out of my body for only a very short time, and this dream consciousness could be acquired only at intervals of several weeks. To begin with, my progress was very slow; but presently I made two more discoveries:

(1) The mental effort of prolonging the dream produced a pain in the region of the pineal gland—dull at first, but rapidly increasing in intensity —and I knew instinctively that this was a warning to me to resist no longer the call of my body.

(2) In the last moments of prolonging the dream, and while I was subject to the above pain, I experienced a sense of dual consciousness. I could feel myself standing in the dream and see the scenery; but at the same time I could feel myself lying in bed and see my bedroom. As the call of the body grew stronger the dream scenery became more faint; but by asserting my will to remain dreaming I could make the bedroom fade and the dream-scenery regain its apparent solidity.

And at this stage of my research a new query arose: what would happen if I disregarded the warning pain and fought it to a climax? As a matter of fact I was horribly afraid of making the experiment but a sense of duty urged me on. After flunking one or two opportunities, I made the battle and won. Just when it seemed I must be beaten, something went *click* in my brain; the pain vanished, and also the sense of dual consciousness. I was locked out in the dream, which was apparently the glorified counterpart of the seashore about a mile from my home. It was all very beautiful and absolutely real—so real that the idea of "waking up" seemed quite absurd —but my triumph was marred by an uneasy feeling that I was now to face quite new conditions. Two things worried me: I had no idea how time was passing on the physical earth, and I was evidently invisible to the few people who crossed my path. This experience was subtly different from my previous excursions; for no longer did there seem to be the slightest link between me and that once-tiresome physical body. Came the thought: was I dead?

I did not like it and willed to return, but nothing happened. I tried again and again, and nothing happened. Then I got frightened—the utter loneliness became dreadful—but I knew that a panic might prove fatal. I waited a little, then tried once more. Again there came that strange cerebral click, and instantly I was back in my body. But, though I could hear the clock ticking and my grandfather moving about in the next room, I was blind and could not move a muscle. I could not even raise an eyelid. That was my first experience of the seeming *cataleptic* rigor of the self-induced trance. Inch by inch I broke it, and it was an agonizing business. As it was impossible to move my body as a whole, I concentrated upon moving my little finger; then finger by finger I got my whole hand free; and then my arm. This done, I gripped the bed-rail above my head and pulled hard. Suddenly the trance broke, my eyes opened, and I was free. I jumped out of bed with great joy, and immediately collapsed upon the floor, being overwhelmed by nausea. I felt ill for two or three days afterwards.

For a time this fright had a sobering effect, and then the rashness of youth broke out once more. Again I sought the pineal pain and went through a very similar experience, though this time the seeming cataleptic trance was not so difficult to break; but then my nerve gave out. I was in love and life seemed sweet. I decided that I would continue my experiments; but that I would never again disregard the warning pain. And I think it was well for me that I came to this decision.

THE DANGERS

As these are very real and great, I think I had better enumerate them before proceeding further with the record. Anyone who, without being under the guidance of an Adept or Master, investigates on my lines exposes himself to the following grave risks—at least, so I believe:

(1) Heart failure, or insanity, arising from shock. This dream world is very lovely, but it has its horrors also.

(2) Premature burial.

(3) Obsession.

(4) Severance of cord.

(5) Repercussion effects upon the physical vehicle, caused by injuries to the astral.

Of course, the last three would be scorned by the orthodox experimenter. I would advise no one, motivated by curiosity alone, to adopt my methods; for I know from experience that they are very dangerous. . . .

THE SECOND STEP

To distinguish them from the ordinary variety, I named these dreams (in which I knew that I was dreaming) Dreams of Knowledge. I come now to my next discovery, which was that a dream of knowledge was often followed by a false awakening; *i.e.*, upon returning to my body I was under the impression that I was awake, until some supernormal occurrence—such as a sudden apparition—frightened me and caused me really to awake. I found then, after many experiences, that a Dream of Knowledge frequently led to a false awakening, in which my body was not dreaming in the ordinary sense, but was in a curious state, which I named the Trance Condition. These are its chief characteristics:

The body appears to be in a semi-rigid position. . . .
Though the eyes are closed, the room is plainly visible. . . .
Physical sounds are distinctly audible.
In this condition one is liable to any imaginable hallucination of sight or sound. . . . One is conscious of strange atmospheric stresses—the before-a-storm feeling, but enormously intensified.
On the whole the Trance Condition is extremely unpleasant.

The question now arose: Can the Trance Condition be a prelude to a Dream of Knowledge as well as an after-effect? Time showed that the answer was, Yes. In those days I had not discovered how to induce the Trance Condition at will; but I occasionally found myself in it, sometimes before dropping off to sleep, sometimes after an ordinary or unremembered dream, and sometimes after a Dream of Knowledge. As I grew able to recognize this state, so multiplied my opportunities for experimenting. I was getting things clearer and building very slowly my theory for liberating the soul at will; but I did not yet realize that it was possible to pass from the Trance Condition into the Dream of Knowledge *without any break in consciousness*. . . .

THE THIRD STEP

It was meditating upon the warning pain, which I imagined to be located in the pineal gland, that led at last to my new discovery. In the ordinary way I could not step out of my body when in the Trance Condition. Before this was possible a mysterious something had to happen—and in those earlier experiments it probably occurred during the break in consciousness and at last it flashed upon me what this something was; I had to force my incorporeal self through the doorway of the pineal gland, so that it clicked behind me. Then a further stage—a stage beyond the Trance Condition with its terrifying sensation, shapes and sounds—was reached. Then, and only then, could I step out of my physical body (now invisible), experience the dual consciousness, and be in the Dream of Knowledge (or a traveler on the astral plane) without any previous break in consciousness. It was done, when in the Trance Condition, simply by concentrating upon the pineal gland and willing to ascend through it. The sensation was as follows: my incorporeal self rushed to a point in the pineal gland and hurled itself against the imaginary trapdoor, while the golden light increased in brilliance, so that it seemed the whole room burst into flame. If the impetus was insufficient to take me through, then the sensation became reversed; my incorporeal self subsided and became again coincident with my body, while the astral light died down to normal. Often two or three efforts were required before I could generate sufficient will-power to carry me through. It felt as though I were rushing to insanity and death; but once the little door had clicked behind me, I enjoyed a mental clarity far surpassing that of the earth-life. And the fear was gone. With a few exceptions, I never felt afraid once I had got clear of my body; it was the Trance Condition, before and after, that I dreaded. The tempest over, one passed into calm and sunlit waters. Leaving the body was then as easy as getting out of bed; but I was always unable to see it—perhaps because its astral counterpart was withdrawn with me—though I could see my wife's form quite plainly. The dual consciousness was generally lost after I left the house. . . .

THE FOURTH STEP

Now one thing was needed: to be able to pass at will into the preliminary Trance Condition. This was to prove most difficult to accomplish. The initial symptoms were fairly easy to produce; but the trouble was that this self-induced state was of such extremely short duration. The very slightest disturbance sufficed to break the trance in its early stages. Nine times out of ten this happened, and the trance was broken before it had become sufficiently deep to allow of any attempt being made to force the pineal door. And often when I had succeeded in inducing a strong trance I would suddenly lose consciousness and find myself, after an unremembered gap, free to move as I would upon the astral plane. Nevertheless, I have induced the trance and passed out the pineal doorway without any break in consciousness whatever; I have returned to my body to strengthen the trance and left it again and returned again, etc., as many as six times in one night, without a single break in the mental continuity of the experience. To induce the trance I would lie down, with muscles relaxed, turning my consciousness inward upon the pineal door and excluding all other thoughts; the body was passive, but the mind positive in its concentration upon this inner point. My eyelids were closed; but I believe the eyes were rolled upward and slightly squinting—that was the sensation. The first symptom was the effect of seeing through my eyelids the room full of the golden light. Then came the numbness, beginning at the feet and extending upward. When the trance was deep this became quite painful, especially in the muscles of the jaw; there was also a sense of enormous pressure in the brain.

This, then, was the climax of my research. I could now pass from ordinary waking life to this new state of consciousness (or from life to "death") and return, without any mental break. It is easily written, but it took fourteen years to accomplish.

A Reincarnation Dream

HERBERT GREENHOUSE

Three days after her five-year-old daughter Alexandrina died, a Sicilian lady named Adela Samona saw the child in a dream. Alexandrina told her mother to stop grieving for she would soon be born again. But Señora Samona had had an operation the previous year that made it medically difficult, if not impossible, for her to have any more children.

Three days later she had the same dream. Later she attended a seance with her husband, and the spirit of little Alexandrina appeared and predicted that she would be born again to her mother, along with a twin sister. This was in March, 1910. In November Señora Samona gave birth to twin girls. One of the girls bore a striking resemblance to the dead girl and was given the same name, Alexandrina. As she grew up she seemed identical in personality as well as appearance to the dead Alexandrina. She was also left-handed and had birthmarks on the left eye and right ear exactly as the dead child had had. Her twin sister was totally unlike the dead girl, both physically and in behavior.

When Alexandrina II was ten years old, her mother promised to take her and her twin for a vacation in the town of Monreale. Although the children had never been there before, Alexandrina insisted that she had visited the town with a "lady who had horns" and that there were some "red priests" in the town. Señora Samona recalled that a few months before the death of the first Alexandrina, she had taken the girl to Monreale in the company of a woman who had cysts on her forehead. In Monreale they saw a group of priests wearing red robes.

Two Parallel (Reciprocal) Dreams
1. Three Dreams of the Same Murder

HERBERT GREENHOUSE

If a man dreams that he will be killed and two other men have the same dream at the same time with the identical gory details, he would certainly have cause for alarm. But Henry Armitt Brown, a young law student living in New York City during the nineteenth century, refused to believe that the burly man with a hatchet depicted in the dream was seeking him out with intent to kill.

One night in the year 1865 Henry lay down at exactly twelve midnight and dozed off. Almost immediately he dreamed that a strong hand was clutching his throat while he lay on his back on a New York street. A bearded, unkempt man of great strength was holding him down, one hand strangling him while the other held a hatchet over his head. Brown heard the anguished cries of friends who were running to his rescue, but before they could intervene, the hatchet split his forehead and he felt the blood spurt over his face. The dream ended with the sound of his friends' weeping in his ears.

The next day a classmate excitedly told him of having the same dream at twelve midnight the night before. In the dream the other student was passing by and heard the sound of scuffling and Brown's cries for help. He saw Brown on his back with the killer on top of him but before he could rush over, the hatchet was buried in Brown's head. Other friends of Brown had also arrived but were too late to save him.

The following week Brown visited friends in Burlington, New Jersey. His hostess told him that her husband had had a horrible dream the week before. "He dreamed a man killed you in a street fight. He ran to help you, but before he reached the spot, your enemy had killed you with a great club." Her husband interrupted her account: "Oh no, he killed you with a hatchet."

Fortunately, the dream killer never appeared and Brown was spared the horror of being murdered this way. The three dreams are a striking example of reciprocal dreaming, where telepathy, if not precognition, seems to be operating. There are hundreds, perhaps thousands, of cases of reciprocal dreaming on record, dreams shared by persons who are friends or otherwise emotionally close to each other.

2. A Romantic Parallel Dream

ROGER CAILLOIS

Ancient Indians knew the mystery of parallel dreams in which two persons, unaware of each other, have a common destiny announced to them. In the *Kathāsaritsagara* (*Ocean of the Streams of Story*), Somadeva, a twelfth-century author, tells how King Vikrāmāditya saw in a dream, in a country unknown, a girl with whom he fell in love. He dreamed that he was embracing her, when his happiness was suddenly interrupted by the cry of the night watchman. At the same time, in a distant country, Princess Malayavatī, who had a horror of men, dreamed that she saw a great personage emerging from a monastery. She married him and was tasting with him the joys of love on the nuptial couch when she was awakened by her chambermaid. After many vicissitudes the king and princess meet, recognize each other, and are united in real life as they had been earlier in their dreams.

E. THE DREAM THAT KEEPS RETURNING

R. L. MÉGROZ

OLD ARTEMIDORUS observed that dreams recurring at short intervals had a similar significance for the dreamer, while one that recurred after a long interval would no longer have the same meaning. This is probably true of many dreams, but modern psychology has shown that the same type of dream, with the same psychic significance, though possibly altered symbolic imagery, may persist for a long time, simply because of the temperamental colour of the dreamer. We are, however, not concerned here with the dreams that reveal an emotional "complex," but with the dreams that obviously repeat themselves, in their story and imagery. It seems to be quite common to experience recurring dreams, and some instances have been quoted in other chapters owing to a different context, like that of childhood.

An account of repeated dream experiences is more interesting in relation to a particular dreamer than a single dream, however vivid, can be, because the very repetition stresses certain imaginative and emotional characteristics of the dreamer's mind. I am therefore fortunate to be able to quote contemporaries of exceptional intelligence and personality to illustrate this type of dreaming. Indeed it will be unnecessary, and owing to limitations of space undesirable, to hark back to dreamers of the past, although their dreams may be as vivid and haunting as De Quincey's. The famous opium eater, however, is recalled by the confession of a fine novelist, Mr. Chris Massie:

THE NIGHT OF A THOUSAND DREAMS

"I am not so affected by dreams that can be explained. The vast, ghostly panorama that De Quincey so eloquently describes, with its contending hosts, its hither and thither passion, its impending salvation or doom, has, like the celebrated overture to *Tannhäuser*, a logical, and even a profound moral significance. That dream is the astral setting of a battle which is taking place on the stage of life; it is the counterpart of that conflict which is ceaseless in the waking consciousness of man; it belongs to reason and reality—the reason and reality we are familiar with as inhabitants of the earth.

"But there stalks abroad an unreason and an unreality in this hinterland of subjective activities which is the country of the exiled soul. Not all the subtleties of literature could impart even a faint reflection of what happens when, for some reason, the drug is withheld, and the ego leaps out of time into eternity, like a planet that has lost its sun. Then follows the night of a thousand dreams. It is as if all the film dramas that have been or ever will be created were being shown simultaneously on the same screen; as if all the gramophones in the world were operating together, and the mind had a detailed sense of every vocal particular, and a general conception of the stupendous whole. Fragments torn out of superhuman dramas, flashes of sublime poetry, spectacles unsurpassable. . . .

"And through it all the soul voyages on its own individual adventures, exploring endless vistas of existence, encountering saints, savages, and slaves that are not of the world, gods and men of some remote universe.

"Incidents? What incidents can be chosen from the passage of a million years? . . . Somewhere in my mind lingers the sinuous grace of strange and wonderful dances to music of ineffable sweetness, in a sunbathed arena, with ascending tiers of enthusiastic life that was unlike human life. I was a stranger there, until across a drifting twilight came the gentle Presence, the adorable One, who knows me. She turned over the pages of my life, and read them, every one, to the last word. She whom I have sought in sweat and blood! My undiscovered affinity of earth! The sweetness that had made me thirst! The hidden shrine! The altar of my offering to God! The sister-spirit who would cleanse me of sin! Beloved; alas, Beloved! . . .

"I wake with a burning, destroying thirst; and I ask myself in terror— 'Is this what my brain can do; or is this what my soul has done?' "

Mr. Massie's account of his dreaming was written for this book ten years ago. Recently, in 1937, Mr. Herbert Palmer sent me the following description of a recurring dream that has a visionary quality. He entitles it:

A DREAM OF HELL

"I have often of recent years dreamed that I was dead and in Hell. Not a Hell of fire and brimstone and physical pain. Not even a Hell of moral suffering and remorse. But a Hell of greyness and drabness and piercing monotony. The landscape is grey and intangible, my actions grey and intangible, and the people I am with though real enough, are grey and incommunicable. Sometimes I am walking or riding through a dismal industrial landscape; but more often I am sitting in grey drab rooms. The whole atmosphere is that of a large dingy railway-station. But one night, about a year after the termination of the war, my Hell was flooded with piercing moonlight. I was alone, vastly and terribly alone, walking through a wide wilderness of rolling country covered with pine-trees.

"Over it soared the moon, a round white moon of piercing anguish, and around me rolled invisible waves of dreadful loneliness. The loneliness was intenser than any earthly loneliness, for it was felt almost as a physical pain. And I was seeking to rid myself of it, seeking to get into touch with human beings, with communicating souls. But nobody and nothing seemed to populate that unending wilderness, nothing save pine-trees. I was dead and in Hell, and quite alone. By and by I came to a house two storys high. I ascended the stairs and entered a room with a table in the centre. On the other side of the table sat my mother, painting a picture that would never come right. I felt that she would paint for all eternity and it would never come right. She was moaning. The whole room was moaning. The whole lonely world around me was moaning. I wanted to get in touch with her, to get in touch with somebody, but I was cut off. All contact was impossible. Our souls could not touch. Slowly the white moonlit world passed away and the dawn arose. But it was a grey, comfortless dawn of pelting rain. For a day, nay for a whole season it rained, and then suddenly the sun shone. But what a sun! it was so hot and blazing. And the loneliness had not changed; it was only the temperature of the loneliness that had changed. I was cut off—from both man and God, and still my mother oblivious of me sat on the other side of the table painting a picture that would never come right. But suddenly I was aware of other people. They were playing tennis in a little court just under the window on the right. Little girls in pink sun-bonnets. I wanted to go out to them, to play and speak with them, but I felt that I could not. Up and down bounced the balls, breaking pleasantly into the unutterable blankness and monotony of my self-centered life in death. I could not communicate, I could not speak, I could not go down the stairs. I was alone, unutterably alone. Then I awoke."

Readers of Mr. Palmer's poetry will realize how characteristic is his dreaming.

Mr. E. H. W. Meyerstein's dreams include the following record of a repeated dream:

METAPHYSICAL

"During an Oxford summer vacation (1910 or 1911) at Chagford, when I was reading philosophy, I had repeatedly a sort of metaphysical nightmare. I would see a point, like either end of a pin; it would advance towards me, or I towards it (I am not sure which), growing in magnitude, until it became a globe into which I was absorbed and whirled violently about until the vertigo was a positive agony. This experience I have described in my Ode on Nothing."

Here we come to the "examination dream," which Dr. Seligman has classed among the universal types of dream. Its frequency as a recurrent dream is no doubt due to the persisting influence over the mind of anxiety about one's work. A simple form of it was described by the late St. Loe Strachey:

"I am worried," he wrote, "by the sense of not being able to pack in time to catch my train, or else compelled to go back to Oxford to pass an examination under impossible and humiliating conditions."

Mr. Bernard Shaw confessed to sharing this experience:

DREAMING FROM OVERWORK

"My experience is practically the same as Strachey's, except that instead of his occasional examination ordeal I find myself madly about to walk on to the stage to perform a part of which I do not know a word, or to sing an operatic role without knowing a note of it.

"This is clearly a variation of the examination dream. No examination could cause me the slightest anxiety, partly because the result would be a foregone conclusion (in the negative), and partly because I have no ambition in that direction. These dreams are overwork dreams. With me, as I gather with Mr. Strachey, they are nearly always connected with travelling and are confined to railway and hotel difficulties. Motoring never comes into them."

Sir Oliver Lodge also confesses to this kind of recurring dream, and says that he remembers no pleasant dreams at all, in which Thomas Carlyle would have sympathized with him, except that Sir Oliver could not share Carlyle's view of the utter unimportance of his dreams. Sir Oliver Lodge writes:

LOSING TRAINS

"My usual nightmare relates to travelling, especially the losing of trains. A particular dream-station has a number of platforms and staircases and passages along which the patient is hurrying and, wrongly directed, ultimately arrives on the first platform to see the train just going out. Sometimes the train is caught, but turns out to be the wrong one. There is a dream-station, which I might recognize if it exists, but it is so unwieldy and confusing that the malice of man can hardly have erected it.

"Another recurrent dream used to trouble me at the beginning of term, namely, that I had forgotten a lecture. Sometimes I found myself apparently listening to a distant noise which—it gradually dawned on me—was made by the students stamping in impatience; but, in hurrying, in an obstructed manner, to the theatre, I found them just dispersed. This may have happened in real life, but it certainly happened in dreams: and waking was a relief.

"Travelling annoyances are with me, however, the most frequent kind of nightmare. Fortunately I seldom dream, for I do not remember any pleasant dreams."

That learned critic, Mr. George Saintsbury, wrote: "No small proportion of my dreams have recurred with little or no variation. The most persistent has been one which, in this or that way, makes me pre-occupied, till I suddenly discover that the hour of some fixed engagement at newspaper office, lecture-room, or what not, has passed."

F. "I KNOW I AM DREAMING" —THE LUCID DREAM

C. E. GREEN

WHAT IS A lucid dream? Here is an example:

Without any preliminary ordinary dream experience, I suddenly found my-self on a fairly large boat travelling at a normal speed up what appeared to be the mouth of a river, just before it issues into the sea. There was some sort of pleasant scenery on either side, with trees and greenery, and straight in front, the water stretched to infinity. The deck was smooth and clean and warmed by the sun, and I felt the warm breeze on my skin. This startled me, because I knew that in a dream one does not feel actual physical sensations with the same intensity and subtlety as in real life, and I was sufficiently mistress of my own thoughts and movements to pinch my arm in order to assure myself that it was only a dream. I felt the flesh under my fingers and the slight pain in my arm, and this filled me with real alarm, because I knew that I ought not to be on that boat, in the daylight. I did not *see* my own body, but I was sufficiently lucid to imagine it, lying inert in my own bed here in Paris. . . .

A lucid dream is a dream in which the subject is aware that he is dreaming.

Plainly a lucid dream constitutes something of a test case. Dreaming is usually defined by reference to its irrationality and discontinuity with waking experience. That is to say, the events of the dream do not obey the usual laws of the physical world and the subject does not relate what is happening to memories of his past life and of the normal world, so that the dream is "discontinuous" with the rest of his experience.

Certain subjects claim that in lucid dreams they retain the greater part, or even all, of the memories which they possess in the waking state. If this is so, the "discontinuity of personal experience" is evidently at a minimum.

Further, some lucid dreams seem to be very accurate imitations of waking life. The case which has been quoted at the beginning of this chapter is an example of this. In this case, we might say that there was no discontinuity with the physical world of ordinary experience other than an apparent displacement of the observer's point of view to a different spatial location.

If the dreamer dreams that he is lying in bed in his own bedroom, as is sometimes reported, even this discontinuity is absent.

A further problem arises about the use of the word "aware," or its synonym "conscious." In our definition, we said that a person having a lucid dream is "aware that he is dreaming." But Malcolm observes: ". . . Having some conscious experience or other, no matter what, is not what is meant by being asleep. . . ." It certainly seems very odd to say that the subject quoted at the beginning of this chapter was not "conscious" at the time of the experience described. The problem might be solved by distinguishing between "physiological unconsciousness" and "psychological unconsciousness." "Physiological unconsciousness" might be defined as a state characterized by unresponsiveness to certain external stimuli. "Psychological unconsciousness" would be more difficult to define. It is difficult to state any criterion of uncriticalness, amnesia, unawareness and so on, which is not found at times in a "normal waking" state. . . .

FALSE AWAKENING

This is a phenomenon which, although otherwise rare, seems to happen frequently to subjects who have completely lucid dreams as well. After a lucid dream, they may have a subsequent dream in which they seem to wake up in bed in the normal way. After some experience of this, it may occur to them to doubt whether they are really awake, and they may then proceed to examine their environment in the hope of obtaining clues. Sometimes they do realize that this is still a dream, and another lucid dream may follow. Or alternatively, the dream may remain pre-lucid. The following two examples illustrate both these possibilities.

I dreamed that my wife and I awoke, got up, and dressed. On pulling up the blind, we made the amazing discovery that the row of houses opposite had vanished and in their place were bare fields. I said to my wife, "This means I am dreaming, though everything seems so real and I feel perfectly awake. Those houses could not disappear in the night, and look at all that grass!" But though my wife was greatly puzzled, I could not convince her it was a dream. "Well," I continued, "I am prepared to stand by my reason and put it to the test. I will jump out of the window, and I shall take no harm." Ruthlessly ignoring her pleading and objecting, I opened the window and climbed out on to the sill. I then jumped, and floated gently down into the street. When my feet touched the pavement, I awoke. My wife had no memory of dreaming.

As a matter of fact, I was very nervous about jumping; for the atmosphere *inside* our bedroom seemed so absolutely real that it nearly made me accept the manifest absurdity of things outside.

Seemed to wake; X. entered the room, switched on the electric light and drew the curtains to exclude the sunlight. (I had been sleeping late, so it was in fact late morning.) This appeared natural but of course should have seemed illogical. I told X. of the lucid dream I had just been having, and thought of the possibility that this was still a dream. I discussed this with X., but dismissed it because of the naturalness of everything—papers spread out on the carpet under the window, spotted with rain that had come in through it. (In actual fact, I did not at this time have any papers spread out in this way—I don't think I ever did while I lived there. However, it would not have been out of the ordinary for me to have decided to do some work on the floor in order to have more room to arrange different groups of papers.) I thought that it could not be a dream, because it could not so accurately reproduce so much in such detail—looking at the numerous papers, feeling their texture, thickness, etc., as I thought this.

PART II

DREAM THEORIES THROUGHOUT THE WORLD

Introduction to Part II

HERBERT GREENHOUSE

THROUGHOUT HISTORY *and in every culture people have wondered what causes the bizarre drama that unfolds in their minds each night as they sleep. In ancient times and in primitive societies it was thought that the mind itself or the soul travelled during dreams, or that actual persons, human or divine, came to visit the dreamer with warnings of danger or instructions for his waking life. Some primitive tribes anticipated Freud in their belief that a dreamer's own soul reveals his hidden desires and that he must fulfill these desires when he is awake. The present-day Senoi of the Malay Peninsula practice dream therapy without benefit of psychoanalysis. At breakfast a Senoi family discusses the dreams of the night before and tries to understand their message.*

The biblical prophets looked upon dreams as visions that revealed the will of Jehovah for their people. The Egyptians thought that through prayer one might be rewarded with a dream in which a god gives him counsel. The Greeks dreamed of receiving divine word of illness or trouble, good health or good fortune, sent to them by Zeus through minor gods. The most noteworthy feature of the Greek cult of dreams was the elaborate art of divination and the recognition of dream oracles in temples established for the cure of bodily ills. The Babylonians and Assyrians placed great emphasis on demonology. Devils and demons were believed to be evil influences encountered in dreams, to be defeated by the practice of magic.

Philosophers such as Plato and Socrates, Schopenhauer and Liebnitz, took their dreams seriously, and Socrates tells of dreams that advised him to "make music." But there were also the detractors of dreams such as Cicero and Aristotle, and later rationalists like Thomas Paine, who ridiculed the notion that dreams were divinely inspired. Although the early Christian theologians thought that God and spirits were very much a part of dreams, in the seventeenth century Jeremy Taylor, a divine of the Church of England, wrote that "dreams follow the temper of the body." Interest in the significance of dreams fell off after the age of science began, and in the nineteenth century writers such as Wundt wrote that dreams were no more than images excited by gastric disturbances or stimulation of the senses.

With the publication of Freud's The Interpretation of Dreams, *attention was turned once more to dreams as a meaningful reflection of the mind and personality, not just something left over from the night before. Freud emphasized the* latent *content of the dream, that is, repressed sexuality and other unrealized wishes, that somehow eluded the censor and appeared in the dream in disguised forms. The psychiatrists and psychologists who followed Freud have used his theories as a starting-point for their own, either expanding or modifying Freud's views, or taking off in completely new directions.*

Part II, on Dream Theories thoughout the World, in general follows the sequence outlined in this introduction: primitive, pagan, Oriental, biblical, and theological theories, followed by the pre-Freudian philosophical and physiological explanations of dreaming, and culminating in the psychiatric breakthrough. Also discussed are nightmares and other disorders of sleep, dozing-off dreams, and artificially induced dreams.

A. A PRIMITIVE VIEW OF

The Soul Goes Hunting and

SIR EDWARD B. TYLOR

CERTAIN OF THE GREENLANDERS . . . consider that the soul quits the body in the night and goes out hunting, dancing and visiting; their dreams, which are frequent and lively, having brought them to this opinion. Among the Indians of North America, we hear of the dreamer's soul leaving his body and wandering in quest of things attractive to it. These things the waking man must endeavor to obtain, lest his soul be troubled and quit the body altogether. The New Zealanders considered the dreaming soul to quit the body and return, even traveling to the region of the dead to hold converse with its friends. The Tagals of Luzon object to waking a sleeper, on account of the absence of his soul. The Karens, whose theory of the wandering soul has just been noticed, explain dreams to be what this *là* sees and experiences in its journeys when it has left the body asleep. They even account with much acuteness for the fact that we are apt to dream of people and places which we knew before; the *leip-pya*, they say, can only visit the regions where the body it belongs to has been already. Onward from the savage state, the idea of the spirit's departure in sleep may be traced into the speculative philosophy of higher nations as in the Vedanta system, and the Kabbala. St. Augustine tells one of the double narratives which so well illustrate theories of this kind. The man who tells Augustine the story relates that, at home one night before going to sleep, he saw coming to him a certain philosopher, most well known to him, who then expounded to him certain Platonic passages, which when asked previously he had refused to explain. And when he (afterwards) inquired of this philosopher why he did at this house what he had refused to do at his own:

not do it," said the philosopher, "but I dreamt I did." And thus,
Augustine, that was exhibited to one by phantastic image while wak-
, which the other saw in a dream. (De Civ. Dei XVIII. 18.) European
folklore has preserved interesting details of this primitive dream-theory,
such as the fear of turning a sleeper over lest the absent soul should miss
the way back. King Gunthram's legend is one of a group interesting from
the same point of view. The king lay in the wood asleep with his head in
his faithful henchman's lap; the servant saw as it were a snake issue
from his lord's mouth and run to the brook, but it could not pass, so the
servant laid the sword across the water, and the creature ran along it and
up into a mountain; after a while it came back and returned into the
mouth of the sleeping king, who waking up told how he had dreamt that
he went over an iron bridge into a mountain full of gold. This is one of
those instructive legends which preserve for us, as in a museum, relics of
an early intellectual condition of our Aryan race, in thoughts which to
our modern minds have fallen to the level of quaint fancy, but which
still remain sound and reasonable philosophy to the savage. . . .

This opinion, however, only constitutes one of several parts of the
theory of dreams in savage psychology. Another part has also a place
here, the view that human souls come from without to visit the sleeper,
who sees them as dreams. These two views are by no means incompatible.
The North American Indians allowed themselves the alternative of supposing a dream to be a visit from the soul of the person or object
dreamt of, or a sight seen by the rational soul, gone out for an excursion
while the sensitive soul remains in the body. So the Zulu may be visited
in a dream by the shade of an ancestor, who comes to warn him of danger,
or he may himself be taken by the *itongo* in a dream to visit his distant
people, and see that they are in trouble; as for the man who is passing
into the morbid condition of the professional seer, phantoms are continually coming to talk to him in his sleep, till he becomes, as the expressive
native phrase is "in a house of dreams." In the lower range of culture,
it is perhaps most frequently taken for granted that a man's apparition in
a dream is a visit from his disembodied spirit, which the dreamer, to use
an expressive Ojibwa idiom, "sees when asleep." Such a thought comes
out clearly in the Fijian opinion that a living man's spirit may leave the
body, to trouble other people in their sleep; or in a recent account of an
old Indian woman of British Columbia sending for the medicine man to
drive away the dead people who came to her every night. A modern observer's description of the state of mind of the Negroes of South Guinea
in this respect is extremely characteristic and instructive. "All their
dreams are construed into visits from the spirits of their deceased friends.
The cautions, hints and warnings which come to them through this source
are received with the most serious and deferential attention, and are always acted upon in their waking hours. The habit of relating their dreams,

which is universal, greatly promotes the habit of dreaming itself, and hence their sleeping hours are characterized by almost as much intercourse with the dead as their waking are with the living. This is, no doubt, one of the reasons of their excessive superstitiousness. Their imaginations become so lively, that they can scarcely distinguish between dreams and their waking thoughts, between the real and the ideal, and they consequently utter falsehood without intending, and profess to see things which never existed. . . .

Visits from the dead are matters of personal experience and personal testimony. In dream or vision the seer beholds the spirits of the departed, and they give him tidings from the other world, or he may even rise and travel thither himself, and return to tell the living what he has seen among the dead. It is sometimes as if the traveler's material body went to visit a distant land, and sometimes all we are told is that the man's self went, but whether in body or in spirit is a mere detail of which the story keeps no record. Mostly, however, it is the seer's soul which goes forth, leaving his body behind in ecstasy, sleep, coma or death. Some of these stories, as we trace them on from savage into civilized times, are no doubt given in good faith by the visionary himself, while others are imitations of these genuine accounts. Now such visions are naturally apt to reproduce thoughts with which the seer's mind was already furnished. Every idea once lodged in the mind of a savage, a barbarian, or an enthusiast, is ready thus to be brought back to him from without. It is a vicious circle; what he believes he therefore sees, and what he sees he therefore believes. Beholding the reflection of his own mind like a child looking at itself in a glass, he humbly receives the teaching of his second self. The Red Indian visits his happy-hunting grounds, the Togan his shadowy island of Volotu, the Greek enters Hades and looks on the Elysian Fields, the Christian beholds the heights of Heaven and the depths of Hell.

Among the North American Indians, and especially the Algonquin tribes, accounts are not unusual of men whose spirits, traveling in dreams or in the hallucinations of extreme illness to the land of the dead, have returned to re-animate their bodies, and tell what they have seen. Their experiences have been in great measure what they were taught in early childhood to expect, the journey along the path of the dead, the monstrous strawberry at which the *jebi-ug* or ghosts refresh themselves, but which turned to red rock at the touch of their spoons, the bark offered them for dried meat and great puff balls for squashes, the river of the dead with its snake-bridge or swinging log, the great dog standing on the other side, the villages of the dead beyond. The Zulus of our own day tell of men who have gone down by holes in the ground into the underworld, where mountains and rivers and all things are as here above, and where a man may find his kindred, for the dead live in their villages, and may be seen milking their cattle, which are the cattle killed on earth and come to life anew. The Zulu Umpengula, who told one of these stories to Dr. Callaway, remembered when he was a boy seeing an ugly little hairy man called Uncama, who once, chasing a porcupine who ate his mealies, followed it down a hole in the ground. When he came back to his home on earth he found that he had been given up for dead himself, his wife had duly burnt and buried his mats and blankets and vessels, and the wondering people at sight of him again shouted the funeral dirge. Of this Zulu Dante it used to be continually said, "There is the man who went to the underground people. . . ."

It is frequently observed or implied that the religious beliefs of the lower races are in no small measure based on the evidence of visions and dreams, regarded as actual intercourse with spiritual beings. From the earliest phase of culture upwards, we find religion in close alliance with ecstatic physical conditions. These are brought on by various means of interference with the healthy action of body and mind, and it is scarcely needful to remind the reader that, according to philosophic theories antecedent to those of modern medicine, such morbid disturbances are explained as symptoms of divine visitation, or at least of superhuman spirituality. Among the strongest means of disturbing the functions of the mind so as to produce ecstatic vision is fasting, accompanied as it so usually is with other privations, and with prolonged solitary contemplation in the desert or forest. Among the ordinary vicissitudes of savage life, the wild hunter has many a time to try involuntarily the effects of such a life for days and weeks together, and under these circumstances he soon comes to see and talk with phantoms which are to him visible personal spirits. The secret of spiritual intercourse thus learnt, he has thenceforth but to reproduce the cause in order to renew the effects.

The rite of fasting, and the utter objective reality ascribed to what we call its morbid symptoms, are shown in striking detail among the savage tribes of North America. Among the Indians (the accounts mostly refer to the Algonquin tribes), long and rigorous fasting is enjoined among boys and girls from a very early age; to be able to fast long is an enviable distinction, and they will abstain from food three to seven days, or even more, taking only a little water. During these fasts, especial attention is paid to dreams. Thus Tanner tells the story of a certain Net-no-kwa, who at twelve years old fasted ten successive days, till in a dream a man came and stood before her, and after speaking of many things gave her two sticks, saying, "I give you these two to walk upon, and your hair I give it to be like snow"; this assurance of extreme old age was through life a support to her in time of danger and distress. At manhood the Indian lad, retiring to a solitary place to fast and meditate and pray, receives visionary impressions which stamp his character for life, and especially he waits till there appears to him in a dream some animal or thing which will be henceforth his "medicine," the fetish-representative of his monitor or protecting genius. For instance, an aged warrior who in his youth had dreamed of a bat coming to him, wore the skin of a bat in the crown of his head henceforth, and was all his life invulnerable to his enemies as a bat on the wing. In after life, an Indian who wants anything will fast till he has a dream that his *manitu* will grant it to him. While the men are away hunting, the children are sometimes made to fast, that in their dreams they may obtain omens of the chase. Hunters fasting before an expedition are informed in dreams of the haunts of the game, and the means of appeasing the wrath of the bad spirits; if the dreamer fancies he sees an Indian who has been long dead, and hears him say, "If thou wilt sacrifice to me thou shalt shoot the deer at pleasure," he will prepare a sacrifice, and burn the whole or part of a deer, in honor of the apparition. The Ojibwa prophetess, known in after life as Catherine Wabose, in telling the story of her early years, relates how at the age of womanhood she fasted in her secluded lodge till she went up into the heavens and saw the spirit at the entrance, the Bright Blue Sky; this was the first supernatural communication of her prophetic career. The account given to Schoolcroft by Chingwauk, an Algonquin chief deeply versed in the mystic lore and picture writing of his people, is as follows: "Chingwauk began by saying that the ancient Indians made a great merit of fasting. They fasted sometimes six or seven days, till both their bodies and minds became free and light, which prepared them to dream. The object of the ancient seers was to dream of the sun; as it was believed that such a dream would enable them to see everything on earth. And by fasting long and thinking much on the subject, they generally succeeded. Fast and dreams were at first attempted at an early age. What a young man sees and experiences during these dreams and fasts, is adopted by him as truth, and it becomes a principle to regulate his future life. If he has been favored much in his fasts, and the people believe that he has the art of looking into futurity, the path is opened to the highest honors. The prophet, he continued, begins to try his power in secret, with only one assistant, whose testimony is necessary should he succeed. As he goes on, he puts down the figures of his dreams and revelations, by symbols, on bark or other material, till a whole winter is sometimes passed in pursuing the subject, and he thus has a record of his principal revelations."

The Secret Helper in Dreams

WILLIAM MACDOUGALL

An important institution among some of the Ibans (a pagan tribe of Borneo) which occurs but in rare instances among the other peoples is the *ngarong* or secret helper. The *ngarong* is one of the very few topics in regard to which the Ibans display any reluctance to speak freely. So great is their reserve in this connection that one of us lived for fourteen years on friendly terms with Ibans of various districts without ascertaining the meaning of the word *ngarong*, or suspecting the great importance of the part played by the notion in the lives of some of these people. The *ngarong* seems to be usually the spirit of some ancestor or dead relative, but not always so, and it is not clear that it is always conceived as the spirit of a deceased human being. This spirit becomes the special protector of some individual Iban, to whom in a dream he manifests himself, in the first place in human form, and announces that he will be his secret helper; and he may or may not inform the dreamer in what form he will appear in the future. On the day after such a dream the Iban wanders through the jungle looking for signs by which he may recognize his secret helper; and if an animal behaves in a manner at all unusual, if a startled deer stops a moment to gaze at him before bounding away, if a gibbon gambols about persistently in the trees near him, if he comes upon a bright quartz-crystal or a strangely contorted root or creeper, that animal or object is for him full of a mysterious significance and is the abode of his *ngarong*. Sometimes the *ngarong* then assumes the form of an Iban and speaks with him, promising all kinds of help and good fortune. If this occurs the seer usually faints away, and when he comes to himself again the *ngarong* will have disappeared. Or, again, a man may be told in his dreams that if he will go into the jungle he will meet his *ngarong* in the form of a wild boar. He will then, of course, go to seek it, and if by chance other men of his house should kill a wild boar that day, he will go to them and beg for its head or buy it at a good price if need be, carry it home to his bed-place, offer it cooked rice and kill a fowl before it, smearing the blood on the head and on himself, and humbly begging for pardon. Or he may leave the corpse in the jungle and sacrifice a fowl before it there. On the following night he hopes to dream of the *ngarong* again, and perhaps he is told in his dream to take the tusks from the dead boar and that they will bring him good luck. Unless he dreams something of this sort, he feels that he has been mistaken, and that the boar was not really his secret helper.

Perhaps only one in a hundred men is fortunate enough to have a secret helper, though it is ardently desired by many of them. Many a young man goes to sleep on the grave of some distinguished person, or in some wild and lonely spot, and lives for some days on a very restricted diet, hoping that a secret helper will come to him in his dreams.

When, as is most commonly the case, the secret helper takes on the form of some animal, all individuals of that species become objects of especial regard to the fortunate Iban; he will not kill or eat any such animal, and he will as far as possible restrain others from doing so. A *ngarong* may after a time manifest itself in some new form, but even then the Iban will continue to respect the animal-form in which it first appeared.

In some cases the cult of a secret helper will spread through a whole family or household.

Sex Dreams of the African Ashantis

R. S. RATTRAY

To the Ashanti mind dreams are caused either by the visitation of denizens of the spirit world, or by spirits, *i.e.*, volatile souls of persons still alive, or by the journeyings of one's own soul during the hours of sleep.

I have heard of a case of a sexual dream where the disclosure of the dream cost the owner his life. It would not be easy to obtain a better example of how real events are held to be which pass before the sleeper. Such dreams mean that "your soul desires that woman's soul," stated my informant. "If you dream that you have had intercourse with a woman with whom you have never had sexual relations, it means that you will never in all your life have sexual intercourse with that woman, because 'your soul has already devoured her.' "

If you dream that you have had sexual intercourse with another man's wife and any one hears of it, and tells her husband, then you will be fined the usual adultery fee, for your soul and hers have had sexual intercourse. If you ever dream such a dream you should not tell anyone, but very early next morning you should go to the midden heap, which is also the women's latrine, and whisper to it and say *Suminna ma so dae bone emma no nye sa.* (O midden heap, I have dreamed an evil dream, grant that it may never happen like that.) Any bad dream you must carry away to the refuse heap, where everything bad is put.

If you dream that you have sexual intercourse with someone who is now dead and with whom you have had sexual relations during her life, then your penis will surely die; but this does not happen if the dream is about some woman now dead, but with whom you have never had sexual relations during her life.

The Dream Is the Cause of the Wish

BRONISLAW MALINOWSKI

Dreams and day-dreams are not an easy subject for study among the Melonesians of the Trobriand Islands. It is a remarkable and characteristic feature of these natives, in which they seem to differ from other savages, that they apparently dream little, have little interest in their dreams, seldom relate them spontaneously, do not regard the ordinary dream as having any prophetic or other importance, and have no code of symbolic explanation whatever. When I tackled the subject directly, as I often did, and asked my informants whether they dreamt, and, if so, what their dreams had been, the answer was usually negative, with rare exceptions, to which we will return. Is this absence of dreams, or rather of interest in dreams, due to the fact that we are dealing with a non-repressed society, a society among whom sex, as such, is in no way restricted? Is it so because their "complex" is weak, appears late, and has few infantile elements? This rarity of free dreams and the absence of strong affect, hence absence of remembrance, points to the same conclusion as the absence of neurosis, that is, to the correctness in broad outline of the Freudian theory. For this theory affirms that the main cause of dreams is unsatisfied sexual appetite, and especially such sexual or quasi-sexual impulses as are repressed violently in infancy. To this question one could only obtain a satisfactory answer by collecting rich comparative material among two communities of similar culture and mode of living but with different repressions.

I have used so far the expression "free dreams," for there is a class of dreams which it is difficult to range, whether with the free or with the fixed fantasies, since they run on lines prescribed by tradition and could be called "official dreams." Such, for instance, are dreams in which a man leading an enterprise or carrying out some task is supposed to dream under certain circumstances about the object of his enterprise. The leaders of fishing excursions dream about the weather, about the place where the shoals may appear, about the best date for the expedition, and they give their orders and instructions accordingly. Those in charge of the overseas expeditions called *Kula* are often supposed to have dreams about the success of their ceremonial trading. Above all, the magicians have dreams associated with the performance of their magic. There is also another form of typical or traditional dream associated with magic, that, namely, which comes about as the direct result of a spell or of a rite. Thus, in the ceremonial overseas trading there is a certain spell which acts directly on the mind of the partner, induces in him a dream, and this dream makes the partner desire the exchange. Most love magic is supposed to produce a dream which awakens the amorous wish.

Thus, these natives, remarkably enough, reverse the Freudian theory of dreams, for to them the dream is the cause of the wish. In reality, this class of traditional dreams is very much within the lines of the Freudian theory. For they are constructed as a projection of the magician's own desires. The victim of love magic feels in her dream an itching, a craving which is the same as the state of mind of the performer of the magic. The *Kula* partner under the influence of magic is supposed to dream of glorious scenes of exchange which form the very vision dominating the wishes of the performer.

Nor are such dreams merely spoken and only supposed to exist. Very frequently the magician himself would come to tell me that he had dreamt about a good yield in fishing, and would organize an expedition on the strength of it. Or a garden wizard would speak of a dream he had had about a long drought, and therefore order certain things to be done. During the annual ceremonial feast in honor of dead ancestors I had on two occasions opportunities of noting dreams of natives. In both cases the dream referred to the proceedings, and in one the dreamer claimed to have dreamt that he had had a conversation with the spirits, who were not satisfied with things. Another class of typical dream is concerned with the birth of babies. In these the future mother has a sort of dream annunciation from one of her dead relatives.

Now one of the typical or official dreams is the sexual dream, which interests us here more especially. A man will dream that a woman visits him at night; in dream he will have congress with her, and he will awake finding the discharge of semen on the mat. This he will conceal from his wife, but he will try to follow up the dream actively in real life and initiate an intrigue with the woman. For the dream means that she who visited him had performed love magic and that she desires him.

The Culture Shapes the Dream*

DOROTHY EGGAN

Automatic physiological protective and regenerative mechanisms during sleep are accepted facts, and there is also much evidence which indicates that emotional release through fantasy at night frequently enables an individual to live with himself more easily through the day, as for instance the coward whose dreams constantly make of him a hero. Consequently we find the *protective device of mild amnesia or waking censorship* in the form of defective memory, so that the recorded manifest content of any one dream rarely gives a clear picture.

Consider, for instance, the following dream in which a Hopi Indian dreamer goes hunting with some white men and secures several deer. He takes a load of venison to a clan relative who is an old war chief in another village. The people there are very grateful for the rare delicacy. The old chief invites the dreamer to replace a man, now ill, who was to lead a religious dance. After the dance the dreamer is highly praised for his performance by three men: (1) the old war chief, (2) the sick dance leader and (3) the leader's brother. While this is going on, a runner tells these men that the village is about to be destroyed by enemies. The three men are in a panic and begin to cry, but the dreamer swallows the lump in his own throat and, rebuking their cowardice, says, "I'm only a common man but *I* can stand on my feet and fight. Stand on your feet and fight like men. I was kinda mad when I made this speech to my men." The dreamer wakes from this dream sweating and says it wasn't a very good dream. Nor was it, but it would have been far worse if his waking mind had remembered the dream thoughts which had helped to construct the dream.

The facts are these: some thirty years before this dream occurred, the dreamer was a candidate for tribal initiation into manhood. He was afraid of this initiation, and the old war chief of this dream was prominent among those who forced him into it. One requirement for tribal initiation was the killing of a large number of rabbits. Being an incred-

* This article consists of excerpts from a paper by the late Miss Eggan: "The Manifest Content of Dreams: A Challenge to Social Science," *American Anthropologist* 1952, vol. 54, pp. 469–485. A footnote on page 472 of the article reads: "Dreams cited in this paper are taken from a collection of Hopi Indian dreams which was begun by the writer in 1939 in connection with an investigation of social and cultural change by F. Eggan. The data now consist of more than 600 dreams obtained from twenty informants in five villages."

ibly poor hunter the dreamer failed to get even one rabbit after hunting for two days. The sick dance leader whom he replaced in this dream and the leader's brother—who with the war chief became *three incompetent cowards in this dream thirty years later*—patted the neophyte on the back in a condescending manner and offered to hunt for him. They secured forty rabbits for him in one day, which allowed the initiation to proceed.

The entire dream handles this old hurt in a healing manner: the dreamer hunts with white men which gives him status in his own eyes; he returns quantities of venison for the lowly rabbits of his boyhood; and he angrily shames the cowardice of all three men who contributed to his former humiliation. But, even so, the dream was not as effective as it needed to be, and the dreamer awakened in sweating discomfort. The discomfort became vague, however, when he was thoroughly awake; his associations evaded the painful memories, and dwelt instead on the pleasant qualities of the dream. He commented with a smile that these people were very proud of him in the dream. In this dream, as is often the case, the protective mechanism of mild amnesia enables the individual, when awake, to evade for a time at least the inner stresses which arose out of unpleasant experiences, and to a certain extent to accept instead whatever comfort their reworking is able to give him.

When using dreams as data there is sometimes a temptation to find a way around the interpretative problems presented by amnesic censorship by seizing upon one or two elements in the dream and calling the dream "interpreted" when the meaning of equivalent Freudian symbols has been assigned to it. Examples of this oversimplified procedure, in which material is often of necessity so greatly abridged that it seems virtually meaningless to the reader, is then used by other scientists as an argument against the use of dreams, since it seems obviously to be not only questionable science but questionable sense. . . .

From among the many examples in our material which illustrate the inadequacy of oversimplified symbolic interpretation, *per se*, a few illustrations can be given: A female informant, age 27, is an acculturated individual, extremely anxious both in dreams and waking performance. Her dreams are short and more heavily symbolized at the manifest level than are most Hopi dreams. An item frequently found in her dreams is a dark, canyon- or box-like passage. Dreams in which this element is found are usually classified by her as "bad" dreams. An obvious interpretation of this element might be made as a womb symbol, associated with sexual anxiety. But we must also consider the fact that this woman lived for a time at the Grand Canyon where she was constantly and quite properly afraid that her small, active son would fall into it. Moreover, in discussing one of these canyon dreams she suddenly interrupted herself to say, "I don't know why I think of this now, but did I ever tell you how I used to hate those trips to Mishongnovi with my mother? I rode on her back all the way. My mother would be crying because she hated to go there and she always stopped in that *dark entrance to the plaza* to dry her eyes. I hated that most. She cried harder when she stopped there and I didn't know why and *I* was afraid of dark places after that." The inform-ant herself cried quietly for several minutes, and then asked to be re-minded of what we had been talking about before what she considered a digression from our conversation.

The canyon-desiccated country in which she lives, her experiences at the Grand Canyon, and the painful association of a specific dark passage with a troubled mother whom she adored—all of these do not rule out other connections in her dream thoughts, of course. On the contrary, an intimate knowledge of the dreamer and her mother—and particularly of the dreamer's intense identification with her mother—plus other associative material, shows many connections, part of them undoubtedly sexual. But had a blind symbolic explanation been given to "canyon-like passages," without reference to geographic and cultural background, and to dreamer associations, a wealth of material too complicated for this brief discus-sion would have been missed. On the cultural side, inter-village connec-tions and relations were clarified; and on the personal, two women's attitudes toward a group of paternal relatives were eventually under-stood. . . .

In another dream a man has some teeth pulled. Does he have a castra-tion complex? This is quite possible, since he had a traumatic castration shock as a child, and now finds the castration of animals a difficult task. But he is also known to be a physical coward. He comments that the dream "means bad" because the doctor has been telling him that his knee is lame because of two ulcerated teeth, and this is "nonsense talk," be-cause how could his teeth make his knee hurt? The doctor must be after him, though, he says, or he wouldn't have this dream; and he ends by ask-ing whether the recorder ever had a tooth pulled, and did it hurt? Again the deeper level of dream work is *not* ruled out by the obvious immediate concern. It is merely emphasized that in this simple dream, as is often the case, the dreamer's discomfort called attention to a *reality situation* in the manifest content of the dream. . . .

If, then, the assumption is justified that dreams are a probable univer-sal form of mental activity, at once idiosyncratic and culturally molded, there follows the inevitable conclusion that their communication is a chal-lenge to the social scientist as well as the therapist. And since both sci-entific mandates and the informant's welfare indicate the necessity of devising methods by which this communication may be made more intelli-gible at the manifest level, it is suggested that any experimental approach to this problem is useful, even though it must be considered tentative. . . .

Among the cultural problems where an oblique approach can fre-quently discover information which might otherwise be overlooked are those connected with culture change. The problems of acculturation must, of course, be approached in many ways. But it is possible to conduct a very thorough examination of observable manifestations in culture change, such as borrowed techniques, property inheritance, missionary church membership, and school attendance, and to record changes in marriage customs, kinship patterns and the less esoteric religious rites, and in the end to find oneself dissatisfied with an analysis which, lacking vitality and depth, fails to reveal significant aspects of culture change.

The fact is that individuals in the process of adapting to intruding influences can seldom give very accurate direct information regarding the depth of such penetration, either with respect to themselves or to the tribe as a whole. There is a distinct lag between the modification of an "ideal" culture construct and the society's conscious acceptance of the reality situation. Thus, among the Hopi, the strength of tribal attitudes toward cooperative obligations to the tribe, frequently masked by surface changes, is well illustrated in dreams, as is also the superficiality of Hopi conversion to Christianity. A survey may show that 30% of a village is Christian in that they attend a missionary church; but their dreams indicate that the majority of the old Hopi who list themselves as Christian have as much respect for Masau'u, and many other Hopi deities, as they ever had.

These people sometimes come back from college to bow to the will of the old grandmother who is the head of their clan. One such woman, an excellent pianist, who lists among her possessions a piano, a refrigerator, and a washing machine, notes in an interview that she belongs to a church in Los Angeles where she lives most of the year. But may we judge accurately by these things the degree of this woman's acculturation when she says, in associations to a dream, "Oh, I'm going to leave my husband [in spite of the piano and washing machine] because I have my girl baby at last and don't need him any more. They [the clan] have given me my fields and my brothers will plant for me." . . .

The *form* a dream takes, then, is a very personal arrangement of affectual events, but it is limited by the dreamer's perception of his universe, and both the form and the processes underlying dream and reality experiences—as well as the verbalizations regarding these—are sharply shaped in practice, and subsequently as definitely defined, by cultural perception of them. It seems quite possible, for instance, that individuals in a society where infants are pushed and shaken from a squatting mother might, at an unconscious level, symbolize birth quite differently from those born on a comfortable bed, the whole process being aided by relaxing drugs and gentled in every conceivable way. For although birth is a "constant" in human experience, the cultural manipulation of the "process" among the Hopi would seem to increase the fatigue and discomfort for both mother and child, something western culture minimizes. However, this process, as culturally directed by the Hopi, is perceived by them to be entirely compatible with the safety of both mother and infant; but seen through the observer's "cultural screen," it is perceived as being exceedingly precarious for both, and will be so verbalized both in dreams and waking thought. Furthermore, the Hopi regard certain western birth customs with fear and distaste. Certainly, too, a cannibalistic feast—either in reality or dream—would be perceived quite differently by a university professor and a cannibal, though the practice of cannibalism, particularly as a ritual where the vital organs of an enemy are eaten for magical power, and the covert ambitious drives of a college professor, may originate in the same level of the unconscious.

Thus dreams and the elaborations introduced into the recital of them, an integral part of the dreamer's associations with the dream, are all facets of a *projective* process in which the dreamer responds to his own mind's images of his culturally oriented world as it is, or as he wishes or fears it to be. The consistency with which any individual responds to these inner images is very marked, so that among recorded Hopi dreams, individual patterns of dreaming are discernible, in spite of a high degree of cultural uniformity both in the dreams and in the society.

B. DREAMS IN THE ANCIENT WORLD

Dreaming an Intermediate State[*]

From the Brihadârmyaka-Upanishad.

Translated by F. Max Müller

GANAKA VAIDEHA SAID: "Who is that Self?"

Yâgñavalkya replied: "He who is within the heart, surrounded by the Prânas (senses), the person of light, consisting of knowledge. He, remaining the same, wanders along the two worlds, as if thinking, as if moving. During sleep (in dreams) he transcends this world and all the forms of death (all that falls under the sway of death; all that is perishable).

"On being born that person, assuming his body, becomes united with all evils; when he departs and dies, he leaves all evil behind.

"And there are two states for that person, the one here in this world, the other in the other world, and, as a third, an intermediate state, the state of sleep. When in that intermediate state, he sees both these states together, the one here in this world, and the other in the other world. Now whatever his admission to the other world may be, having gained that admission, he sees both the evils and the blessings.

"And when he falls asleep, then after having taken away with him the material from the whole world, destroying and building it up again, he sleeps (dreams) by his own light. In that state the person is self-illuminated.

[*] *The* Upanishads *are philosophical treatises, and part of the ancient Vedic literature, the foundation of the literature of India. It was through the* Upanishads *that the Western World made its first exploration of Vedic literature. Scholars have traced their genesis back as far as the Mantras period—or about* 1000 B.C. *The* Upanishads *belong to what has been called the "revealed literature" of India. The* Brihadârmyaka-Upanishad *is one of the eleven fundamental* Upanishads *of the* Vedânta *philosophy.*

"There are no (real) chariots in that state, no horses, no roads. There are no blessings there, no happiness, no joys, but he himself sends forth (creates) blessings, happiness and joys. There are no tanks there, no lakes, no rivers, but he himself sends forth (creates) tanks, lakes and rivers. He indeed is the maker.

"On this there are two verses:

"After having subdued by sleep all that belongs to the body, he, not asleep himself, looks down upon the sleeping (senses). Having assumed light, he goes again to his place, the golden person, the lovely bird.

"Guarding with the breath (prâna, life) the lower nest, the immortal moves away from the nest; the immortal one goes wherever he likes, the golden person, the lovely bird.

"Going up and down in his dreams, the god makes manifold shapes for himself, either rejoicing together with women, or laughing (with his friends), or seeing terrible sights.

"People may see his playground, but he himself no one ever sees. Therefore they say, 'Let no one wake a man suddenly, for it is not easy to remedy, if he does not get back (rightly to his body).'

"Here some people (object and) say:

" 'No, this (sleep) is the same as the place of waking, for what he sees while awake, that only he sees when asleep.' No, here (in sleep) the person is self-illuminated (as we explained before)....

"That (person) having enjoyed himself in that sleep (dream), having moved about and seen both good and evil, hastens back again as he came, to the place from which he started to be awake. And whatever he may have seen there, he is not followed (affected) by it, for that person is not attached to anything....

"As a large fish moves along the two banks of a river, the right and left, so does that person move along these two states, the state of sleeping and the state of waking.

"And as a falcon, or any other (swift) bird, after he has roamed about here in the air, becomes tired, and folding his wings he is carried to his nest, so does that person hasten to that state where, when asleep, he desires no more desires, and dreams no more dreams.

"There are in his body the veins called Hitâ, which are as small as a hair divided a thousandfold, full of white, blue, yellow, green and red. Now when, as it were, they kill him, when, as it were, they overcome him, when, as it were, he falls into a well, he fancies, through ignorance, that danger which he (commonly) sees in waking. But when he fancies that he is, as it were, a god, or that he is, as it were, a king, or 'I am this altogether,' that is his highest world."

The Prophetic Dream of Buddha's Father

SIR EDWIN ARNOLD

And all that night
The King Suddhōdana dreamed the troublous dreams.
The first fear of his vision was a flag
Broad, glorious, glistening with a golden sun,
The mark of Indra; but a strong wind blew,
Rending its folds divine, and dashing it
Into the dust; whereat a concourse came
Of shadowy Ones, who took the spoiled silk up
And bore it eastward from the city gates.
The second fear was ten huge elephants,
With silver tusks and feet that shook the earth,
Trampling the southern road in mighty march;
And he who sate upon the foremost beast
Was the King's son—the others followed him.
The third fear of the vision was a car,
Shining with blinding light, which four steeds drew,
Snorting white smoke and champing fiery foam;
And in the car the Prince Siddārtha sate.
The fourth fear was a wheel which turned and turned,
With nave of burning gold and jewelled spokes,
And strange things written on the binding tire,
Which seemed both fire and music as it whirled.
The fifth fear was a mighty drum, set down
Midway between the city and the hills,
On which the Prince beat with an iron mace,
So that the sound pealed like a thunderstorm,
Rolling around the sky and far away.
The sixth fear was a tower, which rose and rose
High o'er the city till its stately head
Shone crowned with clouds, and on the top the Prince
Stood, scattering from both hands, this way and that,
Gems of most lovely light, as if it rained
Jacynths and rubies; and the whole world came,
Striving to seize those treasures as they fell
Toward the four quarters. But the seventh fear was
A noise of wailing, and behold six men

Who wept and gnashed their teeth, and laid their palms
Upon their mouths, walking disconsolate.

These seven fears made the vision of his sleep,
But none of all his wisest dream-readers
Could tell their meaning. Then the King was wroth,
Saying, "There cometh evil to my house,
And none of ye have wit to help me know
What the great gods portend sending me this."
So in the city men went sorrowful
Because the King had dreamed seven signs of fear
Which none could read; but to the gate there came
An aged man, in robe of deer-skin clad,
By guise a hermit, known to none; he cried,
"Bring me before the King, for I can read
The vision of his sleep"; who, when he heard
The sevenfold mysteries of the midnight dream,
Bowed reverent and said, "O Maharāj!
I hail this favored House, whence shall rise
A wider-reaching splendor than the sun's!
Lo! all these seven fears are seven joys,
Whereof the first, where thou didst see a flag—
Broad, glorious, gilt with Indra's badge—cast down
And carried out, did signify the end
Of old faiths and beginning of the new;
For there is change with gods not less than men,
And as the days pass kalpas pass—at length.
The ten great elephants that shook the earth
The ten great gifts of wisdom signify,
In strength whereof the Prince shall quit his state
And shake the world with passage of the Truth.
The four-flame breathing horses of the car
Are those four fearless virtues which shall bring
Thy son from doubt and gloom to gladsome light;
The wheel that turned with nave of burning gold
Was that most precious Wheel of perfect Law
Which he shall turn in sight of all the world.
The mighty drum whereon the Prince did beat,
Till the sound filled all lands, doth signify
The thunder of the Preaching of the Word
Which he shall preach; the tower that grew to heaven
The growing of the Gospel of this Buddh
Sets forth; and those rare jewels scattered thence

The untold treasures are of that good Law
To gods and men dear and desirable.
Such is the interpretation of the tower;
But for those six men weeping with shut mouths,
They are the six chief teachers whom thy son
Shall, with bright truth and speech unanswerable,
Convince of foolishness. O King! rejoice;
The fortune of my Lord the Prince is more
Than kingdoms, and his hermit-rags will be
Beyond fine cloths of gold. This was thy dream!
And in seven nights and days these things shall fall!"
So spake the holy man, and lowly made
The eight prostrations, touching thrice the ground;
Then turned and passed; but when the King bade send
A rich gift after him, the messengers
Brought word, "We came to where he entered in
At Chandra's temple, but within was none
Save a gray owl which fluttered from the shrine."
The gods come sometimes thus.
    But the sad king
Marvelled, and gave command that new delights
Be compassed to enthral Siddārtha's heart
Amid those dancers of his pleasure-house;
Also he set at all the brazen doors
A double guard.
                Yet who shall shut out Fate?

Dream Magic of Ancient Egypt

E. A. WALLIS-BUDGE

The Egyptians believed that the divine powers frequently made known their will to them by means of dreams, and they attached considerable importance to them; the figures of the gods and the scenes which they saw when dreaming seemed to them to prove the existence of another world which was not greatly unlike that already known to them. The knowledge of the art of procuring dreams and the skill to interpret them were greatly prized in Egypt as elsewhere in the East, and the priest or official who possessed such gifts sometimes rose to places of high honor in the state, as we may see from the example of Joseph, for it was universally believed that glimpses of the future were revealed to man in dreams. . . .

Since dreams and visions in which the future might be revealed to the sleeper were greatly desired, the Egyptian magician set himself to procure such for his clients by various devices, such as drawing magical pictures and reciting magical words. The following are examples of spells for procuring a vision and dreams, taken from the British Museum Papyrus, No. 122, lines 64 ff. and 359 ff.

"To obtain a vision from [the god] Besa. Make a drawing of Besa, as shown below, on your left hand, and enveloping your hand in a strip of black cloth that has been consecrated to Isis (?) and lie down to sleep without speaking a word, even in answer to a question. Wind the remainder of the cloth round your neck. The ink with which you write must be composed of the blood of a cow, the blood of a white dove, fresh (?) frankincense, myrrh, black writing-ink, cinnabar, mulberry juice, rainwater, and the juice of wormwood and vetch. With this write your petition before the setting sun [saying], 'Send the truthful seer out of the holy shrine, I beseech thee, Lampsuer, Sumuata, Baribas, Dardalam, Iorlex: O Lord send the sacred deity Anuth, Salbana, Chambré, Breïth, now, now, quickly, quickly. Come in this very night.' "

"To procure dreams: Take a clean linen bag and write upon it the names given below. Fold it up and make it into a lampwick, and set it alight, pouring oil over it. The word to be written is this: 'Armiuth, Lailamchoüch, Arsenophrephren, Phtha, Archentechtha.' Then in the evening, when you are going to bed, which you must do without touching food [or, pure from all defilement], do thus. Approach the map and repeat seven times the formula given below, then extinguish it and lie down to sleep. The formula is this: 'Sachmu . . . epaëma Ligotereënch: the Aeon, the Thunderer, Thou hast swallowed the snake and dost exhaust the moon, and dost raise up the orb of the sun in his season, Chthetho is thy name; I require, O lords of the gods, Seth, Chreps, give me the information I desire.' "

Cures through Dreams

STRABO

Translated by H. A. JONES

On the road between the Tralleians and Nysa is a village of the Nysaens, not far from the city Acharaca, where is the Plutonium, with a costly sacred precinct and a shrine of Pluto and Core, and also the

Charonium, a cave that lies above the sacred precinct, by nature wonderful; for they say that those who are diseased and give heed to the cures prescribed by these gods resort thither and live in the village near the cave among experienced priests, who, on their behalf, sleep in the cave and through dreams prescribe the cures. These are also the men who invoke the healing power of the gods. And they often bring the sick into the cave and leave them there, to remain in quiet, like animals in their lurking-holes, without food for many days. And sometimes the sick give heed also to their own dreams, but still they use those other men, or priests, to initiate them into the mysteries and to counsel them. To all others the place is forbidden and deadly.

Muhammedan Tâbír, or Dream Interpretation

NATHANIEL BLAND

For the earliest record of dreams, both in practice and as a science, one must look to the East, that part of the world from which have been spread alike the earliest lights of knowledge and the first shadows of superstition: and it is in the pages of the Mosaic history that we must seek for such records in their very highest antiquity. We find there examples of dreams of the most awful importance—dreams through which were conveyed revelations of the Supreme Being for the protection and guidance of His creatures, and denunciations against unbelievers, or others who offended against His law. In all these instances the sacred dignity of dreams is asserted by the evidence of their being direct communications from on high. . . .

After the Chaldean sages and the Wise Men of Egypt, dream interpretation continued to be exercised in all parts of the East to the time of Muhammed; and ordinances so far from abolishing this, with many others of the ante-Islamic superstitions, confirmed its authority as a revelation of the Divine decrees, and the sacredness of its character was sealed by the declaration that "Dreams are a portion of prophecy." (The saying in full is, "Dreams constitute one of the forty-six portions of the prophetic mission." Muhammed was forty years old when he first received inspiration, between which time and the age of sixty-three, when he died, were twenty-three years; during this interval, whatever he desired was communicated to him in dreams.) The practice and precepts of Muhammed himself, of his companions and their followers, contribute largely to the traditions on the subject. Allusions to dreams and their interpretation are nearly as abundant in the pages of the Koran as in those of Holy Writ; and the skill of Joseph, as exercised in prison and at the court of the Pharaoh of Egypt, is related in a chapter, declared from inspiration to be "the most beautiful of narratives." The very infancy of Muhammedism is identified with the history of this belief; for (even rejecting the less orthodox theory which attributes to a night-vision the *Mârâj*, or miraculous ascent [of Muhammed]), the earliest announcement of Muhammed's mission, and the revelation of the first portion of the Koran which was made known to him, were in a dream; while a similar mode of communication cheered the disheartened partisans of Islam in the expedition to Hudaibiyah, by the promise of their triumphal entry, in the following year, into "the holy temple" of Mecca.

Without collecting the numerous sayings of Muhammed from their various sources of tradition, mere reference to the Mishkát ul Masábih alone will show the importance the Prophet attached to dreams and their signification. He used each morning to ask his disciples what they had dreamed in the night, interpret or reject their communications, according to their soundness or unsoundness, and relate his own dreams. One, in particular, of very great length, with its interpretation, is recorded in the Mishkát. By another dream equally attributed to him, the Sunnís justify the still-disputed rights of his three successors; and the origin of a strife, political and religious, which convulsed the whole Muhammedan empire and threatened its destruction, and which still divides the followers of Islam by a schismatic and irreconcilable hatred, is founded on a revelation made to its founder in his sleep.

In all subsequent periods the same influence was powerfully exercised over the Muhammedan rulers, by encouraging them in enterprise or warning them against calamity. Thus, Omar the Khalif was warned of his approaching end, by a white cock thrice pecking him with its beak, the manner of his death being verified in the number of stabs he received from the hand of Firúz; and it is probable the color of the bird (white) also symbolized the notion of the assassin. The well-known story of the arm holding a handful of red earth, which appeared to Hárún in a dream at Raccah, indicating the place of his death, is perhaps one of the most romantic of numerous instances of the kind. His son Amínu's fear of the encroaching power of the Tahirite family is said to have been derived by him from a warning in sleep; and it is recorded of Mutahad, one of his later descendants, the sixteenth Khalif of the Ben Abbás, that his whole reign was troubled with dreams of various import. The commencement of new and powerful dynasties, and the birth of men destined to convulse the world by revolution and conquest, have been thus announced. The advent of the Muhammedan apostle and the consequent fall of the Pagan power were disclosed in a dream to Khusru, one of the last of the Sasanians. A flame of fire, spreading over heaven and earth, foretold to the obscure father of the first three Buwaihide princes the foundation of the glory of his family; and the radiant stars in the dream of the Moghul Kachúli Behádur predicted the birth of his descendant Timúr, and the devastating influence of the empire of Chengíz Khán and his successors.

It is not surprising that a principle, involving, as was believed, the prescience of great events, and controlling so powerfully the decisions and actions of the most enlightened princes, should have invited attention to its study, and that its professors should have been encouraged and rewarded. Dream interpreters, accordingly, were in as high favor at the courts of the Muhammedan princes as the Chaldean sages had been with the rulers of Babylon and Assyria, or the soothsayer Aristander with the Macedonian conqueror. An example of munificence in the rewards which were bestowed on the interpreter, even for a single instance of his skill, especially if displayed in the successful announcement of a prosperous event, is shown in the Khalif al Mehdi, who is said to have dreamed that his face was black; an omen which caused him much alarm on waking. None of those he consulted were able to explain its import, till he was advised to apply to Ibrahím ben Abdallah Kírmáni, who was considered to have more experience and skill than all others, and who foretold him that he should be the father of a female child. Mehdi gave him a thousand pieces of silver for converting a supposed evil omen into good, and that same day a daughter was born to the Khalif, who thereupon presented the successful expounder of his dream with ten thousand dirhems more. The interpretation was according to this passage of the Koran: "And when any of them is told the news of the birth of a female, his face becometh black, and he is deeply afflicted." ...

The art itself, dignified as a science, took its place among the higher orders of natural philosophy, under the name of *Ibn ul Tâbír*, or the Science of Dream Interpretation, and its study gave rise to numerous Tâbír Námehs, or Dream Books, in which the nature of sleep and dreams, and the rules for their interpretation, and the import of their various objects, are discussed with all the analytical minuteness which distinguishes the Encyclopediacs of Eastern nations. Such works are found in all the principal Muhammedan languages, the Arabic, the Persian, the Turkish, and the Hindustani. ...

The code established by the Muhammedan lawgivers of Oneirocritics [dream-interpretation] may be divided into these four general heads: the different kinds of dreams; the mode of interpreting them, and time and manner of their accomplishment; the duties of the dreamer, both in obtaining true and auspicious revelations, and in the proper mode of having them explained; and lastly, the duties and qualifications of an interpreter of dreams, a function, or branch of knowledge entitling its possessor to a very high rank among the learned in the East. The interpreter of dreams is considered by the Muhammedan to stand in the place of the prophets, and to enjoy a portion of their miraculous gifts. In all their works on the subject, Tâbír is set forth as being a noble science, first taught by God himself to Adam, from Adam passing to Seth, and from Seth to Noah, by whom the Deluge was foretold in his explanation of a dream to Canaan's mother. . . .

Dreams in general are divided according to their kinds, or according to their import; their kinds, as to being real and true dreams, or deceptions and unsound. The first are called Ahkám, and are considered genuine inspirations from the Deity, warnings from a protective power, or revelations of coming events, in which the angel Gabriel exhibits to man in his sleeping state the records and ordinances inscribed on the Lauhi Mahfúz, the Recording Tablet of Fate. All others are merely phantoms and ill visions, and are termed Ahlám, and sometimes Azghas, a word signifying, properly, handsful of dried grass and weeds, but applied figuratively to dreams, probably from their resemblance in worthlessness and want of arrangement. These Azghás are laid to the suggestions of some Div or agent of Iblís, who takes an opportunity to lead mankind astray by pretending revelations during sleep. But they are said to arise from mutual causes. Jâfar Sádic says they occur to four classes of persons: those of evil-disposed minds; drinkers of wine; eaters of melancholy food, as lentils, love-apples, and salt meat; and to young children, or else are suggestions of the evil spirits. . . .

Dreams have different meanings, according to the class of persons to whom they occur; for which reason the Nuâbbir is to inform himself of the rank and condition of those who consult him; whether the seer be a king, a learned man, a jurisconsult, a holy man or Súfi, one of the common class of men, etc. Of all these classes, the dreams of a king are the soundest and most entitled to belief, from the exalted nature of his station, and the virtues with which royalty is adorned; and so of Cázis, or Judges, from the upright character and attributes which should distinguish a judge. Of mankind in general, the dreams of males have the advantage over those of females, because God chose the male as the first object of creation, and dignified that sex by selecting from it a hundred and twenty-four thousand of his prophets, and in His wisdom has allotted to men the most noble qualities and the highest powers of intellect. Of females, matrons have the advantage, a preference which is conceded to the chastity and dignified virtues of a married woman. The rich man's dreams are excellent, according to the Khalif Abú Bekr, because he is able to pay the Zakát, or alms, and do many good and charitable actions, perform the pilgrimage, and make bridges and caravanserais. . . . Those of poor men, indeed, seem to be of little or no authority, for they are constantly in grief and anxiety for their children and families, and if they have good predicted, its fulfilment is distant, and if evil it is accomplished almost immediately.

A Soothsayer's Dream Book

ARTEMIDORUS

Dreams and visions are infused into men for their advantage and instruction. And both sacred and profane Histories furnish such a variety of examples concerning the true event of Dreams, that it would argue incredulity and ignorance not to credit them. Hippocrates is of opinion, that whilst the body sleeps, the spirit is awake, and transported to all places where the body could have access, and it sees and knows all things which the body could know and see when awake, and touches all that it could touch. In short, that it hath all the operations that the body, now asleep, can be capable of when awake.

There are Five Sorts of Dreams, that have different qualities. The first is a Dream: the second a Vision: the third an Oracle: The fourth a Phantasy or vain Imagination: The fifth an Apparition.

That is called a Dream which discovers the truth under a hidden figure; as when Joseph interpreted Pharaoh's Dream of the seven lean kine that should devour the seven fat ones, and the same of the ears of corn, etc.

A Vision is this: When a man really sees awake, what he did asleep; as it happened to Vespatian, when he saw the Surgeon that drew out Hero's tooth.

An Oracle is a revelation or advertisement made to us in our sleep by some Angel, or other Saint, to perform God's will according to their information; as it happened to Joseph, the husband of the Holy Virgin, and the Three Wise Men.

The Phantasy, or vain Imagination, happens in that instant when the affections are so vehement that they ascend up to the brain during our sleep, and meet with the more watchful spirits; thus what the thoughts are employed about in the day, we fancy in the night; so a lover, who in the daytime thinks on his fair one, in the night when asleep meets with the same thoughts. It happens also, that he that fasts all day, dreams at night that he is feeding; or if thirsty in the daytime, in the nighttime he dreams of drinking, and is very much delighted with it. And the miser and userer dream of bags, nay, will discourse of them in their sleep.

An Apparition is no other than a nocturnal Vision that presents itself to weak infants and ancient men, who fancy they see chimeras approaching to intimidate or offend them.

There are Two principal kinds of Dreams: First, Speculative or Contemplative. The Second is Allegorical or Figurative.

Speculative Dreams have an immediate event; but the Allegorical not so soon, for there is a day or two between a Dream and the event thereof. Sometimes there are Dreams which cannot possibly happen; as when you dream that you fly, have horns, go down into Hell, and the like: These are Allegorical, and carry a different signification.

Dreams are proportioned according to the party dreaming. Thus those of eminent persons, will be great, as, if good, they signify great benefits, and, on the contrary, great misery. If the party that dreams be of a mean condition, the dreams, with their events, will be mean also; if poor, their dreams will be very inconsiderable; for the rules of dreaming are not general, and therefore cannot satisfy all persons, seeing they often, according to times and persons, admit of varied interpretations.

[*Circa* A.D. 140]

C. JUDEO-CHRISTIAN SPECULATIONS ON DREAMS

Famous Biblical Dreams

HOLY BIBLE (GEN. XXVIII. 10–16)

Jacob's Ladder

AND JACOB WENT OUT from Beersheba, and went toward Haran.

And he lighted upon a certain place, and tarried there all night, because the sun was set: and he took of the stones of that place, and put them for his pillow, and lay down in that place to sleep.

And he dreamed, and, behold, a ladder set up on the earth, and the top of it reached to heaven: and, behold, the angels of God ascending and descending on it.

And, behold, the LORD stood above it, and said, I am the LORD GOD of Abraham thy father, and the God of Isaac: the land whereon thou liest, to thee will I give it, and to thy seed:

And thy seed shall be as the dust of the earth: and thou shalt spread abroad to the west, and to the east, and to the north, and to the south: and in thee and in thy seed shall all the families of the earth be blessed.

And, behold, I am with thee, and will keep thee in all places whither thou goest, and will bring thee again into this land: for I will not leave thee, until I have done that which I have spoken to thee of.

And Jacob awaked out of his sleep, and he said, Surely the LORD is in this place, and I knew it not.

HOLY BIBLE (GEN. XXXVII. 3–11)

Joseph's Dream

Now Israel loved Joseph, more than all his children, because he was the son of his old age: and he made him a coat of many colours.

And when his brethren saw that their father loved him more than all his brethren, they hated him, and could not speak peaceably unto him.

And Joseph dreamed a dream, and he told it his brethren: and they hated him yet the more.

And he said unto them, Hear, I pray you, this dream which I have dreamed:

For, behold, we were binding sheaves in the field, and, lo, my sheaf arose, and also stood upright; and, behold, your sheaves stood round about, and made obeisance to my sheaf.

And his brethren said to him, Shalt thou indeed reign over us? And they hated him yet the more for his dreams, and for his words.

And he dreamed yet another dream, and told it his brethren, and said, Behold, I have dreamed a dream more: and, behold, the sun, and the moon, and the eleven stars, made obeisance to me.

And he told it to his father, and to his brethren: and his father rebuked him, and said unto him, What is this dream that thou hast dreamed? Shall I and thy mother and thy brethren indeed come to bow down ourselves to thee to the earth?

And his brethren envied him; but his father observed the saying.

HOLY BIBLE (GEN. XL; XLI)

Joseph's Dream Interpretations at Pharaoh's Court

And it came to pass after these things, that the butler of the king of Egypt and his baker had offended their lord the king of Egypt.

And Pharaoh was wroth against two of his officers, against the chief of the butlers, and against the chief of the bakers.

And he put them in ward in the house of the captain of the guard, into the prison, the place where Joseph was bound.

And the captain of the guard charged Joseph with them, and he served them: and they continued a season in ward.

And they dreamed a dream both of them, each man his dream in one night, each man according to the interpretation of his dream, the butler and the baker of the king of Egypt, which were bound in the prison.

And Joseph came in unto them in the morning, and looked upon them, and, behold, they were sad.

And he asked Pharaoh's officers that were with him in the ward of his lord's house, saying, Wherefore look ye so sadly today?

And they said unto him, We have dreamed a dream, and there is no interpreter of it. And Joseph said unto them, Do not interpretations belong to God? tell me them, I pray you.

And the chief butler told his dream to Joseph, and said to him, In my dream, behold, a vine was before me;

And in the vine were three branches: and it was as though it budded, and her blossoms shot forth: and the clusters thereof brought forth ripe grapes:

And Pharaoh's cup was in my hand; and I took the grapes, and pressed them into Pharaoh's cup, and I gave the cup into Pharaoh's hand.

And Joseph said unto him, This is the interpretation of it: The three branches are three days:

Yet within three days shall Pharaoh lift up thine head, and restore thee unto thy place: and thou shalt deliver Pharaoh's cup into his hand, after the former manner when thou wast his butler.

But think on me when it shall be well with thee, and shew kindness, I pray thee, unto me; and make mention of me unto Pharaoh, and bring me out of this house:

For indeed I was stolen away out of the land of the Hebrews; and here also have I done nothing that they should put me into this dungeon.

When the chief baker saw that the interpretation was good, he said unto Joseph, I also was in my dream, and, behold, I had three white baskets on my head:

And in the uppermost basket there was of all manner of bakemeats for Pharaoh: and the birds did eat them out of the basket upon my head.

And Joseph answered and said, This is the interpretation thereof: The three baskets are three days:

Yet within three days shall Pharaoh lift up thy head from off thee, and shall hang thee on a tree: and the birds shall eat thy flesh from off thee.

And it came to pass the third day, which was Pharaoh's birthday, that he made a feast unto all his servants: and he lifted up the head of the chief butler and of the chief baker among his servants.

And he restored the chief butler unto his butlership again; and he gave the cup unto Pharaoh's hand:

But he hanged the chief baker; as Joseph had interpreted to them.

Yet did not the chief butler remember Joseph, but forgat him.

Chapter 41

And it came to pass, at the end of two full years, that Pharaoh dreamed; and, behold, he stood by the river.

And, behold, there came up out of the river seven well favoured kine, and fat-fleshed; and they fed in a meadow.

And, behold, seven other kine came up after them out of the river, ill favoured and lean-fleshed, and stood by the other kine upon the brink of the river.

And the ill favoured and lean-fleshed kine did eat up the seven well favoured and fat kine. So Pharaoh awoke.

And he slept and dreamed the second time: and, behold, seven ears of corn came up upon one stalk, rank and good.

And, behold, seven thin ears, blasted with the east wind, sprung up after them.

And the seven thin ears devoured the seven rank and full ears. And Pharaoh awoke, and, behold, it was a dream.

And it came to pass in the morning, that his spirit was troubled: and he sent and called for all the magicians of Egypt, and all the wise men thereof: and Pharaoh told them his dream; but there was none that could interpret them unto Pharaoh.

Then spake the chief butler unto Pharaoh, saying, I do remember my faults this day.

Pharaoh was wroth with his servants, and put me in ward in the captain of the guard's house, both me and the chief baker.

And we dreamed a dream in one night, I and he; we dreamed each man according to the interpretation of his dream.

And there was there with us a young man, an Hebrew, servant to the captain of the guard; and we told him, and he interpreted to us our dreams; to each man according to his dream he did interpret.

And it came to pass, as he interpreted to us, so it was; me he restored unto mine office, and him he hanged.

Then Pharaoh sent and called Joseph, and they brought him hastily out of the dungeon: and he shaved himself, and changed his raiment, and came in unto Pharaoh.

And Pharaoh said unto Joseph, I have dreamed a dream, and there is none that can interpret it: and I have heard say of thee, that thou canst understand a dream to interpret it.

And Joseph answered Pharaoh, saying, It is not in me: God shall give Pharaoh an answer of peace.

And Pharaoh said unto Joseph, In my dream, behold, I stood upon the bank of the river:

And, behold, there came up out of the river seven kine, fat-fleshed and well favoured; and they fed in a meadow.

And, behold, seven other kine came up after them, poor, and very ill favoured and lean-fleshed, such as I never saw in all the land of Egypt for badness:

And the lean and ill favoured kine did eat up the first seven fat kine:

And when they had eaten them up, it could not be known that they had eaten them; but they were still ill favoured, as at the beginning. So I awoke.

And I saw in my dream, and, behold, seven ears came up in one stalk, full and good:

And, behold, seven ears, withered, thin, and blasted with the east wind, sprung up after them:

And the thin ears devoured the good ears. And I told this unto the magicians: but there was none that could declare it to me. And Joseph said unto Pharaoh, The dream of Pharaoh is one: God hath shewed Pharaoh what he is about to do.

The seven good kine are seven years: and the seven good ears are seven years: the dream is one.

And the seven thin and ill favoured kine, that came up after them, are seven years: and the seven empty ears, blasted with the east wind, shall be seven years of famine.

This is the thing which I have spoken unto Pharaoh: What God is about to do, he sheweth unto Pharaoh.

Behold, there come seven years of great plenty throughout all the land of Egypt:

And there shall arise after them seven years of famine; and all the plenty shall be forgotten in the land of Egypt; and the famine shall consume the land:

And the plenty shall not be known in the land, by reason of that famine following: for it shall be very grievous.

And for that the dream was doubled unto Pharaoh twice; it is because the thing is established by God, and God will shortly bring it to pass.

Now, therefore, let Pharaoh look out a man discreet and wise, and set him over the land of Egypt.

Let Pharaoh do this, and let him appoint officers over the land, and take up the fifth part of the land of Egypt in the seven plenteous years.

And let them gather all the food of those good years that come, and lay up corn under the hand of Pharaoh, and let them keep food in the cities.

And that food shall be for store to the land against the seven years of famine, which shall be in the land of Egypt; that the land perish not through the famine.

And the thing was good in the eyes of Pharaoh, and in the eyes of all his servants.

And Pharaoh said unto his servants, Can we find such a one as this is, a man in whom the Spirit of God is?

And Pharaoh said unto Joseph, Forasmuch as God hath shewed thee all this, there is none so discreet and wise as thou art:

Thou shalt be over my house, and according unto thy word shall all my people be ruled: only in the throne will I be greater than thou.

And Pharaoh said unto Joseph, See, I have set thee over all the land of Egypt.

HOLY BIBLE (I KINGS, III. 5-15)

Solomon Receives the Gift of Wisdom in a Dream

In Gideon the LORD appeared to Solomon in a dream by night: and God said, Ask what I shall give thee.

And Solomon said, Thou has shewed unto thy servant David my father great mercy, according as he walked before thee in truth, and in righteousness, and in uprightness of heart with thee: and thou hast kept for him this great kindness, that thou hast given him a son to sit on his throne, as it is this day.

And now, O LORD my God, thou hast made thy servant king instead of David my father: and I am but a little child: I know not how to go out or come in.

And thy servant is in the midst of thy people which thou hast chosen, a great people, that cannot be numbered nor counted for multitude.

Give therefore thy servant an understanding heart to judge thy people, that I may discern between good and bad: for who is able to judge this thy so great a people?

And the speech pleased the LORD, that Solomon had asked this thing.

And God said unto him, Because thou hast asked this thing, and hast not asked for thyself long life; neither hast asked riches for thyself, nor hast asked the life of thine enemies; but hast asked for thyself understanding to discern judgment;

Behold, I have done according to thy words: lo, I have given thee a wise and understanding heart; so that there was none like thee before thee, neither after thee shall any arise like unto thee.

And I have also given thee that which thou hast not asked, both riches and honour; so that there shall not be any among the kings like unto thee all thy days.

And if thou wilt walk in my ways, to keep my statutes and my commandments, as thy father David did walk, then I will lengthen thy days.

And Solomon awoke: and, behold, it was a dream. And he came to Jerusalem and stood before the ark of the covenant of the LORD, and offered up burnt offerings, and offered peace offerings, and made a feast to all his servants.

HOLY BIBLE (JOB, VII. 13-16)

Job Protests Against his Dreams

When I say, My bed shall comfort me, my couch shall ease my complaint;

Then thou scarest me with dreams, and terrifiest me through visions;

So that my soul chooseth strangling, and death rather than my life.

I loathe it; I would not live always: let me alone: for my days are vanity.

HOLY BIBLE (JEREMIAH, XXIII. 25–32; XXVII. 9–10; XXIX. 8–9)

Jeremiah Condemns False Dream Interpreters

I have heard what the prophets said, that prophesy lies in my name, saying, I have dreamed, I have dreamed.

How long shall this be in the heart of the prophets that prophesy lies? they are prophets of the deceit of their own heart:

Which think to cause my people to forget my name by their dreams, which they tell every man to his neighbour, as their fathers have forgotten my name for Baal.

The prophet that hath a dream, let him tell a dream; and he that hath my word, let him speak my word faithfully. What is the chaff to the wheat? said the LORD.

Is not my word like as a fire? saith the LORD; and like a hammer that breaketh the rock in pieces?

Therefore, behold, I am against the prophets, saith the LORD, that steal my words every one from his neighbour.

Behold, I am against the prophets, said the LORD, that use their tongues, and say, he saith.

Behold, I am against them that prophesy false dreams, saith the LORD, and do tell them, and cause my people to err by their lies, and by their lightness; yet I sent them not, nor commanded them: therefore they shall not profit this people at all, saith the LORD.

Therefore harken not ye to your prophets, nor to your diviners, nor to your dreamers, nor to your enchanters, nor to your sorcerers, which speak unto you, saying, Ye shall not serve the king of Babylon:

For they prophesy a lie unto you, to remove you far from your land; and that I should drive you out, and ye should perish.

For thus said the LORD of hosts, the God of Israel, Let not your prophets and your diviners, that be in the midst of you, deceive you, neither harken to your dreams which ye cause to be dreamed.

For they prophesy falsely unto you in my name; I have not sent them, saith the LORD.

HOLY BIBLE (DANIEL, II; IV. 1–34)

Daniel Interprets Nebuchadnezzar's Dreams

And in the second year of the reign of Nebuchadnezzar, Nebuchadnezzar dreamed dreams, wherewith his spirit was troubled, and his sleep brake from him.

Then the king commanded to call the magicians, and the astrologers, and the sorcerers, and the Chaldeans, for to shew the king his dreams. So they came and stood before the king.

And the king said unto them, I have dreamed a dream, and my spirit was troubled to know the dream.

Then spake the Chaldeans to the king in Syriac, O king, live for ever: tell thy servants the dream, and we will shew the interpretation.

The king answered and said to the Chaldeans, The thing is gone from me: If ye will not make known unto me the dream, with the interpretation thereof, ye shall be cut in pieces, and your houses shall be made a dunghill:

But if ye shew the dream, and the interpretation thereof, ye shall receive of me gifts, and rewards, and great honour: therefore shew me the dream and the interpretation thereof.

They answered again, and said, Let the king tell his servants the dream, and we will shew the interpretation of it.

The king answered and said, I know of certainty that ye would gain the time, because ye see the thing is gone from me.

But if ye will not make known unto me the dream, there is but one decree for you: for ye have prepared lying and corrupt words to speak before me till the time be changed: therefore tell me the dream, and I shall know that ye can shew me the interpretation thereof.

The Chaldeans answered before the king, and said, There is not a man upon the earth that can shew the king's matter: therefore there is no king, lord, nor ruler, that asked such things at any magician, or astrologer, or Chaldean.

And it is a rare thing that the king requireth: and there is none other that can shew it before the king, except the gods, whose dwelling is not with flesh.

For this cause the king was angry and very furious, and commanded to destroy the wise men of Babylon.

And the decree went forth that the wise men should be slain; and they sought Daniel and his fellows to be slain.

Then Daniel answered with counsel and wisdom to Arioch the captain of the king's guard, which was gone forth to slay the wise men of Babylon:

He answered and said to Arioch the king's captain, Why is the decree so hasty from the king? Then Arioch made the thing known to Daniel.

Then Daniel went in, and desired of the king that he would give him time, and that he would shew the king the interpretation.

Then Daniel went to his house, and made the thing known to Hananiah, Mishael, and Azariah, his companions:

That they would desire mercies of the God of heaven concerning this secret, that Daniel and his fellows should not perish with the rest of the wise men of Babylon.

Then was the secret revealed unto Daniel in a night vision. Then Daniel blessed the God of heaven.

Daniel answered and said, Blessed be the name of God for ever and ever: for wisdom and might are his:

And he changeth the times and the season: he removeth kings, and setteth up kings: he giveth wisdom unto the wise, and knowledge to them that know understanding.

He revealeth the deep and secret things: he knoweth what is in the darkness, and the light dwelleth with him.

I thank thee, and praise thee, O thou God of my fathers, who hast given me wisdom and might, and hast made known unto me now what we desired of thee: for thou hast now made known unto us the king's matter.

Therefore Daniel went in unto Arioch, whom the king had ordained to destroy the wise men of Babylon: he went and said thus unto him, Destroy not the wise men of Babylon: bring me in before the king, And I shew unto the king the interpretation.

Then Arioch brought in Daniel before the king in haste, and said thus unto him, I have found a man of the captives of Judah that will make known unto the king the interpretation.

The king answered, and said to Daniel, whose name was Belteshazzar, Art thou able to make known unto me the dream which I have seen, and the interpretation thereof?

Daniel answered in the presence of the king, and said, The secret which the king hath demanded, cannot the wise men, the astrologers, the magicians, the soothsayers, shew unto the king:

But there is a God in heaven that revealeth secrets, and maketh known to the king Nebuchadnezzar what shall be in the latter days. Thy dream, and the visions of thy head upon thy bed, are these:

As for thee, O king, thy thoughts came into thy mind upon thy bed, what should come to pass hereafter; and he that revealeth secrets maketh known to thee what shall come to pass.

But as for me, the secret is not revealed to me for any wisdom that I have more than any living, but for their sakes that shall make known the interpretation to the king, and that thou mightest know the thoughts of thy heart.

Thou, O king, sawest, and, behold, a great image. This great image, whose brightness was excellent, stood before thee, and the form thereof was terrible.

The image's head was of fine gold, his breast and his arms of silver, his belly and his thighs of brass.

His legs of iron, his feet part of iron and part of clay.

Thou sawest till that a stone was cut out without hands, which smote the image upon his feet that were of iron and clay, and brake them to pieces.

Then there was the iron, the clay, the brass, the silver, and the gold, broken to pieces together, and became like the chaff of the summer threshing floors; and the wind carried them away, that no place was found for them: and the stone that smote the image became a great mountain, and filled the whole earth.

This is the dream; and we will tell the interpretation thereof before the king.

Thou, O king, art a king of kings: for the God of heaven hath given thee a kingdom, power, and strength, and glory.

And wheresoever the children of men dwell, the beasts of the field, and the fowls of the heaven, hath he given into thine hand, and hath made thee ruler over them all. Thou art this head of gold.

And after thee shall arise another kingdom inferior to thee, and another third kingdom of brass, which shall bear rule over all the earth.

And the fourth kingdom shall be strong as iron: forasmuch as iron breaketh in pieces and subdueth all things: and as iron that breaketh all these, shall it break in pieces and bruise.

And whereas thou sawest the feet and toes part of potters' clay and part of iron, the kingdom shall be divided; but there shall be in it of the strength of the iron, forasmuch as thou sawest the iron mixed with mirey clay.

And as the toes of the feet were part of iron and part of clay, so the kingdom shall be partly strong, and partly broken.

And whereas thou sawest iron mixed with mirey clay, they shall mingle themselves with the seed of me; but they shall not cleave one to another, even as iron is not mixed with clay.

And in the days of these kings shall the God of heaven set up a kingdom which shall never be destroyed: and the kingdom shall not be left to other people, but it shall break in pieces and consume all these kingdoms, and it shall stand for ever.

Forasmuch as thou sawest that the stone was cut out of the mountain without hands, and that it brake in pieces the iron, the brass, the clay, the silver, and the gold, the great God hath made known to the king what shall come to pass hereafter: and the dream is certain, and the interpretation thereof sure.

Then the king, Nebuchadnezzar fell upon his face, and worshipped Daniel, and commanded that they should offer an oblation and sweet odours unto him.

The king answered unto Daniel, and said, Of a truth it is, that your God is a God of gods, and a Lord of kings, and a revealer of secrets, seeing thou couldest reveal this secret.

Then the king made Daniel a great man, and gave him many great gifts, and made him ruler over the whole province of Babylon, and chief of the governors over all the wise men of Babylon.

Then Daniel requested of the king, and he set Shadrach, Meshach, and Abednego, over the affairs of the province of Babylon: but Daniel sat in the gate of the king.

Nebuchadnezzar the king, unto all people, nations, and languages, that dwell in all the earth: Peace be multiplied unto you.

I thought it good to shew the signs and wonders that the high God hath wrought towards me.

How great are his signs! and how mighty are his wonders! his kingdom is an everlasting kingdom, and his dominion is from generation to generation.

Nebuchadnezzar was at rest in mine house, and flourishing in my palace:

I saw a dream which made me afraid, and the thoughts upon my bed and the visions of my head troubled me.

Therefore made I a decree to bring in all the wise men of Babylon before me, that they might make known unto me the interpretation of the dream.

Then came in the magicians, the astrologers, the Chaldeans, and the soothsayers: and I told the dream before them: but they did not make known unto me the interpretation thereof.

But at last Daniel came in before me, whose name was Belteshazzar, according to the name of my god, and in whom is the spirit of the holy gods: and before him I told the dream, saying,

O Belteshazzar, master of the magicians, because I know that the spirit of the holy gods is in thee, and no secret troubleth thee, tell me the visions of my dream that I have seen, and the interpretation thereof.

Thus were the visions of mine head in my bed: I saw, and, behold, a tree in the midst of the earth, and the height thereof was great.

The tree grew, and was strong, and the height thereof reached unto the heaven, and the sight thereof to the end of all the earth.

The leaves thereof were fair, and the fruit thereof much, and in it was meat for all: the beasts of the field had shadow under it, and the fowls of the heaven dwelt in the boughs thereof, and all flesh was fed of it.

I saw in the visions of my head upon my bed, and, behold, a watcher and an holy one came down from heaven.

He cried aloud and said thus, Hew down the tree, and cut off his branches, shake off his leaves, and scatter his fruit: let the beasts get away from under it, and the fowls from his branches.

Nevertheless, leave the stump of his roots in the earth, even with a band of iron and brass, in the tender grass of the field; and let it be wet with the dew of heaven, and let his portion be with the beasts in the grass of the earth;

Let his heart be changed from man's, and let a beast's heart be given unto him; and let seven times pass over him.

This matter is by the decree of the watchers, and the demand by the word of the holy ones; to the intent that the living may know that the Most High ruleth in the kingdom of men, and giveth it to whomsoever he will, and setteth up over it the beasts of men.

This dream I king Nebuchadnezzar have seen. Now thou, O Belteshazzar, declare the interpretation thereof, forasmuch as all the wise men of my kingdom are not able to make known unto me the interpretation: but thou art able; for the spirit of the holy gods is in thee.

Then Daniel, whose name was Belteshazzar, was astonied for one hour, and his thoughts troubled him. The king spake and said, Belteshazzar, let not the dream, or the interpretation thereof, trouble thee. Belteshazzar answered and said, My lord, the dream be to them that hate thee, and the interpretation to thine enemies.

The tree that thou sawest, which grew, and was strong, whose height reached unto the heaven, and the sight thereof to all the earth;

Whose leaves were fair, and the fruit thereof much, and in it was meat for all; under which the beasts of the field dwelt, and upon whose branches the fowls of the heaven had their habitation:

It is thou, O king, that art grown and become strong; for thy greatness is grown, and reacheth unto heaven, and thy dominion to the end of the earth.

And whereas the king saw a watcher and an holy one coming down from heaven, and saying, Hew the tree down and destroy it; yet leave the stump of the roots thereof in the earth, even with a band of iron and brass, in the tender grass of the field; and let it be wet with the dew of heaven, and let his portion be with the beasts of the field, till seven times pass over him;

This is the interpretation, O king, and this is the decree of the Most High, which is come upon my lord the king:

That they shall drive thee from men, and thy dwelling shall be with the beasts of the field, and they shall make thee to eat grass as oxen, and they wet thee with the dew of heaven, and seven times shall pass over thee, till thou knowest that the Most High ruleth in the kingdom of men, and giveth it to whomever he will.

And whereas they commanded to leave the stump of the tree roots, thy kingdom shall be sure unto thee, after that thou shalt have known that the heavens do rule.

Wherefore, O king, let my counsel be acceptable unto thee, and break off thy sins by righteousness, and thine iniquities by shewing mercy to the poor; if it may be a lengthening of thy tranquillity.

All this came upon the king Nebuchadnezzar.

HOLY BIBLE (MATT. I. 18–21; II. 12–14, 19–21; XXVII. 17–20)

Dreams from the New Testament

Now the birth of Jesus Christ was on this wise: When as his mother Mary was espoused to Joseph, before they came together, she was found with child of the Holy Ghost.

Then Joseph her husband, being a just man, and not willing to make her a public example, was minded to put her away privily.

But while he thought on these things, behold, the angel of the LORD appeared unto him in a dream, saying, Joseph, thou son of David, fear not to take unto thee Mary thy wife, for that which is conceived in her is of the Holy Ghost.

And she shall bring forth a son, and thou shalt call his name JESUS: for he shall save his people from their sins.

And being warned of God in a dream that they should not return to Herod, they departed into their own country another way. And when they were departed, behold, the angel of the LORD appeareth to Joseph in a dream, saying, Arise, and take the young child and his mother, and flee unto Egypt, and be thou there until I bring thee word: for Herod will seek the young child, to destroy him.

When he arose, he took the young child and his mother by night, and departed into Egypt. . . .

But when Herod was dead, behold, an angel of the LORD appeareth in a dream to Joseph in Egypt,

Saying, Arise, and take the young child and his mother, and go into the land of Israel: for they are dead which sought the young child's life.

And he arose, and took the young child and his mother, and came into the land of Israel.

Therefore, when they were gathered together, Pilate said unto them, Whom will ye that I release unto you? Barabbas, or Jesus which is called Christ?

For he knew that for envy they had delivered him.

When he was set down on the judgment seat, his wife sent unto him, saying, Have thou nothing to do with that just man; for I have suffered many things this day in a dream because of him.

But the chief priests and elders persuaded the multitude that they should ask Barabbas, and destroy Jesus.

Dream Interpretation in the Talmud

(BABYLONIAN AND GRAECO-ROMAN PERIOD)

SANDOR LORAND, M.D.

In surveying the scientific literature on dreams Freud remarked on the attitude toward dreams which prevailed during classical antiquity: "They took it as axiomatic that dreams were connected with the world of super-human beings in whom they believed and that they were revelations from gods and daemons." In the present study I wish to present the thinking of the Hebrews of that same period with regard to the meaning of dreams. Their attitudes and beliefs about the origin, meaning, and interpretation of dreams are embodied in the Babylonian Talmud, which was compiled during the period extending from 200 B.C. to about A.D. 300, which may be referred to as the Graeco-Roman Period.

The Talmud is a compilation of the contributions of over 2,000 scholars from various countries, principally Palestine and Babylon. These contributions date from 450 B.C. to about A.D. 500. The Talmud, containing some 6,000 folio pages, is divided into the Palestinian and the Babylonian Talmud. These two separate sets of books are referred to collectively as the Talmud. The Palestinian Talmud is the earlier; the Babylonian was compiled about 200 years later and is considerably larger than the Palestinian.

The Talmud consists of two parts: the Mishnah, containing the first codification of Jewish law since the Bible, and edited by the Patriarch Rabbi Jehuda about 200 B.C.; and the Gemara, which is a commentary on the Mishnah. The scholars of the Mishnah are called the teachers (Tannaim), and the scholars of the Gemara are known as the interpreters (Amoraim). From the literary point of view, the Talmud is composed of two main parts: the Halakah and the Haggadah. The Halakah deals with law. The Haggadah contains metaphysical, theological, philosophical, and historical material; in addition it contains a great deal on traditions, astronomy, mathematics, botany, medicine, psychology, demonology, and dream interpretation.

According to Freud, Herophilus, the Greek physician who lived under the first Ptolemy around 320 B.C., was the first to speak explicitly of dreams as deriving from wishes. Freud also refers to the Dream Book of Artemidorus of Daldis who lived in the second century A.D. Artemidorus' book he considers as the most complete study of dreams and dream-interpretation as practised in the Graeco-Roman period. In referring to the

Hebrew sources of dream interpretations, Freud mentions the biblical dream of Joseph; no reference, however, is to be found in his writings to the extensive dream literature in the Talmud.

In preparing this study, a careful examination was made of the volumes of the Babylonian Talmud and the various extensive writings based on it, yielding no less than 217 references to dreams in the Talmudic literature. These references cover the Hebrew's thoughts about the origin of dreams, their purpose and meaning, wish-fulfilment in dreams, the relation of dreams to reality, the technique of dream interpretation, etc. If assembled in a separate volume this Talmudic material would make a quite impressive Dream Book.

In writing on the origins of the dream theories of the Hebrews, one cannot omit the period of history preceding that of classical antiquity in which the Talmud originated. This pre-history of the Hebrews with its myths, religious beliefs, and customs entered into and influenced later formulations which finally found expression in the Talmud.

The pre-historical period of the Hebrews can be traced back to about 1000 B.C. when David conquered Jerusalem. With this conquest the Hebrews gave up their nomadic life and settled down among the Canaanites, Assyrians, Babylonians, and Egyptians. The religious doctrines and mysticism as well as the social and cultural life of the surrounding peoples influenced the Hebrews' mode of life and customs. This influence, of course, extended also to their concept of dreams. They were particularly influenced by Babylonian customs and traditions, and by Greek and Roman culture.

The sages of the Talmudic period, who understood their people well, knew how to use this mystical material to shape Hebrew life. Dream interpretation was used by the sages and rabbis for that purpose; dreams were interpreted as having ethical and religious significance as well as prophesying the future, and thus were used to mould religious, social, and political behaviour and thought. Dreams became a source of guidance for the heads of the colleges in making decisions on moral and spiritual matters, and were used quite frequently in this manner. Teachers were able to appeal to the popular imagination through dream interpretations.

This dream literature in the Talmud clearly bears the marks of Babylonian, Greek, and Roman influence, as indicated earlier. Many passages in the Haggadah describe dialogues between the various leaders and princes of the Hebrews on the one hand, and the Caesars, Cleopatra, and Ptolemy on the other.

The Hebrew conceptions must also have influenced Artemidorus' ideas about dreams. In his wide travels, Artemidorus collected many ideas on the subject. He cites many dreams, along with their interpretations, which are similar to the Talmudic dream interpretations. The symbols which Artemidorus uses are identical with those which appear in Talmudic dreams, but their meaning and the interpretation of the symbols are frequently not identical.

In general, ancient peoples believed that dreams were sent by the gods to guide human beings in their decisions and actions. Moreover, they regarded dreams as either favourable or hostile manifestations. This belief was held by the Phoenicians, Egyptians, and especially by the Babylonians, with whom the Hebrews had so much contact, especially during the Diaspora, and from whose culture they borrowed so extensively. The Haggadah contains many references to the divine nature and prophetic significance of dreams, as well as to their wish-fulfilment aim. In addition, the Hebrews considered the antagonistic forces in the human mind to be a source of dreams. Among the supernatural powers which may be the source of dreams, they included evil spirits, daemons, the returning dead, and the wandering soul.

The wandering soul was described as consisting of two parts—Ruach and Neshomo. Neshomo departs in sleep and travels all over the world. What it sees and experiences forms the content of the dream. Emissaries of the supernatural power may appear to the dreamer, the emissary being either an angel or a daemon. They appear to help, to warn or to punish. Sometimes a dead father will appear to his son in a dream to advise him in the solution of a difficult problem. Many examples of such dreams are cited in the Haggadah. Living persons may also appear in a dream for the above purposes, but in the literature they appear to do so less frequently.

Artemidorus also believed in the divine origin of dreams and considered daemons instrumental in their production. Socrates thought of dreams as originating from the gods, and thus ascribed a prophetic meaning to them.

The influence of Graeco-Roman dream concepts and theories is clearly shown in the Talmud in connection with the Hebrews' visits to dream oracles in cases of sickness, and also their indulgence in divining and probing dreams stimulated artificially. We find many instances of warnings and prohibitions against such practices on the part of the teachers and the heads of the various academies.

It was probably under pressure of the custom prevalent among the general population of imitating the Greeks and Romans that the Hebrews also visited the Temple of Aesculapius in order to practise incubation for provoking dreams, the purpose of which was the healing of the sick. The repeated warnings and prohibitions indicate that the artificial provoking of dreams was widely practised.

We find occasional expressions of opinion on the part of some Rabbis that dreams have no meaning. Rabbi Meir, for example, was of this opinion; Rabbi Nathan, on the other hand, believed that they do have meaning. Later, however, Talmudic sages completely accepted the idea that dreams have meaning and that they can be excited artificially, but it was strictly forbidden to use artificial means such as incubation.

We can ascertain two trends according to which the origin of dreams is explained in the Talmud: first, dreams have an *external* source—they come from higher powers, from God or His angels (prophetic dreams), or from daemons (warning, threatening, and punishment dreams); second, they have an *internal* source: they have a psychological origin. Rabbi Jonathan expressed this as follows: "The man is shown in the dream what he thinks in his heart." There are references to dreams originating from mental activity, the inner powers of the sleeper. In this category the Talmud places dreams originating from the thoughts of the day, and cites as an example the case of Rabbi Joshua and the Emperor Hadrian. The Emperor asked the Rabbi, "Of what shall I dream tonight?" Rabbi Joshua told him that he would dream of how the Persians would mishandle him. The Emperor Hadrian thought about this the whole day and did dream about it at night.

In ascribing the origin of the dream to the individual's inner powers, the Hebrew concept was and is that there is always a struggle in man's soul between two inclinations—the good, the higher ambitions (Yetzer Tob) and the impulses which are immoral and impure (called Yetzer Hara). This struggle finds expression in dreams.

The various references to dreams in the Talmud can be grouped under the following categories: the origin of dreams; the purpose of dreams; prophetic and wish-fulfilment dreams; nightmares and erotic dreams; punishment dreams, expiation, and changing bad dreams to good; and the technique of dream interpretation. In addition to these topics there are also discussions of the relation of the dream to reality, dreams without meaning, and the problem of not dreaming.

As to the purposes of dreams, the Talmud considered them important in influencing the life and behaviour of the individual. Mention is made, for example, of the importance a king's dream has, which will concern the whole world, i.e. the king's action as a result of the dream may have a great influence on the world situation. This has its parallel in Artemidorus' description of the importance of a ruler's dream. The Talmud further enumerates dreams with political content, which may have the effect of influencing politics; dreams which may influence an individual to change his religion; dreams which may make one remember important rulings and laws—for instance, the dream of Rab, who was reminded of a forgotten Halakals (Law) in his dream.

The Talmud attributed many meanings to a dream, just as our present concept attributes several wish-fulfilment elements to the same dream. The general Talmudic opinion added to this the belief that no dream is ever fully realized, whether good or bad, because every dream contains both truth and untruth. The Talmud compares it to rye which does not exist without straw; in the same way, no dream exists without being partly worthless.

The dreams in which a wish is most likely to be fulfilled are the early morning dreams. This realization of the dream wish is especially emphasized in the relationship of dreams to sickness. Rabbi Abraham enumerates the following bodily activities as good omens for recovery when they occur in sickness: sneezing, perspiration, sleeping, dreaming, and seminal emission. This is paralleled by Aristotle's contention that dreams show signs of what goes on inside the body; he cautions physicians to take careful account of their patients' dreams.

The belief that dreams foretell the future led people to try to produce dreams by means of incubation. These magical ways of producing dreams are given special attention in the Talmud. As mentioned above, the Rabbis preached against it, but it was practised nevertheless; as time went on, however, it became a partly approved practice. The Talmud mentions that Rabbi Jose, who lived during the reign of Diocletian, fasted eighty days in order to see the dead Rabbi Chiyya the Great, who finally appeared to him. The practice of incubation was due to the influence of the Romans and Greeks, who frequently consulted oracles of the dead. In the tractate *Sanhedrin* it is mentioned that one may sleep on the grave of a dead person so as to dream and receive some message from the dead. But sleeping on a grave was considered dangerous because of the evil spirits which hover over the graves. Artemidorus held a contrary belief, that one cannot ask the gods for a dream, nor can dreams be artificially produced. According to his theory only unexpected or unlooked-for dreams can be considered as of divine origin.

Another method of producing dreams, according to the Talmud, is to pray for good dreams or for the nullification or changing of bad dreams. Prayers against bad dreams were established by Rabbi Jona. Rabbi Jehuda's advice was to ask God for good dreams. He remarks that one should wish for three things which are of great importance: a good king, a good year, and a good dream. Before going to sleep one prays for peaceful sleep and also asks not to be troubled by bad thoughts or bad dreams. One should pray for good dreams because dreams always deal with the future. This custom has survived up to the present. On the High Holy Days, when the *cohen* blesses the community during service, the community prays for the elimination, nullification, and changing of bad thoughts and dreams. In *Berakoth* we read, "If a dream spirit tells a man 'Tomorrow you will die,' he should not despair. Prayer and good deeds help."

The custom of praying for dreams probably derived from the Babylonians, who had prayers for good dreams. The Greeks offered sacrifices for good dreams: they offered sacrifices of wine, etc., to Hermes in order not to have bad dreams.

Another mode of changing bad dreams to good was suggested by Rabbi Huna, according to whom a disturbing dream should be told to three persons, who then pronounce, "It is good and will remain good. God will turn it into good." Among the Greeks an individual told his bad dreams to the Sun, for the belief held by the Greeks was that the light breaks the bad spell and disperses the demons of darkness.

Rabbi Chisda believed that a bad dream is worse than being punished by beating. Good dreams were important because, as the Talmud puts it, good dreams were considered the cause of happy feelings. Whenever the Talmud refers to bad dreams it also refers to demons who appear in these dreams, and who torture the sleeper. The Talmud has many references to fights between human beings and demons, and these were looked upon as punishment dreams. They frighten the dreamer, and the fright itself is a punishment. Dreams in which one is tortured by demons or evil spirits can be influenced by prayer and good deeds as well as by fasting. One may also pray to forget a dream, but the strongest antidote to bad dreams is fasting.

Nightmares the Talmud connects with sexual sensations and excitement. The demon who causes erotic dreams is described in the Talmud as hairy and resembling a goat (very much like the faun of the Romans). Another well-known demon who causes such erotic dreams is Lilith. The Talmud believes that she attacks those persons who sleep alone in the house. Lilith may take on a masculine or a feminine form. She appears in a female form when approaching men and in a male form when approaching women.

Lilith was probably taken over by the Hebrews from the Babylonians ("Lilu" and "Lilitu" in Assyrian and Babylonian). The Greeks knew her under the form of Empusae (forcers-in) = Incubus.

These demons torture the sleeper with erotic feelings, especially during afternoon sleep. The Rabbis of the Talmud made provisions for the dreamer of such erotic dreams so that he may not feel guilty. They declared that seminal emissions as a result of such dreams were not the responsibility of the dreamer. Rabbi Huna states, "Even if the emission is connected with feelings of gratification, the dreamer is not responsible, because it was not real sexual intercourse."

The symbols in the Talmudic dream interpretation correspond to the symbols which appear in the proverbs in Hebrew folklore and myths. A woman was symbolized in a dream by a house. The door of the house also symbolized a woman. A dream of Raba is as follows: "I saw the outer door of a house collapse." Interpretation: a woman will die.

Teeth in a dream refer to members of the family. Birds in a dream refer to human beings, and may also function as sexual symbols. Pigeons in a dream always represent women; for example, a man tells a dream in which he saw a pigeon returning to his bed; interpretation: the man had intercourse with many women. The raven is usually a male sexual symbol. A dream is told in which someone sees a raven return to his wife's bed. Interpretation: the woman had sex relations with many men. Artemidorus also refers to the raven as a wrecker of marriages and a thief; this interpretation is suggested to him by the black colour of the raven and by the changing of his voice. The owl and the bat appear in the Talmud as bad omens because they are night birds and prey upon other birds. They were thought of as the embodiment of the spirits of the dead. The snake in the Talmud, however, was a good omen. This interpretation was shared by the Greeks and the Romans, for whom snakes were household gods. Artemidorus speaks of snakes as dangerous, but at times he considers them to be of good omen. The hen in the Talmud refers to fertility, suggested by her many eggs.

The various fruits and plants had symbolic sexual significance. A dream in which a man poured oil on an olive tree was interpreted to mean that he slept with his mother in the dream, a tree branching out representing the woman, and the oil having its obvious significance. (This is one of many incest dreams mentioned in the Talmud.) Another dream is cited in which a man saw the shadow of a myrtle tree above him as he was lying under the tree. Interpretation: he slept with a woman in the dream, the woman on top and the man underneath. In general, the myrtle symbolized the engaged girl, because of its universal use for the bride at weddings. The grapevine also symbolized woman because of the vines pregnant with grapes, the grapes referring to the breasts.

Oedipal and incestuous dreams were well known and were correctly interpreted. A dream in which a man slept with his mother is interpreted euphemistically: "You slept with rationality." This interpretation attempts to spare the dreamer's embarrassment and possible sense of guilt. The interpretation refers to a Biblical verse which reads: "Call rationality Mother." In the same fashion, a dream in which a man sleeps with his sister was interpreted by citing the Biblical verse: "Speak to wisdom— you are my sister." The dream then would mean that the dreamer will be wise, just as in the first dream the dreamer will be rational.

He who dreams about sleeping with a married woman will have a share in the hereafter; this applies only if he does not know her and did not think of her in the evening. The interpretation refers to the belief that sexual intercourse constitutes a sixtieth part of the pleasures of Paradise. Artemidorus considered such dreams as of evil intent because they may lead to the breaking up of a marriage.

To be nude in the dream meant to be without sin, the nudity probably symbolizing the purity of the new-born baby. The moon always symbolized a woman, just as for the Romans the moon was feminine and the sun always represented a man.

A man came to Rabbi Ishmael and said: "I dreamed that one of my eyes kissed the other eye." The Rabbi replied: "You should be dead; you slept with your sister." According to Artemidorus also, the right eye symbolizes the son, brother, and father; the left eye symbolizes the daughter, sister, and mother.

Dreams with castration content are also mentioned in the Talmud, the loss of parts of the body—hands, legs, teeth, or hair. These were interpreted in a euphemistic way. The general interpretation was that a person afflicted by such a loss in his dreams would have an easier life. If one has no hands, one will not have to use one's hands for work and struggle. If one loses a foot, he will ride on a horse or be carried about, which also will make his life easier.

The dream interpreters in the Talmud sometimes used anagrams or plays on words, and at times interpreted from the double meaning of a word. In order to find a meaning for a dream, a word was divided into parts, or the interpretation was taken from the sound of the word in the dream. Interpretation through play on words: Bar Qappara said to Rabbi Jehuda ha-Nasi (compilator of the Mishnah), "In my dream I saw that my nose fell down." Rabbi Jehuda answered, "Violent anger was diverted from you." "Nose" in Hebrew, "ap"—also means "anger."

Dreams may mean the opposite of their manifest content. Rabbi Chisda says: "A bad dream is better than a good dream."

The interpretation was always provided solely by the interpreter, and not through the dreamer's associated thoughts. Talmudic and ancient interpretation in general was based on the associations which the dream evoked in the interpreter's mind.

Aristotle in *De Divinatione per Somnum* states (as quoted by Freud): "The best interpreter of dreams was the man who could best grasp similarities; . . . the most successful interpreter is the man who can detect the truth from the misshapen picture."

The Talmud makes a distinction between good and bad interpreters, and mention is made of the great number of interpreters in the same community. *Berakoth* notes that there were twenty-four dream interpreters in Jerusalem at one time, and Rabbi Bana stated that he visited all of them. He remarked, "What one did not interpret to me the other did, and all interpretations were realized in the end." The Talmud advises that the interpreter should be paid lest he be influenced in his interpretation.

The interpreter's rôle was important because his interpretation might have an important bearing on the subsequent actions of the dreamer in waking life.

The dream interpreter is advised by the Talmud to consider the dreamer's personality, his various life circumstances, his age, his occupation, economic circumstances, state of happiness or unhappiness, how troubled or relaxed he was at the time of dreaming, etc. The dream can then be interpreted from many angles and in different ways. For instance, the occupation of the dreamer is important because the dream may be interpreted in relation to it. Naturally, the interpreter must be well versed in the various languages which the dreamer speaks, so that the idioms of those languages will be known to him.

The Rabbis advised that some dreams should not be interpreted at all, because they might contain some unfavourable predictions.

The outstanding characteristics of Talmudic dream interpretation were to prophesy the future and to serve the wish-fulfilment function. Both contain much truth. As Freud said, ". . . The ancient belief that dreams foretell the future is not wholly devoid of truth. By picturing our wishes as fulfilled, dreams are, after all, leading us into the future. But this future which the dreamer pictures as the present has been moulded by his indestructible wish into a perfect likeness of the past."

The Dream Follows the Mouth

ROGER CAILLOIS

In postbiblical literature the idea was put forward that the dream itself was unimportant and that it was the interpretation that counted, becoming itself the effective forecast, and thereby forcing reality to follow suit. "There were twenty-four interpreters of dreams in Jerusalem. Once I had a dream and went to everyone of them and what any one interpreted, none of the others interpreted in the same way, and yet all of them were fulfilled. This is in pursuance of the saying: *The dream follows the mouth* [of the one who interprets it]."

Certain stories exemplify the truth of this doctrine and suggest its theoretical basis.

The Dream of the Cracked Granary

A certain woman came to Rabbi Eliezer and said to him: "I saw in a dream that the granary of my house came open in a crack." He answered: "You will conceive a son." She went away, and that is what happened.

She dreamed again the same dream and told it to Rabbi Eliezer who gave the same interpretation, and that is what happened.

She dreamed the same dream a third time and looked for Rabbi Eliezer. Not finding him, she said to his disciples: "I saw in a dream that the granary of my house came open in a crack."

They answered her: "You will bury your husband." And that is what happened.

Rabbi Eliezer, surprised by the lamentations, inquired what had gone wrong? His disciples told him what had happened. He cried out, "Wretched fools! You have killed that man. Is it not written: 'As he interpreted to us, so it was?' (Gen. 41:13). And Rabbi Yohannan concludes: "Every dream becomes valid only by its interpretation."

Dreams Take the Soul to "the Superior Region"

SYNESIUS OF CYRENE

Translated by Isaac Myer

If dreams prophesy the future, if visions which present themselves to the mind during sleep afford some *indicia* whereby to divine future things —dreams will be at the same time true and obscure, and even in their obscurity the truth will reside. "The Gods with a thick veil have covered human life." (Hesiod.)

I am not surprised that some have owed to a sleep the discovery of a treasure; and that one may have gone to sleep very ignorant, and after having had in a dream a conversation with the Muses, awakened an able poet, which has happened in my time to some, and in which there is nothing strange. I do not speak of those who have had, in their sleep, the revelation of a danger which threatened them, or the knowledge of a remedy that would cure them. But when sleep opens the way to the most perfect inspections of true things to the soul which previously had not desired these inspections, nor thought concerning the ascent to intellect and arouses it to pass beyond nature and reunite itself to the intelligible sphere from which it has wandered so far that it does not know even from whence it came, *this*, I say, is most marvelous and obscure.

If one thinks it extraordinary that the soul may thus ascend to the superior region, and does not believe that the way to this felicitous union lies through the imagination, let him hear the sacred oracles when they speak about the different roads which lead to the higher sphere. After enumerating the various *subsidia* which help the ascent of the soul by arousing and developing its powers, they say:

> By lessons some are enlightened,
> By sleep others are inspired.
> SYBILLINE ORACLES

You see the distinction which the oracle establishes; upon the one side, inspiration; upon the other, study; the former, it says, is instruction whilst one is awake, the latter when asleep. Whilst awake, it is always a man who is the instructor: but when asleep, it is from God that the knowledge comes. . . .

Thanks to its character divination by dreams is placed within the reach of all: plain and without artifice, it is pre-eminently rational; holy, because it does not make use of violent methods, it can be exercised anywhere: it dispenses with fountain, rock and gulf, and it thus is that which is truly divine. To practice it there is no need of neglecting any of our occupations, or to rob our business for a single moment. . . . No one is advised to quit his work and go to sleep, especially to have dreams. But as the body cannot resist prolonged night-watches, the time that nature has ordained for us to consecrate to repose brings us, with sleep, an accessory more precious than sleep itself: that natural necessity becomes a source of enjoyment and we do not sleep merely to live, but to learn to live well. . . .

But in divination by dreams, each of us is in himself his proper instrument; whatever we may do, we cannot separate ourselves from our oracle: it dwells with us; it follows us everywhere, in our journeys, in war, in public life, agricultural pursuits, in commercial enterprises. The laws of a jealous Republic do not interdict that divination; if they did they could do nothing: because how can the offense be proven? What harm is there in sleeping? No tyrant is able to carry out an edict against dreams, still less proscribe sleep in his dominions; that would be at once fully to command the impossible, and an impiety to put himself in opposition to the desires of nature and God.

Then let us all deliver ourselves to the interpretation of dreams, men and women, young and old, rich and poor, private citizens and magistrates, inhabitants of the town and of the county, artesans and orators. There is not any privileged, neither by sex, neither by age, nor fortune or profession. Sleep offers itself to all: it is an oracle always ready, to our infallible and silent counselor; in these mysteries of a new species each is at the same time priest and initiate. It, as well as divination, announces to us the joys to come, and through the anticipated happiness which it procures for us, it gives to our pleasures a longer duration; and it warns us to the misfortunes that threaten us, so that we may be put on our guard.

The charming promises of hope so dear to man, the farseeing calculations of fear, all come to us through dreams. Nothing is more qualified in its effect to nourish hope in us; this good, so great and so precious that without it we could not be able, as said the most illustrious Sophists, to support life. . . .

I have not yet stated my own indebtedness to dreams. And yet it is to the minds given to Philosophy that dreams especially come, to enlighten them in their difficulties and researches, so as to bring them during sleep the solutions which escape them when awake. We seem in sleeping at one time to apprehend, at another to find, through our own reflection. As for me, how often dreams have come to my assistance in the composition of my writings! Often have they aided me to put my ideas in order and my style in harmony with my ideas; they have made me expunge certain expressions, and choose others. When I allowed myself to use images and pompous expressions, in imitation of the new Attic style, so far removed from the old, a god warned me in my sleep, censured my writings, and making the affected phrases to disappear, brought me back to a natural style. At other times, in the hunting season, I invented, after a dream, traps to catch the swiftest animals and the most skillful in hiding. If, discouraged from too long waiting, I was preparing to return to my home, dreams would give me courage, by announcing to me, for such or such a day, better result: I then patiently watched some nights more; many animals would fall in my nets or under my arrows. All my life has been spent among books or in hunting, except the time of my embassy; and would to the gods I had never lived those three cursed years! But then again divination has been singularly useful to me: it has preserved me from ambushes that certain magicians laid for me, revealed their sorceries and saved me from all danger; it sustained me during the whole duration of the mission which has caused to prosper the greatest good in the cities of Libya; it conducted me even before the Emperor, in the midst of his court, in which I have spoken with an independence, of which no Greek ever before had given an example.

[*Circa* A.D. 400]

Dreams Are Usually False

JEREMY TAYLOR

The observation of dreams and fears commenced from the fancies of the night. For the superstitious man does not rest even when he sleeps; neither is he safe, because dreams are usually false, but he is afflicted for fear they should tell true. Living and waking men have one world in common, they use the same air and fire, and discourse by the same principles of logic and reason; but that men are asleep, have every one a world to himself, and strange perceptions; and the superstitious hath none at all: his reason sleeps, and his fears are waking; and all his rest, and his very securities, to the fearful man turn into affrights and insecure expectations of evil, that shall never happen; they make their rest uneasy and changeable, and they still vex their weary soul, not considering there is no other sleep for sleep to rest in: and therefore, if the sleep be troublesome, the man's care be without remedy till they be quite destroyed. Dreams follow the temper of the body, and commonly proceed from trouble or disease, business or care, an active head and a restless mind, from fear or hope, from wine or passion, from fullness or emptiness, from fantastic remembrances, or from some common demon, good or bad: they are without rule and without reason, they are as contingent, as if a man should study to make a prophecy, and by saying ten thousand things may hit upon one true, which was therefore not foreknown, though it was forespoken; and they have no certainty, because they have no natural causality nor proportion to those effects, which many times they are said to foresignify. The dream of the yolk of an egg importeth gold (saith Artemidorus); and they that use to remember such fantastic idols, are afraid to lose a friend when they dream their teeth shake, when naturally it will rather signify a scurvy; for a natural indisposition and an imperfect sense of the beginning of a disease, may vex the fancy into a symbolical representation; for so the man that dreamed he swam against a stream of blood, had a pleurisy beginning in his side; and he that dreamt he dipped his foot into water, and that it was turned to a marble, was enticed into the fancy by a beginning dropsy; and if the events do answer in one instance, we become credulous in twenty. For want of reason we discourse ourselves into folly and weak observation and give the devil power over us in those circumstances, in which we can least resist him. "A thief is confident in the twilight"; if you suffer impressions to be made upon you by dreams, the devil hath the reins in his own hands, and can tempt you by that, which will abuse you, when you can make no resistance. Dominicica, the wife of Valens the emperor, dreamed that God threatened to take away her only son for her despiteful usage of St. Basil: the fear proceeding from this instance was safe and fortunate; but if she had dreamed in the behalf of a heretic, she might have been cozened into a false proposition upon a ground weaker than the discourse of a waking child.

[*Circa* 1650]

Both God and the Devil Appear to Us in Dreams

DANIEL DEFOE

There may be dreams without apparitions, as there may be apparitions without dreams; but apparition in dream may be as really an apparition as if the person who saw it was awake; the difference may be here, that the apparition in a dream is visible to the soul only, for the soul never sleeps; and an apparition to the eyesight is visible in common perspective.

How is it then that we see in our dreams the very faces and dress of the persons we dream of; nay, hear their voices, and receive due impressions from what they say, and often times speak to them with our own voices articulately and audibly, though we are fast asleep? What secret power of the imagination is able to represent the image of any person to itself, if there was not some appearance, something placed in the soul's view, by a secret, but invisible hand, and in an imperceptible manner? which something is in all respects, and to all purposes, as completely an apparition, as if it was placed in open sight when the person was awake.

The Scripture confirms this opinion by many expressions directly to the purpose, and particularly this of appearing, or apparition in dream. . . .

Certainly dreams in those days were another kind of thing than they are now. God spoke to them, and they answered; and when they were awake they knew that it was God that spoke, and gave heed to the vision or apparition of God to them.

There are many . . . instances of the like in the sacred history; as first in the remarkable case of King Solomon, I Kings iii. 5. *The Lord appeared to Solomon in a dream by night, and God said, ask what I shall give thee.*

This is called in the Scripture a dream, ver. 15. *And Solomon awoke, and behold it was a dream;* and yet it is all confirmed; and the petition that Solomon made, though in his sleep, or dream, is accepted and answered as his real act and deed, as if he had been awake. A good hint, by the way, that we may both please and offend in our dreams, as really as if we were awake; but that is a hint, I say, by itself.

That passage of Solomon is very remarkable to the case in hand. If my readers please to believe that there was such a man as Solomon, and that he had such a dream, they must allow that it was a real apparition; God appeared to him in a dream.

To bring it down a step lower; as God has thus personally appeared to men in dreams, so have inferior spirits, and we have examples of this too in the Scripture. . . .

As it has pleased God to appear in this manner, and to cause angels to appear also in the same manner, and upon special occasions, so I make no question but the Devil often appears in dreams too. . . .

Now as the dreams in those days, and our dreams at this time, are exceeding different; and that as our heads are so full of impertinent thoughts in the day, which in proportion crowd the imagination at night, so our dreams are trifling and foolish; how shall we know when they are to be taken notice of, and when not? when there is a real apparition, haunting us, or showing itself to us, and when not? in a word, when an angel, or when a devil, appears to us in dream?

It is a nice question, and as it does not particularly relate to the present inquiry, so it would require too long a digression to discourse critically upon it; but I shall dismiss it with this short answer; we must judge, as I said before in the case of open apparitions, by the weight, and by the nature of the message or errand which the apparition comes about; evil messengers seldom come of good errands, and angels good or bad seldom come on trifling messages.

Trifling dreams are the product of the mind being engaged in trifling matters; a child dreams of its play, a housewife dreams of her kitchen, a nurse of the children, a tradesman of his shop; these have nothing of apparition in them; nothing of angels or spirits, God or devil, but when dream comes up to vision, and the soul is embarked in a superior degree, to a commerce above the ordinary rate, then you may conclude you have had some extraordinary visitors, that you have been in some good or bad company in the night, and you are left to judge of what kind, by the substance or terror of the vision. If it be to open the understanding, to increase knowledge, to seal instruction; in a word, if it is for direction to good actions, or stirring up the soul of man to perform his duty to God or man, it is certainly from above; it is an apparition from God, it is a vision of angels and good spirits. . . .

If it be an allurement to vice, laying before you an opportunity to steal, presenting an object of beauty, an enticement to commit an unlawful action; depend upon it, it is from the dark regions, it is an apparition of the Devil, and he employs his agents and perhaps attends in person to draw you into mischief.

N.B. Here it is worth a wise man's considering, whether the Devil representing a temptation to any person in a dream, and the person complying, he is not guilty of the fact as really as if he had been awake; I leave it only as a head of reflection.

[1727]

D. PHILOSOPHERS LOOK AT THEIR DREAMS

The Dream Theory of Socrates

PLATO

Translated by H. Davis

SUCH AS ARE EXCITED IN SLEEP, when the rest of the soul—which is rational, mild, and its governing principle—is asleep, and when that part which is savage and rude, being satisfied with food and drink, frisks about, drives away sleep, and seeks to go and accomplish its practices: in such an one, you know, it dares to do everything, because it is loosed and disengaged from all modesty and prudence: for, if it pleases, it scruples not at the embraces, even of a mother, or of any one else, whether gods, men, or beasts; nor to commit murder, nor abstain from any sort of meat—and in one word, it is wanting neither in folly nor shamelessness. You speak most truly, replied he. But when a man is in good health, methinks, and lives temperately, and goes to sleep after exciting his reason, and feasting it with noble reasonings and investigations, having thus attained to an internal harmony, and given up the appetites neither to want nor repletion, that they may be at rest, either by joy or grief, but suffer it by itself alone without interruption to inquire and long to apprehend what it knows not—either something of what has existed, or now exists, or will exist hereafter; and so also, having soothed the spirited part of the soul, and not allowed it to be hurried into transports of anger, or to fall asleep with agitated passion; but after having quieted these two parts of the soul, and roused to action that third part, in which wisdom dwells, he will thus take his rest; you know, that by such an one the truth is best apprehended, and the visions of his dreams are then least of all portrayed contrary to the law. I am quite of this opinion, said he. We have digressed indeed a little too far in talking of these things; but what we want to know is this, that in every one resides a certain species of desires that are terrible, savage, and irregular, even in some that we deem ever so moderate: and this indeed becomes manifest in sleep.

Socrates Obeys a Dream

PLATO

Translated by Benjamin Jowett

Cebes said: I am very glad indeed, Socrates, that you mentioned the name of Aesop. For that reminds me of a question which has been asked by others, and was asked of me only the day before yesterday by Evenus the poet, and as he will be sure to ask again, you may as well tell me what I should say to him, if you would like him to have an answer. He wanted to know why you who never before wrote a line of poetry, now that you are in prison are putting Aesop into verse, and also composing that hymn in honor of Apollo.

Tell him, Cebes, he replied, that I had no idea of rivalling him or his poems; which is the truth, for I knew that I could not do that. But I wanted to see whether I could purge away a scruple which I felt about certain dreams. In the course of my life I have often had intimations in dreams "that I should make music." The same dream came to me sometimes in one form, and sometimes in another, but always saying the same or nearly the same words: Make and cultivate music, said the dream. And hitherto I had imagined that this was only intended to exhort and encourage me in the study of philosophy, which has always been the pursuit of my life, and is the noblest and best of music. The dream was bidding me to do what I was already doing, in the same way that a competitor in a race is bidden by the spectators to run when he is already running. But I was not certain of this, as the dream might have meant music in the popular sense of the word, and being under sentence of death, and the festival giving me a respite, I thought that I should be safer if I satisfied the scruple, and, in obedience to the dream, composed a few verses before I departed. And first I made a hymn in honor of the god of the festival, and then considering that a poet, if he is really to be a poet or maker, should not only put words together but make stories, and as I have no invention, I took some fables of Aesop, which I had ready at hand and knew, and turned them into verse.

Dream Divination

ARISTOTLE

Translated by Thomas Taylor

Concerning divination subsisting in sleep, and which is said to happen from dreams, it is neither easy to despise, nor to assent to it. For the opinion of all, or most men, that dreams have some signification, procures belief, as an assertion derived from experience. And that there is a divination concerning some things in dreams is not incredible, for it possesses a certain reason. Hence some one may fancy that the like takes place with respect to other dreams. But as no rational cause is seen why this divination should take place, this causes it to be incredible. For that it is divinity who sends dreams, together with being in other respects unreasonable, is attended with this absurdity, that dream [significant of future events] should be sent not to the best and wisest men, but to any casual persons. But the cause which is far from divinity being taken away, no other cause appears to be reasonable. For as some persons have foreseen transactions about the pillars of Hercules, or those which have happened in Barysythenes, to discover the origin of these, appears to be beyond our sagacity. It is necessary, therefore, that dreams should either be the causes, or signs, or accidents of events, or that they should be all, or some of these, or one of them only. But I say the cause, indeed, as the moon is the cause of an eclipse of the sun, and labor of a fever. But the sign of an eclipse is the egress of the stars [while the sun exists above the horizon]. And the roughness of the tongue is the sign of a fever. But that while some one is walking, the sun is eclipsed, is an accident; for this is neither a sign, nor the cause of the eclipse, nor is the eclipse the cause of walking. Hence no accident is either always, or very frequently produced. These then, indeed, are the causes, but those are the signs of dreams; as of accidents pertaining to the body. The most elegant of physicians, therefore, say that it is necessary to pay very great attention to dreams. Hence it is reasonable thus to think, and not to disbelieve in dreams, since they are observed by artists, by speculative men and by philosophers. For the motions which take place in the day, unless they are very great and strong, are concealed from us by the great motions with which we are occupied when awake. But the contrary takes place in sleep, for then small appears to be great motions. This, indeed, is evident from those things which frequently happen in sleep; for we then fancy that it thunders and lightens in consequence of a small sound being produced in the ears; that we enjoy honey and sweet sapors, in consequence of the defluxion of the least part of phlegm; and that we walk through fire, and are vehemently heated, when a small heat is produced about certain parts. But when we wake, it is evident to us, that those particulars subsist after this manner. Hence, since the principles of all these are small, it is evident that this is the case with the principles of all diseases, and of the other passions which are about to take place in the body. It is evident, therefore, that these things are necessarily more apparent in sleep, than when we are awake. Moreover, it is not unreasonable to suppose, that some of the phantasms which present themselves in sleep are the causes of the action which we perform [when awake]; just as when intending to act, we frequently see that we act in a dream clearly indicative of futurity. But the cause of this is, that the motion is prepared from principles which occur in the day. Thus again it is necessary that the motions which take place in sleep, should frequently be the principle of diurnal actions, in consequence of the cogitation of these being again prepared in nocturnal phantasms. Thus, therefore, it is possible that some dreams may be signs and causes; but many of them resemble accidents, and especially all such as are transcendent, and of which the principle is not in us; as for instance, a naval battle, and things which happen at a distance. For it is likely that these dreams are verified after the same manner as when a thing happens to take place while we are speaking about it; for what hinders this from being the case in sleep? But it is more probable that many things of this kind accidentally occur. As, therefore, the mention of a thing is neither a sign, nor the cause of its existence, so neither is a dream a sign or the cause of an event happening as it appeared to the dreamer, but it is a fortuitous circumstance. Hence many dreams do not happen to be verified; for things fortuitous have neither a perpetual nor a frequent subsistence.

In short, since some other animals dream, dreams will not be sent from divinity, nor are they produced for the sake of this. They are, nevertheless, demoniacal, but not divine; of which this is an indication, that very degenerate men are prescient, and clearly see future events in dreams, as not being sent by divinity. But those whose nature is, as it were, loquacious and melancholy, see all-various visions. Because, however, they are more according to many things, and multifariously, they meet with these visions; just as some have contended for a long time, gain at last the prize of contention; for, as it is said, if you throw many darts, you will, some time or other, hit the mark. This, also, happens to be the case in dreams. But it is not at all absurd that many dreams do not happen: for neither in bodies do the effects always follow indicated by signs and the celestial orbs, as rain and wind; for if another motion predominates over this form the effect is produced, the sign is not attended with a corresponding event. And many things which have been well deliberated on, of such as ought to be done, are dissolved on account of other principles which possess greater authority. For, in short, not everything is produced which [according to the preparation of causes] ought to be produced; nor is that which will be, and that which is about to be, the same thing. But at the same time it must be said, that there are certain principles, from which they are not perfected, and that these are naturally adapted to be signs of certain things which do not take place. Concerning, however, those dreams which have not such principles as we have mentioned, but such as are distant either in time, or place, or magnitude, or in no one of these, yet those who see the dream do not contain in themselves the principles [of what they see] unless the foreseeing is from accident; concerning these, the cause will be rather such as follows, than that assigned by Democritus, who asserts, that images and effluxions are the cause. For, as when some one moves water or air, this moves something else, and that ceasing its motion, it happens that a motion of this kind proceeds as far as to a certain thing, he who moves not being present; thus nothing hinders but that a certain motion and sense may arrive to souls that dream, from which Democritus produces images, and effluxions; and that wherever these motions and sense happen to arrive, they are more sensible by night, because those which are borne along in the day are dissolved. For the air of the night is more undisturbed, because the night is more tranquil [than the day]. These motions and senses may, also, produce a sense in the body, in consequence of sleep; on which account, also, those that are asleep have a greater perception of small inward motions than those that are awake. But these motions produce phantasms, from which future events about things of this kind are foreseen. Hence this passion happens to anyone indiscriminately, and not to the most wise. For it would take place in the day, and with wise men, if it were sent by divinity. But it is thus probable that any casual persons foresee. For the minds of these are not thoughtful, but, as it were, solitary and void of all things, and being moved, is led by that which moves. The cause, too, why certain persons in an ecstasy foresee future events is, because the proper or appropriate motions do not disturb, but are expelled. Hence these motions that are foreign are especially perceived. But those certain persons clearly perceive future events, and that familiars especially foresee things pertaining to familiars happens, because familiars are particularly solicitous about each other. For as when at a distance, they especially know and have a sensible perception of each other, thus, also, they have a perception of each other's motions; for the motions of familiars are more known. But the melancholy, on account of their vehemence [in thinking], as those who hurl a dart at a distant object, tend directly to the mark, in consequence of the permitation, rapidly imagine that which follows and is annexed. For just as with the poems of Philaegidas, those who are inspired with prophetic fury, assert and think of that which is consequent to the similar, as, for instance, instead of Venus, the epithet foam-begotten, and thus connect that which is first. Again, in consequence of the vehemence of their thoughts, the motion of them is not expelled by another motion. He, however, is a judge of dreams according to the most consummate art, who is able to survey similitudes; for everyone is capable of forming a judgment of dreams which manifestly indicate future events. But I say similitudes because phantasms occur in dreams similar to images in water, as we have before observed. There, however, if the motion is abundant, the representation is in no respect similar, and the images do not resemble the true substances [of which they are the images]. But he will be skilled in forming a sufficient judgment, who is able rapidly and intimately to perceive dissipated and distorted images, and to see that they are the images of a man, or a horse, or anything else. And in like manner he is the best interpreter of dreams who can similarly discern the similitudes in these; for motion in these disturbs the clear perception of future events. What, therefore, sleep and dreams are, and from what cause each of these is produced, we have shown; and we have also spoken concerning divination from dreams.

No Divine Energy Inspires Dreams

CICERO

Translated by C. D. Yonge

The first thing for us to understand is, that there is no divine energy which inspires dreams; and this being granted, you must also grant that no visions of dreamers proceed from the agency of the gods. For the gods have for our own sake given us intellect sufficiently to provide for our own future welfare. How few people then attend to dreams, or understand them, or remember them. How many, on the other hand, despise them, and think any superstitious observation of them a sign of a weak imbecile mind!

Why then should God take the trouble to consult the interest of this man, or to warn that one by dreams, when he knows that they do not only not think them worth attending to, but they do not even condescend to remember them. For a god cannot be ignorant of the sentiments of every man, and it is unworthy of a god to do anything in vain, or without a cause; nay, that would be unworthy of even a wise man. If, therefore, dreams are for the most part disregarded, or despised, either God is ignorant of that being the fact, or employs the intimation by dreams in vain. Neither of these suppositions can properly apply to God, and therefore it must be confessed, that God gives men no intimations by means of dreams.

Again, let me ask you, if God gives us visions of a prophetic nature, in order to apprise us of future events, should we not rather expect them when we are awake than when we are asleep? For, whether it be some external and adventitious impulse which affects the minds of those who are asleep, or whether those minds are affected voluntarily by their own agency, or whether there is another cause why we seem to see and hear or do anything during sleep, the same impulses might surely operate on them when awake? And if for our sakes the Gods effect this during sleep, they might do it for us while awake. . . .

But let us now treat of those dreams which you term clear and definite, such as that of the Arcadian whose friend was killed by the innkeeper at Megara, or that of Simonides who was warned not to set sail by an apparition of a man whose interment he had kindly superintended. The history of Alexander presents us with another instance of this kind, which I wonder you did not cite, who, after his friend Ptolemy had been wounded in battle by a poisoned arrow, and when he appeared to be dying of the wound, and was in great agony, fell asleep while sitting by his bed, and in his slumber is said to have seen a vision of the serpent which Mother Olympias cherished, bringing a root in his mouth, and telling him that it grew in a spot very near at hand, and that it possessed such medicinal virtue, that it would easily cure Ptolemy if applied to his wound. On awakening Alexander related his dream and messengers were sent to look for that plant, which, when it was found, not only cured Ptolemy, but likewise several other soldiers, who during the engagement had been wounded by similar arrows. . . .

As to those dreams that have occurred in our personal experience, what can we say about them—about your dream respecting my horse being submerged close to the bank, or mine, that Marius with the laurelled fasces ordered me to be conducted into his monument?

All these dreams, my brother, are of the same character, and, by the immortal gods, let us not make so poor a use of our reason, as to subject it to superstition and delusions. For what do you suppose the Marius was that appeared to me? His ghost or image, I suppose, as Democritus would call it. Whence, then, did his image come from? For images, according to him, flow from solid bodies and palpable forms. What body then of Marius was in existence? It came, he would say, from that body which had existed; for all things are full of images. It was, then, the image of Marius that haunted me on the Atinian territory, for no forms can be imagined except the impulsion of images.

What are we to think then? Are those images so obedient to our word that they come before us at our bidding as soon as we wish them; and even images of things which have no reality whatever? For what form is there so preposterous and absurd that the mind cannot form to itself a picture of it? so much so indeed that we can bring before our minds even things which we have never seen; as for instance, the situations of towns and the figures of men.

When, then, I dream of the walls of Babylon, or the countenance of Homer, is it because some physical image of them strikes my mind? All things, then, which we desire to be so, can be known to us, for there is nothing of which we cannot think. Therefore, no images steal in upon the sleeper from without; nor indeed are such eternal images flowing about at all: and I never knew anyone who talked nonsense with greater authority. . . .

If, then, dreams do not come from God, and if there are no objects in nature with which they have a necessary sympathy and connection, and if it is impossible by experiments and observations to arrive at a sure interpretation of them, the consequence is that dreams are not entitled to any credit or respect whatever.

And this I say with the greatest confidence, since those very persons who experience these dreams cannot by any means understand them, and those persons who pretend to interpret them, do so by conjecture, not by demonstration. And in the infinite series of ages, chance has produced many more extraordinary results in every kind of thing than it has in dreams; nor can anything be more uncertain than that conjectural interpretation of diviners, which admits not only of several, but often of absolutely contrary sense.

Let us reject, therefore, this divination of dreams, as well as all other kinds. For, to speak truly, that superstition has extended itself through all notions, and has oppressed the intellectual energies of all men, and has betrayed them into endless imbecilities.

The Witchcraft of Sleep

RALPH WALDO EMERSON

The witchcraft of sleep divides with truth the empire of our lives. This soft enchantress visits two children lying locked in each other's arms, and carries them asunder by wide spaces of land and sea, and wide intervals of time:

> There lies a sleeping city, God of dreams!
> What an unreal and fantastic world
> Is going on below!
> Within the sweep of yon encircling wall
> How many a large creation of the night,
> Wide wilderness and mountain, rock and sea,
> Peopled with busy, transitory groups,
> Finds room to rise, and never feels the crowd.

'Tis superfluous to think of the dreams of multitudes, the astonishment remains that one should dream; that we should resign so quietly this deifying Reason, and become the theatre of delirious shows, wherein time, space, persons, cities, animals, should dance before us in merry and mad confusion; a delicate creation outdoing the prime and flower of actual nature, antic comedy alternating with horrid pictures. Sometimes the forgotten companions of childhood reappear:

> They come, in dim procession led,
> The cold, the faithless, and the dead,
> As warm each hand, each brow as gay,
> As if they parted yesterday:

or we seem busied for hours and days in peregrinations over seas and lands, in earnest dialogues, strenuous actions for nothings and absurdities, cheated by spectral jokes and waking suddenly with ghastly laughter, to be rebuked by the cold, lonely, silent midnight, and to rake with confusion in memory among the gibbering nonsense to find the motive of this contemptible cachination. Dreams are jealous of being remembered; they dissipate instantly and angrily if you try to hold them. When newly awakened from lively dreams, we are so near them, still agitated by them, still in their sphere—give us one syllable, one feature, one hint, and we should repossess the whole; hours of this strange entertainment would come trooping back to us; but we cannot get our hand on the first link or fibre, and the whole is lost. There is a strange wistfulness in the speed with which it disperses and baffles our grasp.

A dislocation seems to be the foremost trait of dreams. A painful imperfection almost always attends them. The fairest forms, the most noble and excellent persons, are deformed by some pitiful and insane circumstance. The very landscape and scenery in a dream seems not to fit us, but like a coat or cloak of some other person to overlap and encumber the wearer; so is the ground, the road, the house, in dreams, too long or too short, and if it served no other purpose would show us how accurately nature fits man awake.

There is one memory of waking and another of sleep. In our dreams the same scenes and fancies are many times associated, and that too, it would seem, for years. In sleep one shall travel certain roads in stagecoaches or gigs, which he recognizes as familiar, and has dreamed that ride a dozen times; or shall walk alone in familiar fields and meadows, which road or which meadow in waking hours he never looked upon. This feature of dreams deserves the more attention from its singular resemblance to that obscure yet startling experience which almost every person confesses in daylight, that particular passage of conversation and action have occurred to him in the same order before, whether dreaming or waking; a suspicion that they have been with precisely these persons in precisely this room, and heard precisely this dialogue, at some former hour, they know not when.

Animals have been called "the dreams of nature." Perhaps for a conception of their consciousness we may go to our dreams. In a dream we have the instinctive obedience, the same torpidity of the highest power, the same unsurprised assent to the monstrous as these metamorphosed men exhibit. Our thoughts in a stable or in a menagerie, on the other hand, may well remind us of our dreams. What compassion do these imprisoning forms awaken! You may catch the glance of a dog sometimes which lays a kind of claim to sympathy and brotherhood. What! somewhat of me down there? Does he know it? Can he too, as I, go out of himself, see himself, perceive relations? We fear lest the poor brute should gain one dreadful glimpse of his condition, should learn in some moment the tough limitations of this fettering organization. It was in this glance that Ovid got the hint of his metamorphoses; Calidasa of his transmigration of souls. For these fables are our own thoughts carried out. What keeps those wild tales in circulation for thousands of years? What but the wild fact to which they suggest some approximation of theory? Nor is the fact quite solitary, for in varieties of our own species where organization seems to predominate over the genius of man, in Kalmuck or Malay or Flathead Indian, we are sometimes pained by the same feeling; and sometimes too the sharpwitted prosperous white man awakens it. In a mixed assembly we have chanced to see not only a glance of Abdiel, so grand and keen, but also in other faces the features of the mink, of the bull, of the rat, and the barn-door fowl. You think, could the man overlook his own condition, he could not be restrained from suicide.

Dreams have a poetic integrity and truth. This limbo and dust-hole of thought is presided over by a certain reason, too. Their extravagance from nature is yet within a higher nature. They seem to us to suggest an abundance and fluency of thought not familiar to the waking experience. They pique us by independence of us, yet we know ourselves in this mad crowd, and owe to dreams a kind of divination and wisdom. My dreams are not me; they are not Nature, or the Not-me; they are both. They have a double consciousness, at once sub-and-ob-jective. We call the phantoms that rise, the creation of our fancy, but they act like mutineers, and fire on their commander; showing that every act, every thought, every cause, is bipolar, and in the act is contained the counteraction. If I strike, I am struck; if I chase, I am pursued.

Wise and sometimes terrible hints shall in them be thrown to the man out of a quite unknown intelligence. He shall be startled two or three times in his life by the justice as well as the significance of this phantasmagoria. Once or twice the conscious fetters shall seem to be unlocked, and a freer utterance attained. A prophetic character in all ages has haunted them. They are the maturation often of opinions not consciously carried out to statements, but whereof we already possessed the elements. Thus, when awake, I know the character of Rupert, but do not think what he may do. In dreams I see him engaged in certain actions which seem preposterous, out of all fitness. He is hostile, he is cruel, he is frightful, he is a poltroon. It turns out prophecy a year later. But it was already in my mind as character, and the sibyl dreams merely embodied it in fact. Why then should not symptoms, auguries, forebodings be, as one said, the moanings of the spirit?

We are let by this experience into the high region of Cause, and acquainted with the identity of every unlike-seeming effects. We learn that actions whose turpitude is very differently reputed proceed from one and the same affection. Sleep takes off the costume of circumstance, arms us with terrible freedom, so that every will rushes to a deed. A skillful man reads his dreams for his self-knowledge; yet not the details, but the quality. What part does he play in them—a cheerful, manly part, or a poor driveling part? However monstrous and grotesque their apparitions, they have a substantial truth. The same remark may be extended to the omens and coincidences which may have astonished us. Of all it is true that the reason of them is always latent in the individual. Goethe said: "These whimsical pictures, inasmuch as they originate from us, may well have an analogy with our whole life and fate."

The soul contains in itself the event that shall presently befall it, for the event is only the actualizing of its thoughts. It is no wonder that particular dreams and presentiments should fall out and be prophetic. The fallacy consists in selecting a few insignificant hints when all are inspired with the same sense. As if one should exhaust his astonishment at the economy of this thumbnail, and overlook the central causal miracle of his being a man. Every man goes through the world attended with innumerable facts pre-figuring (yes, distinctly announcing) his fate, if only eyes of sufficient heed and illumination were fastened on the sign. . . .

Dreams retain the infirmities of our character. The good genius may be there or not, our evil genius is sure to stay. The Ego partial makes the dream; the Ego total the interpretation. Life is also a dream on the same terms.

E. THE PHYSIOLOGICAL
THEORY OF DREAMS

Dreams Caused by Bodily Agitation

THOMAS HOBBES

THE IMAGINATION of them that sleep are those we call *Dreams*. And these also (as all other Imaginations) have been before, either totally, or by parcels in the Sense. And because in sense, the Brain, and Nerves, which are the necessary Organs of sense, are so benumbed in sleep, as not easily to be moved by the action of External Objects, there can happen in sleep, no Imagination; and therefore no Dream, but what proceeds from the agitation of the inward parts of man's body; which inward parts, for the connection they have with the Brain and other organs, when they be distempered, do keep the same in motion; whereby the Imaginations there formerly made, appear as if a man were waking; saving that the Organs of Sense being now benumbed, so as there is no new object, which can master and obscure them with a more vigorous impression, a Dream must needs be more clear, in this silence of sense, than are our waking thoughts. And hence it comes to pass, that it is a hard matter, and by many thought impossible to distinguish exactly between Sense and Dreaming. For my part, when I consider, that in Dreams, I do not often, nor constantly think of the same Persons, Places, Objects and Actions that I do waking; nor remember so long a train of coherent thoughts, Dreaming, as at other times; and because waking I often observe the absurdity of Dreams, and never dream of the absurdities of my waking Thoughts; I am well satisfied that being awake, I know I dream not; though when I dream, I think myself awake.

And seeing dreams are caused by the distemper of some of the inward parts of the Body; divers distempers must needs cause different Dreams.

And hence it is, that lying cold breedeth Dreams of Fear, and raiseth the thought and Image of some fearful object (the motion of the brain to the inner parts, and from the inner parts to the Brain being reciprocal.) And that as Anger causeth heat in some parts of the Body, when we are awake; so when we sleep, the overheating of the same parts causeth Anger, and raiseth up in the brain the Imagination of an Enemy. In the same manner, as natural kindness, when we are awake causeth desire and desire makes heat in certain other parts of the body; so also, too much heat in those parts, while we sleep, raiseth in the brain an imagination of some kindness shown. In sum, our Dreams are the reverse of our waking Imaginations; the motion when we are awake, beginning at one end; and when we Dream, at another.

The most difficult deceiving of a man's Dream, from his waking thoughts, is then, when by some accident we observe not that we have slept, which is easy to happen to a man full of fearful thought; and whose conscience is much troubled; and that sleepeth, without the circumstances, of going to bed, or putting off his clothes, as one that noddeth in a chair. For he that taketh pains and industriously lays himself to sleep, in case any uncouth and exorbitant fancy comes unto him, cannot think it easily other than a Dream. We read of Marcus Brutus (one that had his life given him by Julius Caesar, and was also his favorite, and notwithstanding murdered him), how at Phillipi, the night before he gave battle to Augustus Caesar, he saw a fearful apparition, which is commonly related by Histories as a Vision: but considering the circumstances, one may easily judge to have been but a short Dream. For sitting in his tent, pensive and troubled with the horror of his rash act, it was not hard for him, slumbering in the cold, to dream of that which most affrighted him: which fear, as by degrees it made him wake: so also it must needs make the Apparition by degrees to vanish: and having no assurance that he slept, he could have no cause to think it a Dream, or any thing but a Vision. And this is no very rare accident: for even they that be perfectly awake, if they be timorous, and superstitious, possessed with fearful tales, and alone in the dark, are subject to the like fancies; and believe they see spirits and dead men's ghosts walking in the Churchyards; whereas it is either their Fancy only, or else the knavery of such persons, as make use of such superstitious fear, to pass disguised in the night to places they would not be known to haunt.

From this ignorance of how to distinguish Dreams, and other strong Fancies, from Vision and Sense, did arise the greatest part of the Religion of the Gentiles in time past, that worshipped Satyres, Fawnes, Nymphs, and the like; and nowadays the opinion that rude people have of Fairies, Ghosts and Goblins; of the power of Witches. . . . Nevertheless, there is no doubt, but God can make unnatural apparitions. But that he does it so often, as men need to fear such things, more than they fear the stay, or change, of the course of Nature, which he also can stay, and change, is no point of Christian Faith.

[*Circa* 1650]

Dreams Caused by Sense Stimulation

WILHELM WUNDT, M.D.

Translated by Charles H. Judd

The ideas which arise in dreams come, at least to a great extent, from sensations, especially from those of the general sense, and are therefore mostly illusions of fancy, probably only seldom pure memory ideas which hence become hallucinations. The decrease of apperceptive combinations in comparison with associations, is also striking and goes to explain the frequent modifications and exchanges of self-consciousness, the confusion of the judgment, etc. The characteristics of dreams which distinguish them from other similar psychical states, are to be found, not so much in these positive attributes, as in certain negative attributes. The increase of excitability is limited entirely to the *sensory* functions, the external volitional activity being completely inhibited in ordinary sleep and dreams. When the fanciful ideas of dreams are connected with corresponding volitional acts, we have the very infrequent phenomena of *sleepwalking,* which are related to certains forms of hypnosis. Motor concomitants are generally limited to articulations, and appear as talking in dreams. . . .

Sleep, dreams and hypnosis are, in all probability, essentially the same in their psycho-physical conditions. These conditions consist in the specially modified dispositions to sensations and volitional reactions, and can, therefore, like all such dispositions, be explained on their physiological side only by assuming changes in the activity of certain central regions. These changes have not yet been investigated directly. Still, we may assume from the psychological symptoms that the physiological conditions consist, as a rule, in the inhibition of activity in the regions connected with processes of volition, and apperception, and in increased excitability of the sensory centers.

It is, then, strictly speaking, a physiological problem to formulate a theory of sleep, dreams and hypnosis. . . .

Dreams and hypnosis are often made the subject of mystical and fanciful hypotheses, in some cases even by psychologists. We hear of increased mental activity in dreams and of influence of mind on minds at distance in dreams and by hypnosis. Especially hypnotism has been used in this way, to support superstitious spiritualistic ideas. In connection with "animal magnetism," which may be completely explained by the theory of hypnosis and suggestion, and in connection with "somnambulism," there are a great many cases of self-deception and intentional humbug. In reality all that can stand the light of thorough examination in these phenomena is in general readily explicable on psychological and physiological grounds; what is not explicable in this way has always proved on closer examination to be superstitious self-deception or intentional fraud.

[1896]

Dreams Caused by Retinal Excitement

GEORGE TRUMBULL LADD

Let me briefly describe the method of my very simple experiments. To appreciate them it must be remarked that the retina of my eyes are probably somewhat unusually sensitive to excitement from intra-organic and cerebral stimulation. I have found by inquiry that a large proportion of persons unaccustomed to observe themselves for purposes of scientific discovery are entirely unacquainted with the phenomena of retinal *Eigenlicht*. Ask them what they customarily see when their eyes are closed in a dark room and they will reply that they see nothing. Ask them to observe more carefully and describe what they see, and they will probably speak of a black mass or wall before their eyes, with a great multitude of yellow spots dancing about on its surface. Some few will finally come to a recognition of the experience with which I have long been familiar in my own case. By far the purest, most brilliant, and most beautiful colors I have ever seen, and the most astonishing artistic combinations of such colors, have appeared with closed eyes in a dark room. I have never been subject to waking visual hallucinations, but I verily believe there is nothing I hope to have known to me by perception or fancy, whether of things on earth or above the earth or in the water, that has not been schematically represented by the changing retinal images under the influence of intra-organic stimulation. And as Müller, Maury and others have noticed, any form of unusual cerebral excitement is conducive to very lively activity among the retinal phantasies.

Equipped, then, with the instrument of such a psycho-physical mechanism for the production of visual images, I have been accustomed to experiment in the following way: I "set" this mechanism so that it will dip down into sleep and dream-life, with a gradual curvature, as it were, and then come out of dream-life in an instant; *i.e.*, by a steep curve. When I wake in this way, I am ready to do two things pretty nearly simultaneously —namely, to retain in mind the visual images of the dream from which I am awaking, and also without opening my eyes (which would, of course, spoil the experiment) to note in terms of objective waking consciousness the schematic phantasms which are fading from the retina. Thus a comparison between the phantasm, as objectively observed and localized in the retinal field, and the visual images of the dream, as detained and remembered for a brief time, becomes possible. To set the psycho-physical mechanism of sleep so that it shall run down, and I awake from it within two to five minutes after falling asleep is much easier for me than to set it so as to wake at any given hour in the early morning. Indeed, the latter I find it difficult or impossible to do with much approach to accuracy. I am therefore inclined to think that with a little effort and practice many will find themselves able to perform upon themselves my simple experiments.

It will be observed that the method I have employed, when it is successful, actually catches the retinal schemata as they are vanishing from the retinal field, and then compares them with the visual images they have already produced. The method employed by Maury watches these schemata as they are engaged in the process of producing visual dream-images. I arrest the impish phantasms before they can get off the stage of my dream. I see clearly what they have been doing. Maury arrests them rather while they are coming upon this stage, and endeavors to catch them in the act of beginning their dramatic transformations. It seems to me that my method is preferable; especially since, when it succeeds, it conducts the crucial part of the experiment under the eye of a clear objective waking consciousness.

By this method of experiment, then, I have established as good in my own case, the following conclusions:

The visual "stuff" of those dreams which occur soon after falling asleep is largely, if not wholly, due to excitement of the retina by intra-organic stimulation. These dreams, as respects their origin, are thus distinguished from those which occur under ordinary circumstances in the morning hours. The latter are oftener due to external stimulation—*i.e.*, to the rays of light penetrating to the retina through the closed eyelids. But inasmuch as the sleep of many persons during several hours of the night is a succession of naps interrupted by more or less partial awaking, both the retina and the visual centers of the brain may prove sources of origin for visual dreams.

Those visual dreams, however, which follow almost immediately on going to sleep in a dark room originate, wholly or chiefly, in the *Eigenlicht* of the retina. The vital action of the retina (and hence the variety and rapid movement and wonderful transformation of the retinal schemata) diminishes rapidly with the duration of sleep. The dreams into which the retinal phantasm have woven themselves are forgotten beyond recovering before the morning hours. Hence the visual dream-images which are remembered on awaking, will be more likely to be derived from external stimulation. . . .

Almost without exception, when I am able to recall the visual images of my dreams and to observe the characters of the retinal field quickly enough to compare the two, the schemata of the luminous and colored retinal phantasms afford the undoubted clue to the origin of the things just seen in my dream-life. This is emphatically true whenever the imagery of the dream is purely imaginative rather than accompanied by memory and recognition. . . .

The most elaborate visual dreams may originate in intra-organic retinal excitement. Perhaps a harder problem could not be given to my experiments to solve than the following:

How can one be made by such excitement to see a printed page of words clearly spread out before one in a dream? How can so orderly a visual phenomenon owe its origin to chance arrangements of the "retinal dust"? But I have several times verily caught my dreaming automaton in the feat of having just performed this transformation. On waking from a dream, in which I had distinctly seen lines of printed letters forming words and sentences and had been engaged in reading these lines by sight, I have clearly detected the character of that retinal field which had originated such an extraordinary hallucination. The minute light and dark spots which the activity of the rods and cones occasion, had arranged themselves in parallel lines extending across the retinal field. In other words, the clearly printed page which I was reading in my dream faded into an object that appeared to my waking consciousness like a section of an actual page of print when seen through an oval hole in a piece of paper at too great a distance to distinguish more than an occasional fragment of a word, and even that dimly.

If the superior psycho-physical mechanism of vision can in dream-life seize upon what is really nothing but rows of meaningless blackish spots upon the retina and can convert them into imagined pages of print which may be read with great satisfaction offhand in a dream, what is it not capable of achieving?

[1892]

Producing Dreams by Whispering

JOHN ABERCROMBIE, M.D.

There are remarkable cases in which, in particular individuals, dreams can be produced by whispering into their ears when they are asleep. One of the most curious as well as authentic examples of this kind has been referred to by several writers. I find the particulars in the papers of Dr. Gregory, and they were related to him by a gentleman who witnessed them. The subject of it was an officer in the expedition to Louisburg in 1758, who had this peculiarity in so remarkable a degree that his companions in the transport were in the constant habit of amusing themselves at his expense. They could produce in him any kind of dream by whispering into his ear, especially if this was done by a friend with whose voice he was familiar. At one time they conducted him through the whole process of a quarrel, which ended in a duel; and when the parties were supposed to be met, a pistol was put into his hand, which he fired, and was awakened by the report. On another occasion they found him asleep on the top of a locker or bunker in the cabin, when they made him believe he had fallen overboard, and exhorted him to save himself by swimming. He immediately imitated all the motions of swimming. They then told him that a shark was pursuing him, and entreated him to dive for his life. He instantly did so with such force as to throw himself entirely from the locker upon the cabin floor, by which he was much bruised, and awakened of course. After the landing of the Army at Louisburg, his friends found him one day asleep in his tent, and evidently much annoyed by the cannonading. They then made him believe that he was engaged, when he expressed great fear, and showed an evident disposition to run away. Against this they remonstrated, but at the same time increased his fears by imitating the groans of the wounded and the dying; and when he asked, as he often did, who was down, they named his particular friends. At last they told him that the man next himself in the line had fallen, when he instantly sprang from his bed, rushed out of the tent, and was roused from his danger and his dream together by falling over the tent-ropes. A remarkable circumstance in this case was, that after these experiences he had no distinct recollection of his dreams, but only a confused feeling of oppression or fatigue, and used to tell his friends that he was sure they had been playing some trick upon him.

[*Circa* 1830]

F. THE PSYCHIATRIC BREAKTHROUGH

Dreams Are the Royal Road to the Unconscious Mind

SIGMUND FREUD, M.D.

Translated by James Strachey

THE INTERPRETATION *of dreams is the royal road to a knowledge of the unconscious activities of the mind....*
Every attempt that has hitherto been made to solve the problem of dreams has dealt directly with their *manifest* content as it is presented in our memory. All such attempts have endeavoured to arrive at an interpretation of dreams from their manifest content or (if no interpretation was attempted) to form a judgement as to their nature on the basis of that same manifest content. We are alone in taking something else into account. We have introduced a new class of psychical material between the manifest content of dreams and the conclusions of our enquiry: namely, their *latent* content, or (as we say) the "dream-thoughts," arrived at by means of our procedure. It is from these dream-thoughts and not from a dream's manifest content that we disentangle its meaning. We are thus presented with a new task which had no previous existence: the task, that is, of investigating the relations between the manifest content of the dreams and the latent dream-thoughts, and of tracing out the processes by which the latter have been changed into the former....
Dreams are not to be likened to the unregulated sounds that rise from a musical instrument struck by the blow of some external force instead of by a player's hand; they are not meaningless, they are not absurd; they do not imply that one portion of our store of ideas is asleep while another portion is beginning to wake. On the contrary, they are psychical phenomena of complete validity—fulfillments of wishes; they can be inserted

into the chain of intelligible waking mental acts; they are constructed by a highly complicated activity of the mind.

But no sooner have we begun to rejoice at this discovery than we are assailed by a flood of questions. If, as we are told by dream-interpretation, a dream represents a fulfilled wish, what is the origin of the remarkable and puzzling form in which the wish-fulfillment is expressed? What alteration have the dream-thoughts undergone before being changed into the manifest dream which we remember when we wake up? How does that alteration take place? What is the source of the material that has been modified into the dream? What is the source of the many peculiarities that are to be observed in the dream-thoughts—such, for instance, as the fact that they may be mutually contradictory? . . . Can a dream tell us anything new about our internal psychical processes? Can its content correct opinions we have held during the day? . . .

It is easy to prove that dreams often reveal themselves without any disguise as fulfillments of wishes; so that it may seem surprising that the language of dreams was not understood long ago. For instance, there is a dream that I can produce in myself as often as I like—experimentally, as it were. If I eat anchovies or olives or any other highly salted food in the evening, I develop thirst during the night which wakes me up. But my waking is preceded by a dream; and this always has the same content, namely, that I am drinking. I dream I am swallowing down water in great gulps, and it has the delicious taste that nothing can equal but a cool drink when one is parched with thirst. Then I wake up and have to have a real drink. This simple dream is occasioned by the thirst which I become aware of when I wake. The thirst gives rise to a wish to drink, and the dream shows me that wish fulfilled. In doing so it is performing a function —which it was easy to divine. I am a good sleeper and not accustomed to be woken by any physical need. If I can succeed in appeasing my thirst by *dreaming* that I am drinking, then I need not wake up in order to quench it. This, then, is a dream of convenience. . . .

Here is another dream in which once again the stimulus produced its effect during actual sleep. One of my women patients, who had been obliged to undergo an operation on her jaw which had taken an unfavourable course, was ordered by her doctors to wear a cooling apparatus on the side of her face day and night. But as soon as she fell asleep she used to throw it off. One day, after she had once more thrown the apparatus on the floor, I was asked to speak to her seriously about it. "This time I really couldn't help it," she answered. "It was because of a dream I had in the night. I dreamt I was in a box at the opera and very much enjoying the performance. But Herr Karl Meyer was in the nursing-home and complaining bitterly of pains in his jaw. So I told myself that as I hadn't any pain I didn't need the apparatus; and I threw it away." The dream of this poor sufferer seems almost like a concrete representation of a phrase that sometimes forces its way on to people's lips in unpleasant situations: "I must say I could think of something more agreeable than this." The dream gives a picture of this more agreeable thing. The Herr Karl Meyer on to whom the dreamer transplanted her pains was the most indifferent young man of her acquaintance that she could call to mind.

The wish-fulfillment can be detected equally easily in some other dreams which I have collected from normal people. A friend of mine, who knows my theory of dreams and has told his wife of it, said to me one day: "My wife has asked me to tell you that she had a dream yesterday that she was having her period. You can guess what that means." I could indeed guess it. The fact that this young married woman dreamt that she was having her period meant that she had missed her period. I could well believe that she would have been glad to go on enjoying her freedom a little longer before shouldering the burden of motherhood. It was a neat way of announcing her first pregnancy. Another friend of mine wrote and told me that, not long before, his wife had dreamt that she had noticed some milk stains on the front of her vest. This too was an announcement of pregnancy, but not of a first one. The young mother was wishing that she might have more nourishment to give her second child than she had had for her first.

A young woman had been cut off from society for weeks on end while she nursed her child through an infectious illness. After the child's recovery, she had a dream of being at a party at which, among others, she met Alphonse Daudet, Paul Bourget, and Marcel Prévost; they were all most affable to her and highly amusing. All of the authors resembled their portraits, except Marcel Prévost, of whom she had never seen a picture; and he looked like . . . the disinfection officer who had fumigated the sick-room the day before and who had been her first visitor for so long. Thus it seems possible to give a complete translation of the dream: "It's about time for something more amusing than this perpetual sick-nursing."

These examples will perhaps be enough to show that dreams which can only be understood as fulfillments of wishes and which bear their meaning upon their faces without disguise are to be found under the most frequent and various conditions. . . .

If I proceed to put forward the assertion that the meaning of *every* dream is the fulfillment of a wish, that is to say that there cannot be any dreams but wishful dreams, I feel certain in advance that I shall meet with the most categorical contradiction. . . . Indeed two ladies, Florence Hallam and Sarah Weed, have actually given statistical expression, based on a study of their own dreams, to the preponderance of unpleasure in dreaming. They find that 57.2 per cent of dreams are "disagreeable" and only 28.6 per cent positively "pleasant." And apart from these dreams, which carry over into sleep the various distressing emotions of life, there are anxiety dreams, in which that most dreadful of all unpleasurable feelings holds us in its grasp till we awaken. . . .

It does in fact look as though anxiety-dreams make it impossible to assert as a general proposition (based on the examples quoted in my last chapter) that dreams are wish-fulfillments; indeed they seem to stamp any such proposition as an absurdity.

Nevertheless, there is no great difficulty in meeting these apparently conclusive objections. It is only necessary to take notice of the fact that my theory is not based on a consideration of the manifest content of dreams but refers to the thoughts which are shown by the work of interpretation to lie behind dreams. We must make a contrast between the *manifest* and the *latent* content of dreams. There is no question that there are dreams whose manifest content is of the most distressing kind. But has anyone tried to interpret such dreams? to reveal the latent thoughts behind them? If not, then the two objections raised against my theory will not hold water: it still remains possible that distressing dreams and anxiety dreams, when they have been interpreted, may turn out to be fulfillments of wishes. . . .

In cases where the wish-fulfillment is unrecognizable, where it has been disguised, there must have existed some inclination to put up a defence against the wish; and owing to this defence the wish was unable to express itself except in a distorted shape. . . .

A similar difficulty confronts the political writer who has disagreeable truths to tell to those in authority. If he presents them undisguised, the authorities will suppress his words—after they have been spoken, if his pronouncement was an oral one, but beforehand, if he had intended to make it in print. A writer must beware of the censorship, and on its account he must soften and distort the expression of his opinion. According to the strength and sensitiveness of the censorship he finds himself compelled either merely to refrain from certain forms of attack, or to speak in allusions in place of direct references, or he must conceal his objectionable pronouncement beneath some apparently innocent disguise: for instance, he may describe a dispute between two Mandarins in the Middle Kingdom, when the people he really has in mind are officials in his own country. The stricter the censorship, the more far-reaching will be the disguise and the more ingenious too may be the means employed for putting the reader on the scent of the true meaning.

The fact that the phenomena of censorship and of dream-distortion correspond down to their smallest details justifies us in presuming that they are similarly determined. We may therefore suppose that dreams are given their shape in individual human beings by the operation of two psychical forces (or we may describe them as currents or systems); and that one of these forces constructs the wish which is expressed by the dream, while the other exercises a censorship upon this dream-wish and, by the use of that censorship, forcibly brings about a distortion in the expression of the wish. It remains to enquire as to the nature of the power enjoyed by this second agency which enables it to exercise its censorship.

When we bear in mind that the latent dream-thoughts are not conscious before an analysis has been carried out, whereas the manifest content of the dream is consciously remembered, it seems plausible to suppose that the privilege enjoyed by the second agency is that of permitting thoughts to enter consciousness. Nothing, it would seem, can reach consciousness from the first system without passing the second agency; and the second agency allows nothing to pass without exercising its rights and making such modifications as it thinks fit in the thought which is seeking admission to consciousness. . . .

The more one is concerned with the solution of dreams, the more one is driven to recognize that the majority of the dreams of adults deal with sexual material and give expression to erotic wishes. A judgement on this point can be formed only by those who really analyze dreams, that is to say, who make their way through their manifest content to the latent dream-thoughts, and never by those who are satisfied with making a note of the manifest content alone. . . . Let me say at once that this fact is not in the least surprising but is in complete harmony with the principles of my explanation of dreams. No other instinct has been subjected since childhood to so much suppression as the sexual instinct with its numerous components . . . from no other instinct are so many and such powerful unconscious wishes left over, ready to produce dreams in a state of sleep. In interpreting dreams we should never forget the significance of sexual complexes, though we should also, of course, avoid the exaggeration of attributing exclusive importance to them.

We can assert of many dreams, if they are carefully interpreted, that they are bisexual, since they unquestionably admit of an "over-interpretation" in which the dreamer's homosexual impulses are realized—impulses, that is, which are contrary to his normal sexual activities. To maintain, however, as do Stekel and Adler, that *all* dreams are to be interpreted bisexually appears to me to be a generalization which is equally undemonstrable and unplausible and which I am not prepared to support. In particular, I cannot dismiss the obvious fact that there are numerous dreams which satisfy needs other than those which are erotic in the widest sense of the word: dreams of hunger and thirst, dreams of convenience, etc. So, too, such statements as that "the spectre of death is to be found behind every dream" (Stekel), or that "every dream shows an advance from the feminine to the masculine line" (Adler), appear to me to go far beyond anything that can be legitimately maintained in dream-interpretation.

The assertion that all dreams require a sexual interpretation, against which critics rage so incessantly, occurs nowhere in my *Interpretation of Dreams*. It is not to be found in any of the numerous editions of this book and is in obvious contradiction to other views expressed in it.

I have already shown elsewhere that strikingly innocent dreams may embody crudely erotic wishes, and I could confirm this by many new instances. But it is also true that many dreams which appear to be *indifferent* and which one would not regard as in any respect peculiar lead back on analysis to wishful impulses which are unmistakably sexual and often of an unexpected sort. . . .

When I insist to one of my patients on the frequency of Oedipus dreams, in which the dreamer has sexual intercourse with his own mother, he often replies: "I have no recollection of having had any such dream." Immediately afterwards, however, a memory will emerge of some other inconspicuous and indifferent dream, which the patient has dreamt repeatedly. Analysis then shows that this is in fact a dream with the same content— once more an Oedipus dream. I can say with certainty that *disguised* dreams of sexual intercourse with the dreamer's mother are many times more frequent than straightforward ones. . . .

Dreaming is on the whole an example of regression to the dreamer's earliest condition, a revival of his childhood, of the instinctual impulses which dominated it and of the methods of expression which were then available to him. . . . The fact that dreams are hypermnesic and have access to material from childhood has become one of the cornerstones of our teaching. Our theory of dreams regards wishes originating in infancy as the indispensable motive force for the formation of dreams. . . . A dream might be described as *a substitute for an infantile scene modified by being transferred on to a recent experience*. The infantile scene is unable to bring about its own revival and has to be content with returning as a dream. . . .

In every dream it is possible to find a point of contact with the experiences of the previous day. This view is confirmed by every dream that I look into, whether my own or anyone else's. Bearing this fact in mind, I am able, on occasion, to begin a dream's interpretation by looking for the event of the previous day which set it in motion; in many instances, indeed, this is the easiest method. . . .

Every analysis of a dream shows some recent impression woven into its texture and . . . this recent element is often of the most trivial kind. I may add that . . . the reason why these recent and indifferent elements so frequently find their way into dreams as substitutes for the most ancient of all the dream-thoughts is that they have least to fear from the censorship imposed by resistance. But while the fact that *trivial* elements are preferred is explained by their freedom from censorship, the fact that *recent* elements occur with such regularity points to the existence of a need for transference. Both groups of impressions satisfy the demand of the repressed for material that is still clear of associations—the indifferent ones because they have given no occasion for the formation of many ties, and the recent ones because they have not yet had time to form them. . . .

All dreams are in a sense dreams of convenience: they serve the pur-

pose of prolonging sleep instead of waking up. *Dreams are the* GUARD-
IANS *of sleep and not its disturbers. . . . Thus the wish to sleep . . .
must in every case be reckoned as one of the motives for the formation of
dreams, and every successful dream is a fulfillment of that wish.*

Freud's Theory Modified

WALTER A. STEWART, M.D.

Accepted psychology of dream function and formation states that the
dream serves as the guardian of sleep via hallucinatory wish-fulfillment of
infantile strivings. Since too direct representation of the forbidden wishes
would create anxiety and end in wakening, they must be censored and distorted by the dream work. The stimulus to the dream, the day residue, is
usually some current experience, often of an innocuous nature. Since this
experience has not been worked over in consciousness and is susceptible
to cathexis by unconscious wishes, it is particularly useful as the vehicle
for these wishes.

As a corollary to this formulation, the manifest content was related to
preconscious thoughts and to current events. The day residue was portrayed as the "entrepreneur" of the dream and the manifest content described as a "façade." In contrast, the latent content derived from unconscious sources and infantile experiences and wishes, and was the
"capitalist" in dream formation. The unconscious sources utilized the
day residue in an effort to reach consciousness; the dream work defended
against this via primary process distortions and allowed only derivatives
to emerge in the manifest content. The interpretation of the dream required associations which "undid" the dream work and permitted the
latent dream wish to emerge. These aspects of dream dynamics can be
summarized as follows: A. *One purpose of the dream* is hallucinatory
gratification of forbidden infantile wishes. B. *The manifest content* is
related to: 1, the preconscious; 2, current events (day residue, which
functions as the "entrepreneur"). C. *The latent content* is related to: 1,
the unconscious; 2, childhood experience and fantasies (which function
as the "capitalist"). D. *The dream work* functions to disguise the forbidden wish and therefore permits the hallucinatory fulfilment without
disturbing the sleeper. . . .

Certain dreams seemed to be exceptions to this wish-fulfilling function.
They included punishment dreams, which were only apparent exceptions
since they assuaged the sense of guilt and served the wish for punishment.

The general class of anxiety dreams was easily explained as a failure in the dream work. The opposite to this situation occurred in so-called "dreams from above," where the dream work was totally successful. These were dreams in which no representative of infantile unconscious wishes could be seen in the manifest dream, even via derivatives or in distorted form, nor did it emerge in the associations. The dream work was conceived as having performed its work so well that the essential infantile strivings simply could not be uncovered.

This was the situation until 1920 when Freud, because of his further experience with traumatic dreams and in order to explain the frequent allusions in dreams to painful childhood events, modified his earlier formulation. He wrote, "This would seem to be the place, then, at which to admit for the first time an exception to the proposition that dreams are fulfilments of wishes." Freud continues, "Thus it would seem that the function of dreams, which consists in setting aside any motives that might interrupt sleep, by fulfilling the wishes of the disturbing impulses, is not their *original* function. It would not be possible for them to perform that function until the whole of mental life had accepted the dominance of the pleasure principle. If there is a 'beyond the pleasure principle' it is only consistent to grant there was also a time before the purpose of dreams was the fulfilment of wishes." He then describes the function of those dreams, which are genuine exceptions to the rule that dreams are directed toward "wish-fulfilment," as serving the effort toward mastery of the stimulus. These "genuine exceptions" to the rule have received surprisingly little attention in the literature, possibly because of their rarity in analysis and the fact the truly traumatic dream is less directly useful in the therapeutic effort.

Later Freud again tried to answer "two serious difficulties . . . against the wish-fulfilment theory of dreams . . . people who have experienced a shock . . . are regularly taken back in their dreams into a traumatic situation. . . . What wishful impulse could be satisfied by harking back . . . to . . . distressing traumatic experience?" He answers this paradox in two parts. First, he explains the memories of sexual trauma from childhood which are referred to in dreams as occurring because the dream work succeeds most of the time in "denying the unpleasure by means of distortion and to transforming disappointment into attainment." Second, dealing with traumatic neuroses, Freud explains, "In their case the dreams regularly end in the generation of anxiety. We should not, I think, be afraid to admit that here the function of the dream has failed." In the first explanation, where the traumatic events are from childhood and are represented in the latent dream thoughts, the explanation refers to the success of the dream work. In contrast, the explanation of current traumatic events occurring in the manifest dreams depends on the failure of the dream work. . . .

A further complication to the psychology of dreams is posed by the class of dreams where the manifest dream directly represents infantile sexual strivings and is therefore "openly incestuous, sadistic, or immoral." Freud, when considering this class of dreams, wrote with his usual candor and honesty, "The answer is not easy to come by and may perhaps not seem completely satisfying." He again explains these dreams, which end in anxiety and awakening, in terms of the failure of the dream work, thus fitting the understanding of them into the general explanation of anxiety dreams. Of other, similar dreams which occur without anxiety, he suggests that the ego simply "tolerates" them.

These explanations are questionable in terms of scientific methodology, since by employing the concept of the total success or failure of the dream work no further understanding was required; all possible outcomes could be easily explained or possibly even "explained away." . . .

[There is] another class of dreams, apparently rare, . . . in which the manifest content of the dream portrays large parts or the whole of forgotten and often traumatic events from early childhood. Freud cites a number of dream examples which show the hyperamnesic aspect of dreams, in which a forgotten childhood experience reappears in the manifest content of the dream without modification by the dream work. One example is the dream of a young man who dreamed of seeing his former tutor in bed with his nurse. The young man had no memory of this being an actual event which he had witnessed, but found, on asking his older brother, that the incident had actually occurred as he described it and that he had observed it as a three-year-old. Freud describes this type of dream as "quite unusual" but does not comment further on it.

Another example is reported by Nunberg. He describes the dream of a young woman who dreams she is a child "frantically running along a road looking for someone." The dream, occurring during a threatened separation from the analyst, reproduced the exact setting, recognized by the mother, of the road on which the father left town to come to America when the patient was a child of three. Nunberg describes the dream as a traumatic dream and the function of the dream as an effort toward mastery by reliving the experience over and over. He writes, "The dream represents then the only memory of a forgotten experience, which cannot be remembered in any other way."

These dreams pose a final challenge to the accuracy of relating manifest dream to current events and describing their function as that of the entrepreneur, and of relating the latent content to unconscious infantile sexual strivings and childhood experiences which function as the "capitalist."

An extremely interesting series of dreams illustrating the problem has been described by Horowitz. These were dreams of an adult patient in which the manifest content contained overtly incestuous material and repetitive references to a forgotten childhood experience. At the beginning of treatment the patient reported a dream which had occurred earlier and was one of the causes for seeking treatment. The dream was of her having sexual relations with her father. She awoke in terror and then tried to return to sleep in order to continue the dream. However, she could not sleep because of a frightening fantasy that her mother was outside her room with a gun and would kill her. She had been afraid that the dream meant that she was psychotic.

In other dreams of this patient there were constant references to stairs, not knowing, covering up, the fear of someone knowing, coming home early, being unexpected, hiding things from mother, etc. The recurring references led to the reconstruction of a childhood event in which the patient came home unexpectedly early and discovered her mother in a compromising sexual situation. There is also a recurring and peculiar structure in the manifest content of the dreams in that there are commentary side phrases in most of them. For example, "but I knew he was there"; "but everything looks all right, so it is clear no one will ask questions."

Two aspects are of particular relevance in this fascinating clinical excerpt. First, the manifest content of the dreams contained frankly sexual and often incestuous elements. Second, it is noteworthy that the patient had few associations to the elements in the manifest content of the dream which dealt with the reconstructed childhood experience, nor could specific day residue be discovered which led to the insertion of these elements into the manifest content of the dream. They seemed to be "foreign bodies" inserted into already "unusual dreams" which, possibly based on the transference motivation to communicate, came into the dream in an effort to recall the childhood traumatic event.

DISCUSSION

Problems presented by this and similar dreams require further understanding since they do not fit into our usual formulation of dream psychology. They suggest that we must re-evaluate the role of the dynamic forces which lead to dream formation and the interaction between these forces. . . .

The role of the unconscious wish-fulfilling motive in dream formation is well recognized. The question raised here pertains to the relative importance of another motive which concerns mastery of a trauma. This motive is the one described by Freud as serving the "original function" of the dream. It appears to be more accessible to consciousness and can be related to past as well as present events. In our usual formulation of dream psychology it appears as the day residue dealing with preconscious conflicts of current life and, in its most attenuated form, is represented by the innocuous current experiences often used for this purpose. In the "usual" dream the threat to awakening is represented by instinctual wishes which are then gratified and bound in a distorted hallucinatory fashion.

Clinical experience leads us to call these dreams "usual," since in "civilized society" the availability of food and shelter is generally adequate and immediate threat to life is minimal. However, the frustration of the sexual and aggressive drives, because of taboos and inhibition, is maximal. Therefore, in most dreams the unconscious sexual impulses would be the source of danger and the major potential disturber of sleep. This situation was described by Freud: "Dreaming has taken on the task of bringing back under control of the preconscious the excitation in the Ucs, which has been left free; in so doing it discharges the Ucs excitation, serves it as a safety valve and at the same time preserves the sleep of the preconscious for a small expenditure of waking activity."

In marked contrast to this situation stands the traumatic dream. Here the "original function" of the dream is most apparent. In these dreams the wish-fulfilling function is apparently reduced in dynamic importance and the major function of the dream is a mastery of a past or present traumatic event. It then becomes apparent that these two forces do not for any length of time remain independent of each other. In fact, they are uniquely capable of mutual assistance and soon develop an interdependent, reciprocal relationship. . . .

I suggest that more of the dreams will be understood if we conceive of them as modeled along the lines of the traumatic dream, in the sense that they serve the original function of mastery. Because of the early points of fixation and the arrest in development, the conflicts in severely ill patients are less completely internalized than in the neurotic patient and are represented in terms of the relation of self to object. For example, one patient reported a dream in which she was walking down the street. Everyone was afraid of her because she was radioactive. Since these patients live in a world conceived of as dangerously destructive, each day is filled with frightening and traumatic events, and each day is marked by a preoccupation with the question of survival. The dreams can often be understood in terms of this fear of the outbreak of uncontrolled primitive aggression and the fear of the loss of the sense of identity. The dreams represent an effort to master these primitive fears and, as in the traumatic dream, show a greater dependence on the preconscious component of and the original function of the dream.

Finally, further support to this genetic view of dreaming is suggested by those persons who are grieving over the death of a person they loved. Often these patients express a hope that they will have a dream in which the dead person will appear in the manifest content and are appeased and reassured when this occurs. They seem intuitively to understand the restrictions which the loss and the mental pain has imposed on their freedom to think of the lost object. The dream they wait for, besides giving some magical reassurance, may also be an early signal of this loss of inhibition and the mastery of the painful grief. During the period of mastery, dreams are often forgotten or anxiety provoking. After the appearance in the dream of the dead person dreaming can return to its more usual function and structure.

SUMMARY

A review of Freud's discussion of dream psychology points up his modification of the wish-fulfilling function of the dream. His modification introduced the concept that the original function of the dream was the mastery of traumatic stimuli.

A question is raised and discussed as to the relationship of preconscious and unconscious elements of the dream. Usually we relate manifest content to preconscious source and current life, and latent content to unconscious source and infantile life. Brief clinical examples question these relationships.

In the unusual dreams considered, actual traumatic childhood experiences appear directly in the manifest content of the dream. These dreams were also often openly incestuous. It is suggested that this does not represent a failure of the dream work, but rather a use of unconscious instinctual wishes to defend against the recall of the traumatic childhood experience. This invites a re-evaluation of the role of the forces which lead to dream formation. The preconscious forces represented in the day residue are related to the original function of the dream—that of mastery. A reciprocal relationship between these forces, comparable to the mutual influence between ego and id, is suggested.

The Dream Has a Compensatory Function

C. G. JUNG, M.D.

Translated by Dr. Constance E. Long

An arbitrary translation of the dreams is absolutely inadvisable. That would be a superstitious practice based on the acceptance of well-established symbolic meanings. But there are no fixed symbolic meanings. There are certain symbols that recur frequently, but we are not able to get beyond general statements. For instance, it is quite incorrect to assume that the snake, when it appears in dreams, has a merely phallic meaning; just as incorrect as it is to deny that it may have a phallic meaning in some cases. Every symbol has more than one meaning. I can therefore not admit the correctness of exclusively sexual interpretations, such as appear in some psychoanalytic publications, for my experience has made me regard them as one-sided, and therefore insufficient. As an example of this I will tell you a very simple dream of a young patient of mine. It was as follows: "*I was going up a flight of stairs with my mother and sister. When we reached the top I was told that my sister was soon to have a child.*"

I shall now show you how, on the strength of the hitherto prevailing point of view, this dream may be translated so that it receives a sexual meaning. We know that the incest phantasy plays a prominent part in the life of a neurotic. Hence the picture "with my mother and sister" might be regarded as an allusion in this direction. The "stairs" have a sexual meaning that is supposedly well established; they represent the sexual act, because of the rhythmic climbing of steps. The child that my patient's sister is expecting is nothing but the logical result of these premises. The dream, translated thus, would be a clear fulfilment of infantile desires, which as we know play an important part in Freud's theory of dreams.

Now I have analyzed this with the aid of the following process of reasoning: If I say that the stairs are a symbol for the sexual act, whence do I obtain the right to regard the mother, the sister and the child as concrete, that is, as not symbolic? If, on the strength of the claim that dream pictures are symbolic, I give to certain of these pictures the value of symbols, what right have I to exempt certain other dream parts from this process? If, therefore, I attach symbolic value to the ascent of the stairs, I must also attach a symbolic value to the pictures that represent the mother, the sister, and the child. Therefore I do not translate the dream, but really analyze it. The result was surprising. I will give you the free associations with the separate dream parts, word for word, so that you can form your own opinions concerning the material. I should state in advance that the young man had finished his studies at the university a few months previously; that he found the choice of a profession too difficult to make; that he thereupon became a neurotic. In consequence of this he gave up his work. His neurosis took, among other things, a decidedly homosexual form.

The patient's associations with his mother are as follows: "I have not seen her for a long time, a very long time. I really ought to reproach myself for this. It is wrong of me to neglect her so." "Mother," then stands here for something which is neglected in an inexcusable manner. I said to the patient: "What is that?" And he replied, with considerable embarrassment, "My work."

With his sister he associated as follows: "It is years since I have seen her. I long to see her again. Whenever I think of her I recall the time when I took leave of her. I kissed her with real affection; and at that moment I understood for the first time what love for a woman can mean." It is at once clear to the patient that his sister represents "love for woman."

With the stairs he has this association: "Climbing upwards; getting to the top; making a success of life; being grown up; being great." The child brings him the ideas: "New born; a revival; a regeneration; to become a new man."

One has only to hear this material in order to understand at once that the patient's dream is not so much the fulfilment of infantile desires, as it is the expression of biological duties which he has hitherto neglected because of his infantilism. Biological justice, which is inexorable, sometimes compels the human being to atone in his dreams for the duties which he has neglected in real life.

A careful observer should have no difficulty in discovering that a dream is not entirely severed from the continuity of the conscious, for in almost every dream certain details are found which have their origin in the impressions, thoughts, or states of mind of one of the preceding days, in so far as a certain continuity does exist, albeit a *retrograde* one. But any one keenly interested in the dream problem cannot have failed to observe that a dream has also a *progressive* continuity—if such an expression be permitted—since dreams occasionally exert a remarkable influence upon the conscious mental life, even of persons who cannot be considered superstitious or particularly abnormal. These occasional aftereffects are usually seen in a more or less distinct change in the dreamer's frame of mind.

It is probably in consequence of this loose connection with the conscious contents, that the recollected dream is so extremely unstable. Many dreams baffle all attempts at reproduction, even immediately after waking, others can only be remembered with doubtful accuracy, and comparatively few can be termed really distinct and clearly reproducible. This peculiar reaction with regard to recollection may be understood by considering the characteristics of the various elements combined in a dream. The combination of ideas in dreams is essentially *fantastic*, they are linked together in a sequence which, as a rule, is quite foreign to our current way of thinking, and in striking contrast to the logical sequence of ideas which we consider to be a special characteristic of conscious mental processes.

It is to this characteristic that dreams owe the common epithet of "meaningless." Before pronouncing this verdict, we must reflect that dreams and their chain of ideas are something that *we* do not understand. Such a verdict would therefore be made a projection of our non-comprehension upon its object. But that would not prevent its own peculiar meaning being inherent in a dream.

In spite of the fact that for centuries our endeavor has been made to extract prophetic meaning from dreams, Freud's discovery is practically the first attempt to find their real significance. His work merits the term "scientific" because this investigator has evolved a technique which, not only he, but many other investigators also assert, achieves its object, namely, the understanding of the meaning of the dream. This meaning is not identical with the one to which the manifest dream content makes fragmentary allusion. . . .

A young patient dreams as follows: *I am standing in a strange garden and pluck an apple from a tree. I look about cautiously, to make sure no one sees me.*

The associated dream material is a remembrance of having once, when a boy, plucked a couple of pears surreptitiously from another person's garden.

The feeling of having a bad conscience, which is a prominent feature in the dream, reminds him of a situation which he experienced on the previous day. He met a young lady in the street—a casual acquaintance —and exchanged a few words with her. At that moment a gentleman passed whom he knew, whereupon our patient was suddenly seized with a curious feeling of embarrassment, as if he had done something wrong. He associated the apple with the scene in Paradise, together with the fact that he had never really understood why the eating of the forbidden fruit should have been fraught with such dire consequences for our first parents. This has always made him feel angry; it seemed to him unjust of God, for God had made men as they were, with all their curiosity and greed.

Another association was, that sometimes his father had punished him for certain things in a way that seemed to him incomprehensible. The worst punishment had been bestowed after he had secretly watched girls bathing.

That led up to the confession that he had recently begun a love affair with a housemaid, but had not yet carried it through to a conclusion. On the night before the dream he had had a *rendezvous* with her.

Upon reviewing this material we see that the dream contains a very transparent reference to the incident of the previous day. The connecting associative material shows that the apple episode is palpably meant for an erotic scene. For various other reasons, too, it may be considered extremely probable that this experience of the previous day is still operative even in this dream. In the dream the young man plucks the apple of Paradise, which in reality he has not yet plucked. The remainder of the material associated with the dream is concerned with another experience of the previous day, namely, with the peculiar feeling of a *bad conscience*, which seized the dreamer when he was talking to his casual lady acquaintance; this, again, was connected with the fall of man in Paradise, and finally with an erotic misdemeanor of his childhood, for which his father had punished him severely. All these associations are linked together by the idea of guilt. . . .

I maintain that there exists in the dreamer an unconscious propensity or *tendency to conceive his erotic experiences as guilt.* It is most characteristic that the association with the Fall of Man should ensue, the young man having never really grasped why the punishment should have been so drastic. This association throws light upon the reasons why the dreamer did not think simply, "I am doing what is not right." Obviously he does not *know* that he might condemn his own conduct as morally wrong. This is actually the case. His conscious belief is that his conduct does not matter in the least, morally, as all his friends were acting in the same way; besides, for other reasons too, he is unable to understand why such a fuss should be made about it.

Whether this dream should be considered full, or void, of meaning depends upon a very important question, *viz.*, whether the standpoint of morality, handed down to us through the ages by our forefathers, is held to be full or void of meaning. I do not wish to wander off into a philosophical discussion of this question, but would merely observe that mankind must obviously have had very good reasons for devising this morality, otherwise it would be truly incomprehensible why such restraints should be imposed upon one of man's strongest cravings. If we attach due value to this fact, we are bound to pronounce this dream to be full of meaning, for it reveals to the young man the necessity of facing his erotic conduct boldly from the view point of morality. Even primitive races have in some respects extremely strict legislation concerning sexuality. This fact proves that sexual morality in particular is a not-to-be despised factor in the soul's higher functions, but deserves to be taken fully into account. In this case it should be added, that the young man—influenced by his friends' example—somewhat thoughtlessly let himself be guided exclusively by his erotic cravings, unmindful of the fact that man is a morally responsible being and must perforce submit—voluntarily or involuntarily—to a morality that he himself has created.

In this dream we can discern a compensating function of the unconscious, consisting in the fact that *those thoughts, propensities, and tendencies of a human personality which in conscious life are too seldom recognized, come spontaneously into action in the sleeping state, when to a large extent the conscious process is disconnected.*

Jung on the Collective Unconscious

C. G. JUNG, M.D.

Translated by Stanley M. Dell

The hypothesis of the collective unconscious belongs to the class of ideas that people at first find strange, but soon come to possess and use as familiar conceptions. This has been the case with the general notion of the unconscious. When the philosophic idea of the unconscious, in the form presented chiefly by Carus and von Hartmann, had gone down under the overwhelming wave of materialism and empiricism without leaving any traces of moment, it timidly reappeared in the domain of a medical psychology that shared the aims of natural science.

At first the concept of the unconscious was limited, and denoted the state of subliminal or forgotten contents. Even with Freud, who makes the unconscious—at least metaphorically—take the stage as an active subject, it is really nothing but the gathering place of forgotten and suppressed contents, and has significance as a function only thanks to these. With Freud, accordingly, the unconscious is exclusively of a personal nature, although, on another side, he was aware of its archaic and mythological thought-forms.

A more or less superficial layer of the unconscious is undoubtedly personal. I call it the *personal unconscious*. Yet this personal unconscious appears to rest upon a deeper layer that does not derive from personal experience and achievement but is inborn. This deeper layer I call the *collective unconscious*. I have chosen the term "collective" because this part of the unconscious is not individual, but universal; in contrast to the personal psyche, it has contents and modes of behavior that are more or less the same everywhere and in all individuals. The collective unconscious, so far as we know, is self-identical in all Western men and thus constitutes a psychic foundation, superpersonal in its nature, that is present in everyone of us.

Any kind of psychic existence can be recognized only by the presence of contents that can be made sufficiently conscious for recognition. We can, therefore, speak of an unconscious only in so far as we are able to point out its contents. The contents of the personal unconscious constitute the personal and private side of psychic life. They are chiefly the so-called *feeling-toned complexes*. The contents of the collective unconscious, on the other hand, are the so-called *archetypes*.

The term "archetypes" derives from St. Augustine. . . . For our purposes this designation is appropriate and helpful, for it tells us that with the collective unconscious contents we are dealing with ancient or, better yet, with primordial types—that is to say, with images impressed upon the mind since of old. Primitive tribal lore treats of archetypes that are modified in a particular way. To be sure, these archetypes are no longer contents of the unconscious, but have already changed into conscious formulas that are taught according to tradition, generally in the form of esoteric teaching. This last is a typical mode of expression for the transmission of collective contents originally derived from the unconscious.

Another well-known expression of the archetype is myth and fable.

An Archetypal Dream*

C. G. JUNG, M.D.

Translated by Richard and Clara Winston

This was the dream. I was in a house I did not know, which had two stories. It was "my house." I found myself in the upper story, where there was a kind of salon furnished with fine old pieces in rococo style. On the walls hung a number of precious old paintings. I wondered that this should be my house, and thought, "Not bad." But then it occurred to me that I did not know what the lower floor looked like. Descending the stairs, I reached the ground floor. There everything was much older, and I realized that this part of the house must date from about the fifteenth or sixteenth century. The furnishings were medieval; the floors were of red brick. Everywhere it was rather dark. I went from one room to another, thinking, "Now I really must explore the whole house." I came upon a heavy door, and opened it. Beyond it, I discovered a stone stairway that led down into the cellar. Descending again, I found myself in a beautifully vaulted room which looked exceedingly ancient. Examining the walls, I discovered layers of brick among the ordinary stone blocks, and chips of brick in the mortar. As soon as I saw this I knew that the walls dated from Roman times. My interest by now was intense. I looked more closely at the floor. It was of stone slabs, and in one of these I discovered

---

* From *Memories, Dreams, Reflections.*

a ring. When I pulled it, the stone slab lifted, and again I saw a stairway of narrow stone steps leading down into the depths. These, too, I descended, and entered a low cave cut into the rock. Thick dust lay on the floor, and in the dust were scattered bones and broken pottery, like remains of a primitive culture. I discovered two human skulls, obviously very old and half disintegrated. Then I awoke.

What chiefly interested Freud in this dream were the two skulls. He returned to them repeatedly, and urged me to find a *wish* in connection with them. What did I think about these skulls? And whose were they? I knew perfectly well, of course, what he was driving at: that secret death-wishes were concealed in the dream. "But what does he really expect of me?" I thought to myself. Toward whom would I have death-wishes? I felt violent resistance to any such interpretation. I also had some intimation of what the dream might really mean. But I did not then trust my own judgment, and wanted to hear Freud's opinion. I wanted to learn from him. Therefore I submitted to his intention and said, "My wife and my sister-in-law"—after all, I had to name someone whose death was worth the wishing!

I was newly married at the time and knew perfectly well that there was nothing within myself which pointed to such wishes. But I would not have been able to present to Freud my own ideas on an interpretation of the dream without encountering incomprehension and vehement resistance. I did not feel up to quarreling with him, and I also feared that I might lose his friendship if I insisted on my own point of view. On the other hand, I wanted to know what he would make of my answer, and what his reaction would be if I deceived him by saying something that suited his theories. And so I told him a lie.

I was quite aware that my conduct was not above reproach, but *à la guerre, comme à la guerre!* It would have been impossible for me to afford him any insight into my mental world. The gulf between it and his was too great. In fact Freud seemed greatly relieved by my reply. I saw from this that he was completely helpless in dealing with certain kinds of dreams and had to take refuge in his doctrine. I realized that it was up to me to find out the real meaning of the dream.

It was plain to me that the house represented a kind of image of the psyche—that is to say, of my then state of consciousness, with hitherto unconscious additions. Consciousness was represented by the salon. It had an inhabited atmosphere, in spite of its antiquated style.

The ground floor stood for the first level of the unconscious. The deeper I went, the more alien and the darker the scene became. In the cave, I discovered remains of a primitive culture, that is, the world of the primitive man within myself—a world which can scarcely be reached or illuminated by consciousness. The primitive psyche of man borders on the life of the animal soul, just as the caves of prehistoric times were usually inhabited by animals before men laid claim to them.

During this period I became aware of how keenly I felt the difference between Freud's intellectual attitude and mine. I had grown up in the intensely historical atmosphere of Basel at the end of the nineteenth century, and had acquired, thanks to reading the old philosophers, some knowledge of the history of psychology. When I thought about dreams and the contents of the unconscious, I never did so without making historical comparisons; in my student days I always used Krug's old dictionary of philosophy. I was especially familiar with the writers of the eighteenth and early nineteenth century. Theirs was the world which had formed the atmosphere of my first-story salon. By contrast, I had the impression that Freud's intellectual history began with Büchner, Moleschott, Du Bois-Reymond, and Darwin.

The dream pointed out that there were further reaches to the state of consciousness I have just described: the long uninhabited ground floor in medieval style, then the Roman cellar, and finally the prehistoric cave. These signified past times and passed stages of consciousness.

Certain questions had been much on my mind during the days preceding this dream. They were: On what premises is Freudian psychology founded? To what category of human thought does it belong? What is the relationship of its almost exclusive personalism to general historical assumptions? My dream was giving me the answer. It obviously pointed to the foundations of cultural history—a history of successive layers of consciousness. My dream thus constituted a kind of structural diagram of the human psyche; it postulated something of an altogether *impersonal* nature underlying that psyche. It "clicked," as the English have it—and the dream became for me a guiding image which in the days to come was to be corroborated to an extent I could not at first suspect. It was my first inkling of a collective a priori beneath the personal psyche. This I first took to be the traces of earlier modes of functioning. Later, with increasing experience and on the basis of more reliable knowledge, I recognized them as forms of instinct, that is, as archetypes.

I was never able to agree with Freud that the dream is a "façade" behind which its meaning lies hidden—a meaning already known but maliciously, so to speak, withheld from consciousness. To me dreams are a part of nature, which harbors no intention to deceive, but expresses something as best it can, just as a plant grows or an animal seeks its food as best it can. These forms of life, too, have no wish to deceive our eyes, but we may deceive ourselves because our eyes are shortsighted. Or we hear amiss because our ears are rather deaf—but it is not our ears that wish to deceive us. Long before I met Freud I regarded the unconscious, and dreams, which are its direct exponents, as natural processes to which no arbitrariness can be attributed, and above all no legerdemain. I knew no reasons for the assumption that the tricks of consciousness can be extended to the natural processes of the unconscious. On the contrary, daily experience taught me what intense resistance the unconscious opposes to the tendencies of the conscious mind.

The Dreams of Freud and Jung

CALVIN S. HALL and BILL DOMHOFF

When psychiatric research, normally content to draw on frailer men for its material, approaches one who is among the greatest of the human race, it is not doing so for the reasons so frequently assigned to it by laymen. 'To blacken the radiant and drag the sublime into the dust' is no part of its purpose, and there is no satisfaction for it in narrowing the gulf which separates the perfection of the great from the inadequacy of the objects that are its usual concern. But it cannot help finding worthy of understanding everything that can be recognized in these illustrious models, and it believes there is no one so great as to be disgraced by being subject to the laws which govern both normal and pathological activity with equal cogency.

["Leonardo Da Vinci and a Memory of His Childhood," by Sigmund Freud]

It is hard to imagine two more "illustrious models" in the matter of dream analysis than Freud and Jung. Both men analyzed their own dreams —and, at times, each other's—so it is fitting to demonstrate the usefulness of a new analytic method by applying it to *their* dreams.

What follows is a comparative and quantitative study of the dreams of Freud and Jung as they reported them in their writings. Its main purpose is to demonstrate the value of quantitative content analysis of dreams and to relate the information conveyed by the dreams to known facts about the character and behavior of the two men.

Freud reported 28 dreams in two books, *The Interpretation of Dreams* and *On Dreams*. Jung reported 31, in his autobiographical study, *Memories, Dreams, Reflections*. Although we would like to have had more dreams to work with, previous studies that we have conducted show that as few as 20 dreams reveal significant aspects of a dreamer's personality.

Moreover, the two men's choice of dreams to report might be prejudiced. For example, Freud might have selected dreams favorable to *his* theory, and Jung might have selected dreams favorable to *his* theory. It does seem evident that the two men's reasons for relating their dreams in the first place were quite different. Freud used his own dreams to illustrate various aspects of his dream theory; Jung's purpose was the more personal one of illuminating the nature of his inner life and development. This difference in purpose is evidenced by the books in which the dreams appear. Freud's are published in scientific treatises; Jung's are reported in his autobiography.

In spite of differing purposes, we expected that objective methods of dream analysis would reveal differences between the two men that were congruent with differences in their biographies. We also expected to find many similarities in their dreams. There is, we think, a hard core of universality in the dreams of all human beings, no matter *when* they live, *where* they live, or *how* they live. Each dream was typed on a five by eight card. Freud's 28 dreams and Jung's 31 dreams were shuffled together before they were scored.

One of us (Dr. Hall) did all the scoring, using content scales described in *The Content Analysis of Dreams* by Calvin Hall and Robert Van de Castle. In order to achieve greater accuracy, each dream was scored twice. The dreams were scored for the following variables: length, characters, objects, aggressive and friendly interactions, success and failure, good fortune and misfortune, oral incorporation and oral emphasis, and castration anxiety, castration wish, and penis envy.

To find out what was typical about Freud's and Jung's dreams, their scores were compared with the scores obtained for 500 dreams reported by 100 young American men and, in some cases, with other norms. Although the exact age at which each of Freud's and Jung's dreams occurred is known in only a few cases, it is believed that, with one exception, they were all dreamed during adult life. The exception is a dream Jung reports having had when he was three or four years old.

Here, then, are the results of our investigation into the dreams of Freud and Jung.

The total number of lines in Freud's 28 dream narratives is 286, just a shade more than 10 lines per dream. His longest dream is 34 lines, his shortest is one line. The total number of lines in Jung's 31 dreams is 458, just shy of 15 lines per dream. His longest dream is 51 lines, his shortest is four lines.

This fairly marked difference in average length of dream report is in keeping with the writing styles of the two men. Freud published as much if not more than Jung did, but Freud's style is compact and Jung's discursive. One cannot imagine Freud as the author of Jung's rambling *Memories, Dreams, Reflections*, nor Jung Freud's spare *Autobiographical Study*.

There are certain universal facts about the characters in all dreams. One of them, taken so much for granted that it is rarely commented upon, is that the dreamer is a character in virtually all his own dreams. Freud and Jung are no exceptions: they appear in all their own dreams. (In the Hall-Van de Castle system of content analysis, however, the dreamer is not counted as a character.)

Another universal is that men dream more about men than about women but women dream about equally of the two sexes. Freud and Jung abide by this general rule. They have almost identical sex ratios. The ratio of men to women in Freud's dreams is 2.56 to 1, and in Jung's dreams it is 2.50 to 1. These ratios are somewhat higher than the average ratio for American college men, which is about 2 to 1. It is known, however, that the sex ratio increases with age.

Still another universal is the proportion of single and plural characters. (A plural character is an undifferentiated group or crowd.) The typical proportion is .70 single characters to .30 plural characters. Jung's dreams show exactly that proportion, and Freud's a proportion that is only slightly different, .73 single characters to .27 plurals.

Dreams reported by adults are always peopled by many more adult characters than adolescents, children and babies. The proportion of adults in college men's dreams is .97. Freud's and Jung's proportions are .91 and .93, respectively, which are not significantly different from the norm.

Finally, there is a standard proportion of familiar and unfamiliar characters. A familiar character is a member of the dreamer's family, a relative, a friend or acquaintance, or a prominent person. An unfamiliar character is one who is not known to the dreamer in waking life. In typical dreams of men, .45 of the characters are familiar and .55 are unfamiliar. Freud's proportions are .53 for familiar characters and .47 for unfamiliar characters. Jung's proportions are .57 and .43. This difference between Freud and Jung is not significant, nor is the difference between their proportions and those of the normative group.

Up to this point, the results of the analysis of dream characters merely demonstrate that both Freud and Jung belonged to the male half of the human race. But there are also differences in the dream characters of the two men.

Freud has more characters in his dreams than Jung does, 85 to Jung's 70, although Jung reports more dreams and longer ones. The number of lines per character is 3.4 for Freud and 6.5 for Jung. The density coefficient of people in Freud's dreams is much higher than it is for Jung. Jung's dreams are filled with scenery, architecture and objects rather than with people.

This difference appears to be compatible with what is known about the two men. Freud was a sociable person. He had many close friends and disciples with whom he had very personal relationships. One imagines him surrounded by an entourage wherever he went. Jung was more solitary and kept would-be disciples at a distance. He spent much time in scholarly pursuits, poring over old manuscripts, and he was a lover of nature. Jung said of himself, "Today as then [in childhood] I am a solitary."

A difference in sociability between the two men is indicated by other evidence from their dreams and writings as well. Animals appear more frequently in Jung's dreams than in Freud's, which suggests that Jung identified more closely with the world of nature than with the world of men. He writes in *Memories, Dreams, Reflections,* "I loved all warmblooded animals. . . . Animals were dear and faithful, unchanging and trustworthy. People I now distrusted more than ever." Mystical, fictional and historical figures turn up more often in Jung's dreams than in Freud's. This suggests that Jung lived more in the past whereas Freud lived more in the present. Indeed, Jung said that for years he felt more closely attuned to the past, especially to the Middle Ages and the 18th Century, than to the present.

Jung dreams more about members of his family; Freud dreams more about friends and acquaintances. This implies that Jung's sociability expressed itself within his immediate family, and Freud's social life was centered more outside the family. It is interesting that, although Jung was an only child for nine years and then had only one sister, and Freud grew up in the midst of a large family, both men raised large families of their own. Freud had six children, and Jung had five. Nonetheless, Freud seems to have looked persistently for intimate and even paternal relations outside his family.

A letter written by Freud to Jung is characteristic of this search for intimacy. Here is a passage from the letter, which is reproduced in *Memories, Dreams, Reflections.* "It is remarkable that on the same evening that I formally adopted you as an eldest son, anointing you as my successor and crown prince etc. . . . I therefore don once more my horn-rimmed paternal spectacles and warn my dear son to keep a cool head. . . ." Given Jung's solitariness, his preference for nature and architecture, and his familial concerns, and also given his unsatisfactory relationship with his own father, it is not difficult to imagine how repelled Jung was by Freud's adhesiveness or to believe how quickly the two men went their separate ways.

Here, we think, lies the real secret of their break. After all, Swiss intellectuals such as Oscar Pfister, a Protestant minister, and Ludwig Binswanger, who introduced existentialism and phenomenology into psychiatry, remained personal friends with Freud despite considerable intellectual differences. But Freud did not try to make sons out of Pfister and Binswanger; and Pfister and Binswanger, unlike Jung, did not have depressive, moody fathers who lost their faith and spent time in mental institutions.

There are 12 classes of objects and a miscellaneous class in the Hall-

Van de Castle system of content analysis. Three of the classes—architecture, implements and body parts—have subclasses. There are many more objects in Jung's dreams than in Freud's, 297 versus 196. This suggests, as does the larger number of human characters in Freud's dreams, that Jung was more object-oriented and Freud was more person-oriented.

Further support is given to this statement by the kinds of objects each man dreamed about. Jung dreamed more about houses, buildings and architectural details—especially windows, doors and walls—and more about nature and landscape than either Freud or the norm group did. Freud, on the other hand, dreamed much more about parts of the body, particularly parts of the head, than either Jung or the norm group did.

It is interesting to speculate on the symbolic meaning of these differences. If architecture and nature are female symbols, for the most part, and if body parts, especially the head, are displacements of the male genitals, then it could be inferred that Jung was more oriented toward the female and Freud was more oriented toward the male. This inference ties in with other data to be presented below.

Jung's dreams contain no references to money, whereas Freud dreams of money about as often as the norm group. Freud also refers more often than Jung to food, a fact which will be commented on later. Both men seldom mention implements, especially weapons and recreational equipment, which is probably not surprising considering that they were intellectuals and scholars.

In Freud's dreams, there are 16 aggressive and 16 friendly interactions; in Jung's dreams, 14 and 11, respectively. When these figures are divided by the number of characters, the proportions are much the same for Freud and Jung. Moreover, they are in close accord with the proportions for male dreamers between the ages of 30 and 80.

Other universal characteristics of Freud's and Jung's dreams are the large proportion of dreamer-involved aggression and friendliness as compared with witnessed aggression and friendliness, and the equal number of times that the dreamer is aggressor and victim.

With regard to the role of befriender and befriended, however, the two men are poles apart. Every time Jung is involved in a friendly interaction, he initiates the friendliness. Freud, on the other hand, is more often the recipient of friendliness (eight out of 11 times). The norm is midway between the figures for Freud and Jung. Does this signify that Freud wanted people to respond to him in a friendly manner and was sensitive about being rejected? It does seem that Freud was sensitive about being slighted: for example, his feelings were hurt that Jung did not make an effort to visit him when Freud made a trip to Switzerland. And Freud's biographer, Ernest Jones, says that Freud became quite annoyed when friends to whom he had written did not reply at once.

Another indication of Jung's greater social autonomy is that, when we consider only the dreams in which aggression of friendliness occurs (and not the total number of aggressive and friendly encounters in all the dreams), Freud has almost twice as many "interactional" dreams as Jung has. Freud's frequency agrees with the norm. In other words, Jung has fewer dreams in which he interacts in significant ways with other characters than does Freud.

By far the most interesting finding with respect to aggression and friendliness, however, is the striking difference in Freud's and Jung's aggressive and friendly encounters with male and female characters. The typical man has more aggressive interactions with men than with women, and more friendly interactions with women than with men. Jung's aggressive and friendly encounters with men and women are fairly typical. He has an aggressive interaction with about one out of four male characters in his dreams, and none at all with females. As for friendly encounters, Jung has about an equal number with men and women, which deviates slightly from the norm.

In Freud's dreams, the typical pattern is reversed. He has an aggressive encounter with one out of every four *female* characters, and almost none with males. On the other hand, he has many more friendly encounters with men than with women. These results suggest that Freud had an inverted Oedipus complex. The Oedipus complex is characterized by hostility toward other men and friendliness or love toward women. In an inverted Oedipus complex, the tables are turned. There is a friendly attitude toward men and a hostile one toward women. (Freud's pattern of aggression and friendliness with men and women is not like that of the typical woman, who is both more aggressive and friendlier toward men than toward women. Nor is it like the pattern of a group of male patients in a mental hospital, who showed more aggression than friendliness toward both men and women.)

Is there any evidence from his biography that Freud had an inverted Oedipus complex? Many people have concluded after reading Freud that he was hostile toward women. Ernest Jones says that Freud's attitude toward women was "old fashioned": Freud considered that their main function was to serve as "ministering angels to the needs and comforts of men." He thought women "enigmatic" ("What do they want?" he asked Marie Bonaparte); he was attracted to masculine women; he was "quite peculiarly monogamous." Jones says that "the more passionate side of married life subsided with him [Freud] earlier than it does with many men." We assume this means that Freud stopped having intercourse with his wife fairly early in their married life. That he was "quite peculiarly monogamous" suggests that he did not have affairs with other women.

As regards Freud's feelings for men, we know that he had a very intense relationship with Wilhelm Fliess. Freud spoke of overcoming his emotional homosexuality and admitted that alternations of love and hate affected his relationships with men. Jones also speaks of Freud's "mental bisexuality." By using the word "mental" as a qualifier, Jones implies that the bisexuality was never physically expressed. Freud wrote to his friend and colleague, Max Eitingon, "The affection of a group of courageous young men is the most precious gift that psychoanalysis has bestowed upon me." This remark is reminiscent of Michelangelo (whose art Freud greatly admired), who also found joy in being surrounded by young men.

It appears from his dreams, then, that Freud had an inverted Oedipus complex, and what biographical material is available supports this conclusion. Jung, on the other hand, seems to have had a fairly ordinary Oedipus complex, in the sense that hostility toward the father is inevitable. Nothing that is known of Jung's life changes the picture. He says in his autobiography that he felt much closer to his mother than he did to his father. When his father died he immediately assumed the role of father in the household, even to the point of moving into his father's room. Small wonder that Jung did not want to become a son again, least of all the son of a father with an inverted Oedipus complex.

Success and failure in dreams are almost always experienced by the dreamer himself, and this holds true for Freud and Jung. Most men have an equal amount of success and failure in their dreams. So does Jung, but Freud has much more success than failure. In fact, he succeeds six times and only fails once. This suggests that Freud was more strongly motivated to succeed than Jung was. Jones' remark that fame meant very little to Freud does not square with the fairly obvious fact that Freud aspired to greatness.

Jung, on the other hand, though he may have had the same aspiration, did not do many of the things that would have helped him achieve fame. Unlike Freud, he did not found an international organization with its own journals and publishing house. He did not establish a chain of institutes throughout the world to promote his ideas. He did not encourage disciples. He preferred his stone tower to the bustle of the scientific market place. He did not seek worldly success, though he did not refuse it when it knocked at his door. Near the end of his life Jung wrote, "Today I can say it is truly astounding that I have had as much success as has been accorded me." Good fortune in dreams is rare; misfortune is commonplace. Freud and Jung, true to this universal pattern, have more misfortune than good fortune in their dreams. In fact, Freud has no good fortune at all. Jung, however, has more good fortune than is to be expected. Good fortune is defined as something favorable that happens to a person without any effort on his part, and without a friendly intent upon another character's part. Freud's lack of good fortune, taken together with his large amount of success relative to failure, suggests that he saw success as the result of his own efforts, and not as luck. Jung was more likely to view the world, at least in his dreams, as a cornucopia of benefits. The impression one gets from Jung's autobiography is that he was more fatalistic than Freud. He was inclined to let things happen to him, to let his life be lived rather than to live it. His life "developed naturally and by destiny"; he felt that it was ruled by forces over which he had no control, and which (though he spent much of his adult life trying) he did not completely understand. Freud was more rationalistic. By exercising reason, he felt that one could master the world.

It is customary in dreams for misfortune to befall the dreamer more often than other characters. This is the case in Jung's dreams, but the reverse is true for Freud. In his dreams, more misfortune comes to other characters than to himself. If misfortune to the dreamer is interpreted as an expression of self-punishment, then misfortune to others may be interpreted as a disguised expression of hostility. The dreamer intends harm to another person but he does not want to express it directly through an aggressive act. We have not been able to find any biographical substantiation for the high incidence of indirect hostility in Freud's dreams.

We do know from a previous study that having more misfortunes happen to characters other than the dreamer is less usual for men than for women. In this respect, then, Freud's dreams are more like those of women.

Oral incorporation is scored whenever there is mention of food, eating, drinking, cooking, restaurants and the like in the dream report. Oral emphasis consists of references to the mouth and to oral activities other than eating and drinking, as, for example, smoking, singing and so forth. On both scales, Freud scores higher than Jung, whose scores agree with the norms. Freud probably had a lot of orality in his makeup. We know he smoked a large number of cigars. Jones informs us that Freud had a horror of ever having to be dependent upon others—a reaction formation against oral dependence. Freud's orality is also consistent with the fact that he received friendliness in his dreams more often than he initiated it. It is as if he wanted to be taken care of but fought this infantile wish. Orality is also consistent with the relatively high incidence of success and low incidence of good fortune in Freud's dreams. He wanted to achieve success through his own efforts partly in order to deny his underlying need to be dependent.

Orality does not appear to have played much of a role in Jung's life, nor does he seem to have had conflicts about being dependent upon others. On the contrary, Jung preferred to go it alone rather than be dependent on others.

The castration anxiety, castration wish, and penis envy scales reflect different aspects of the castration complex. Castration anxiety is shown in a dream by injury to part of the dreamer's body or damage to one of his possessions. Castration wish is shown when the same thing happens to another character in the dream. Penis envy reveals itself through the dreamer's acquisition of impressive phallic objects such as cars or guns. These three scales have been shown by Hall and Van de Castle to differentiate between male and female dreamers in a way consistent with Freudian theory.

There is little castration anxiety and no penis envy in either Freud's or Jung's dreams. Freud does express a wish to castrate others in a few of his dreams, but it does not exceed the norms. We may conclude that as far as their dreams tell us, neither of the men was unusually afflicted with this basic anxiety.

This completes our survey of some of the scorable features of the dreams of Freud and Jung. The results show, as we thought they would, that the dreams have universal characteristics as well as individual ones. In this instance, the individual traits are the more interesting because the subjects are Freud and Jung.

Our findings suggest that "scores," that is, frequencies and proportions, obtained from counting various elements in reported dreams bear a meaningful relationship to the personality and behavior of the dreamer. This fact not only demonstrates the value of the system of content analysis devised by Hall and Van de Castle. It also shows that there are important continuities between dreams and waking life: our evidence from the dreams of Freud and Jung supports the idea that their dream behavior is congruent with their behavior in waking life. And the dreams shed considerable light on the breakup of their friendship.

These findings are really not very astonishing when one considers that dreaming is as much a form of behavior as anything a person does in waking life. It would be surprising if dreams failed to reflect the same basic wishes and fears that govern waking behavior, since behavior—all behavior, in our opinion—is to a large degree a product of the timeless unconscious. It is the timeless unconscious (Freud's term) that confers a pattern upon a personality and that grinds out the same forms of behavior over and over again, in dreams as in waking life. To the old question, "Am I a butterfly who dreams he is an awake person or a sleeping person who dreams he is a butterfly?" we reply, "It makes no difference." The dream state merely reveals more clearly the wishes and fears that guide our actions in waking life.

Dreams Reveal the Life Style

ALFRED ADLER, M.D.

From the time when I first attempted to solve the problem of dreams, it seemed clear to me that a man who is dreaming is in a worse position to foretell the future than a man who is awake and in more complete possession of his faculties. It seemed clear that dreams would be found, not more intelligent and prophetic than everyday thinking, but more confused and confusing. Yet we must take note of this tradition of mankind, that dreams are somehow connected with the future; and perhaps we shall find it, in some sense, not entirely false. If we look on it in true perspective, it may provide us with the very key which has been missing. We can see already that men have regarded dreams as offering a solution to their problems. We may conclude that the individual's purpose in dreaming is to seek guidance for the future, to seek a solution for his problems. This is very far from committing us to a prophetic view of dreams. We have still to consider what sort of a solution he seeks and where he hopes to get it from. It still seems evident that any solution offered by a dream would be worse than a solution arrived at by common-sense thinking, with the whole situation before us. Indeed, it is not too much to say that in dreaming an individual is hoping to solve his problems in sleep. . . .

If we really discover the purpose of dreams, moreover, we must also be helped to see what purpose it serves to forget dreams or not to understand them.

This was the most vexing problem before me when I started, some quarter of a century ago, to try to find the meaning of dreams. I could see that the dream is not a contradiction to waking life; it must always be in the same line as other movements and expressions of life. If, during the day, we are occupied with striving toward the goal of superiority, we must be occupied with the same problem at night. Every one must dream as if he had a task to fulfill in dreaming, as if he had to strive toward superiority also in his dreams. The dream must be a product of the style of life, and it must help to build up and enforce the style of life.

One consideration helps immediately to make clear the purpose of dreams. We dream, and in the morning we generally forget our dreams. Nothing is left. But is this true? Is nothing left at all? Something remains— we are left with the feelings our dreams have aroused. None of the pictures persist; no understanding of the dream is left—only the feelings which remain behind. The purpose of dreams must be in the feelings they arouse.

The dream is only the means, the instrument, to stir up feelings. The goal of the dream is the feelings it leaves behind. . . .

Our sleep can be undisturbed only if we are free from tension and sure of the solution of our problems. One disturbance of calm and tranquil sleep is dreaming. We can conclude that we dream only if we are not sure of the solution of our problems, only if reality is pressing in on us even in our sleep and offering us difficulties. This is the task of the dream: to meet the difficulties with which we are confronted and to provide a solution. Now we can begin to see in what way our minds will attack problems in our sleep. Since we are not dealing with the whole situation, the problem will appear easier, and the solution offered will demand as little as possible adaptation from our own side. The purpose of the dream will be to support and back the style of life, to arouse the feelings suited to it. But why does the style of life need support? What can attack it? It can only be attacked by reality and common sense. The purpose of dreams, therefore, is to support the style of life against the demands of common sense. This gives us an interesting insight. If an individual is confronted by a problem which he does not wish to solve along the lines of common sense, he can confirm his attitude by the feelings which are aroused in his dreams. . . .

But if nothing remains behind from a dream but feelings, what has happened to common sense? Dreaming is the adversary of common sense. We shall probably find that people who do not like to be deluded by their feelings, who prefer to proceed in a scientific way, do not dream often or do not dream at all. Others, who are further away from common sense, do not want to solve their problems by normal and useful means. Common sense is an aspect of co-operation; and people who are badly trained for co-operation dislike common sense. Such people have very frequent dreams. They are anxious that their style of life should conquer and be justified; they wish to avoid the challenge of reality. We must arrive at the conclusion that dreams are an attempt to make a bridge between an individual's style of life and his present problems without making any new demands of the style of life. The style of life is the master of dreams. It will always arouse the feelings that the individual needs. We can find nothing in a dream that we shall not find in all the other symptoms and characteristics of the individual. We would approach problems in the same way whether we dreamed or not; but the dream offers a support and justification for the style of life.

If this be true, we come to a new and most important step in understanding dreams. In dreams we are fooling ourselves. Every dream is an auto-intoxication, self-hypnosis. Its whole purpose is to excite the mood in which we are prepared to meet the situation. We should be able to see in it exactly the same personality that we find in everyday life; but we should see him, as it were, in the workshop of the mind, preparing the feelings which he will utilize during the day. If we are right, we shall be able to see self-deception even in the construction of a dream, in the means which it employs. . . .

On what other means does a dream draw? From the earliest times it has been observed, and in our day Freud has especially emphasized, that dreams are mainly built up out of metaphors and symbols. As one psychologist says, "We are poets in our dreams." Now why does a dream not speak in simple straightforward language instead of in poetry and metaphors? If we speak plainly, without metaphors or symbols, we cannot escape common sense. Metaphors and symbols can be abused. They can combine different meanings; they can say two things at the same time, one of which, perhaps, is quite false. Illogical consequences can be drawn from them. They can be employed to stir up feelings. . . .

The fact that dreams are designed to fool us and intoxicate us accounts for the fact that they are so rarely understood. If we understood our dreams they could not deceive us. They could no longer arouse in us feelings and emotions. We should prefer to proceed in common-sense ways, and we should refuse to follow the promptings of our dreams. If dreams were understood they would lose their purpose. The dream is a bridge between the present real problem and the style of life; but the style of life should need no reinforcement. It should be directly in contact with reality. There are many varieties of dreams and every dream reveals where reinforcement of the style of life is felt to be necessary in view of the particular situation which confronts the individual. It is impossible to interpret symbols and metaphors by formula; for the dream is a creation of the style of life, drawn from the individual's own interpretation of his own peculiar circumstances. If I describe briefly some of the more typical forms of dreams, I am not doing it to provide a rule-of-thumb interpretation; but only to help toward understanding dreams and their meaning.

Many people have experienced dreams of flying. The key to these dreams, as to others, is in the feelings they arouse. They leave behind them a mood of buoyancy and courage. They lead from below to above. They picture the overcoming of difficulties and the striving for the goal of superiority as easy; and they allow us to infer, therefore, a courageous individual, forward looking, and ambitious, who can not get rid of his ambition, even when he is asleep. They involve the problem, "Should I go on or not?"; and the answer suggested is, "There are no obstacles in my way." There are very few people who have not experienced dreams of falling. This is very remarkable; it shows that the human mind is more often occupied with self-preservation and the fear of defeat than with a striving to overcome difficulties. This becomes comprehensible when we remember that our tradition of education is to warn children and put them on their guard. Children are always admonished, "Don't get on the chair! Leave the scissors alone! Keep away from the fire!" They are always being surrounded by fictitious dangers. Of course, there are real dangers too; but to make an individual cowardly will never help him in meeting these dangers.

When people dream frequently that they are paralyzed or that they fail to catch a train the meaning is generally, "I should be glad if this problem would pass by without any need for interference on my part. I must make a detour, I must arrive too late, so that I am not confronted. I must let the train go by." Many people dream of examinations. Sometimes they are astonished to find themselves taking an examination so late in life, or having to pass an examination on a subject in which they have already passed long ago. With some individuals the meaning would be, "You are not prepared to face the problem before you." With others it would mean, "You have passed this examination before and you will pass the test before you at present." One individual's symbols are never the same as another's. What we must consider chiefly in the dream is the mood residue and its coherence with the whole style of life.

Every Dream Is a Confession

WILHELM STEKEL, M.D.

Translated by Eden and Cedar Paul

A knowledge of the *Art* of dream interpretation is of supreme importance to the analyst and the psychotherapeutist of no matter what school. Freud speaks of the dream as "the royal road leading into the unconscious." I like to call it "a signpost which shows the way to the life conflict." It might be regarded as superfluous; surely people know their own life conflict, and are ready to talk about it to all and sundry? Those who think so do not reckon with the fact that our patients are actors who play-act even to themselves. When they tell us their dreams, we become privileged spectators of the drama, and can soon learn to distinguish the false coin. In their works, imaginative writers best reveal their conflicts when they do not know that they are doing so. Similarly every dream is a confession, a resurrection of the suppressed, an outcrop of hidden truth. Hebbel wrote: "Every writer writes his autobiography, and his self-portraiture is most skillful when he is unaware that he is painting his own portrait." This is equally true of the dream. It provides us with fragments of autobiography. Though fragmentary, they are never insignificant.

No dream is unimportant and therefore negligible. If a dream appears unimportant, it is because we do not understand it.

Weeks may elapse before the analyst understands a dream, when its significance has been disclosed by the subsequent course of the analysis. That is why I make every patient keep a dream book, in which the dreams are recorded day by day, or rather night after night. Many patients are rebellious in this matter, but can be placated by being told that the dream book will remain their own property, although the analyst must be allowed to see it at each sitting in order to ascertain what dream motifs are recurrent. This will inform the doctor about the patient's, the dreamer's, dominant aims in life, his leit-motifs.

I often hear of patients who never dream; but so far as my personal experience as an analyst is concerned, such patients are almost unknown to me. Those who never have remembered dreams, learn to do so when properly trained, and produce dreams almost daily. I have known some in whom the desire to remember and record a dream has caused grave disorder of sleep. Those were patients who had made ready pencil and a writing block on the bedside table, that they might record the dream immediately on awaking. In such cases I forbid them to rouse themselves and write down the dream, but nevertheless it is usually possible to get hold of the dream images. . . .

Dreams of which the dreamer says to himself in an interlude of nocturnal wakefulness, "That was a very important dream, and you must not forget to tell the doctor about it tomorrow," are seldom remembered. In such cases the hypocritical self-assurance functions as the guardian of sleep, lulling the patient's conscience as regards his will-to-health by telling him that he has satisfactorily fulfilled his duty to be candid. One important element in the art of dream interpretation is that the analyst should refrain from prematurely communicating his interpretation to the patient. The frictionless course of the analysis may often be hindered by undue activity in this respect. The doctor should remember that the patient must be more ripe for revelation, that a condition of receptivity must be induced. Since the analyst will continually return to the topic of former dreams, will never cling to a single dream but will interpret a series, he will have ample opportunity for communicating his interpretation to the patient as soon as he thinks the apt moment has arrived. . . .

ASSOCIATIONS

There would seem to be no sense in wasting words over the dispute whether the psychotherapist should try to interpret a dream without aid from the dreamer. For my part, I believe myself to have proved, and feel entitled to maintain, that (to take one instance) the death symbolism of the dream would still be unknown if we had always scrupulously waited for the dreamer's "evidential associations." A thoroughly adequate psychoanalyst should be so familiar with the language of the dream that he would be able to understand the meaning of any dream without the dreamer's associations. As yet, unfortunately, we cannot invariably do so; but I look forward to the coming of the day when it will be possible. Even now, as regards most dreams, I am able from the manifest content to draw important inferences as to the secret thoughts of the dreamer, and I hope that in a few years I shall do better still. . . .

One of my patients arrived with a dream and a hundred pages of associations to it he had written before leaving home. The examination of this material took a week, and the result was ludicrously small. The parapath graciously flings the analyst a few fragments, and laughs up his sleeve because he is not unmasked. How seldom are we presented with associations which can effectively unriddle a dream. This is most likely to happen at the first sittings, and when the patient has never been analyzed before. At this stage the patient is not yet master of his craft. Soon, however, he will produce dreams intended to lead the doctor astray, and is so skillful with his association that they give no clue to the latent content of the dream. He may relate dreams which he never dreamed, and disclose memories that are no more than fantasies. Woe to the analyst who accepts all associations as good money.

I have often analyzed the dreams of doctors who were well-informed about analytical matters, and have almost invariably found the associations served to conceal the patient's secret thoughts. Only when I had shown the analysand that I was aware of his devices, did valuable material begin to appear.

Universal (Typical) Dreams

EMIL A. GUTHEIL, M.D.

TYPICAL DREAMS

Typical dreams are dreams which occur with only few variations to most people. There are several groups of typical dreams: (1) tooth dreams; (2) kinesthetic dreams; (a) flying dreams; (b) falling dreams; (3) exhibition dreams; (4) examination dreams; and (5) coming-too-late dreams.

Tooth Dreams

These dreams attracted the attention of men for thousands of years. The first attempts to give them a significance based on scientific interpretation were made by the Greek Artemidoros of Daldos, one of the first writers of a scientific dream book. Because of the time in which he lived he was not yet free from the tendency to consider the dream as a prophetic expression and so he interpreted tooth dreams as having a relation to death.

Even today primitive people are inclined to believe that a dream of teeth falling out is an omen indicating that a relative shall die.

The analysts see the patient's *death wishes* toward his relatives expressed in this way. The appropriateness of this symbolic representation is made clear to us when we consider the fact that a tooth falling out from its place among other teeth leaves an empty place in its group, just as a dying person leaves an empty place in the midst of his family. In both cases a preceding illness is the usual cause of the disappearance.

Other interpretations of a tooth dream are dependent upon the accompanying emotion which has to be reported with the dream by the patient. If extraction of teeth means removal of something rotten and putrid (well-known symbols of the *treatment* and the overcoming of difficulties), then we shall find in the dream a feeling of relief or at least an indifferent reaction by the dreamer. . . .

Masturbation problems, as well as, occasionally, the "castration complex" may be represented by teeth falling out, or being pulled out (in which case the "tooth" symbolizes the genital) and may have an attendant feeling of anxiety. . . .

We find anxiety in dreams of losing teeth, when the symbolism represents the idea of *getting old*. The anxiety in this case is equivalent to the fear of death, or of becoming impotent, ugly, undesirable.

An example of a simple tooth dream follows:

"I dreamed that I broke off one of my upper front teeth. I put my hand into my mouth and pulled the tooth out. I woke up. Emotion indifferent."

The dreamer was a forty-year-old woman who was unhappily married. The "upper front tooth" was her husband. To interpret this dream as a fear of growing old is out of the question because of the indifferent reaction of the patient. The loss of a front tooth means very much to a woman; it is a disfigurement and is fraught with pain. We would have found something of this reaction in the dream. It means less to her to get rid of her husband. . . .

We also sometimes find dreams in which the tooth symbolizes the *female genital* or another opening of the human body, as, for example, the mouth or the anus, particularly in connection with dental operations. In these cases it is not the tooth which matters as a symbol but rather the cavity of the tooth as the object of the therapeutic efforts (boring and drilling).

A male patient whose high degree of latent homosexuality was discovered in analysis and who had a rather feminine attitude toward men, dreamed:

"I was at the dentist's. He put an oblong instrument into my hollow tooth. I felt a strong pain." . . .

Flying Dreams

Almost all modern psychologists have made contributions to the interpretation of this type of dream. Freud has emphasized that the impressions which we retain in our early life of such things as swinging and rocking arouse in us the desire to revive the pleasure of these sensations. He thinks, therefore, that flying dreams help us to re-experience this pleasure. Freud also has emphasized the close connection of the flying dream to the erection in men and coitus fantasies in women.

Stekel saw symbols of death in some flying dreams. According to him, flying means being suspended in the air like angels and ghosts.

Jung is inclined to see in flying dreams the tendency to overcome the difficulties of life, to overcome all gravity pulling us down to the ground.

According to his general conception of the neurosis, Adler considers flying as an expression of our will to dominate, to elevate our own personality over that of others.

People standing under a compulsion, people who are forced to endure certain unhappy circumstances, unhappy marriage, unpleasant job, or the like, experience their desire for freedom in their flying dreams.

To a certain extent each of the above-mentioned interpretations may be correct. For the investigator, it is necessary to be acquainted with all of them and to apply individual interpretations to individual dreams. . . .

Falling Dreams

These dreams occur frequently, and usually are attended by strong anxiety. Falling is a losing of the equilibrium. (To sink slowly and to float, in the dream, usually is to be considered among the flying dreams.) The analyst regards the equilibrium as mental. Thus the "falling" may be interpreted as "loss of temper," "loss of self-control," "yielding," "falling down from the accepted moral standard," etc. Persons who fear the loss of self-control frequently suffer fits of anxiety after dreams of falling.

The loss of the ego consciousness which occurs during the moment of falling asleep may sometimes create such a feeling of fear in the dreamer that he awakens after having had a dream flash similar to the following:

"I am falling down a precipice into an endless depth."

One of my patients perceived the moment of falling asleep (losing the ego consciousness) in his dream as *a candle going out.*

"Falling" in dreams of women may signify intercourse. We speak of "fallen women" meaning "morally fallen."

Dreams in which we see other persons falling are usually the result of unconscious death wishes. . . .

Exhibition Dreams

Freud has observed how often we dream of walking naked in the streets. In his opinion these dreams contain a wish-fulfillment idea based on the infantile exhibitionist tendency. Everyone represses the infantile exhibitionist desire. Therefore, everyone is inclined to indulge in this desire through the medium of the dream.

Another interpretation of this type of dream is that it expresses the dreamer's feeling of guilt or feeling of inferiority. Being naked, he shows his "shortcomings" freely; he can be criticized by people, he has reason to be ashamed of himself, etc. A dream of this kind is the following, dreamed by a twenty-four-year-old student:

"I was on the way to the university. Suddenly I noticed that I was naked. I felt terribly embarrassed and thought of hiding somewhere. Minnie came and gave me her cape."

The patient has a reason to be ashamed. He is suffering from an infantile paraphilia, masochism, in which he craves being humiliated by a woman. If people knew that his serious manner is but a mask hiding a ridiculous infantile fantasy life, they would despise him. Minnie is a friend who plays a great role in his fantasies.

(Q) "Do real exhibitionists dream the same way?"

(A) No. Dreams of real exhibitionists have entirely different contents. Exhibitionism is, as experience teaches, based on the patient's unsatisfied desire to see some tabooed person undressed (scoptophilia). Because of this unsatisfied desire, the patient feels compelled to take active part. In his fantasy he identifies himself with the person who has refused to fulfill his desires. He attempts to do by himself what he really wants to be done to him by the tabooed person. In other words, exhibitionists are, in reality, unconscious "voyeurs." It is this situation and not the exhibition that we find in their dreams. . . .

Examination Dreams

These are frequently had by persons who have already passed the concerned examinations. Freud interprets this type of dream in the following way: "Don't be afraid of tomorrow. Think of the fear you suffered before the examination and, in view of the fact that everything turned out well, see how senseless it was to be afraid."

An examination can also signify the "final" examination as to one's "good" and "bad" deeds, the examination before the Highest Examiner:

"I had to take the final examination in Church Law. I did not know anything and was very much excited."

This dream expresses the patient's feeling of guilt. Since it is the first dream in the treatment, it also shows the patient's resistance toward the examiner, the doctor.

The dreamer is usually unprepared and unsuccessful. He goes through a turmoil of tension and excitement. He has to repeat an examination but has forgotten all the information he had when he first took his examination. He becomes frightened and upset, and sometimes his distress can be relieved only by awakening. And what is his reaction immediately after he awakens? "Am I glad this is over!" "Am I glad that I don't have to take this exam again!"

Examination dreams often occur at the threshold of important decisions, when the dreamer's self-confidence is at stake. For instance, there is the young man who is about to marry and who doubts his success during the wedding night; or someone who has to undertake new responsibilities (a new job), and is uncertain of passing the "test" which life imposes upon him.

In our mental ledger, as a rule, there are items which, as time goes on, we can check off as successes and achievements. Following an examination nightmare one can say to oneself, "The problems with which you are now confronted may be difficult; but don't worry, during your lifetime you have also achieved success." In this way it is possible for the patient to counter his anxieties; the dream "rallies the assets" for the individual to bolster his morale.

Coming-too-Late Dreams

The train is about to leave. The dreamer is afraid he may not make it. The train leads toward a goal. The dreamer is afraid he may not reach it. However, since it is usually a neurotic goal he is trying to attain, his effort is doomed in advance. We are dealing here mostly with neurotic life plans such as incestuous or other antimoral schemes. For instance, a man may develop the idea that some day he will join his sister in an incestuous relationship. Such a life plan may be maintained for many years, although its "coefficient of reality," that is, its chance of fulfillment, is rather low. Neurotic goals of this sort can be found expressed in coming-too-late dreams. The patient always has the feeling that he must be there "before it is too late." Why? Because he secretly realizes that it *is already too late*, that his life plan is futile.

In dreams of this type we sometimes see also signs of resistance to analysis. They are often followed by tardiness at sessions, or sometimes the patients arrive far too early for their appointments and, in this manner, compensate for the original desire not to come at all.

Coming-too-late dreams belong to the category of *frustration dreams*. The latter occur in people who harbor such contrasting desires which neutralize each other and produce zero as a result. The "wish to go" and the "wish not to go" may lead to the dream picture of "not being able" to get there. The goal in such cases is a neurotic one.

In addition to the above, we find coming-too-late dreams in conditions of extreme *fatigue*. They contain a warning that the vital resources of the individual are getting low, and that the effort to find a proper adaptation to the outside world is frustrated by physical exhaustion. This condition, as you know, has been called the "effort syndrome." The dreams of this type are usually accompanied by other frustration dreams, by repetitive patterns and other manifestations of disturbed adaptation. . . .

Dreams in which one is rooted to the ground also belong to typical dreams. A dream of this type is that of *the woman who is pursued by a man. She would like to run away but she is rooted to the ground and cannot help herself except by awakening.*

Two conflicting tendencies are responsible for this reaction. One is to remain and face the forbidden sexual experience, the other is to withdraw. The conflict cannot be solved and, as a last resort, awakening occurs.

Typical dreams, on the whole, do not enlighten us much unless they are connected with other more specific images or with an outspoken emotional reaction.

The Dreamer Lives in a Real World

MEDARD BOSS, M.D.

"Tonight I had a strange dream of an urn," this woman reported to me on the 3rd of August, 1950. "At first I dreamt that I was sitting at the dinner table with my husband and children. The table was in our dining-room, which I had made even more cosy by moving the sideboard. I felt safe and peaceful in this room which was so dear to me. On the walls I could see the really good pictures which my husband loved to collect: in the windows I could see flowers, and in front of me the very attractively set table. On it was a lovely beefsteak with roast potatoes and a juicy lettuce. I can still feel the seductive odour of the roast beef pleasantly tickling my nose, and the mere thought of the delicious juiciness of the lettuce still makes my mouth water. Greedily I took one bite after another, for I was very hungry. I was fully absorbed in eating, and my husband and my children were tucking in as well. 'Do you remember,' I asked my husband a little while later, 'that we had exactly the same menu on the first day of our honeymoon in Cannes?' He confirmed it with a smile, adding, 'It was exactly a year ago.' In the dream I was not in the least disturbed by this ridiculous assertion, and by the fact that our children, five and six years old, were sitting at the table. We had actually been married for ten years. Indeed I was fully convinced that my husband was right, and I replied, 'I feel as if it had only been yesterday.' I then thought quietly of those happy days. At the same time I was grateful for the happiness of today. I looked at my husband and my children, and I felt extremely fond of them and very near to all of them, especially to my eldest son. While he had originally been sitting in his usual place at the opposite corner of the table he was suddenly and strangely transported right next to me. In the dream it did not appear strange that he had suddenly changed places without any movement on his or anybody else's part. It was quite reasonable. Nor did it strike me as peculiar that while I was sitting so happily amongst my family, there suddenly appeared colourful bridges, reminiscent of very bright rainbows. They extended across the table between me and my family. A large and golden urn hovered on these bridges between us, and particularly near my favourite son.

While I was so absolutely happy, I suddenly thought: 'Who knows how long we shall be together? Who knows what the future will hold? Won't the Russians be here shortly?' I imagined how the Russians might suddenly enter our house one night and kill all of us. But just as quickly I thought of turning our garage into a hiding-place. I did all this in such vivid detail that, in my imagination, I could already see a troop of wildly gesticulating soldiers storming the house. And as so often happens in dreams, it was no longer a matter of imagination, but now I could actually see the Russians approaching. However, I immediately pulled myself together and with great effort of will I dispelled all these dark images. I was determined to feel only the happiness of the present and to leave the future to God. Full of eagerness I again turned to my husband and children and began to devise a plan for a drive in the afternoon.

I then awoke, because the maid had been knocking at the door. But for quite some time I did not know where I was. The luncheon table around which all of us had just been chatting so merrily, had been so real and vivid in all its detail, that it confused me utterly to find myself in bed. At first I could not decide which of the two was real: the luncheon which I had just dreamt of, or my bed." . . .

Most dream interpreters would agree that in these nocturnal events and experiences we are dealing with dream images in which certain instinctual drives, strivings, or characteristics of the dreamer find their hallucinatory satisfaction or expression. But does not this unquestioned acceptance of such psychological determination by-pass the phenomena themselves so that they are lost sight of from the very start? Does the viewpoint of psychopathology that dream experiences are a type of hallucination deal with the dream as such, or does it not rather do violence to it from the perspective of waking thought? Who could guarantee that this treatment of dream phenomena is not capricious, or that its validity is proved in the slightest, and that we have not distorted the phenomena, and therefore used quite an inadequate measuring rod? Have we not persuaded ourselves all too readily that the dreamer is no more than a person asleep in whom the dream images can run their course as merely subjective and unreal fantasies or ideas? Can the definition of such a dream as a hallucinatory image mean anything else than the fact that its phenomena are prejudged as mere hallucinations and representations of the corresponding objects of the waking world?

All this tells us nothing about the dream as dream. Indeed, on careful reflection, this definition of dream objects as mere hallucinations is guilty not only of misunderstanding the object to be investigated, but of a double misinterpretation: for, first, to designate the dream object as a hallucination implies that it is a sensory confusion. This is a devaluation of the phenomenon from the standpoint of waking life and does not contribute anything to its elucidation. Secondly, we use this devaluation (which does not even apply to so-called hallucinations) in interpreting the dream. The dream phenomenon itself, however, teaches us unequivocally that the usual talk of unreal hallucinatory dream images by no means does justice to its immediate reality. How often does a dreamer not prize the reality of dream events beyond that of waking experience? The poet Franz Grillparzer, for instance, thought that the waking world compared with a recent dream of his was like a drawing compared with a painting, or a foggy day compared with a sunny one. Our dreamer, too, did not merely see pictures that were only the reproduction of physical reality. Rather she experienced with all her body and soul a world as completely real as she had ever felt during waking life. How else could she have wondered, on waking up, which was the real world: that of the luncheon table in the dream, or her bedroom?

If, then, our dream was no hallucination, neither was it a pure vision of an imperceptible pictorial reality in the sense of Ludwig Klages. Our dreamer was physically and perceptually aware of the glowing green colour of the lettuce, and the odour of the roast tickled her nose most pleasantly. . . .

How did our dreamer in fact experience the room, the time, and the objects and persons of her dream environment, before subsequent evaluation on the part of her waking consciousness and without any theoretical reconstruction? Certainly she did not only see images, but lived in so real a world that her surprise on suddenly awaking reminds us of the poser of Chwang-Tse, which serves as the motto of this book. Let us recall her question, "Am I actually the person who is lying in bed and who just dreamt that she had lunched with her family, or did I in fact fall asleep after luncheon and do I now dream that the maid has just woken me up?" At the very beginning of the dream she experienced being in her dining-room so realistically that, just as in waking life, there can be no question of a mere bare, spatial relationship between her body and the space of the room. The room of her dream was from the very beginning the happily attuned space of her whole existence. She had "housed" herself in the room in a pleasant mood, and had "felt at home" in it. How artificial and false, compared with this immediate dream experience, is the usual division of such a relationship into the two parts of an external and an internal world: into a mere external object in space such as the volume of the room on the one hand, and some quite independent psychic experiences, conditions, and behaviour patterns on the other!

Nor was the object "beefsteak" confronted by her as an object encysted in itself. She tells us rather that she was with it body and soul, and that she felt so attracted by it that she became completely absorbed in eating it, that she as a whole human being was no longer anything but this eating-relationship with the meat. . . .

Were the dream urn and the dream bridge merely symbols and representations in the form of images of her inner subjective disposition? Could not both urn and bridge be considered as objects in themselves? By what right do dream psychologists . . . deny the fact that they are objects in themselves, and interpret them as mere symbols projected by the dreamer's psyche? What if there are no dream symbols at all? . . .

The intense physical experience of the dreamer herself clearly shows that the dream phenomena are neither perceived as images nor as symbols. In our dreams we experience real physical facts: a thing is a real thing, an animal is a real animal, a man is a real man and a ghost is a real ghost. In our dreams we are in just as real a material world as in our waking life and in both cases we express our individuality in our behavior and relationships with the objects and fellow beings around us. . . .

Although interpretations on the objective and subjective levels have undoubted therapeutic effects despite their lack of understanding of the dream, we can expect a cure in a much deeper sense from an understanding of the full meaning of the dream world. For if, in spite of all the rationalist depreciations of waking thought, man learns to respect dream phenomena in their own full reality, then the complete and inherent content of his dream world may reveal to him the actual measure of his life accomplishments. This happens to a far greater extent and much more deeply than is the case when he considers these dream phenomena as mere reproductions of symbols, projections or other "psychic realities" on the part of a subject, or even of a psyche, however highly individuated. Such a cure is dependent on the fact that the analysand either accepts or learns to accept phenomenological dream interpretations, and that existential analysis does not remain a mere intellectual pastime of his but that through it he is enlightened and completely transformed. We can only say that a sufferer has the roots of his suffering torn out when he has proceeded beyond a merely "psychological" or anthropological attitude to things, fellow-beings and to himself, and has been led to the healing experience of belongingness to man and to a new and true relationship with the essence of all things.

Our attempt to preserve dreams as much as possible in their full phenomenal state and to demonstrate them as such has led to the most important recognition that dreams cannot be divorced from man as mere objects, in order to be compared with other man-made objects. We learnt that man when dreaming, no less than when awake, always exists in his relationships with things and with people. We have learnt, indeed, that these relationships go to make up his entire existence. We also learnt that man can realize his existence in dreams, just as in waking life, through the most varied relationships and attitudes.

Are there more possibilities of being related to things and people in the dream than in waking life? Or are there certain possibilities of living which occur exclusively in dreams? In other words, is it the number of possible attitudes which is the essential and not yet adequately formulated difference between waking and dreaming existence? Or could both forms of existence only be distinguished by particular modes of behaviour which are exclusively their own? The answer to these questions will emerge from an examination of all those dreams that we have studied in which a particular relationship between the dreamer and his dream world appears with special clarity. . . .

Our discussion of some dozens of individual dreams has merely been able to strengthen our earlier belief that we cannot consider dreaming and waking as two entirely different spheres. In reality there is no such thing as an independent dream on the one hand, and a separate waking condition on the other, which we could distinguish from each other by their characteristics, as for instance the species "fox" is distinguished from the species "eagle." Any such attempt at a distinction is doomed to failure from the very beginning. For it is always the identical human being who awakens from his dreams and who maintains his identity throughout all his waking and dreaming. What we must realize more clearly at the end of our investigation is the fact that we must recognize the dream as a form of human existing in its own right, just as we call the waking state a particular form of man's life.

Formation and Evaluation of Hypotheses in Dream Interpretation

ERIKA FROMM and THOMAS M. FRENCH

The authors consider dreams to be artistic products of the thinking, groping mind. The dreamer uses simultaneously ideation and more formally organized logical thought in producing the dream, just like the poet or the composer, or the painter do in their creative activities. And dreams, when once fully understood, are fascinating works of beauty.

In order to understand a dream, the interpreter must involve himself open-mindedly in a parallel re-creative, non-schematic process. It is an intuitive activity. But if it is to be more than a hit-or-miss spouting off of the analyst's own brainstorms it requires also scientific self-discipline and the willingness to evaluate critically and conscientiously the ideas and hypotheses one has arrived at intuitively. Only then can the interpreter find out whether his intuitive hypotheses are correct, need modification and/or refinement, or whether they should be discarded because they are wrong.

At the start of a dream interpretation the interpreter is in a situation similar to that of M. Broussard when he came upon the Rosetta Stone. The message of the dream—or parts of it—are written in hieroglyphs (the language of the patient's Unconscious) on a slab of black basalt. It must be translated faithfully into consciously understandable language (the language of the Conscious). How does the interpreter go about this task?

The interpreter should not just decode the "symbols." Like the *good* translator of poetry from a foreign language and culture, who tries faithfully and artistically to recreate in the language of the translation the specific poetic atmosphere and quality of the original poem, so the dream interpreter must also re-create the dream's specific, elusive atmosphere in order to understand it fully and make it meaningful to the patient's conscious mind.

Sometimes the interpreter intuitively grasps the central meaning of a dream. He then must proceed to see whether all the details fit in as parts of the whole—with his hypothesis. (If they do not, he must discard his hypothesis as being wrong, or modify it.) The following dream and its interpretation may serve as an example of an intuitive (re-) creative, correct hypothesis:

A. THE CEMENT DREAM

1. Dream

In the fifteenth analytic hour a 35-year-old male married patient, father of three children, who came to analysis in order to be cured of his neuro-dermatitis, reported that a few nights ago he dreamt he "was mixing cement." That was all.

2. Associations

Immediately upon awakening he felt as if he really knew exactly how to mix cement. But actually, he says, he does not.

He associates in the analytic hour that his house recently needed tuck-pointing; that he was going to do it himself, but did not know how to mix concrete. So, he hired somebody. The patient further associated: "My dear wife went to a bingo game last night." He had to take care of the children, put them to bed, and wait till she got home. Because she went out to play bingo, he came too late to his night job.

Then he talked about a hit-and-run driver who killed a child. The patient "cannot see how people can leave the scene—I couldn't do such a thing."

Later he tells of his wife's accusing him of wanting to get rid of every-thing, not enjoying his family, just tolerating them.

3. Interpretative Process

That the hiring somebody might refer to the analyst whom he had just hired recently to help him with his problems, was easy to figure out (on the basis of parallels). And the dream in connection with the first associa-tion upon awakening stated clearly that "mixing cement" was a "prob-lem" that the patient felt he could not solve alone (again a parallel).

But *what* is the specific problem that the patient wants the analyst to help him with at this time? That is the basic question we had to answer in interpreting this dream.

In order to do so we let our imaginative processes play over the mate-rial. We visualized a house, tuckpointing, cement.

Suddenly it occurred to us that in "tuckpointing" cement is used to *hold the bricks of a house together*. The *function* of tuckpointing is to prevent the house from crumbling apart. . . . Our next thoughts were: A house is a home, a home for a *family*.

In a flash, we felt that now intuitively we may have grasped the central meaning of the dream; and we hypothesized that the patient's problem may be one of holding his family together.

This hypothesis immediately proved to be the key for understanding all the associations as well as the dream:

In all of the associations the patient refers to a wish to be a good family man . . . and a fear that he is not. He asks himself: Am I or am I not a good family man? He wants to be. He says his wife is the one who neglects her duties to the family and acts like a "hit-and-run" driver, he "couldn't do such a thing." But his wife accuses him of "wanting to get rid of" the family, just tolerating them. The dream expresses the patient's hope that in therapy the analyst will help him to hold his family together. The patient dreamt the dream in an *effort to solve* the problem of how to be a good family man. But this problem is expressed in the dream in a de-animated, de-vitalized symbolic form: instead of interacting with his wife and children directly, he "mixes (lifeless) cement."

Rarely are a dream and its associations so concise, short, clear and simple that the dream's total latent meaning can be grasped by the interpreter at once, as a whole with all its constituent subparts.

Usually dreams are too complicated to be encompassed by the interpreter's integrative Ego span right at the beginning of the interpretive process.

This process starts in the majority of the cases with *scanning* of the material (usually followed by letting it "simmer" in the analyst's mind). Like a radar instrument, the interpreter lets his thoughts and feeling processes sweep, in a random fashion, over the patient's dream material, the associations and the preceding hour, until he gets one or more clues.

Listening for clues . . . what are these clues?

There may be parallels in the material of the dream and the associations. Or incongruencies. Or a feeling of empathic resonance within the analyst. Or the interpreter may look first for the general affect of the dream which so often indicates the reactive motive. Or perhaps the totality of the situation in which the patient puts himself in the dream—or with which dream and associations seem to be pervaded—become a first clue to the interpreter.

Perhaps, on the other hand, the interpreter may be struck by strange, curious parts of the dream and get the feeling: this detail must mean something . . . but what? . . .

B. THE ARMY MESS HALL DREAM

In the ninety-eighth hour, the analyst praised the patient whose Cement Dream we discussed above, for having been able to allow himself to become aware of tender feelings towards his wife. The patient expressed pleasure and embarrassment in relation to this compliment at the end of the ninety-ninth hour. The next night the patient had a dream.

1. Dream

I was in the Army again. Went into the mess hall with another guy. Had a little trouble getting food. Then saw a couple of guys I recognized. A Southerner, called "the Colonel"—he was really a private—said: "Sit down, I'll take care of you. I'll serve you like a king, on gold plates." I replied: "Never mind the plates, just get me good food." Then this guy's appearance changed . . . he looked like Jack Benny. He said he was Jack Benny's brother. I said: "Are you related?" Everybody laughed. Then the scene changed. We were both being chased. We were going through a tunnel. I said: "This is ridiculous! If you are Jack Benny's brother and he owns millions, why doesn't he help out?"

2. Associations

The patient associated that he had been close to "the Colonel" in the Army. The "Colonel" had been willing to do quite a bit for him.

The gold plate business seemed odd to the patient. He said he "didn't care for a lot of bullshit, just facts—don't flower it up. Sometimes people will give you a medal and then lay an egg."

He returned to thinking about the "Colonel," and about a lieutenant in the Army (a medical officer) for whom the "Colonel" worked. This doctor was rough. He said the patient was goldbricking, using his dermatitis as an excuse for discharge. The patient denied it. The lieutenant's superior officer overruled the lieutenant and got the patient discharged.

3. Interpretive Process

The manifest content of this dream as a whole at first seems ununderstandable. Perhaps the interpreter is struck by a curious detail of the dream, the "Colonel's" words: "I'll take care of you . . . will serve you on gold plates."

It is incongruous to be served on gold plates in an Army mess hall. The juxtaposition of these two details seemed odd to the patient, too. Obviously they must be an important clue to the latent content of the dream.

The interpreter may make a mental note that an Army mess hall is a stark, uncozy, purely masculine place; a place where men use rough language (see the word bullshit in the associations) in order to hide or disparage sentiments.

Then the interpreter's attention may turn to the patient's next association: "Sometimes people will give you a medal and then lay an egg." A curious association. It sticks out like a sore thumb. To what perceptions, thoughts or feelings could the patient refer by quoting this saying?

As a working hypothesis, the interpreter may begin now to ask himself: does the patient symbolize in the dream the thought that someone who serves him is trying to flatter him? (Serve him—a mere army sergeant—"on gold plates like a king"; "flower it up"; "give a medal.") Who could the flatterer who takes care of him be? The analyst? Very possibly so. The analyst, after all has praised the patient recently about being able to express tender feelings towards his wife.

Now the association "Sometimes people will give you a medal and then lay an egg" falls into place and a part of the dream's puzzle becomes intelligible. The patient is pleased by the analyst's praise, but also intensely embarrassed about his tender feelings; and he fears the analyst's praise will lead to something unpleasant. What this unpleasant consequence is, we don't know yet. Nor can we be *fully* sure at this point that the " 'Colonel' who really was a private" stands for the analyst.

Why does the "Colonel" change into the brother of Jack Benny, i.e., the brother of a famous and rich man? And why is he chased out through a tunnel together with the patient? We could find no answer to these two questions and thus could not understand the last half of the dream until it occurred to us that the young analyst was the Chief Psychiatric Resident at the clinic at which the patient was seen, that he occupied an office next to the office of the Chief Psychiatrist who was a famous man, and that a tunnel connected the Psychiatric Clinic with other parts of the hospital—and led out to the street.

We can now be certain that the " 'Colonel' who really was a private," and whose physiognomy changes so he looks like Jack Benny's brother represents the analyst. What is more, now the total latent dream content forms an organic, intelligible, cognitive whole.

The patient felt pleasure at being warmly praised by the analyst for expressing gentle tenderness towards his wife. But he blusteringly must deny this in the dream because he also feels shame. According to his Teutonic ego ideal, a real he-man should not be tender. Therefore, in the second half of the dream his thoughts turn to depreciating his analyst's importance. ("He said he was Jack Benny's brother. I said: Are you related? Everybody laughed.") Furthermore, the patient fears that the hospital authorities will chase him out of treatment—and the "sissy" analyst with him —if they hear that this resident who takes care of him has "flattered" him for being able to express tenderness. As the patient's masculine pride disapproves of gentle tenderness within himself, so he thinks the men in charge of the hospital must do; and the director of the psychiatric clinic, his resident psychiatrist's big brother, "doesn't help out."

Which method of approach the interpreter will use in solving the riddle of a dream is an intuitive decision.

In some cases the nature of the dream material itself "demands" a particular interpretative approach. In trying to open a heavy, tightly nailed-down wooden case you don't use your finger nails, you use a crow bar—that's what "the thing asks for."

In other cases the manner of approach may be determined by subtle factors residing within the interpreter's own personality structure—and we don't mean counter-transference. Neo-Gestalt theoretical research on perception . . . has shown that, within certain subtle limits, personality characteristics and/or the particular psychic and somatic state a person is in (e.g., hunger) determine whether and how he perceives an objective stimulus or a problem. It is for these reasons that certain clues may immediately be perceived (in a certain context) by one interpreter, and not by another.

Also: on the basis of their own personality structure and their characteristic mode of working, some interpreters may naturally tend to use one interpretive approach rather than another.

Frequently, without necessarily being consciously aware of it, one uses several methods in succession . . . or in combination . . . in the interpretation of one dream.

There is only *one* fully correct Focal Conflict interpretation for every dream . . . but there is not just one road that leads to it. Important is only that one gets there, and is not satisfied with being merely somewhere in the vicinity of the correct understanding.

The question arises now: What makes for failure in dream interpretation?

Failure can be due to the interpreter's unwillingness to evaluate critically his intuitive hunches. It occurs when instead of checking and rechecking for correctness, he deïfies his intuition and allows no doubt about it. If challenged, some analysts will burn at the stake those that advocate scientific controls.

In the more enlightened, less fanatic believer in "pure" intuition, failure to find the Focal Conflict frequently is due to his getting side-tracked on a Sub-Focal Conflict.

Another possible cause of failure may be the interpreter's commitment to an (incorrect) hypothesis he has made at an earlier stage of the interpretative process, and his resistance to letting go of it. . . .

An intuitively made hypothesis is the interpreter's artistic creation. He has a great deal of Ego involvement in it. The *purely* intuitive analyst makes *one* hypothesis. He puts all of his eggs in *one* basket. Naturally, he is not willing to drop it.

The intuitive interpreter with the Scientific Critical Attitude—he who looks for evidence that could prove or disprove his hypothesis and who also looks for possible gaps—is committed to his hypothesis too. But he is *mainly* committed to his hypothesis, *not solely*. Some of his Ego involvement is taken up by the sporty pursuit of proving his own hypothesis wrong or insufficient.

Actually, after his hypothesis has occurred to him he makes two more: (*a*) my hypothesis is correct; and (*b*) it may be wrong; with the major Ego involvement, of course, on (*a*).

Because he is not totally committed to his one artistic-intuitive creation, he has some free-floating "committability" left and is able to evaluate his own creation critically, to let intuitive emphases shift, and to find new solutions if necessary.

Still another cause for failure is the fact that so frequently an important clue to the dream lies right under the interpreter's nose but is not recognized as a clue. Or it is recognized only after a good deal of "simmering," incubating about the dream—and shifting of emphasis for and against certain hypotheses the interpreter has made. The clue has been "camouflaged" as a subpart in the context of another cognitive whole. Suddenly the overlooked clue jumps out of its camouflaged position and stands out by itself (or ties up with another part into a more meaningful whole). And the interpreter asks himself: Why, in Heaven's name, didn't I see that before? . . .

How, in the end, can the interpreter be sure that he has faithfully, i.e., correctly, caught the Focal Conflict and the exact total meaning of a dream?

The answer to this question is: The interpretative hypothesis is correct if it illuminates or explains every bit of the dream text plus every single association given to it as parts of *a total response the dreamer has made to his actual current emotional situation*. Fidelity is measured by the degree to which the interpretation approximates the ideal of such total illumination and explanation.

Two types of checks are possible. One is of scientific nature. The other is an artistic kind of validation which we shall call the Esthetic Experience.

In the process of seeking scientific evidence, the interpreter carefully, minutely, checks and rechecks the material for inconsistencies with his hypothesis. The interpretative hypothesis about the dream is correct, if in the end the interpreter does not need to resort to subsidiary or extraneous side hypotheses to tie up loose ends; and furthermore, if he has been totally honest in his critical evaluation as to whether or not all the material fits in with his hypothesis. . . .

The other evidence for the correctness of an interpretation is a more subjective artistic experience the interpreter has with some—not all—interpretations he makes. This is what we propose to call *the Esthetic Experience*. . . .

What happens in the interpreter—who may be the therapist, or the patient, or preferably both searching together—while he is trying to solve the riddle of the dream?

He has found some clues. Perhaps has brought some or even most of them into a meaningful relationship with each other. But there has remained some part of the material that has defied explanation. Or the whole did not make "real sense" to him. The analyst sits back and "simmers," lets his radar-like, freely suspended attention wander over the dream again.

Suddenly he arrives at a new or modified artistic insight about the dream. And feels: Oh, . . . that's it! That's beautiful! That illuminates the whole meaning of the dream and I now can see it in all its plasticity as the beautiful work of art that it is. He feels exhilarated, excited, joyous, and experiences esthetic pleasure.

Is the Esthetic Experience the interpreter has, real proof that he has arrived at the correct interpretation? Subjectively it certainly feels like it. And frequently it really is. Particularly, if the patient comes to this sudden insight or if the therapist's interpretation "hits home" with the patient and, like a sunburst, illuminates to him too, the dark landscape of his unconscious struggle.

When the interpretation is made in the process of research—from a written record, post hoc, in the absence of the patient—some additional, consensual proof can be gained if the esthetic feeling is experienced by your colleagues when you present to them the patient's dream and your interpretation. We hope you felt it when we gave you the Cement Dream and our interpretation of it. And perhaps some of you felt only what we should like to call the *Hm-hm Erlebnis*. This can be described as the arriving at an insight which proves someone else's hypothesis rather than one's own. It contains insight . . . nodding-agreement insight. But it is not as creative an insight as that experienced . . . in the Esthetic Experience.

Nearly always the Esthetic Experience is subjectively felt by the one who experiences it as pretty strong proof. But it *can* have its pitfalls: The investigator may get so enchanted by it that he fails to finecomb the material for details that might not fit in with his hypothesis. The Esthetic Experience does not necessarily suffice. It always must be followed, at least for check-up purposes, by the process of finding the Scientific Evidence.

Much of what has been said in relation to dream interpretation here perhaps applies to all creative scientific hypothesis formation and evaluation.

G. AN EXPERIMENTAL APPROACH TO DREAMS THROUGH HYPNOSIS AND DRUGS

The Visions Induced by Mescal

SILAS WEIR MITCHELL, M.D.

AT TWELVE NOON of a busy morning I took fully one and one-half drachm of an extract of which each drachm represented one mescal button. . . . At 1 P.M. I took a little over a drachm. . . .

I lay down again at 5.20 P.M., observing that the outer field space seemed smoky. Just at this time, my eyes being closed, I began to see tiny points of light, like stars or fireflies, which came and went in a moment. . . . About 5.40 the star points became many and then I began to observe something like fragments of stained-glass windows. The glass was not very brilliant, but the setting, which was irregular in form, seemed to be made of incessantly flowing sparkles of pale silver, now going here, now there, to and fro, like, as I thought, the inexplicable rush and stay and reflux of the circulation seen through a lense. These window patterns were like fragments coming into view and fading.

Hoping for still better things in the way of color, I went upstairs, lay down in a darkened room and waited. In a few minutes the silver stars were seen again, and later I found that these always preceded any other remarkable visions.

The display which for an enchanted two hours followed was such as I find it hopeless to describe in language which shall convey to others the beauty and splendor of what I saw. . . .

During these two hours I was generally awake. . . . Time passed with little sense for me of its passage. . . . Especially at the close of my experience, I must, I think, have been for a while in the peculiar interval between the waking state and that of sleep—the "praedormitum"—the time when we are apt to dream half-controlled stories. . . .

My first vivid show of mescal color effects came quickly. I saw the stars, and then of a sudden, here and there delicately floating films of color—usually delightful neutral purples and pinks. . . . Then an abrupt rush of countless points of white light swept across the field of view, as if the unseen millions of the Milky Way were to flow a sparkling river before the eyes. In a moment this was over and the field was dark. Then I began to see zigzag lines of very bright colors, like those seen in some megrims. . . .

The tints of intense green and red shifted and altered, and soon were seen no more. Here, again, was the wonderful loveliness of swelling clouds of more vivid colors gone before I could name them and sometimes rising from the lower field, and very swiftly altering in color tones from pale purples and roses to grays, with now and then a bar of level green or orange intense as lightning and as momentary.

When I opened my eyes all was gone at once. Closing them I began after a long interval to see for the first time definite objects associated with colors. The stars sparkled and passed away. A white spear of gray stone grew up to huge height, and became a tall, richly furnished Gothic tower of very elaborate and definite design, with many rather worn statues standing in the doorway or on stone brackets. As I gazed every projecting angle, cornice and even the face of the stones at their joinings were by degree covered or hung with clusters of what seemed to be huge precious stones, but uncut, some being more likes masses of transparent fruit. These were green, purple, red and orange; never clear yellow and never blue. All seemed to possess an interior light, and to give the faintest idea of the perfectly satisfying intensity and purity of these gorgeous color-fruits is quite beyond my power. All the colors I have ever beheld are dull as compared to them.

As I looked, and it lasted long, the tower became of a fine mouse hue, and everywhere the vast pendant masses of emerald green, ruby reds, and orange began to drip a slow rain of colors. All this while nothing was at rest a moment. The balls of color moved tremulously. The tints became dull, and then, at once, past belief vivid; the architectural lines were all active with shifting tints. The figures moving shook the long hanging lines of living light, and then, in an instant, all was dark.

After an endless display of less beautiful marvels I saw that which deeply impressed me. An edge of a huge cliff seemed to project over a gulf of unseen depth and my viewless enchanter set on the brink a huge bird claw of stone. Above, from the stem or leg, hung a fragment of some stuff. This began to unroll and float out to a distance which seemed to me to represent Time as well as immensity of Space. Here were miles of rippled purples, half transparent, and of ineffable beauty. Now and then soft golden clouds floated from these folds, or a great shimmer went over the whole of the rolling purples, and things, like green birds, fell from it, fluttering down into the gulf below. Next, I saw clusters of stones hanging into masses from the claw toes, as it seemed to me miles of them, down far below into the underworld of the black gulf.

This was the most distinct of my visions. Incautiously I opened my eyes, and it was gone. A little later I saw interlaced and numberless hoops in the air all spinning swiftly and all loaded with threaded jewels or with masses of color in long ropes of clustered balls. I began to wonder why I saw no opals, and some minutes after each of these circles, which looked like a boy's hoop, became huge opals; if I should say fluid opals it would best describe what was however like nothing earthly.

I set myself later to seeing if I could conjure figures, for so far I had seen nothing human in form, nor any which seemed alive. I had no luck in this, but a long while after I saw what seemed a shop with apothecaries' bottles, but of such splendor green, red, purple, as are not outside of the pharmacies of fairy land.

On the left wall was pinned by the tail a brown worm of perhaps a hundred feet long. It was slowly rotating, like a catherine wheel, nor did it seem loathly. As it turned, long green and red tentacles fell this way and that. On a bench near by two little dwarfs made, it seemed, of leather, were blowing through long glass pipes of green tint, which seemed to me to be alive, so intensely, vitally green were they. . . .

I was at last conscious of the fact that at moments I was almost asleep, and then wide awake. In one of these magic moments I saw my last vision and the strangest. I heard what appeared to be approaching rhythmical sounds, and then saw a beach, which I knew to be that of Newport. On this, with a great noise, which lasted but a moment, rolled in out of darkness wave on wave. These as they came were liquid splendors, huge and threatening, of wonderfully pure green, or red or deep purple, once only deep orange, and with no trace of foam. These water hills of color broke on the beach with myriads of lights of the same tint as the wave. This lasted some time, and while it did so I got back to more distinct consciousness, and wished the beautiful terror of these huge mounds of color would continue.

A knock at my door caused me to open my eyes, and I lost whatever of wonder might have come after.

After dinner I ceased to be able to see any further display of interest. Now and then a purple or pink fragment appeared but that was all. For a day after I noted the fact that my visions could be easily recalled by a memorial effort, but with less and less sharpness.

These shows are expensive. For two days I had headache, and for one day a smart attack of gastric distress. . . . The experience, however, was worth one such headache, and indigestion, but was not worth a second.

The mode of action of mescal is somewhat curious and may vary with the dose and the man. At first, even at the height of the drug action, the visions require one to wait with closed eyes for a minute or more. To open the eyes is to dismiss the vision, no matter how dark be the room. Suggestion availed one but little, and no act of will was competent to hold my dream unaltered.

I found in these seeming laws some resemblance to those which—in my case, at least—appear to govern quite ordinary and normal phenomenon. From childhood, I, like some others, can at night, before sleep arrives, summon visions. These are not always just what I desire. Once present I cannot alter them; they shift, change, and disappear under influences not within my capacity to control or analyze. To open my eyes, even in the most intense darkness, dismisses these visions. Is it true of opium visions? The same law certainly applies to some hysterical phantasms; but the explanation does not yet seem attainable. My normal power to summon visions was entirely lost under mescal action. I tried to see faces, gardens, etc., but none came at command so long as I was under the influence of the drug.

[1896]

Hypnotic Dreams (I)

DAVID BALLIN KLEIN

The subjects selected for hypnosis were kept in ignorance of the nature of the experiment. Only one of them had ever been hypnotized before. The others were not told that hypnosis was to be employed and after being aroused at the end of the first session some of them were astonished at having "fallen asleep." For the most part they were students of elementary psychology who had volunteered to serve as subjects. Upon entering the laboratory they were assured that nothing of a distressing or unpleasant nature was to be tried. It was also pointed out that no details of what was to be attempted could be furnished without militating against the success of the work. To allay their curiosity they were informed the main purpose of the experiment was to ascertain the relative efficacy of various methods of bodily relaxation. In this way any influence attributable to suggestion in the waking state was eliminated.

After the subject was comfortably seated hypnosis was induced by means of visual fixation and by verbal suggestion. Upon being assured of the genuine hypnotic status of the subject as indicated by his inability to open his eyes and to pry his clasped hands apart when the appropriate counter-suggestion had been given, he was told to "relax and sleep for a few minutes." In doing so he was usually made to rest his head on his arms which were placed on the table in front of him. This preliminary "sleep," lasting from one to two minutes, seemed to facilitate the subsequent dreaming, although it was by no means essential. . . .

The subject was now told to sit up but to continue sleeping and the following instructions given:

I want you to watch very carefully for any dreams you might have and as soon as the dream is over tell me all about it.

One of the stimuli, to be described presently, was then presented. Each stimulus was made to act for approximately ten seconds. If the subject failed to respond spontaneously after two minutes, he was asked, "Did you have a dream?" It was found that often the subject had a dream to report, but was waiting to be asked to tell about it. Accordingly, in our later work the suggestion, "Don't wait for me to ask you about it, but tell me about the dream as soon as it is over," was added to the formula of instructions. In this way it was possible to measure the duration of the dreams by means of a stop watch. . . .

Once the subject began on this suggestion to report the dream at once without waiting for special prompting, he continued to do so. After telling about the dream in this spontaneous fashion the subject was questioned by the experimenter on any particular phases of the dream requiring further description. The subject was then told to "sleep some more" and after the lapse of from twenty to thirty seconds, the time necessary to prepare the next stimulus, the suggestions to watch for a dream and to describe it immediately after its experience was repeated and the next stimulus was applied. . . .

Most of the work was done with the following stimuli:

1. Small bottle of creosote held in front of the subject's nose for about ten seconds.

2. Sounds of tuning fork, (100 vibrations) applied to the right ear of subject for about ten seconds.

3. Application of circular piece of metal (cold) to middle of forehead for about ten seconds.

4. Stroking back of right hand with absorbent cotton for about ten seconds.

5. Small bottle of perfume held in front of subject's nose for about ten seconds.

6. Pinching back of right hand between thumb and forefinger with small calipers—three pinches within ten seconds.

7. Sound of organ pipe (G)—three blasts within ten-second interval.

8. Subject is made to handle ordinary wax candle by grasping it with his right hand and holding it for about ten seconds.

9. Bottle of asafoetida held in front of subject's nose for about ten seconds

10. Subject is made to handle a small cardboard triangle covered with absorbent cotton and required to hold it in his right hand for about ten seconds.

In addition to the foregoing stimuli, some of which, as is of course obvious, were used to obtain a direct check on Freudian symbolism, an unambigious type of sex stimulation was used occasionally as a still more cogent bit of evidence along the same line of investigation. This form of stimulation consisted of a gentle stroking of the subject's trousers over the genital region by means of a ruler. For purposes of economy of description this particular stimulus will hereafter be referred to as the genital stimulus.

At times stimuli somewhat different from the foregoing were tried merely to ascertain the scope of the method. This applies particularly to the use of single words spoken to the subject. The latter approach was intended to determine the suitability of the methods as means of evaluating the free association technique of dream analysis as advocated notably by Jung. . . .

Most of the results incorporated in this monograph were secured from eight subjects. Two of them were young women and the others young men. . . .

By way of illustrating the richness and variety of the dreams obtained by this method the following examples chosen more or less at random from our collection are included. In those instances where the duration of the dream was obtained the time is indicated at the beginning of the dream recital. . . .

Dream 1. Subject: Young man, university sophomore.
Stimulus: Stroking right hand with absorbent cotton for about ten seconds.
Dream Response: A cow licked my hand.
Q. Is that all you can tell me? A. Yes.
Q. Tell me more about the cow—what color it was—where you were. A. I was sitting down and the cow reached over my shoulder and bit me.
Q. Did she bite you? A. No. She licked me.
Q. Could you see the cow? A. (Mumbles something in the way of assent.)
Q. What color was she? A. Brown with blue horns.
Q. What else? A. That's all.
Q. What hand did the cow lick? A. On the right hand.
Q. And what did you do when the cow licked your hand? A. Didn't do anything.
Q. Did you recognize this cow? A. No.
Q. Oh, it was a strange cow. Where was it? A. It was in the field.
Q. Do you know what field it was? A. No.
Q. Didn't seem familiar? A. No.
Q. Did you really believe that the cow licked your hand or did you just dream or think that it did? A. I just thought so—I didn't know.
Q. Do you think it was a real cow? A. Yes
Q. You really saw those blue horns or did you dream that? A. No.
Q. What—no? A. I saw them.

Dream 2. Same Subject.
Stimulus: Bottle of asafoetida held to nose for about ten seconds.
Dream Response—Smelled something dead—a horse—a dead horse.
Q. What else? A. He was just dead.
Q. Where was this dead horse? A. He was decomposed.
Q. How do you know? A. I could see it.
Q. What did it look like? A. His stomach was all out.
Q. What else? A. That's all.
Q. Could you only see it? A. I could smell it.
Q. What color was the horse? A. The skin was pulled up. It was brown.
Q. Anything else? A. He had a right front foot.
Q. Where was this? A. It was in some bushes.
Q. Where? In the country? A. Yes.
Q. Whose horse was he? Do you know? A. No.
Q. What did you do when you smelled him? A. Just walked on by.
Q. Did you see him too? A. I smelled him.
Q. Are you positive about that? A. Yes.
Q. This wasn't a dream? A. I don't know.
Q. You think this could have been real—that you really smelled him?
A. Yes. . . .

Dream 5. Subject: Young man, university student.
Stimulus: Pinching back of right hand between thumb and forefinger with small calipers—three pinches within ten-second interval.
Dream Response—Dreamed I was at home and seemed like me and a little boy were scufflin' or boxing and I jumped up and ran across the alley and across a fence to some people across the street. They had some horses over there. I got one of these horses and rode to golf club and rode horse to side of swimming pool. After swimming I went to locker room of golf club and changed clothes. Met girls in dining room of dance hall. (Does not know whether he talked to girls. Seemed he just went up there. One of them had on a light green dress with no sleeves and other sort of yellow dress. Doesn't know whether he knew them or not. Was pleased to see them. In connection with boxing episode: Seemed "like we were all tangled up—like two cats fighting." Didn't know boys. Doesn't remember getting wet in water. No feeling attached to immersion.) . . .

Dream 7. Same Subject.
Stimulus: Bottle of asafoetida held to nose about ten seconds.
Dream Response (35 seconds)—Seemed like I was up at fraternity house and they were having initiation and I went out Mount Bonnell and ran down side of mountain. Crossed lake in a boat and got out and ran across pond and went to bootleggers. Got a bottle of whiskey and ran back to fraternity house.
(Seemed like he smelled something that reminded him of initiation but he doesn't remember what it was. Doesn't know whether it really happened or whether he dreamed it. Did not take long to make the trip. Was very much impressed by the speed at which he traveled. Did not know what to do with whiskey after he arrived at fraternity house. Did not talk to bootlegger. Just

seemed as though he ran up to house and left with whiskey. "Couldn't tell hardly whether it was whiskey or beer. Something I got out of the bootlegger.")

Dream 8—Subject: Young woman, university sophomore.
Stimulus: Odor of perfume presented for about ten seconds.
Dream Response (25 seconds)—Dreamed about having been put to sleep and not being able to wake up when the anesthetic had been given. Dreamed about the operation. Seemed as though she "was going off into a world of nowhere."
Q. Did that seem as though it was real or did you dream it? A. No; it was real—very much.

Dream 9—Same Subject.
Stimulus: Holding wax candle for about ten seconds.
Dream Response (58 seconds)—"I dreamed I was playing golf."
Q. Where? A. At the golf links on the campus.
Q. Who was with you? A. My brother's roommate.
Q. Did you really play? A. Yes.
Q. Did you drive the ball? A. Yes.
Q. Could you really see the ball? A. Yes.

Dream 10—Same Subject.
Stimulus: Holding candle in right hand for about ten seconds.
Dream Response (15 seconds after removal of stimulus)—Dreamed of being in a physical-training class. "I dreamed I was trying to lift the bar and couldn't. They were laughing at me 'cause it was funny. I did not have any strength."
Q. Were you holding on with both hands? A. Yes, we were over at the P. T. shack. I just could not do it.
Q. Did it really happen? A. Yes.
Q. Did it seem real to you? A. Yes.
Q. How did the dream end? A. I just dropped down.
Q. And then what happened? A. That's all.
Q. Did it seem to have taken place? A. Yes, I could see it.

Dream 20—Subject: Young man, university senior.
Stimulus: Word "Help" uttered by experimenter.
Dream Response (20 seconds)—I was driving along the highway at home. Heard yelling and we stopped. A car was turned sideways in the road. I went down and saw the car was turned over on the side of the road. A man was crawling out. Said he wasn't hurt. He told me someone was under the car. I helped turn the car over. There was a woman badly cut. We took her to the hospital.
Q. Did this really happen? A. I just imagined it.
Q. Could you see the car? A. Yes, it was a brown car—a Cadillac.
Q. Where was this? A. On the highway between Wichita Falls and Electra.
Q. Did this actually happen or did you dream it? A. Just saw it and heard the man.
Q. What did you hear? A. He was yelling "Help!"

As the previous list of examples indicates, there is a decidedly convincing unanimity of opinion concerning the relationship between the dreaming during hypnosis and the dreaming during sleep. All of them seemed to agree that the term *dream* is legitimately applicable to the just-experienced hypnotic episodes. What bothers them, though, is the question, "Would you say these dreams are the same as those you have at night when you're asleep?" Some subjects regard them as the same, but others report them as different because they were "not exactly asleep." This latter experience, in other words, does not appear as a difference in dream process so much as a difference in the concomitant setting serving to differentiate hypnosis from actual sleep. . . .

Time and again the subjects would report an inability to specify what had caused the particular dream under consideration at the moment. Stated otherwise, they were apparently oblivious of the instigating stimulus. They also reported a peculiar suddenness of onset and an equal suddenness of termination with reference to their dreams. . . .

One of the most interesting long-standing psychological questions we endeavored to answer by means of our technique was the problem of the *typical dream.* . . . The first of such typical dreams we tried to produce was the familiar oft-reported dream of falling or flying. . . . We reasoned that a typical dream must have a very commonplace and frequently recurring stimulus, otherwise it would be rare and not a typical dream. . . . It also seemed obvious to us that the stimulus for the falling dream must in some way be an integral part of the experience of having one's bodily equilibrium disturbed. Furthermore, since most dreaming takes place while we are sleeping on a bed and stretched out horizontally, the stimulus would very likely be due to the mechanics of this situation. Considerations such as these suggested the possibility of a *sudden and minute drop* of a part of the body, as the sleeper shifted his position on the pillow or mattress, as the adequate stimulus for the falling dream. . . . Accordingly, we decided to subject it to experimental test.

The first person we tried this out on was a young girl who was completely uninformed regarding the nature of our experimentation. She accepted our plausible explanation of studying the relative efficacy of various methods of bodily relaxation. After inducing hypnosis we had her lie in a comfortable position with her head on a pillow. . . . We introduced our supposed stimulus for the falling dream for the first time. It consisted specifically of a sudden pressure on the cot near her ankles and made for a slight inclination of the body, the feet being momentarily lower than the head. The dream response proved so amazing and unexpected confirmation of our theory that we cite in detail:

Q. Did you have a dream? A. Yes.

Q. What was it you dreamed? A. I dreamed I was sliding down—sliding down a shoot the chute.

Q. Could you feel yourself sliding? A. Yes.

Q. Could you feel yourself go down? A. Yes.

Q. Were you going down head first? A. No, feet first.

Q. Were you sitting up? A. No.

Q. Could you feel yourself going down? A. Yes.

Q. Did you go straight or which way? A. It was the way the shoot the chute goes.

Thus encouraged by this success we repeated this type of stimulus during the experimental period and varied its location each time. We were struck by the way in which the dream of falling changed with such variation. For example, a slight pressure on both sides of the cot at the level of the waist resulted in a dream of being shoved under water. Unilateral pressure on the left side of the cot produced a dream centering around an automobile wreck she had been in some eight or ten months before. The following laboratory notes of this dream are worthy of note:

Q. What did you dream about the wreck just now? A. We fell off an 18-foot bluff.

Q. Were you hurt? A. Yes.

Q. Did you live through it again just now? A. Yes. (Placed hand over heart and sighed.)

Q. Did you feel yourself land or were you unconscious? A. I could feel myself falling, falling, falling.

After trying three other stimuli unrelated to the falling dream, and getting dream reports on them, we reverted to the typical dream in question and applied the stimulus of pressure on the right side of the cot at about the level of the subject's waist again. This time she responded (39 seconds):

I was falling, falling, falling down a mountain. Isn't that funny?

Q. What else? What were you going to tell me about the fall? A. I landed in town, and how!

Q. Did it hurt? A. No.

Q. Did you fall a long way? A. I fell from the top of the mountain. It seemed real pleasant.

Q. Did you land on your feet? A. No, on my side and I thought Daddy said something about it.

Q. Was he with you? A. No, but he said it was the way monkeys used to do.

Q. Did this really happen or did you dream it? A. No, it really happened.

Q. Did you tell your Dad about it? A. Yes, when I got home.

Q. From where? A. Seemed like I was on a trip and when I got home I told Daddy about it. It doesn't seem clear.

Q. Is that all? A. Yes.

Incidentally, this subject upon being awakened and asked about the foregoing dreams testified that she realized she had been dreaming. Concerning the one dealing with the automobile accident she stated she had dreamed it about three or four times in her night dreams, "But this one seemed more real, just as though it had just happened."

Our work with this stimulus showed the ease with which the direction of the fall can be predicted. Although we tried this stimulus but eleven times, the fact that we secured "falling" dreams taken in conjunction with the reasons prompting our selection of this stimulus as the one most likely responsible for that type of dream, justifies us in being decidedly confident of the part played by such incipient drops in bodily position during the course of ordinary sleep. The stimulus, we found, does not have to be at all violent. A very slight depression of the pillow or mattress will elicit the dream.

It may well be, of course, that other stimuli may result in such "falling" dreams. All that we contend is that the particular stimulus in question can be *experimentally* demonstrated to result in such dreams. . . .

For a given subject a given stimulus often tends to result in a repetition of the same dream or a repetition of one of several themes. In the case of one of our subjects pinching the hand invariably produced the dream of the black rat. The odor of asafoetida caused him to dream of a dead horse on repeated occasions. For another subject this particular stimulus reinstated an early childhood experience in which one of his schoolmates appeared with a bag of asafoetida around his neck. This dream was reported by him on several occasions. In those cases where a given dream was secured repeatedly, questioning of the subject would indicate that the experience was connected with some rather vivid episode in the subject's life. In general, it appears that Hollingsworth's explanation of the recurrent dream rests on a sound factual basis capable of experimental confirmation. According to him, "Any profound emotional shock . . . establishes persistent patterns of imagery, attitude, and feeling, which thereafter are readily reinstated by a variety of stimuli resembling details of the original situation." . . .

Another problem apparently amenable to experimental solution by means of the hypnotic dream technique is the long-standing question of the duration of the dream experience. Just how the duration of each dream may be determined has already been explained. As the time-measures so far introduced indicate, there is, of course, considerable variation from one dream to the next. Up to the present, however, we have not secured a single dream lasting as long as two minutes. It may well be that the stimuli we employed have had something to do with this matter. . . . Our figures are intended to be no more than suggestive. . . . Up to the present we have secured the duration time for 84 of the dreams. The measure ranges from 5 to 83 seconds, with a mean time of 35.94 seconds. . . .

Convincing of the possibility of demonstrating the inferred phenomena of dreamless sleep is an amnesic condition in the case of Subject J. M. X. This subject in the course of four experimental periods reported 49 dreams during hypnosis. Immediately after waking he was unable to recall any of them, and usually insisted he had merely fallen asleep, and that nothing had taken place.

We also endeavored to arouse his recognition of the dreams he had reported by discussing various salient aspects of them, but he seemed very much mystified by our questions regarding dead horses, black rats, fogs, cows, and other repeatedly mentioned constituent items of his dreams. He talked very freely about his previous experiences with such items, but never connected them with the dreams he had had shortly before the questioning. His amnesia for the dreams was evidently complete enough to insist no dreams had been experienced. . . .

The other subjects usually remembered most of their dreams. Their dream reports after waking were fairly accurate descriptions of the events reported during hypnosis. In fact, we could find no evidence for the psychoanalytic view of the distortions supposed to be characteristic of such reports. On the other hand it is possible that such distortions may be a function of delayed as opposed to immediate recall. Inasmuch as we have not yet subjected this possibility to experimental investigation we are only justified in stating that the Freudian distortions are not revealed when the dream reports are made directly after waking.

As was previously stated, in our selection of stimuli we deliberately chose some that have direct sexual implications in terms of Freudian symbolism. Both the candle and the cardboard triangle covered with cotton were intended to serve as phallic symbols. In addition, what we have already described as the genital stimulus was used as a less ambiguous stimulus of the same sort. It was also hoped the olfactory stimulus of the perfume would serve to incite some amorous associations. Sometimes we even went so far as to kiss the subject on the back of the neck or on his forehead, or to stroke his hair by way of stirring suppressed erotic proclivities to vicarious satisfaction or expression in the dream. We even included such verbal stimuli as "love" or the name of some member of the opposite sex in whom the subject was known to be interested.

If anything, our list of stimuli was weighted unduly in the direction of the sexual so that on *a priori* grounds we were justified in expecting a preponderance of sex dreams in our experiments. In strict justice to the Freudians it should be stated that we are using the term *sexual* in its ordinary and traditional sense and not in the less restricted psychoanalytic sense. It might also be no more than just to point out the fact that Freud, to the best of our knowledge, has never committed himself on the question of the influence of sex symbols presented as stimuli to a sleeping or hypnotized subject.

At the present moment we have 171 hypnotic dreams recorded. In an endeavor to ascertain what percentage of this total might be regarded as sexual we examined the collection and classified every dream in which a member of the opposite sex appeared, no matter how innocent the appearance, as a sex dream. By using such a generous criterion of the sexual, we got a total of 34. This means that almost 20 per cent of the dreams might be construed as sexual if every dream in which a member of the opposite sex appears is regarded as a sex dream.

On the other hand, if we limit our criterion to those dreams in which an erotic or quasi-erotic element figures, such as being kissed, holding hands, going on a journey with a sweetheart, the number of sex dreams is reduced to fifteen. The latter and, under the circumstances, more conservative estimate makes the percentage of sex dreams slightly less than 9 per cent. On the basis of this calculation we venture to say, as a first approximation, that the chances are that not over 10 per cent of dreams are sexual, and even this estimate may be too high if the word sexual is limited to a direct physiological connotation.

[1930]

Hypnotic Dreams (II)

LESLIE H. FARBER and CHARLES FISHER

INTRODUCTION

Because of the difficulty of investigating emotional processes experimentally, the investigation of dream psychology has progressed little since the publication of Freud's Interpretation of Dreams, a fact which Freud noted in 1933 when he complained that analysts "behave as though they had nothing more to say about the dream—as though the whole subject of dream theory were finished and done with." He called attention, as an exception, to the pioneer work of several Viennese investigators who, using hypnosis (Schrötter) and other methods, had made a start in the experimental confirmation of the theory of dream symbolism. Unfortunately this research was not pursued. The last two decades have seen considerable development of hypnotic techniques in the study of various unconscious processes. Erickson, Kubie, Luria, Eisenbud, and others have contributed to this literature.

To develop a method of dream study which might be more objective than the interpretive technique used in analytic therapy, a group of average college students were used as hypnotic subjects. With them as subjects the following problems were investigated:

1. *The capacity of normal individuals under hypnosis to understand dream language and the factors which might influence this understanding.* In hypnotic and other dissociated mental states, individuals show capacity for understanding and interpreting the unconscious psychic productions of others. It is well known that schizophrenic patients are able to interpret dreams. Some artistic individuals manifest a special faculty for understanding the unconscious import of artistic creations. Erickson found that a hypnotized subject in one instance was able to read and understand the automatic writing of another person.

2. *The production of experimental dreams under hypnosis.* Earlier workers have found that they could partially control the form and content of the dream by suggesting under hypnosis what was to be dreamed about. Their suggestions were restricted to a limited number of grossly sexual situations. We hoped to confirm this work and extend its scope to include a variety of dream stimuli.

3. *The nature of the relationship between hypnotist and subject.* Hypnosis fell into comparative disuse as a therapy largely because of the lack of understanding of the hypnotic relationship.

The students who participated in the project as hypnotic subjects were recruited from a Washington university by the professors, who announced to their classes that two psychiatrists were doing research with hypnosis. The volunteers were from 18 to 21 years of age. Those who seemed unstable were immediately excluded, and only those who proved to be naïve about psychology, ignorant of any knowledge of the theory of dreams, were chosen. They were asked not to read about the subject for the duration of the project. Those selected were average students, with no conspicuous personal problems and no special talents, either artistic or intellectual.

DREAM TRANSLATION

Under hypnosis the subjects were directly presented with dreams, of which some were fantasies of the experimenters, some produced by other subjects during hypnosis, some were the dreams of friends and patients, and a few were myths and psychotic productions. For example, an eighteen-year-old girl was told under hypnosis: "Dreams have meaning. Now that you are asleep you will be better able to understand them. A girl dreamt that she was packing her trunk when a big snake crawled into it. She was terrified and ran out of the room. What do you think the dream means?" Almost before the question was finished, the subject blushed, hesitated a second, then said, "Well, I guess she was afraid of being seduced. The snake would be the man's sex organ and the trunk hers."

As a control, subjects were always questioned about the dream before and after hypnosis, and in no instance did the subjects in the waking state make any comment comparable to that obtained under hypnosis. Care was taken not to ask leading questions nor to reveal the experimenters' interpretations of the dreams.

Several female subjects were given this dream: "A boy was sitting at his desk studying when the waste basket caught on fire. He ran and got a pitcher of water and put the fire out." Their immediate response was, "Oh, he wet his bed," or, "He should have gone to the bathroom." However, a dream about a girl putting out a fire made no sense to them.

It was suggested to one subject that as a child she had wet the bed and been severely scolded by her mother. In response to this stimulus she dreamed of falling into a pond in winter and being scolded by her mother. This dream was then related to a second girl, under hypnosis, who was entirely ignorant of the genesis of the dream. Without any hesitation the second subject said, "Oh, that girl must have wet the bed!," thus recovering the stimulus that had produced the dream.

A second example illustrating the sexual differentiation of symbols is the following dream given for translation: "A man is sitting in a dentist's chair while the dentist tries to pull his tooth. He pulls and pulls. The dreamer is in great pain when the dream ends." Several subjects said the dream meant that a man was having his "vital organ" cut off. When the dental patient was a woman, the dream was translated as "giving birth to a baby."

An exclusive appetite for mushrooms, developed by a psychotic patient, was described to a subject under hypnosis, and she was asked what it would mean if it were a dream. She answered, "He was very sexual. He might even be homosexual." Since one of the authors later treated this patient, he can attest to the validity of this student's hypnotic interpretation.

During the first World War, one of the authors had the following vivid nightmare: "I had been captured by the Kaiser and he made ready to execute me. He placed my head on a chopping block and was about to swing the axe which would end my life, when the dream ended." Under hypnosis a student said the Kaiser was really the dreamer's father who was going to chop off his penis, not his head. She believed it was a punishment for something—probably some sexual act.

The story of Moses and the bulrushes presented as a dream to a girl subject evoked the response, "I think somebody was going to have a baby," adding that the bulrushes stood for pubic hair.

Because of the startling unanimity of response offered by hypnotic subjects, one might at first conclude that dreams are like puzzles which have only one answer—a sexual one. We have come to believe that these uniform sexual responses were influenced by the nature of the hypnotic relationship. Hypnosis is not only a state of consciousness, like sleep, in which dreams occur, but it is also a very striking interpersonal relationship. The most obvious characteristic of this relationship is the extreme dependence of the subjects and their feeling that the hypnotist is omnipotent. Their critical capacities, while not eliminated as Freud once thought, are certainly restricted. The hypnotist too is reacting, not only to the subject, but to the hypnotist's rôle of omnipotence. His reaction will in turn influence the subject. The relationship contains all the complexities of any relationship between two people, although the belief has developed, because of certain extraordinary aspects of the process, that in hypnosis one deals with something outside the bounds of normal human experience. The unique interaction at any given moment between the personality of the hypnotist and the personality of the subject will necessarily determine the experimental results. Even under what seem to be the same experimental conditions, different hypnotists evoke totally different responses.

Many observers have compared hypnosis to sexual seduction or assault, and it is a commonplace that a male hypnotist can hypnotize women much more easily than men. It is noteworthy that practically all the erotic dream translations cited were obtained from comparatively uninhibited women, and from one male subject who was a rather passive individual with a marked attachment for the hypnotist. Jung is said to have abandoned hypnosis when an awakening subject coyly thanked him for being so decent. "That demonstrated to me," he said, "the true nature of hypnosis." We have not found that hypnosis is very different in this respect from other transference relationships. Recognition of this factor does not detract from the method, as Jung feared, but increases its scientific validity.

The following example will illustrate how the form of the dream translation will depend on the interpersonal factors described. A shy female subject in hypnosis was told, "Some time ago you were packing your trunk when a snake crawled into it. You became terrified and ran out of the room." She then dreamed, "It was night and I was lost in the jungle. It was muddy and the mud came up to my waist so that I could not move in any direction. There were little snakes on the branches of the trees above me, which kept falling on my arms and shoulders. They kept getting nearer; some of them touched me. Only the mud kept the snakes from going below my waist; they could not touch me where the mud was; they could not get in. I felt safe in the mud." Questioned about this dream when awake, she said that the snakes were something harmful and the mud signified safety—a mere paraphrase of the dream. Hypnotized again, she was questioned by a person other than the hypnotist. Now the snakes represented something desirable, the mud a barrier to the satisfaction of her desire. First she spoke of the snakes as ideas which attracted her but which other people thought too radical; then as people whose political and social beliefs made them attractive, but who were disapproved of by others; finally, she referred to the snakes as experiences she wished to have but which convention, as represented by the mud, denied her. At this point the interlocutor left the room and the subject's hypnotist questioned her alone.

There was then a general relaxation of her facial expression and quite spontaneously she said that the snakes represented a pollution which came from the phallic branches of the trees, and this was the experience she desired. Questioned by a person other than the hypnotist, her translation was on a conventional social level. The dream was perceived in sexual terms in relation to the hypnotist. Both translations are of course parts of the total dream significance.

A similar variation in translation was obtained while attempting to discover how pregnancy would be portrayed in an experimental dream. A hypnotized girl was told, "Not long ago you discovered that a friend of yours had become pregnant; she came to you and told you how terrified she was to be caught in this way. You were shocked and did not know what to do." She then dreamed, "I was on an island and all around me waves were swelling; there were mountains up and down and around. There was a sudden downpour of rain. I felt that everything around me was so powerful that I was just insignificant. I did not know what to do." Several days later the dream was recalled to her under hypnosis by a person other than the hypnotist. Although she felt the dream was about pregnancy, the small island was the social ostracism and isolation enforced by her predicament, while the rain was the gossip and insinuation which fell on her. When her own hypnotist questioned her, she said that the rain was the downpour of semen.

This difference in response raises some interesting questions. Are the sexual translations due to some direct or implied suggestive influence by the hypnotist? Although it is difficult to eliminate this factor, our impression is that neither the hypnotist nor the substitute exerted any suggestion. Or can the dominant-submissive relationship of hypnosis be a sexual experience to the subject and does this serve to determine the form of his translations? It is undoubtedly true that a number of subjects seem to regard hypnosis as a sexual experience. We believe that this specific characteristic of the relationship with the hypnotist makes for a sexual interpretation, but this cannot be stated with certainty.

Only five, or about 20 per cent of the subjects carefully studied, proved to be able translators of dreams. The explanation for the failure of the remainder of the group is not clear. It can be said, however, that these individuals were quite inhibited and rigid compared to the translators. The reasons for both the ability and inability to translate dreams will be elicited only through careful personality studies of the individual subjects.

Even among the selected group it often happened that a hypnotized subject was unable to make any statement about a dream. This type of resistance could usually be overcome by one of two opposite methods. Sometimes a subject was able to translate his own dream only when it was presented as that of another person. At other times it was necessary to transform another person's dream into his own, by suggesting that this was an actual experience which had happened to him, and then asking him to dream about it.

A pregnant woman of our acquaintance dreamt that as she lay in bed one morning she was horrified to find a number of small white worms crawling over her arm. This dream was offered to a hypnotic subject with no result. The subject was then told that she herself had recently suffered the same horrible experience. She dreamt, "There was a white candle resting in a small dish beside my bed. The candle burned lower and lower and little wax particles kept dropping into the base of the dish." When asked about the new dream, she said, "The man came and that's what the dripping of the wax was." The first dream about the worms was recalled to her and she said, "That was the same thing." With another subject, who was likewise unable to find any meaning in the worm dream, this same manœuvre of redreaming elicited a dream that the subject was driving alone in a car with her arm resting on the sill of the open window. It was snowing and snowflakes kept dropping on her exposed forearm. After this dream she commented, "Now I know what the dream about the worms meant. Some girl had had relations with a man and she was afraid of getting pregnant. They hadn't taken any precautions. The worms refer to sperm." For some reason these two subjects translated the worm dream only after they had in effect restated the dream in their own dream language.

THE PRODUCTION OF EXPERIMENTAL DREAMS

The production of experimental dreams under hypnosis was first successfully accomplished many years ago by Karl Schrötter. In 1912 this investigator reported a series of dreams containing the symbols with which psychoanalytic dream interpretation has made us familiar, and the work was offered as experimental proof for the Freudian theory of symbols. This theory received additional confirmation in the investigations of Roffenstein in 1923 and Nachmansohn in 1925. As in sleep, the hypnotized subject will dream spontaneously, and he will also dream about situations that are suggested to him.

The production of such experimental dreams under hypnosis depends, however, upon the capacity of the individual subject to accept in fantasy and live through an emotionally-toned situation suggested to him by the hypnotist. While the situation is being outlined, his facial expressions and bodily movements show that he is experiencing genuine emotion—often painful and sometimes very intense.

The experimental procedure we finally evolved, after considerable trial and error, is as follows: Under deep hypnosis the subject is told, "I am going to recall an experience that happened to you some time ago. You have probably forgotten it, but as I describe it, you will remember it in all its details." The experience is then described and the subject is told: "A dream will come to you. Raise your right hand when the dream begins and lower it when the dream is finished." After one or two minutes of dreaming, the subject will relate his dream. It should be noted that the subject is not instructed to dream about the suggested situation, but merely told that a dream will come to him. We have been more successful in eliciting dreams with this method, probably because it permits greater freedom of fantasy on the part of the subject.

The dream stimuli we have used fall into two categories, first, those which were sexual, comprising experiences of pregnancy, intercourse, bedwetting, masturbation and homosexuality; second, nonsexual stimuli, including experiences of hostility, false accusation, competition, being taken advantage of, and others. Dreams obtained by hypnosis or by posthypnotic suggestion have all the characteristics of spontaneous dreams, and the subjects do not make a distinction between them. Following the dream stimulus, the subject usually first gives us a dream which is a paraphrase of the suggested stimulus, slightly modified by the inclusion of incidents from his own life experience. As he continues dreaming his subsequent productions have more and more the bizarre and pictorial character of dreams.

Why all subjects are not able to dream under hypnosis is not clear. The reaction to a dream stimulus seems to depend upon a combination of factors which include the nature of the dream stimulus, the personality structure of the subject, and his relationship to the hypnotist. Roffenstein had great difficulty in finding a hypnotic subject who would dream, probably because he utilized dream stimuli involving highly traumatic experiences as, for instance, suggesting to a woman that she dream about a homosexual relation. We have used a more indirect method calculated to spare the moral sensibilities of the subject. To elicit a dream about pregnancy, we suggested an experience in which a friend had become pregnant. Since the dream is always personalized, we achieved the desired result in the end. Another method of bringing about the acceptance of reprehensible experiences was to place them in childhood. From one subject we were able to elicit excellent dreams by the instruction: "I am going to recall a certain experience. This did not actually happen to you, but as I tell you about it, you will live through it as if it had." As a final precaution, we always attempted to remove the stimulus at the end of the experiment by telling the subject that the suggested experiences had not really happened to him.

The following experimental dream involves the play on words that is so frequently encountered in dreams. A young woman was told, "When you were a little girl you wet your bed and when you awoke in the morning your mother scolded you." The subject then dreamed that she told a lie which made her parents so angry that they spanked her. In her first account, she omitted the bedwetting, the substance of the lie. Only after considerable questioning by us, and evasion on her part, did she state that what she had lied about was risking being "run over in order to go to the A and P."

We have sometimes asked subjects to draw certain objects or figures that appear in their dreams, which frequently helps to clarify their meaning. Marcinowski first demonstrated in 1912 that landscapes in the dreams of his patients represented parts of the body, unrecognizable from the verbal descriptions. Kubie likewise reported a very instructive case, in which the meaning of a dream was revealed in a drawing representing an airplane as the male genitals.

To investigate symbolization of the female breast, a male subject was given the dream stimulus: "One day you were walking down a street in one of the poorer sections of town and you happened to see a young woman sitting on the steps nursing an infant. Her breast was exposed and you could see the baby take the nipple in its mouth and suck at it." His dream was: "I came to the corner where there was an old, run-down store. I went in to look for a magazine called Famous Fantastic Mysteries. I saw some fruit—apples and oranges—and tobacco and candy. They did not have the magazine so I bought some pipe tobacco and went out. I took the Mount Pleasant street car and rode to the top of a tall hill; it was flat on top; the other side was steep. It was the end of the car line. I got off and stood on the edge and looked down." Under hypnosis he drew a picture of the hill:

The same subject was told that he had once wet his bed and had felt very much ashamed because that was the sort of thing a child did. He dreamt that he called his mother and told her about wetting the bed. The doctor came and advised an operation. He went to the hospital in a cab with his mother, was prepared for the operation, and was greatly frightened as he was taken to the operating room. Next he was walking out of the hospital and down 13th street to a hardware store in order to buy a woodworking tool. Asked under hypnosis to draw the tool, he drew the head of a hammer.

Past experiences are sometimes incorporated into the dream. A girl, given the dream stimulus of an experience in which she had been caught masturbating by her mother, dreamed: "My sister and I, dressed in our best clothes, were making mud pies with mud which we kept in a rusty tomato can. We splattered the front of our dresses and mother scolded us, saying that it was my fault that my sister was doing it too." She later remembered this to be an incident from her childhood, possibly a screen memory.

Another subject, told that while walking through the woods she had been frightened by seeing a snake, dreamed that she and her father climbed a steep, winding path to the top of a hill on which there was a reservoir. As they walked back she leaned on her father's arm. When awake she recalled having made such an excursion to a reservoir with her father. Shortly afterward she went home on vacation and in describing to her father her work with us, she mentioned this dream. He was startled and visibly upset but unwilling to give any explanation. The father's reaction permits the speculation that the girl's casual recollection is a screen memory for an early trauma. As an association to snake, it suggests seeing the father's penis. That experimental dreams might be used to recover forgotten experiences was proposed by Nachmansohn who made similar observations.

We gave a male subject the dream stimulus of having eaten some green apples and developing a severe diarrhœa. We suggested to him in detail the nature of his symptoms and described the number, kind, changing color and consistency of his stools. All through his subsequent narration he coughed and spluttered. This symptom had not been present before, and it disappeared after the experiment. He dreamed that he was ill in bed. The light was turned on and off several times. It got "lighter and then darker." He started and stopped reading several times. He turned on the radio but it kept running on and on, interrupting his thoughts. There was no music—only talk—until finally he turned it off. We believe that the cough and the manner of speaking were symptomatic equivalents of diarrhœa by displacement, similar to the verbal diarrhœa of the radio which ran on and on.

Many subjects will, when asked, produce a dream without any dream stimulus. These spontaneous dreams often have a manifest content corresponding to the chief conscious interests of the individual. A geology major, with a marked interest in architecture, dreamed repeatedly of architectural groupings and landscapes.

On several occasions we asked a woman physician to be present during hypnotic sessions. During these sessions the subject's spontaneous dreams changed in character. With a woman present, he dreamed of climbing a staircase; of a sewer pipe running through a tunnel; of driving a car around the left side of a mountain into a tunnel.

The hypnotic subject is thus found to be not simply a passive object whose dreams can be manipulated at will by an omnipotent hypnotist. Hypnotic behavior is a meaningful, goal-directed striving, its nature determined by the dynamic unconscious. The subject's spontaneous dreams are influenced by his own unconscious needs and the interaction of these with the hypnotist and any other persons included in the hypnotic situation. Similarly, the dreams elicited in response to dream stimuli are not simple reflections of the stimulus but reveal the needs and wishes of the subject.

Manifestly nonsexual dream stimuli usually evoke dreams expressing the social situation in terms of "body language." A young girl was given as a stimulus a situation in which, falsely accused by a friend of cheating in an examination, she became very angry but because of circumstances was unable to deny the accusation. The subject then dreamed that a dentist was trying to pull her tooth despite her frightened protests that the nurse had taken the anæsthetic out of the wrong bottle. In her dream the humiliating accusation is portrayed as bodily assault and deprivation.

A boy was told that he had a rival in his geology class with whom he had trouble competing because he refused to defer to the teacher as the other boy did. The subject then dreamed: "The geology class went on a field trip. We came to an outcropping of rock and I started chipping at it with my hammer. A flying fragment of rock hit the other boy in the face, cutting him. That made me feel fine." Here academic competition becomes a bodily assault on his rival. The examples indicate how a familiar dream symbol may portray a variety of human experiences. Thus, tooth-pulling may represent not only castration and childbirth but also socially insulting predicaments; the attack with the hammer may represent not only homosexual assault but also scholastic rivalry.

SUMMARY

A method is presented for the study of dreams and other unconscious processes by hypnosis. In hypnosis certain subjects have more awareness of the meaning of dream language than in the waking state. This awareness is influenced by the relationship between hypnotist and subject. The similarity of this relationship with other interpersonal relationships was pointed out, as well as the possibility of using this method for the study of transference. A number of experimental dreams, evoked by both sexual and nonsexual dream stimuli, are presented and their special characteristics discussed. The results obtained illustrate the great plasticity of the dream language and argue against too narrow interpretation of symbols.

[1943]

H. THE FRINGE AREA OF DREAMS: NIGHTMARES, SLEEPWALKING, AND DOZING-OFF DREAMS

We Go Mad When We Dream

WILHELM GRIESINGER, M.D.

Translated by C. L. Robertson and James Rutherford

THE SIMPLE TESTIMONY, so frequently given by those who have recovered, that the whole period of their [mental] disease now appears to them as a dream—sometimes a happy, but more frequently a painful and gloomy one; and further, that during insanity, in certain cases, the impression left by their former healthy life was also like a bygone dream—might lead us to the great similarity of insanity to states of dreaming.

It is true that in the insane the principal signs of sleep are absent—the closing of the external senses, the suppression of consciousness of the outer world, and of the influence of the will upon the muscles—all of which we regard as essential to dreaming. But, on the one hand, it is known that we dream the more readily the less profound our sleep is, and that there are states of sleep where an influence similar, indeed almost akin, to a waking state is exerted on the muscles (speaking during sleep, sleeping of the postilion while riding, somnambulism). . . . There are in the insane states of sensation and of emotion—dullness of sensorial impressions, which no longer affect the individual as they formerly did—that weakening of the influence of the will upon the muscles which is manifested in great slowness of movement, and even, at times, in cataleptic persistence of positions enforced—which, in connection with the coexistent obscurity of consciousness, vividly reminds us of what takes place when sleep comes on.

Indeed, the analogy of insanity to dreaming, especially to dreams occurring in the half-waking state, must be admitted. In children, we occasionally see, especially when under slight disease, that they, while sleeping, still speak; for example, they understand the mother, they answer her, they open their eyes and recognize her, but nevertheless they dream on, and in particular they cannot withdraw themselves from uneasy dreaming ideas. Even the intermediate conditions of sleep and waking, which succeed each other in endless gradations, strongly favor the appearance of illusions and hallucinations, and which are distinguished by an irregular activity of the imagination and by incoherence of the intelligence. They are preceded by a state of sleepiness, the individual being dull, torpid and taciturn; the senses become blunt, the impressions of sight fail, sound appears distant, his consciousness is dull, answers are delayed, he forgets himself, and speaks incoherently. These are often observed in the commencement of insanity. . . .

The dream, like insanity, receives its essential color, its certain fundament of tone, from the governing disposition; which may be determined as well by the mental occurrences of waking life, as by the changes of the organic state during sleep; in which, especially, all congestive states and all morbid impressions from the digestive organs, and abdominal organs in general, have a very great influence. The ruling sentiments of pleasure and pain call for their corresponding images, in which objects without form in themselves become sensuous clothed forms, the reality of the actual impressions is delusive, and what enters from without, through the senses, meets in the dreamer, as in the insane man, a center, preoccupied and filled with the given disposition, and becomes perverted and construed in the sense of the ruling sentiments and ideas. On the other hand, however, the same two-foldedness of the personality and the same emotions ensue when groups of ideas and sentiments of unaccustomed hostile intent stand opposed to the I, and the dream, like insanity, is busy to transfer to the external world and to dramatize subjective images (hallucinations) of all the senses. . . .

The dreamer, like the insane, accepts all, even the most adventurous and foolish, representations as possibilities without particular astonishment, and the veriest absurdity becomes the most unquestioned truth if the masses of perception which can rectify it remain dormant. An individual may dream of having solved a scientific problem, and is filled with joy at his fortunate success; he awakes and discovers it as an ordinary false thought. Thus, there are insane persons who suddenly discover perpetual motion, or a mechanical idea which must change the whole surface of the earth, and similar things; they are filled with ecstasy at such discoveries; what they demonstrate, however, is to us folly, and they, after recovery, cannot understand why they could not at once see through such great errors.

Agreeable, ravishing, heavenly dreams are very rare in health; they are most frequent in states of deep bodily or mental exhaustion, and we often observe at such times that the ideas suppressed during waking come forth strongly in dreams. To the individual who is distressed by bodily and mental troubles, the dream realizes what reality has refused—happiness and fortune. The starving Trenck, during his imprisonment, often dreamed of rich repasts; the beggar dreams that he is wealthy, the person who lost by death some dear friend fondly dreams of the most ultimate and lasting reunion. So also in mental disease. . . .

A number of other phenomena of dreaming present an evident analogy to insanity. Thus, sometimes in insanity, as in dreams, all idea of time is wanting; minutes seem hours, as in a dream we live years in a quarter of an hour, and events which would take months to occur in reality, appear to the insane man to pass in the shortest space of time. . . .

Those rarer cases are very interesting which intermitting insanity takes the place of normal sleep, and thereby seems to stand midway between dreaming and somnambulism. Guislain relates such a case, and considers generally that there exists a certain analogy between mental diseases and states of dreaming. . . .

When the seeds of mental disease are actually present, agitating dreams may hasten its outbreak; sometimes the subject of the future delirium is clearly exhibited in them. Results of the existing cerebral irritation, they act destructively on the emotions and their after-affects continue dominant during the waking state.

[*Circa* 1860]

A Classic Description of Nightmare

ROBERT MacNISH, M.D.

Nightmare may be defined as a painful dream, accompanied with difficult respiratory action, and a torpor in the powers of volition. The reflecting powers are generally more or less awake; and, in this respect, nightmare differs from simple dreaming, where they are mostly quiescent.

This affection, the Ephialtes of the Greeks, and Incubus of the Romans, is one of the most distressing to which human nature is subject. Imagination cannot conceive the horrors it frequently gives rise to, or language describe them in adequate terms. They are a thousand times more frightful than the visions conjured up by necromancy or diablere; and far transcend everything in history or romance, from the fable of the writhing and asp-encircled Laocoon to Dante's appalling picture of Ugolino and his famished offspring, or the hidden torture of the Spanish Inquisition.

The whole mind, during the paroxysm, is wrought up to a pitch of unutterable despair; a spell is laid upon the faculties, which freezes them into inaction, and the wretched victim feels as if part alive in his coffin, or overpowered by resistless and unmitigable pressure.

The modifications which nightmare assumes are infinite, but one passion is almost never absent—that of utter and incomprehensible dread. Sometimes the sufferer is buried beneath overwhelming rocks, which crush him on all sides, but still leave him with a miserable consciousness of his situation. Sometimes he is involved in the coils of a horrid, slimy monster, whose eyes have the phosphorescent glare of the sepulchre, and whose breath is poisonous as the marshes of Lerna. Everything horrible, disgusting, or terrific in the physical or moral world, is brought before him in fearful array; he is hissed at by serpents, tortured by demons, stunned by the hollow voices and cold touch of apparitions. A mighty stone is laid upon his breast, and crushes him to the ground in helpless agony; mad bulls and tigers pursue his palsied footsteps; the unearthly shrieks and gibberish of hags, witches, and fiends float around him. In whatever situation he may be placed, he feels superlatively wretched; he is Ixion working for ages at his wheel; he is Sisyphus rolling his eternal stone; he is stretched upon the iron bed of Procrustes; he is prostrated by inevitable destiny beneath the approaching wheels of the car of Juggernaut. At one moment, he may have the consciousness of a malignant demon being at his side; then to shun the sight of so appalling an object, he will close his eyes, but still the fearful being makes its presence known; for its icy breath is felt diffusing itself over his visage, and he knows he is face to face with a fiend. Then, if he looks up, he beholds horrid eyes glaring upon him, and an aspect of hell grinning at him with even more than hellish malice. Or, he may have the idea of a monstrous hag squatted upon his breast—mute, motionless and malignant, an incarnation of the Evil Spirit—whose intolerable weight crushes the breath out of his body, and whose fixed, deadly, incessant stare petrifies him with horror and makes his very existence insufferable.

In every instance, there is a sense of oppression and helplessness; and the extent to which these are carried varies according to the violence of the paroxysm. The individual never feels himself a free agent; on the contrary he is spell-bound by some enchantment, and remains an unresting victim for malice to work its will upon. He can neither breathe, nor walk, nor run, with his wonted facility. If pursued by any imminent danger, he can hardly drag one limb after another; if engaged in combat, his blows are utterly ineffective; if involved in the fangs of any animal, or in the grasp of an enemy, extrication is impossible. He struggles, he pants, he toils, but it is all in vain; his muscles are rebels to the will, and refuse to obey its call. In no case is there a sense of complete freedom: the benumbing stupor never departs from him; and his whole being is locked up in one mighty spasm. Sometimes he is forcing himself through an aperture too small for the reception of his body, and is there arrested and tortured by the pangs of suffocation produced by the pressure to which he is exposed; or he loses his way in a narrow labyrinth, and gets involved in its contracted and inextricable mazes; or he is entombed alive in a sepulchre, beside the moldering dead. There is, in most cases, an intense reality in all that he sees, or hears, or feels. The aspects of the hideous phantoms which harass his imagination are bold and defined; the sounds which greet his ear appallingly distinct; and when any dimness or confusion of imagery does prevail, it is of the most fearful kind, leaving nothing but dreary and miserable impressions behind it.

Much of the horror experienced in nightmare will depend upon the natural activity of the imagination, upon the condition of the body, and upon the state of mental exertion before going to sleep. If, for instance, we have been engaged in the perusal of such works as *The Monk, The Mysteries of Udolpho,* or *Satan's Invisible World Discovered,* and if an attack of nightmare should supervene, it will be aggravated into sevenfold horror by the spectral phantoms with which our minds have been thereby filled. We will enter into all the fearful mysteries of these writings, which, instead of being mitigated by slumber, acquire an intensity which they never could have possessed in the waking state. The apparitions of murdered victims, like the form of Banquo, which wrings the guilty conscience of Macbeth, will stalk before us; we are surrounded by sheeted ghosts, which glare upon us with their cold sepulchral eyes; our habitation is among the vaults of ancient cathedrals, or among the dungeons of ruined monasteries, and our companions are the dead.

At other times an association of ludicrous images passes through our mind; everything becomes incongruous, ridiculous and absurd. But even in the midst of such preposterous fancies, the passion of mirth is never for one moment excited; the same blank despair, the same freezing *inertia,* the same stifling tortures, still harass us; and so far from being amused by the laughable drama enacting before us, we behold it with sensations of undefined horror and disgust.

In general, during an attack, the person has the consciousness of an utter inability to express his horror by cries. He feels that his voice is half choked by impending suffocation, and that any exertion of it, farther than a deep sigh or groan, is impossible. Sometimes, however, he conceives that he is bellowing with prodigious energy, and wonders that the household are not alarmed by his noise. But this is an illusion; those outcries which he fancies himself uttering, are merely obscure moans, forced with difficulty and pain from the stifled penetration of his bosom. . . .

The illusions which occur are perhaps the most extraordinary phenomena of nightmare; and so strongly are they often impressed upon the mind, that, even on awaking, we find it impossible not to believe them real. We may, for example, be sensible of knockings at the door of our apartment, hear familiar voices calling upon us, and see individuals passing through the chamber. In many cases, no arguments, no efforts of the understanding will convince us that these are merely the chimeras of sleep. We regard them as events of actual occurrence, and will not be persuaded to the contrary. With some, such a belief has gone down to the grave; and others have maintained it strenuously for years, till a recurrence of the illusions, under circumstances which rendered their real existence impossible, has shown them that the whole was a dream. Many a good ghost story has had its source in the illusions of nightmare.

[*Circa* 1830]

Nightmare of a Poet*

SAMUEL TAYLOR COLERIDGE

While I am awake, by patience, employment, effort of mind, and walking I can keep the fiend at Arm's length; but the Night is my Hell, Sleep my tormenting Angel. Three nights out of four I fall asleep, struggling to lie awake—and my frequent Night-Screams have almost made me a nuisance in my own House. Dreams with me are no Shadows, but the very Substances and foot-thick Calamities of my life.

The Dreams of Sleepwalkers

DANIEL HACK TUKE, M.D.

Dreaming and Hallucination in relation to sleepwalking and screaming —as might be supposed, as indeed I have intimated, there is in the answers I have received ample evidence of the action of the ideational centers in somnambulists, and the direct influence of a vivid dream upon the actions of the sleepwalker and the screamer.

* From a letter to Thomas Wedgwood.

One girl almost always dreamt that the room was full of boiling water, and that she was trying to escape from it. Another saw a figure, namely, a shepherd with a lady's bonnet on his head; and, what is interesting in her case, the hallucination often remained on the following day. She would stand still, and on being asked the reason for refusing to move, would reply that there was the shepherd in the bonnet in her way.

A lady informs me that an act performed by her daughter was connected with a dream in this wise: She dreamed about a shipwreck, and she awoke finding herself out of bed. In the morning she found she had wrapped a large shawl carefully round the candlestick which was on the chair by her bedside. She then saw clearly that the explanation of the act lay in her having succoured a shipwrecked sailor, for whom the candlestick had done duty.

The physician whose personal experience I have already quoted says: "My sleepwalking has often been associated with dreams. The subjects are generally one of the three following: Fire in the house, (2) burglars, (3) damage to, or death of, some near relative."

Another writes: "Dreams seem always to be associated with my sleepwalking, and it is the almost invariable accompaniment of the dream, *i.e.*, I always put into practice the thing dreamed. Once I dreamed I was drowning, and I jumped out of bed, rushed into the passage, and called for help over the stairs."

A barrister sleepwalker writes: "On one occasion I came downstairs in my nightdress to warn the family not to drink the beer, as I had seen a crow fall into it when it was brewing. This was, of course, only a dream, as no such thing had really occurred." He adds, "Very vivid dreams are always associated with sleepwalking in my case. I always dream when I sleep, if only for a moment, and always did so." "I compose poems and solve problems in my dreams and feel great delight and satisfaction in so doing; but when I awake I find the poems often without any meaning and the solutions of problems are trash and false. I have also words and sentences of horror in my dreams which are nonsense. Moreover, I often awake with an impression of the enormous size of the furniture of my bedroom."

Speech in Sleepwalkers (*Somniloquy*)—Some somnambulists speak with great facility. One writes: "I am quite capable of carrying on a conversation with anyone. I often talk during my sleepwalking, both when addressed, and also when alone. For example, when sleeping with anyone I make up a long story to prove that I am not asleep, that being my great object when I am asleep, as I feel convinced in my own mind that I am awake. When alone I talk also." (He is heard by his family.)

The same gentleman's sister says: "I have usually dreams appropriate to the actions performed. I sometimes am under the delusion that I have swallowed a pair of scissors or a pin, and have a slight cough at the time." A form, it would seem, of globus hystericus.

A medical friend (Dr. Yellowlees) writes to me: "I know an individual who, when a boy, was found standing up in bed and furiously shaking the bedposts. The explanation was, that he had been reading *Uncle Tom's Cabin* and believed, in his dream, that he had got hold of Legree! When a student, he was amazed one morning to find that he had the fire-irons beside him in bed, and could only explain it by remembering that he had dreamt that robbers were going to break into the house, and that he had intended to confront them with the poker." Substitute for the bedpost a child in the bed or room, and clearly this might easily have become a criminal case. . . .

One of the most remarkable of the deeds performed by sleepwalkers communicated to me, occurred in the person of a mental physician when holding the post of assistant officer in a huge asylum, and attested by the unexceptional evidence of another physician. It is a splendid instance of unconscious reflex action of the brain, the train of events originating entirely from without.

On one occasion when making his usual morning visit in a detached ward occupied by the more excited patients, he was about to leave, when the nurse said, "You haven't seen the new patient, sir."

"What new patient?" said Dr. Blank.

"The patient you brought over during the night, sir."

"I brought no patient over during the night," was the reply.

"Dr. Blank," said the amazed nurse, "I'll let you see the woman!" Whereupon she opened the door of a room and showed him a maniacal patient.

The fact was that Dr. Blank had been roused from bed, had dressed, and had gone downstairs and examined the admission papers. He had received the patient, and as she was much excited, had gone out of doors to this detached building to arrange about a room for her; yet in the morning all this was utterly forgotten. Nothing but seeing the patient there would convince the doctor that the event had occurred, and even seeing her did not recall the very faintest recollection of her admission.

[*Circa* 1860]

Dozing-off Dreams

H. A. TAINE

Translated by T. D. Haye

I know this [hypnagogic] state from my own experience, and have many times repeated the observation, above all in the daytime, when fatigued and seated in a chair. It is then sufficient for me to close one eye with a handkerchief; by degrees the sight of the other eye becomes vague, and it closes. By degrees, all external sensations are effaced or cease, at all events to be remarked; the internal images, on the other hand, feeble and rapid during the state of complete wakefulness, become intense, distinct, colored, steady and lasting; there is a sort of ecstasy, accompanied by a feeling of expansion and of comfort. Warned by frequent experience, I know that sleep is coming on, and that I must not disturb the rising vision; I remain passive; and in a few minutes it is complete. Architecture, landscapes, moving figures, pass slowly by, and sometimes remain, with incomparable clearness of form and fullness of being; sleep comes on, and I know no more of the real world I am in. Many times, like M. Maury, I have caused myself to be gently roused at different moments of this state, and have thus been able to mark its characters. The intense image which seems an external object is but a more forcible continuation of the feeble image which an instant before I recognized as internal; some scrap of a forest, some house, some person which I vaguely imagined in closing my eyes, has in a minute become present to me with full bodily details, so as to change into a complete hallucination. Then waking up on a hand touching me, I feel the figure decay, lose color, and evaporate; what had appeared a substance is reduced to a shadow. I have frequently thus watched in turn the filling out by which a simple image becomes an hallucination, and the obliteration which turns the hallucination into a simple image. In this double transition, we are able to notice the differences, and perceive the conditions of the two states.

First, when we are going to sleep. As the image becomes more intense so it becomes more absorbing and independent. On the one hand, it attracts by degrees all the attention; external noises and contacts become less and less sensible; at last they are as if they did not exist. The image, on the other hand, becomes prominent and persistent, we seem no longer actors, but spectators; its transformations are spontaneous and *automatic*.

When attention and automatism are at their height, the hallucination is complete, and it is precisely by the loss of these two characters that it is destroyed. Next, as to waking. On the one hand, at the light touch that arouses us, a part of our attention is brought back to the outer world. On the other hand, as memory returns, reviving images and ideas surround with their train the special image, they come into conflict with it, assume ascendancy over it, depose it from its solitary position, restore it to social life, and replace it in its habitual dependency. This opposition and contention cause the stupefaction of waking, and what we call being thoroughly awake is but the re-establishment of equilibrium. . . .

In every process by which the exaggeration of images is combatted, all we attempt is to set up an equilibrium, not that of a balance in which one scale is lower than the other. In the normal state of wakefulness, the first scale which holds the sensations proper, is the heavier; the second and lighter scale holds images proper. The two scales in the normal state are, for the moment, on a level; but the heavier scale immediately weighs down the other, and our images are recognized as internal. . . .

In addition to the weights constituted by the sensations, there are other, lighter, but still usually sufficient in the healthy state to deprive the image of its externality; I mean recollections. The recollections are themselves images, but connected together and undergoing a recoil which gives them a situation in time. . . . General judgments acquired by experience are associated with them, and form with them a group of elements connected among themselves and so balanced, by their relations to one another, as to form a whole of considerable cohesion, and lending its entire force to each of its elements. Every one may observe in his own case the reductive power of this group. A few days ago, I had a very clear and perfectly connected dream, in which I committed a ridiculous and enormous absurdity, too much so to describe; let us take something less glaring, such as quietly drawing off one's boots in company, and placing them on the mantlepiece beside the clock. It happened in a drawing room I like very much; I saw distinctly the principal guests, their dress, their attitudes, I spoke to them, the scene was long, and the impression so clear that a quarter of an hour after I could have described it with every detail. I felt ill at ease, and was wondering how I could get out of my difficulty. Just then I began to awake, and this state lasted two or three minutes. My eyes were still closed; but probably, through some feeling of color or actual movement, ordinary consciousness was reviving, though feebly. In the first place, I was astonished at having shown such frightful ill-breeding; in other words, the vague recollection of my previous actions rose up and came into opposition with my dream; this recollection became more precise, and brought on others; the lines of the past were reformed, and at the same time and in the same degree, the absurdity I had dreamed of, finding no standing room, disappeared and evaporated. Then came this judgment based on general ideas: "It is all a dream." The ridiculous image, at once and definitely, became distinct and severed from the real recollections, and entered the region of pure phantasm.

[*Circa* 1885]

PART III

THE NEW WORLD OF DREAM RESEARCH

Introduction to Part III

HERBERT GREENHOUSE

WHAT IS *the new world of dream research?*

Freud, his contemporaries, and later psychiatrists and psychologists opened the door to a more profound understanding of the dynamics of the dream—why people dream and what the process is deep within the psyche that shapes the dream. Their theories suffered, however, from a basic weakness—most dreamers either forget their dreams or have only a vague recollection of them. If they are asked by a psychotherapist or dream researcher to recall their dreams hours or days later, much distortion has crept into their accounts. Freud himself wrote of "secondary elaboration" —the tendency of the dreamer upon awakening to reconstruct his dream in rationalistic terms. He sees his dream from the viewpoint of one who is fully awake, not as a participant in the dream itself.

With the discovery in 1952 of the REMS (rapid eye movements), however, it was now possible to record dreams immediately at any time of the night, thus to test the older psychiatric and physiological theories of dream origins. For the last twenty years scores of researchers have been sitting in laboratories night after night, watching the brain wave and eye movement patterns of sleepers in another room. When the EOG pens trace the darting side-to-side movement of the sleeper's eyes, he is awakened and asked to describe his dream. Many new facts about dreaming have been learned through this technique—when people dream, how often they dream, how long they dream, the proportion of dreaming to sleeping time during the night, etc.

Have Freud, Adler, and the other theorists been proven right? Is it true, as Freud claimed, that dreams are the royal road to the unconscious mind, that they discharge the repressed emotions accumulated each day by the dreamer, thus making the dream act as a "safety valve," and that one of the dream's functions is to keep the sleeper from waking up and thus it becomes the "guardian of sleep"? On several counts the insights of the psychologists and psychiatrists have been verified. Dreams are indeed a safety valve that allows the discharge of negative emotions, and they are a depth-phenomenon revealing the personality and motivations of the dreamer. But it may be more accurate to call sleep the guardian of dreams rather than the reverse. Careful charting of dreams has shown that they are a biological as well as a psychological necessity.

As a biologically determined process, dreams occur at regular intervals throughout the night and in more or less predictable patterns. Experiments depriving sleepers of their dreams have resulted in disorientation and often physical and psychotic symptoms. When the sleeper is allowed to dream once more, he makes up in dreaming time for the amount he has lost. There is some evidence that animals dream, too, and show serious psychological and physical degeneration when they are deprived of sleep.

The new world of dream research has also found that even when the sleeper is not dreaming, a kind of thinking goes on all night long that resembles conscious daytime thought. Another form of thinking-dreaming occurs as the sleeper is dozing off—the drowsy or hypnagogic dream that differs both from sleeping but nondreaming thought and from the dreams of the regular cycle that begin ninety minutes later. Hypnagogic dreams are most often in the form of still pictures, comparable to slides flashing in sequence on a screen, while dreams during the regular cycle are like a surrealistic movie complete with characters and action.

Earlier theorists such as Wundt and Abercrombie who thought that dreams were initiated and shaped by sense stimuli or gastric disturbances have been refuted in the laboratory. The Dement-Wolpert experiments in this section show that sense stimuli introduced during dreaming and nondreaming periods—throwing cold water on the sleeper, flashing lights in his eyes, or sounding tones—do not start a dream or markedly affect its content.

Many of the researchers have tried to influence the subject's dreams by showing him exciting films before he goes to sleep. An interesting type of experiment based on the Poetzl effect has proven the Freudian view that dreamers use little-noticed experiences of the day before—the "day's residues"—to construct the manifest or superficial content of the dream. Poetzl was a dream researcher who used the technique of flashing pictures on a screen in milliseconds so that they could not be consciously recorded by the observer. He found, as contemporary researchers have, that the details that have gone unnoticed by the conscious mind help to structure the dream.

Telepathic messages are also incorporated into the dream fabric. At the Division of Parapsychology and Psychophysics of Maimonides Medical Center in Brooklyn, a "sender" sits in one room while the subject sleeps in another, and concentrates through the night on a painting. Often the details of the painting are woven into the dream, but they merely serve the main purpose of the dream—to work out psychological problems and follow the prescribed biological pattern of dreaming.

The new dream research also uses other artificial methods to learn more about dreaming—introducing sense stimuli both before and during the dream, using drugs and hypnosis to influence the extent and content of the dream, comparing controlled daytime naps with nighttime dreams, and depriving the sleeper of both sleep and dreams to see what effect it has on dreaming and on the physical and psychological health of the dreamer. In discussing the effect of drugs and hypnosis on dreams, this section may seem to overlap Part II, but new insights in these areas have resulted from use of REM techniques.

The editors regret that space limitation prevents the inclusion of many excellent articles on dreams, some of them from the 1947 World of Dreams, *some by contemporary researchers such as Frederick Snyder, who has characterized the work since 1952 as "the new biology of dreaming." Certainly no up-to-date book on dreams can neglect mention of Nathaniel Kleitman and Eugene Aserinsky, who first discovered the REMS.*

The material in Part III—The New World of Dream Research—is arranged in this sequence: After Calvin Trillin tells how the REMS were discovered, we take a tour of the dream laboratory and follow the sleep-dream stages of a typical night; our next articles discuss the new findings about dreams, including the possibility that the sleeper's eyes watch the dream action; the following articles describe NREM or nondreaming sleep and the nature of drowsy or hypnagogic dreams; next is a discussion of nappers, narcoleptics, nightmares and sleepwalkers, followed by articles that chart the age differences in dreaming time and the dreaming of animals along the evolutionary scale; then the dramatic relationship between dreams on the same night is shown, followed by the kind of sense impressions that occur in dreams, the presence or absence of color in dreams, and the dreams of the deaf and blind. The final section takes up the many ways of artificially influencing dreams, including dream telepathy, and ends with a discussion of the biological need to sleep and dream.

It must be emphasized that dream researchers, as scientists, are cautious about their own findings. It takes many replications of a dream experiment before the results may be thought of as conclusive. Even as this book goes to press, exciting new experiments and new discoveries are being made and rechecked in other laboratories. It was the experimenters from 1952 to 1974, however, who laid the groundwork, as the pioneers do in every science.

A. DREAMS MOVE INTO THE LABORATORY

The Discovery of Rapid Eye Movements[*]

CALVIN TRILLIN

IN APRIL, 1952, at the University of Chicago, a graduate student of physiology named Eugene Aserinsky noticed that periodically during the night the eyes of people who are asleep move rapidly for several minutes. The movements first showed up on an early-model polygraph that Aserinsky was using—they were recorded by means of tiny electrodes taped near the subject's eyes—and Aserinsky's first reaction was that the machine must be broken. When he finally walked into a room where a subject was sleeping and looked for himself, however, he was amazed to find that his observation did not depend on machinery; he could quite easily see the eyeball bulges darting around under the lids. Difficult though it was for Aserinsky to believe, hundreds of years of scientific research had failed to uncover a phenomenon that can be observed by an insomniac watching his wife sleep in light of early morning. Most scientists first learned of the movements in September of the following year, when, in a section in the back of *Science* magazine called "Technical Reports," there appeared an article entitled "Regularly Occurring Periods of Eye Motility and Concomitant Phenomena During Sleep." The article—written by Aserinsky and Nathaniel Kleitman, a distinguished physiologist and student of sleep in whose laboratory Aserinsky had been working—reported on some remarkable findings gathered from people who had been awakened and questioned during the night. "Of twenty-seven interrogations during ocular motility, twenty revealed detailed dreams," Aserinsky and Kleitman wrote. "Of twenty-three

* From "A Third State of Existence" by Calvin Trillin. Reprinted by permission; © 1965 The New Yorker Magazine, Inc.

interrogations during ocular inactivity, nineteen disclosed complete failure of recall."

Aserinsky's discovery and the discoveries that quickly followed it in Kleitman's laboratory represented one of the rare instances of a scientific breakthrough that opens up an entirely new field of research. There had previously been some reports of slow, pendular eye movements, related to the other movements of the body during the night—Aserinsky was studying these when he made his discovery—and it was later found that as early as 1892 a psychologist named George Trumbull Ladd had speculated that the eyeballs might move during dreaming. By 1953, however, Ladd's speculation had long been forgotten, and the standard scientific belief was that the eyes were in a position of rest during sleep. In demonstrating that this was not true, and that the movements that did occur indicated that a dream was taking place, Aserinsky and Kleitman provided scientists with their first opportunity to identify and study dreaming sleep. Not surprisingly, it turned out to be an opportunity to discover that practically everything that had been believed about the cause and nature of dreaming was not true.

Despite the dramatic appearance of this opportunity, scientists seemed in no hurry to take advantage of it. After Aserinsky obtained his doctorate, he turned to more orthodox physiology, one reason being that the physiology departments that hire researchers seemed to believe that the study of sleep and dreams, while interesting, was not quite a proper pastime for a respectable physiologist. Kleitman, who had often seemed to be alone in the field during forty years of research, was about to retire. From 1954 to 1957, just about the only researcher in the country studying Rapid Eye Movement Sleep (or REM Sleep, to use the acronym that is common among researchers) was a nearly indefatigable medical student named William Dement, who had come to Kleitman's laboratory to do research a few months after Aserinsky first noticed the eye movements. In the three years he remained at the lab (while completing both his M.D. and a doctorate in physiology), Dement began to investigate the basic questions raised by the discovery: Just what is dreaming and what is its function? Most of what was learned up to 1958 about the implications of Aserinsky's discovery can be found in Dement's Ph.D. thesis. In it, he states, "In the development of nearly every new discovery, the initial dramatic observation is followed by a period of painstaking, often tedious investigation to complete the details of the description." Dement's work in those years was undoubtedly painstaking and tedious, even for somebody as fascinated by the phenomenon of dreaming sleep as he was. To this day, sleep research remains one of the most wearing kinds of scientific research, with practical problems that only begin with the necessity of staying awake all night in order to observe somebody else sleep. The field still consists mostly of young men—often sleepy young men—whose occupational difficulties include wives irritated by constant absences, eyes strained from trying to make some manageable record from the tracings on miles of graph paper, and social lives haunted by questions about whether or not dreams are in color. These hardships alone might have been enough to keep some people out of sleep research, but, according to Dement, the problem in those early years was mainly that "physiologists weren't interested in dreams and psychiatrists weren't interested in research."

Dement's completion of the details was an extraordinary start in the attempt to find out what it was that Aserinsky had discovered. For a number of years, scientists had used the electroencephalograph, or EEG—which traces brain waves on graph paper in much the same way that an electrocardiograph traces heart action—to divide sleep into stages of "depth." The division was made to account for the differences in voltage and frequency between the brain-wave pattern of a sleeping person and the pattern of the waking brain—from a "light" stage that was almost the same as being awake to a "deep" stage characterized by a much less active pattern. Dement used the same method; he and Kleitman divided sleep into four stages. But by keeping the electroencephalograph on all night instead of merely taking samplings, he discovered that the stages were not caused, as had previously been thought, by a person's awakening, or nearly awakening, during the night and then gradually falling back into "deep sleep;" instead, the stages occurred every night in a predictable cycle. Dement discovered that the eye movements occurred only in Stage 1, when the brain-wave pattern most resembled the waking pattern. In fact, except for a brief appearance of Stage 1 without eye movements at the beginning of sleep, Stage 1 sleep and dreaming sleep were identical. By remaining awake all night two or three times a week, Dement eventually saw enough sleep recordings to create a simple, predictable pattern for the phenomenon that had so long been considered fortuitous. He knew that dreaming occurred about every ninety minutes, that it could be identified both by a Stage 1 brain-wave pattern and by eye movements, that it lasted for periods that became increasingly long during the night but averaged about twenty minutes, and that each period consisted of several dreams, usually separated by some movement of the body and a brief moment of wakefulness. He found, in other words, that everybody has approximately four to seven periods of dreaming sleep during the night, taking up about twenty per cent of sleeping time and accounting for ten or twenty separate dream episodes.

Dement's research contradicted most of the commonly held notions about dreams. Freud had said that dreams existed to provide a safety valve for the fulfillment of some indestructible instinctual drive, such as hunger or sex, and that they were "the guardian of sleep" in that their stories disguised unacceptable wishes well enough to prevent the anxiety that would otherwise cause arousal. The regularity of dreaming that Dement found did not argue for such a theory, nor did his finding that dreaming did not preserve sleep, for people almost invariably woke up briefly during a dream period. Dement's findings seemed to disprove flatly the extension of the guardian-of-sleep theory to mean that dreams occurred in order to explain away any noise or discomfort that would have awakened the sleeper if it had not been surrounded with a story. He had some success in modifying dreams once the Rapid Eye Movement period had started (people who were squirted with water might dream of sudden rainfalls, leaking roofs, or being squirted with water), but he found that it was impossible to bring on a dream by disturbing a sleeper if the sleeper was not already in a REM period. He also disproved the notion that dreams were caused by gastrointestinal distress brought on by the eating of the previous evening—an opinion held by what is occasionally called the cheese-and-pickle school. Dement found that the dreaming cycle began approximately every ninety minutes, cheese and pickles or no cheese and pickles.

The dozens of awakenings made in these early studies verified the original finding of Aserinsky and Kleitman that if people were awakened during a REM period they could be expected to recall a dream four times out of five. Of course, Dement, who has always been a man of scrupulous skepticism, never accepted the existence of dream recall as being equivalent to the existence of dreams. Theoretically, all dreams could be invented by people as they woke up. However, in his experiments in the Chicago laboratory he found it increasingly difficult to doubt that rapid eye movements were indeed an indication that dreaming was taking place, and that the action of the dream was not instantaneous, as had once been thought, but lasted as long as the REM period lasted. The fact that some dream reports were gathered during non-REM-period awakenings—they were relatively few and usually much less vivid—suggested that some mental activity more abstract than dream adventures took place during the non-REM period, although some of the reports were obviously memories of dreams from the previous REM period. The most interesting evidence that Dement found to support the existence of dreams was a correlation between the dream narrative and the way the eyes moved. Merely by studying the polygraph record of how a person's eyes moved during a dream, Dement could predict in most cases whether or not the dream content had been particularly active. One night, he noticed that a subject was having a series of uninterrupted vertical eye movements, and he decided to awaken subjects from then on whenever their eye movements were consistently vertical or consistently horizontal. He found five more examples of consistently vertical eye movements. The subjects recalled standing at the foot of a cliff and looking up at climbers and down at some equipment; climbing up a series of ladders and looking up and down; throwing basketballs at a net; looking at the top of some stairs; and watching leaflets floating down from a blimp. Dement found one case of steady horizontal movements. When the subject was awakened, he reported that in his dream he had been watching two people throw tomatoes at each other.

The Dream Cycle Throughout the Night

GAY GAER LUCE

THE ELECTROENCEPHALOGRAPH

The progression of cycles that make up a night's sleep have been pieced together by numerous observers through nightlong vigils in sleep laboratories. There are perhaps 2 dozen sleep laboratories in the United States, in university buildings and hospitals. They vary somewhat in size and newness, and complexity of equipment, but laboratories designed for the study of human sleep basically resemble each other. In the control room the visitor will notice the fundamental polygraph instruments, consolidated in the big amplifier system, the electroencephalograph machine, a device through which researchers can watch brain activity. Small conductive electrodes, bits of metal pasted onto the scalp, or in some cases, needles implanted in the brain, transmit the natural beat of a brain region through changes of electric potential. The electroencephalograph (EEG) amplifies these shifts in potential, transmitting them to magnetic tape, or driving a row of ink pens on the desklike panel of the machine. Each pen, driven by a signal from a part of the brain, moves up when the electric charge is negative and down when the charge becomes positive. As a continuous sheet of graph paper moves forward on a roller, at a constant speed, under the oscillating pens, the up-and-down pen movements are traced out as waves—brain waves. Their amplitude indicates the ever shifting amount of voltage generated in a brain region, and their shape can indicate the speed of the electrical changes within. Thus, a glance at the inked record will tell whether the potentials in the brain are shifting in a regular, synchronous fashion, with slow, large voltage changes, or whether the changes are fast and irregular, desynchronized.

Although some body functions can be detected by simply looking at a person, precise and reliable measures of blood pressure, pulse, respiration, muscle tone, temperature require sensing devices that can produce signals to be amplified and recorded in the manner of brain waves. In order to minimize interference with sleep, researchers now use some of the miniature instruments developed for space exploration. For example, a thermistor no bigger than a pin can be used to detect body temperature continuously. This kind of equipment enables simultaneous recordings of heart rate and temperature fluctuations on the same record as the EEG, showing how changes in brain wave patterns are related to changing body functions.

THE SLEEP LABORATORY

On any evening, when most people have settled down to an after-dinner entertainment or are preparing for bed, the sleep scientist has begun to check out his equipment. Inkwells are filled, pens cleaned, wire leads tested for insulation and possible breaks, and a thousand-foot sheet of folded EEG paper inserted between the rollers, reels of magnetic tape set in place. Continual adjustments, requiring some manual and electronic dexterity, are essential to reliable data collection, and before the arrival of a sleep subject, the control room resembles the cockpit of a plane during the instrument check for takeoff.

The aura of the sleep laboratory is similar, whether it is 10-below-zero on the snowbound University of Chicago campus where a solitary row of lights mark the brownstone containing the laboratory, or a balmy California night outside the vast and silent new hospital at UCLA. The sleep researcher collects his data largely during these lonely hours, a strenuous pursuit, sometimes requiring vigils for many consecutive nights, weeks, or even months. It is an endeavor requiring physical and mental endurance, one that places a strain on all personal or social activity, for it may be necessary to monitor the sleep of others on many consecutive nights while fulfilling administrative and academic duties and analyzing the data by day.

Our current picture of a night's sleep is a composite of thousands of nights and thousands of volunteers, most of them young men in their twenties, generally students or professionals. Very often they are paid a small sum to sleep in the laboratory and abide by the rules of the study—which may prohibit napping, drinking coffee or alcohol, and taking drugs. Typically, the young volunteer will arrive before 10 p.m., change into pajamas, and seat himself in some corner of the laboratory to be decorated for the night.

Often, in the strong odor of acetone and collodion, used to fasten electrodes to the skin, the experimenter will conduct a quiet and soothing conversation as he carefully affixes the electrodes to the top of the head, at the temples, near the eyes. Each electrode disc has a brightly colored lead, following a color code, and the many-colored wires are often drawn through a ring at the top of the head like a pigtail. When the preparation is securely finished, the volunteer will go to bed in one of the quiet bedrooms adjacent to the control room. The room is ordinary enough, except for a jackboard at the head of the bed, and an intercom system. The wires from the volunteer's head are plugged into the jack-board, and he settles down. The lights go out. The bed is comfortable, and the volunteer can move freely, although he cannot get up and walk around ordinarily without being unplugged. If he wants anything, however, he can tell the experimenter through the intercom system.

The room is private, the volunteer is comfortable, the technical details of the study well in hand, and one might expect that data collection would be quite routine. In all human studies, however, there is an emotional component, and the somewhat predictable, somewhat elusive interplay of feelings adds a heavy burden to the sleep study. Even a well-balanced medical student may have a hard time falling asleep in his private bedroom although accustomed to being in laboratories; the gentlemen beyond the door are monitoring his brain waves, and although he knows that EEG patterns do not invade mental privacy in the sense that they cannot reveal thought or dream content, the laboratory situation is strange.

"THE LABORATORY EFFECT"

On their first night subjects often do not exhibit the sleep patterns that seem characteristic of them on later nights. A night or two of adjustment may be necessary, in full headdress. Sometimes as many as five or more consecutive nights will be necessary to obtain the baseline—the usual pattern of the individual's sleep—before the experimenter collects a sole night of data. However trivial the bias may be in a particular study, and no matter what precautions have been taken, the so-called "laboratory effect" resides within all the generalizations being drawn from human studies—as illustrated by the fact that among hundreds of young men in the laboratories, nightmares and wet dreams have been extremely rare. Thus, in speaking of the typical night of sleep as we now see it, we must bear in mind some modifications for it is a composite of nights spent in a laboratory.

DROWSINESS

Usually, about 11 p.m., the acclimated volunteer will be relaxed. His body temperature is declining. His eyes are closed, and he is no longer moving. On the graph paper in the control room the jumble of rapid, irregular brain waves is beginning to form a new pattern, a regular rhythm known as the alpha rhythm. This pattern of 9–12 cycles a second indicates relaxed wakefulness. Subjectively, it is a serene and pleasant state, devoid of deliberate thought, into which images may float. A moment of tension or attempt to solve a mental problem will disrupt it.

With further relaxation the alpha waves grow smaller, decreasing in amplitude. As alpha rhythm diminishes, a person's time perception seems to deteriorate, and two rapid flashes of light may seem to blend into one. As his alpha rhythm diminishes, the young volunteer hovers on the borders of drowsiness and sleep, perhaps seeing images, experiencing dreamlike thoughts or fragments.

STAGE 1

Another pattern begins to emerge on the EEG paper. This new script is smaller, indicating lower voltages. It is uneven, desynchronized, and it changes swiftly. At this point one may experience a floating sensation, drifting with idle images as the alpha rhythm gives way to the low voltage, fast irregular rhythm of the first stage of sleep. The volunteer, in this phase, can be easily awakened by a noise or spoken word. His body muscles are relaxing. Respiration is growing more even and heart rate is becoming slower. If awakened at this point a person may assert that he was not really asleep. This phase of consciousness is like a port of entry, a borderland, and lasts only a few minutes. Soon the background rhythm of the EEG grows slower.

STAGE 2

The script grows larger and the pens trace out quick bursts known as spindles, rapid crescendos and decrescendos of waves. The eyes of the young volunteer may appear to be slowly rolling. He is quite soundly asleep, yet it is not hard to awaken him. By now there has been a fundamental change in his brain function. One aspect of this change is suggested by a study in which volunteers slept with their eyes half open; illuminated objects were suspended before their eyes. On the whole they were not awakened by the light, nor did they remember seeing anything, but when awakened by a voice a few seconds later they often insisted they had been wide awake and thinking thoughts that, as narrated, had a vague and dreamlike quality. If awakened at this point a person might feel he had been thinking or indulging in reverie. Let undisturbed, however, he will soon descend into another level of sleep.

STAGE 3

The spindle bursts and somewhat irregular brain wave rhythm begins to be interspersed with large slow waves. These occur at about one a second, and are high in amplitude. The electrical input may run as high as 300 microvolts in stage 3, as compared with the 60 microvolts of the waking alpha rhythm. Now it will take a louder noise to awaken the sleeping person or animal, perhaps a repetition of his name. His muscles are very relaxed. He breathes evenly, and his heart rate continues to slow down. His blood pressure is falling, and his temperature continues to decline. Innocuous sensory events are making almost no impression on the awareness of the sleeper, and were he among the people who do sleep with their eyes half open, he would not be seeing anything.

STAGE 4

This stage might be called a most oblivious sleep. The muscles are very relaxed, and the person rarely moves. It is hard to awaken him with the low noise or buzzer that would have aroused him earlier. His heart rate and temperature are still declining, and his respiration is slow and even. Waken the volunteer now with a loud noise or by calling his name and he may come into focus slowly, and may feel that he was not experiencing any mental activity. The EEG pens scratch out a continuous train of slow, high amplitude waves. The sleeper is utterly removed from the world, although his brain wave responses would indicate that every sound and the lightest touch are received in his brain. Indeed, during this synchronous, slow-wave sleep the brain shows a very large response to outside stimuli such as sounds, but the brain systems that make this stimulation into conscious sensation appear not to be working in their usual way. This may account for the eerie apparition, the somnambulist, who will rise from bed in this stage of sleep, negotiate a room full of furniture, look straight at people with eyes open, yet appear not to perceive them, and return to bed, usually recalling nothing of the interlude when awakened. Stage 4 appears to be one of the times when children commonly wet their beds, a time when a person is, by some criteria, most deeply asleep. Although people can be trained to discriminate between sounds, to hear spoken words, to press a button during another stage of sleep, their performance during stage 4 is not nearly so frequent.

A normal person will spend a considerable portion of the night in this stage, especially if he has lost sleep. If annoyed from outside, he will tend to drift into a lighter phase of sleep, but if annoyances prevent him from spending a certain portion of his night in stage 4, on subsequent nights he will make it up by spending substantially more time in stage 4. Although he seems hard to awaken from this phase, paradoxically he may be even harder to awaken from the first stage of sleep—if he happens to be in the throes of dreaming.

STAGE 1 REM

About an hour or so after falling asleep, the sleeper may begin to drift back up into the lighter phases of sleep. Roughly 90 minutes have passed, and the volunteer's sleep has resumed the pattern of stage 2. Now, suddenly, the pens of the EEG begin to jabber, scratching out wild oscillations. He has turned over in bed, and moved. As the oscillations die away the brain wave record shows an irregular low-voltage, rapidly changing script like that of stage 1. Now two pens that are activated by movements of the eyes make rapid darts, as if the eyes had turned to look at something. Intermittently the pens continue. The eyes move as if following a film. These rapid eye movements, known as REMs, signal a phase of vivid dreaming, a most unique state of consciousness. In this phase, it will take a relatively huge amount of noise to awaken a person—yet a very slight noise, with significance, may quickly alert him.

Sound a click in the sleeper's ear, and his brain wave response will not resemble that of stage 4—but shows a great resemblance to the response during waking. Although it may be hard to awaken a person at this time, in many ways his brain activity paradoxically resembles waking, and REM sleep is often called paradoxical sleep. It is believed by some investigators to be a unique state, totally different from the rest of sleep, and subserved by different brain mechanisms.

The entire body shows pronounced changes now. Gone is the even breath and pulse. The organs that show the most striking changes in sleep are those indicating fright or anger. Everyone is familiar with the blanched skin, wide eyes, rapid heart beat and knotted stomach of fright. These changes are controlled by the closely related nerves of the autonomic nervous system, which regulates the organs of the chest and viscera, changes in the skin and eyes, with the help of hormones secreted by the adrenal glands. The autonomic system modifies its organic domain in unison, and is tuned in to the emotional state of the creature. During slow wave sleep the heart rate, respiration, and blood pressure fall to their lowest levels of the day, falling at sleep onset and continuing to drop until about an hour before awakening. During REM sleep, however, the heart rate, blood pressure, and respiration become exceedingly variable, sometimes fluctuating wildly. Usually there is a long interval of REM sleep during the latter part of the night, the time when a person's temperature has fallen to its nadir. During the REM period in the early hours of morning the activity of the autonomic system often becomes most intense, inducing what have been called "autonomic storms," which may account for the statistically frequent occurrence of heart attacks at this time, and further study of this period may make it possible to anticipate and prevent such coronaries.

Many of the physical changes that attend the REM state can be observed from watching the sleeper. At the onset the muscles of the head and chin will relax completely. This is so regular that the loss of tonus in the muscle under the chin can serve to activate an alarm, signalling the onset of REM sleep. Most teeth-grinding occurs at this time. From infancy through adulthood, the REM period is attended by penile erections in males. Rapid, jerky movements of the eyes can be seen, even in many blind people.

Most striking of all, however, is the now substantial evidence that this is a period of vivid dreaming for all humankind, and the suggestion that it is a period of consciousness in which monkeys and perhaps other animals experience vivid imagery. Awakened during REM sleep, a person will almost inevitably report mentation that differs from waking thought, dramatic, and often bizarre—generally recognized as a dream. Yet, if he is awakened a few minutes after the rapid eye movements cease, when he has lapsed into another phase of sleep, the dream will have evaporated. The average individual spends a total of about 5 years of his life in such vivid dreaming, but for the most part he is amnesic, remembering very little.

The discovery of the REM phase of sleep and subsequent findings about the body and brain during this state have raised many fundamental questions about the organization and function of the central nervous system, and has stimulated a rapidly growing body of research which will be explored at greater length in later sections of this paper.

It has been said that the average adult dreams about every 90 minutes, and that the full cycle of sleep stages spans an interval of 90–120 minutes, corresponding to a subcycle within the circadian temperature rhythm.

This generalization is somewhat misleading, although it has been widely propagated in the press, for dreaming, dreamlike experiences, fragments, images, mentation occur in all phases of sleep, although recall varies. Sleep is a succession of repeated cycles. Nevertheless, one's progression through a night does not resemble the passage of a train on a circular track, arriving at different stations at a predictable time. People of about the same age do not follow such a rigid timetable of sleep, and all humanity does not rise and fall on the waves of a single tide.

THE WHOLE NIGHT

A reexamination of the nightly EEG patterns of sleep has been conducted recently with 16 medical students, each of whom spent four nights in the laboratory. Only two uniform patterns emerged. The entire group showed a greater incidence of REM periods during the last third of the night, and the slow-wave sleep of stage 4 predominated during the first third of the night. Not only was there no consistent time schedule of sleep stages for the group—but individuals showed slightly different patterns on different nights. Excepting for their REM periods they did not spend more than 10 minutes at a time in any EEG phase, and throughout the night stage 2 with its spindles occurred evenly, like a transition period, a bridge. Evidence from a number of studies suggests that each of us has a characteristic sleep pattern, an EEG script that is identifiable and individual, although we vary somewhat from night to night. So far no rules have been found for describing the succession of EEG phases that all people will pass through in a night's sleep, but more sophisticated analyses may indeed reveal an inherent order in the sequence of cycles.

However much people differ in detail, normal people show roughly the same overall pattern. They sleep for a long interval once in 24 hours, at the time of their lowest body temperature. They spend roughly the same proportion of the night in REM sleep and stage 4, distributing them over the night in roughly the same manner.

A Chart of Sleep and Dream Stages

ROBERT L. VAN DE CASTLE

The sequential unfolding of the sleep stages is shown in the accompanying graph. As a subject moves from wakefulness through drowsiness, he passes through a very brief "descending" Stage 1 down to Stage 4 sleep. After having been asleep for an hour or so, the record moves from Stage 4, back up through Stage 3, and eventuates in the appearance of a very brief REM period that may last only about five minutes. Following this REM period he usually returns again to Stage 4 sleep, but usually not for as long a period of time. Approximately ninety minutes after the onset of the first REM period, the subject again evidences another REM period, which may continue for approximately ten minutes or so. Generally the subject does not return to Stage 4 sleep, or does so for only a very brief period of time, after the second REM period. He will generally spend some time in Stage 3, however, before the appearance of the third REM period. As before, the onset of this REM period occurs approximately ninety minutes after the onset of the previous REM period. The typical pattern for the remainder of the night would be for the subject to alternate between Stage 2 sleep and REM sleep, with the remaining REM periods also occurring at approximately ninety-minute intervals.

As the graph shows, most Stage 4 sleep is obtained during the first third

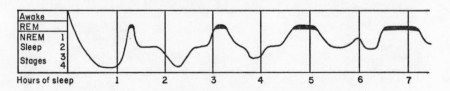

Figure 1. Changes in stages of sleep during the night.

of the night. Each succeeding REM period tends to become progressively longer and the final REM period of the night may last from twenty-five to forty-five minutes. It should be emphasized that the sleep pattern of any individual on a given night may show various departures from the pattern that has been described since the preceding pattern is one based upon averages obtained from a large number of young adult subjects. For the normal adult, REM sleep occupies approximately 22 per cent of his sleep, with the remainder of his sleep spent approximately in the following fashion: Stage 2, 50 per cent; Stage 3, 7 per cent; Stage 4, 14 per cent and Stage 1 NREM, 7 per cent.

B. NEW FACTS ABOUT DREAMS

Everybody Dreams Every Night

STANLEY KRIPPNER, Ph.D., and WILLIAM HUGHES

AT THE UNIVERSITY OF CHICAGO, in April, 1952, a graduate student noticed that periodically during the night the eyes of people who are asleep move rapidly for several minutes. This discovery represents one of the rare instances of a scientific breakthrough that opens up an entirely new field of research. As early as 1892 a psychologist [Ladd] had speculated that the eyeballs might move during dreaming but his speculation was soon forgotten and most physiologists held that the eyes were in a position of rest during sleep. The 1952 discovery led to other psychophysiological findings that demonstrated that most of what had been believed about the dreaming process was not true.

Replacing the notion that dreams last only a few seconds was the finding that the EEG-monitored Rapid Eye Movement (REM) stages of sleep are rarely less than 10 minutes long and may last for an hour or more. In his doctoral dissertation, one investigator (Dement, 1958) demonstrated that the acting out, in waking life, of the content of the dream narrative takes about as long as the duration of the REM stage from which the dream was reported.

Replacing the idea that one dreams only before waking was the discovery that there is an average of four or five REM stages in the course of a typical night's sleep. The average young adult subject spends about 20 per cent of his sleep time in the REM state. During infancy and childhood the proportion is much higher, while during old age it is somewhat lower.

Replacing the assumption that many people dream rarely or never was the finding that virtually everyone dreams every night. It is true that some people *remember* their dreams more frequently than others, but this fact is related to situational and personality variables rather than to the actual amount of dream time. Foulkes has concluded, "Those who generally deny or ignore their world of private and subjective experience during wakefulness seem to recall fewer dreams than do those who accept and exploit this dimension of experience."

The psychophysiological data refute not only the folklore on dreams but also many of the theoretical stances held by Freudian and Adlerian psychoanalysts. Both Freud and Adler felt that individuals dream in proportion to the number and intensity of their personal problems but the data demonstrate that the REM stages recur in a highly predictable cyclic pattern with few variations for each individual studied. Emotional problems often take advantage of the dreaming state and a skilled psychoanalyst can use dream content therapeutically. However, the recent research findings do not support the notion that one's emotional problems precipitate or "trigger" the REM state.

Sleep Longer, Dream More

W. B. WEBB and H. W. AGNEW, JR.

In a general population of humans of the same age there is a wide range of individual differences in average sleep lengths. In a recent self-report survey of 2369 17-year-old students entering the University of Florida, for example, 8 percent reported sleeping less than 6½ hours per night and 13 percent reported sleeping more than 8½ hours per night. These naturally occurring differences in sleep length raise a number of questions about the sleep stage characteristics associated with them. Do short sleepers miniaturize the sleep characteristics of the long sleepers? Are some stages of sleep reduced in short sleepers and others accentuated? More particularly, do short sleepers adapt their sleep process relative to the REM stage or are they relatively deprived of this stage by partial deprivation?

Two senior high school classes of the University of Florida laboratory school were administered a questionnaire about their sleep which included an item on sleep length. Subsequently, the students maintained a sleep log for 2 weeks in which they recorded their daily time of retiring and awakening. Two screening criteria were then introduced: (i) five successive nights of the sleep log entries in which the reported sleep length did not differ by more than 1 hour; (ii) a discrepancy of less than 1 hour between the questionnaire estimate of sleep length and the average of the five successive nights selected above. Subjects meeting these criteria and sleeping less than 6½ hours or more than 8½ hours were selected for further consideration. An independent estimate of the usual time of retiring and awakening of the subject was obtained from a parent or guardian. Again, a 1-hour discrepancy in estimated sleep length was used to eliminate subjects. From the remaining subjects, the long and the short sleepers meeting our 8½ and 6½ criteria were chosen. The selected subjects included six short sleepers (two males and four females) and eight long sleepers (four males and four females). Average lengths of sleep (from the sleep log) ranged in the short sleep group from 5 hours and 50 minutes to 6 hours and 25 minutes; in the long sleep group, from 8 hours and 40 minutes to 9 hours and 40 minutes. All subjects were between 17 and 19 years of age.

The EEG sleep patterns of the subjects were recorded in the laboratory on three consecutive nights. They were asked to continue their daily routines but to report to the laboratory 1 hour prior to their usual bedtime. . . .

For comparison a "control" group was drawn from a previously reported study. This group consisted of 14 males, 17 to 19 years of age, who were not selected on a sleep length criterion. Their data are the second and third nights of experimentally uninterrupted sleep in the same laboratory, recorded and scored by the same procedures.

Table 1 displays the number of minutes slept in each sleep stage by the long sleepers, the short sleepers, and the control group. Figure 1 presents the hour-by-hour mean number of minutes of stage 4 and stage REM for the experimental groups.

Both experimental groups differed significantly from the control group in total time slept. The shortest mean sleep length for the long sleepers was 529 minutes; the longest mean sleep length for the short sleepers was 395 minutes. The short sleep group had less sleep in combined stages 0 and 1 than the long sleepers and probably less than the control group. They had less stage 2 sleep than either the long sleepers or the control group, and less stage 3 sleep than the control. The long sleepers had more stage REM and stage 2 sleep than either the short sleep group or the control group. They probably had more combined stage 0 and stage 1 sleep than the controls. The short sleep group did not differ statistically from the control group in stage 4 and stage REM. The long sleep group did not differ from either the control group or the short sleep group in stage 4 sleep. All statistical tests are two tail tests of the t-test for independent means.

Subjects selected on the basis of naturally occurring long and short

TABLE 1
THE MEAN TIME SPENT IN EACH STAGE OF
SLEEP AFTER THE ONSET OF THE FIRST STAGE 1.

Stage	Duration (minutes) for		
	LONG SLEEPERS	SHORT SLEEPERS	CONTROL GROUP
0	8	2	5
1	32	12	21
REM	155	96	101
2	277	168	215
3	22	18	29
4	72	81	81
Total	566	377	452

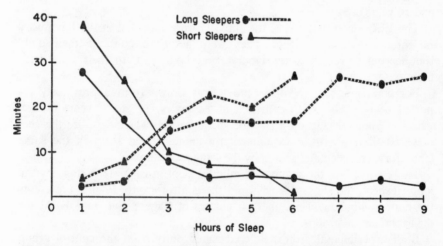

Figure 1. Mean number of minutes of stage 4 and REM sleep by long and short sleepers. The solid line represents stage 4 sleep; the dashed line, REM sleep. Dots represent long sleepers; triangles, short sleepers.

sleep patterns gave evidence of different kinds of sleep processes when these processes were measured in the laboratory and indexed by EEG sleep stages. Short sleepers showed a pattern that may be interpreted as more "efficient." Less time was spent in light sleep and awakenings. Their reduced stage 3 suggests that they made the transition from stage 2 to stage 4 more readily, since stage 3 is essentially a mixed stage 2 and stage 4 record. They received as much stage 4 or REM sleep, generally considered as need stages, as did the unselected sleepers, although they slept 1 hour and 15 minutes less. On the other hand, the long sleep group showed marked increases in REM sleep and in stage 2 sleep when compared with the control group, increases of 53 and 36 percent, respectively. The large relative increase in stage REM would reflect a continuation of the intra-sleep cycling previously noted, in which REM occurs as a prominent aspect of the later part of the natural sleep process.

Jones and Oswald have recently reported the sleep stage characteristics of two subjects who had consistently slept only about 3 hours per night over a long period of time. In both cases the absolute amount of stages 3 and 4 constituted approximately 50 percent (80 to 90 minutes) of sleep periods that averaged 165 minutes; REM sleep, on the other hand, occupied only about 40 minutes of the sleep periods. These data indicate that there is a point at which shortening of the total time available for sleep will result in REM restriction in chronic sleep patterns.

Both our data and those of Jones and Oswald support a hypothesis that the absolute amount of REM will be a function of the length of time of the sleep period. In order to sleep length the average amounts of REM in the four populations examined were: 2 hours and 45 minutes sleep, 48 minutes REM; 6 hours and 17 minutes sleep, 96 minutes REM (short sleepers); 7 hours and 32 minutes sleep, 101 minutes REM (control group); and 9 hours and 26 minutes sleep, 155 minutes REM (long sleepers). There is some evidence to support the hypothesis that initial "strength" of the stage 4 response is a function of the time between sleep periods. It has been previously noted that a strong stage 4 response is typical of total deprivation conditions exceeding 24 hours. In the Jones and Oswald study, stages 3 and 4 constituted 50 percent of sleep with 21 hours between sleep periods. This tendency for a potent stage 4 response had been noted in a study of partial sleep deprivation in which sleep was restricted to 3 hours per night (and hence 21 hours between sleep periods); stage 3 and 4 sleep constituted 55 percent of the 3 hours. Compared with the long sleepers, the short sleepers of this study (with a longer time between sleep periods) showed a higher stage 4 response in the early part of the night (Figure 1).

The three articles that follow are excerpts from papers describing laboratory experiments that disclosed new facts about dreamers and dreaming.

Your Eyes Watch the Dream Action (I)

WILLIAM DEMENT and NATHANIEL KLEITMAN

Specific eye-movement patterns and visual imagery of the dream.—
The quality and quantity of the REM's themselves showed endless variation. There was much or little movement, big or small movements, and so on. As has been stated, the movements occurred in bursts of activity separated by periods of relative inactivity. However, the brain-wave stage during the whole period remained the same whether there was much or little movement at any given moment of the period.

It was hypothesized that the movements represented the visual imagery of the dream, that is, that they corresponded to where and at what the dreamer was looking. An attempt to account for every movement by having S state chronologically in what directions he had gazed in the dream proved futile. The Ss could not recall the dream with such a high order of detail and precision.

In a slightly different approach, Ss were awakened as soon as one of four predominant patterns of movement had persisted for at least 1 min. and were asked to describe in detail the dream content just before awakening. The four patterns were: (*a*) mainly vertical eye movements, (*b*) mainly horizontal movements, (*c*) both vertical and horizontal movements, and (*d*) very little or no movement. The prevalence of the horizontal or vertical components was determined by placing leads both vertically and horizontally around the eyes.

A total of 35 awakenings was accumulated from the nine Ss. Periods of either pure vertical or horizontal movements were extremely rare. Three such periods of vertical movements were seen. After each of these the dream content involved a predominance of action in the vertical plane. One S dreamed of standing at the bottom of a tall cliff operating some sort of hoist and looking up at climbers at various levels and down at the hoist machinery. Another S dreamed of climbing up a series of ladders looking up and down as he climbed. In the third instance the dreamer was throwing basketballs at a net, first shooting and looking up at the net, and then looking down to pick another ball off the floor. Only one instance of pure horizontal movement was seen. In the associated dream S was watching two people throwing tomatoes at each other. On 10 occasions *S*s were awakened after 1 min. of little or no eye movement. In these, the dreams all had the common property that the dreamer was watching something at a distance or just staring fixedly at some object. In two of these awakenings in different *S*s the patterns were the same, as follows: about a minute of ocular inactivity followed by several large movements to the left just a second or two before the awakening. Both instances, interestingly enough, were virtually identical as regards dream content. In one case *S* was driving a car and staring at the road ahead. He approached an intersection and was startled by the sudden appearance of a car speeding at him from the left as the bell rang. In the other, the dreamer was also driving a car and staring at the road ahead. Just before the awakening he saw a man standing on the left side of the road and hailed him as he drove past.

In the 21 awakenings after a mixture of movements *S*s were always looking at things close to them, objects or people. Typical reports were of talking to a group of people, looking for something, fighting with someone, and so forth. There was no recall of distant or vertical activity.

Your Eyes Watch the Dream Action (II)

WILLIAM DEMENT and EDWARD A. WOLPERT

The direction of the eye movement as a direct expression of the spatial orientation of the dream activity.—Actually, it is hypothesized that the eye movements seen in sleep are those that the sleeper executes in the dream. However, since eye movements and fixations are for the most part not conscious, they must be inferred from the activity that one is watching. Thus, vertical eye movements should result when one watches events taking place in a vertical plane. For very short events, a person can usually remember where he "looked," although he does not remember consciously executing the specific eye movement.

In order to test the hypothesis that rapid eye movements are an exact indication of the direction of the dream activity, the very last action reported by *S*, i.e., where he looked, was compared with the very last eye movement (or its lack) before the awakening. Six *S*s were studied over 10 nights of sleep using both horizontal and vertical electrode placements around the eyes. Control fixations were executed while *S* was awake to determine the potential form associated with each of the four directions of eye movement. Of 39 dreams elicited in this series, the last dream activity before awakening could be recalled in 23 instances with sufficient clarity to differentiate the direction of the last eye movement in the dream. The last eye movement in the record was identical with the last reported fixation in the dream in 17 cases. In one example of this procedure, the last recorded eye movement was downward. The last reported dream activity was picking up an object on the floor. In this case, as in others, the eye movement corresponded in direction to what would have been expected if the dreamer had carried out this action in real life. Since Ss had to choose the correct movement from among five possibilities (up, down, right, left, none), the probability of attaining the 74% accuracy by chance alone was vanishingly small.

In addition to the above findings, two anecdotal examples similar to the others previously reported in support of this hypothesis have been obtained. The dreams were elicited after awakenings which followed an interval during which *only* vertical eye-movement potentials were seen in the record. (Instances in which either vertical or horizontal movement persists as a pure component are extremely rare.) In one, S was standing before a staircase leading up into a building. He was anxiously peering at the address which was carved in the sidewalk at his feet, and then looking up toward the top of the stairs. In the other, S was watching a blimp that hovered above him. The occupants of the blimp began dropping leaflets and S recalled alternately looking up at the blimp and down at the dropping leaflets.

Your Body Moves between Dreams

WILLIAM DEMENT and EDWARD A. WOLPERT

DREAMS AND BODY MOVEMENTS

It has been previously observed that the cessation of eye-movement periods was often accompanied by a large body movement on the part of the sleeper, and that during the eye-movement periods the incidence of gross body movement was markedly lower than during the adjacent intervals. This suggested the possibility that body movements interrupting eye-movement periods, yet followed by additional ocular activity, might mark the end of one dream sequence and the beginning of another.

In order to test this possibility, the dream transcriptions were carefully screened for examples of either long narratives of smoothly related, continuously progressing events, or accounts consisting of two or more distinct, seemingly unrelated, dream fragments. Dreams that could unequivocally be placed in one of the two categories were relatively infrequent. Many were eliminated because of poor recording. Others did not obviously fit in either category. An example of the latter was when the dream contained an abrupt shift of scene, as from a restaurant to the home dining room, but with the same people remaining as central characters. Thus, it was neither smoothly continuous nor were the two scenes entirely unrelated.

A total of 46 dreams fulfilled the requirements of being long and continuous, and 31 contained two or more apparently unrelated fragments. The associated electrical recordings were then examined for the presence of artifactual signs of body movement and were separated into those in which no body movements occurred during the eye-movement period, and those containing signs of one or more body movements. A two-by-two contingency table was used in which the presence or absence of body movements was related to recall of continuous or fragmented dreams. From this analysis, it appears that long continuous dreams are more likely to be recalled in the absence of gross body movements while fragmented dreams are more likely to be recalled if the periods contain body activity.

Assuming the execution of a body movement actually marked the end of a discrete dream episode, it seemed possible that this fragment might be forgotten and the recall limited to the dream activity following the movement and preceding the awakening. With this in mind, the transcriptions were again scanned for narratives which were much shorter than would have been expected from the objective duration of the eye-movement period. In 45 instances, dream narratives after 10 to 20 min. of rapid eye movements were as short or shorter than those generally obtained after 4 or 5 min. of eye activity. It was found that in 37 of these 45 cases, a large body movement had occurred several minutes before the awakening.

As a result of these findings, it was decided to awaken Ss during eye-movement periods just *after* a gross body movement was observed. This was done 10 times. In 3, no content was recalled, in 3, the dream was reported as usual, but in the other 4, the following very suggestive remarks were spontaneously made by Ss:

A. "I had just come to the end of a dream, I think, but it was a natural transition point. I had been talking to a friend and . . . [dream described]. Then I had the feeling that the dream ended before I woke up."

B. "I don't know if I was awake when I heard the bell. The dream seemed to be over before the bell rang."

C. "I'm trying to decide if I was dreaming just when you woke me up. I guess I was . . . [described dream]. I kind of had this feeling that just about as I finished the dream just mentioned there seemed to be a kind of little blank space or something and then just a picture of a telephone or something [arousing bell]. I got the idea that I'd finished before the bell sounded."

D. "[Dream described] I had the impression that the dream had reached its natural end, that the TV program I was watching had reached its fade-out point."

It is also worth mentioning that in one *S*, who was awakened during an eye-movement period that had a body movement every 2 or 3 min., the dream recall was extremely disjointed, consisting of six unrelated fragments. The *S* spontaneously commented that he couldn't understand why the dream was so "mixed up." All these findings indicate that body movements during dreams tend to signal a change in the dream activity.

Penile Erections during Dreams

HERBERT GREENHOUSE

LABORATORY EXPERIMENTS HAVE SHOWN that men have penile erections during every REM dreaming period, regardless of the content of the dream. Sometimes these erections have been sustained through REM periods of more than half an hour. Many ingenious devices have been used to measure the erections, including a doughnut-shaped tube filled with water that is placed around the base of the penis. An erection causes a rising water level in a small tube attached to it. In some experiments the sleepers have worn no device but were observed by researchers as they slept in the nude.

Full or partial erections occur about 95 per cent of the time during dreams and are rarely seen during nondreaming sleep. They occur whether or not the sleepers have had recent sexual gratification. In one experiment, a subject had had intercourse five hours before sleeping in the laboratory, another subject eighteen hours before, and several subjects within the previous two days, but all had erections during dreaming. (Charles Fisher, M.D., Joseph Gross, M.D., and Joseph Zuch, M.D., "Cycle of Penile Erection Synchronous with Dreaming (REM) Sleep," *Archives of General Psychiatry*, 1965, vol. 12, pp. 29–45.)

Erections during dreaming tend to decrease somewhat with age, but the only significant difference is between adolescent dreamers and elderly dreamers in their sixties. Erections have even been observed in newborn babies during their REM sleep stages.

Dreams with an element of anxiety tend to inhibit erections. Researcher Charles Fisher found that the sudden loss of erection during a dream could be correlated with events in the dream marked by aggression and anxiety. In one of the dreams the sleeper was attacked by snakes and in another by sharks. Fisher believes that "there may be a greater correlation between dream content and the vicissitudes of the erections than we had originally believed." The proof of such correlation, however, must wait upon future experiments.

Do women have erections during dreaming? It appears that they do. The following is from a paper by I. Karacan, A. L. Rosenbloom, and R. L. Williams ("The Clitoral Erection Cycle during Sleep," *Psychophysiology*, September 1970): "Comparable observations of clitoral erections in females have not been made because of technical difficulties in producing a strain gauge for the normal clitoris. The study of females with congenital clitoral enlargement and the development of a mercury strain transducer have made such observations possible. Two females with genetically enlarged clitorises . . . were compared with two males with the same penile disorder and with two healthy males. EEG sleep patterns and nocturnal erections were monitored on three or more nights for each subject." The females had the same number of (clitoral) erections as the males with most of the erections during the dreaming periods.

C. THE SLEEPING MIND AT WORK

You Think All Night Long

DAVID FOULKES

DEMENT AND KLEITMAN's findings indicated that REM-sleep awakenings almost invariably produced dream reports while arousals during non-rapid eye movement (NREM) sleep did so only very seldom. Their criterion of recall, however, was "detailed" dream description. The failure of NREM awakenings to meet this criterion did not imply that NREM sleep was without mental content of any sort, only that it was without content meeting this criterion, but the earliest feelings of dream researchers seemed to be that NREM sleep was, in fact, altogether devoid of significant psychological experience. In more recent years, however, it has become clear that this is not the case; mental content of a distinctive quality *can* be reliably elicited from NREM sleep, and the nature of this content may be one key to the understanding of the REM-sleep dream....

My doctoral thesis at the University of Chicago, completed in 1960, was the first study to deliberately examine the question of NREM mentation. Eight subjects were tested for seven nights each, with both REM and NREM awakenings made on each night. I sought to determine the extent of NREM (and REM) recall in nocturnal interviews in which the subject was requested to report on his mental experiences in general rather than on his "dreams." This change in interview technique seemed desirable in light of previous evidence that NREM mentation might be less dreamlike than REM mentation and consequently would be unreported by the subject if he felt that the experimenter were interested only in his "dreams." In addition, recordings were made during the nocturnal interviews of the subject's answers to a number of standardized questions concerning the quality of reported mental experiences—for example: Did you have any feelings or emotions? Was the imagery clear?—and the subject also filled out a rating form the next morning for each such experience. These answers and ratings made possible a comparative analysis of the nature of NREM and REM mental content.

REM-sleep recall, with 108 awakenings, was found 87 per cent of the time, and NREM-sleep recall, with 136 awakenings, was found 74 per cent of the time. The difference between these values was statistically significant, but not large. . . .

This very high index of mentation in NREM sleep, compared with Dement and Kleitman's very low index of the same variable, immediately raised a number of questions. Was this NREM recall memory of something other than NREM mental activity? Was it, in particular, recollection of experiences that occurred during REM sleep? My findings demonstrated that the NREM recall rate was identical whether awakenings had been preceded by an uninterrupted REM period or not. The hypothesis that NREM recall consisted of prior REM content thus could not explain NREM reports of mental activity. Did this NREM recall come predominantly from EEG stage-2 sleep adjacent to REM sleep, or was it evenly distributed through the NREM portion of the sleep cycle? Recall from ascending stage 2 was high (74 per cent), but that from stages 3 and 4 (70 per cent) was almost equal to it. Apparently, the entire NREM period was capable of sustaining mentation. How had earlier experimenters failed to achieve the high levels of NREM mental activity obtained in this study?

Part of the difference in findings on the rate of reported NREM mentation may stem from unknown differences in the subjects employed in the several investigations of such mental activity. Dement and Kleitman's study employed only nine subjects, five of whom contributed the bulk of their data, and my research used only eight subjects. With samples as small as these, subject variability, which seems far greater for NREM recall than for REM recall, becomes particularly important. Kamiya's study, with its large number of subjects and awakenings and its NREM value midway between mine and that of Dement and Kleitman, probably yields the most generally representative value of the incidence of reportable NREM mental activity.

In addition to subject variability, however, the difference in findings on NREM mentation is also probably due, in part, to differences in interview technique and in recall criterion, as discussed above. The key element in both of these cases seems to lie in qualitative variations between REM and NREM content. Because NREM mentation is less dreamlike than REM mentation, it was less apt to be elicited in interviews in which subjects were asked to report their "dreams" than in interviews in which they were asked to report their mental experiences in general, and it was less apt to be classified as "recall" (dream recall) by experimenters.

QUALITATIVE DIFFERENCES BETWEEN
REM AND NREM REPORTS

[Here are] some of the major dimensions along which my subjects' REM and NREM reports proved differentiable. There was, first of all, a greater incidence of thinking (conceptual) reports from NREM sleep than from REM sleep, whereas almost all REM reports were of dreams (perceptual).

NREM reports had less content involving hallucinated organismic involvement (emotional processes, in general, and anxiety and hostility-violence, in particular; visual activity; physical movement) than did REM reports. NREM reports were less elaborated than REM reports—it was more likely that there would be only one, rather than several, characters other than the subject; the narrative was less likely to contain several different scenes or parts and less likely to be rated as dramatic in character.

NREM reports showed a greater manifest correspondence to recent events in the subject's life than did REM reports (greater presence of themes from the subject's daily routine—school or work; more likely to represent a continuation of material reported on a previous awakening; more likely to be an undistorted re-creation of some recent event, thought, or situation; more likely to "make sense" to the dreamer in terms of a manifest reference to some recent experience in his life; and less likely to be rated as distorted). . . .

The main outlines of my findings on the qualitative characteristics differentiating REM and NREM reports have been independently verified by Rechtschaffen and his associates, and have more recently been almost totally confirmed by the findings of myself and Rechtschaffen in a study in which a much larger number of subjects, twenty-four, was employed.

Although statistical evidence may give a rough idea of NREM reports, a full feeling for their nature can come only through acquaintance with actual examples. To this end, the following series, obtained from an adult male subject who was employed by the Internal Revenue Service, is presented:

1. He asked an acquaintance at work for a hammer, so that he could fix something in his apartment (NREM).

2. He was thinking of a point made in his tax class, that you have to provide over half of a person's support to claim him as a dependent (NREM).

3. He received a phone call in the middle of the night from a girl identifying herself as from the University of Chicago. She said that it was time for his "35-day evaluation." He chided her for calling so late at

night. She replied that it was the only time they could get him in (REM sleep, 3 minutes after REM onset).

The first two reports, which are typical of this subject's NREM reports, have an everyday quality which the third one lacks. In commenting on the thirty-five-day evaluation by the University of Chicago, with which his only connection was his service in this dream study, the subject noted that he was in a ninety-day probationary period in his new job. He was to receive thirty-five dollars for his services as a dream subject. It seems, then, that experimental and work experiences have been fused in the REM-period dream so that neither is portrayed with complete accuracy. In the second NREM report, however, the subject is re-experiencing, in a completely undistorted manner, the recent event of considering one of the details of his new job. The purely conceptual quality of this report was a fairly typical NREM characteristic for three of my eight subjects.

The others generally had somewhat more "dreamlike" NREM reports. The following samples are from such a subject, an undergraduate major in English literature:

1. He pictures Anna Karenina. She is sitting at a table, then gets up, turns to the left, and walks away (NREM).

2. He is in a sleep laboratory, filling out a pencil and paper form. Someone passes by commenting that the task is a stupid one (NREM).

3. In the first scene, he is standing on a street corner, holding his bicycle and talking to someone about a girl who wanted to be a striptease dancer.

In the second scene, he is in a doctor's study with two women and the doctor. They are discussing two books. The heroine in the first book was a striptease dancer, but is no longer this, but a nurse. The women are discussing how much hardship she has as a nurse. A discussion then ensues of a second book, by John Steinbeck, in which the main character, also a nurse, did not, apparently, endure similar hardship. The women discuss this avidly, as if they were going to go into "this sort of thing" (REM sleep, 3 minutes after REM onset).

The first two reports of this series seem to be tied much more clearly and with much less distortion to recent manifest behaviors or concerns of the subject. In the first, he brings to life a character of a novel that he is reading; in the second, he takes notice of the questionnaire that he must fill out each evening at the laboratory and makes, through a vaguely identified figure, a comment as to how he views this labor. Although these NREM reports are more detailed and dreamlike than those of the previous subject, there is still a striking difference from REM content in terms of distortion and elaboration.

Many more NREM than REM reports were continuations of the theme of a prior narrative. For example, consider the following two reports, the first collected from ascending stage 1, and the second from descending stage 2 as the subject fell asleep following the first awakening:

1. It was about the parkers who are going to this school, letters being sent to all of them. I saw the office with the files of all the people whose name begins with DEL, and then I saw another file, with the L's, with all this taken out, only other names still in there. Letters were going to be sent to those people with the L's.

2. It was about the L people at the University who want to be sent mail. This person had complained because they hadn't gotten the mail, and sent a complaining letter to the registrar. When I was with the person who was writing the letter, it was sort of a gaily rebellious feeling.

The NREM report clearly takes up where the ascending stage-1 dream was broken off. Note that the NREM dream contains the subject's negative reaction to being interrupted the first time, just as the letters were to be sent out. The subject feels "gaily rebellious" as the would-be recipient files his complaint with the registrar (experimenter). Both of these dreams were also scored in the work-school category as well, since the subject had a clerical job in the University Registrar's office that involved the regulation of student parking.

The following report serves as an example of an NREM report that was rated a memory process:

I was thinking about this phone call from home tonight. I got a long-distance call from home, and my parents were very angry with me because I haven't written. They really gave me hell for about twenty minutes on the phone tonight, which bothered me no end. I had been thinking of that this last time you rang the bell, and I had a very unpleasant feeling about it. I was rehearsing their conversation in my mind.

The nature of the qualitative differences between typical NREM and REM content should now be fairly clear. The former is, in Freudian terms, more like secondary-process, or everyday rational, thinking while the latter is more like primary-process, or fanciful and unrealistic, thinking that does not labor under nearly so many constraints imposed by external reality or by inner standards derived from external reality.

Thinking during Non-dreaming Sleep

ROBERT L. VAN DE CASTLE

The typical NREM report is usually: brief, nonemotional, includes very few characters, contains a minimum of sensory imagery, and involves situations from the very recent past. The person will often describe his subjective experience as simply "thinking" about something when he is awakened and he will claim that he felt capable of voluntarily altering the subject matter about which he was thinking. Discovery of NREM mentation indicates that we are constantly engaged in some form of cognitive activity throughout the entire period of sleep and that there is no period during which our "mind is a blank."

The implications of NREM mentation are very far-reaching when we attempt to formulate an adequate theory about dreaming. We are then faced with the necessity of accounting for the 15 or 20 per cent of dreamlike NREM reports that cannot be distinguished from REM reports, as well as accounting for the 20 per cent or so of REM reports that are very bland and nondreamlike in quality. Faced with the necessity of accounting for such overlapping types of mentation, the original black and white association between REM sleep and dreams and between NREM sleep and nondreams can be seen as needing some zones of gray to explain the findings. The boundary lines are much more blurred than originally supposed and recent theoretical efforts have attempted to encompass such findings by conceptualizing a continuum of dreaming intensity.

How Is the Dream Formed?
Another Look at Freud and Adler

DAVID FOULKES

One might theorize about many aspects of dreaming. Psychoanalytic dream theorists have been much concerned with the meaning of dream content. They attempt to provide guidelines for the explanation and interpretation of "manifest" dream content, feeling that such content conceals, but may be made to reveal, information about the dreamer and his conception of his world. Dream theories are also concerned with the functional significance of the dreaming process, with statements as to why we dream at all, what psychological functions are served by dreaming, and at least inferentially, what might happen to us were we unable to dream. Comprehensive dream theories have also been concerned with describing dream formation and development, that is, they purport to describe the processes of construction through which the dream becomes an organized psychological event.

In this paper, we shall consider the implications of recent electrophysiological dream studies for the portions of two major dream theories, those of Freud and Adler, which deal with dream formation and dream development. It is proposed, first, to present an outline of Freudian and Adlerian theories of dream formation and dream development, and then to examine these theories in the light of recent experimental data. In the presentation of Freudian theory, concentration will be focused upon those formulations which lend themselves to some kind of reasonably direct empirical verification.

TWO THEORIES OF DREAM FORMATION

The central propositions of Freud's theory of dream construction or dream formation are:

1. Dream formation and early phases of the organization of the dream will not be represented in the conscious experience of the dreamer. The typical condition of sleep is a state of unconsciousness, a state in which no mental activity is available to personal awareness or to report to others. In discussing the "psychical conditions during the period of sleep which precedes dreams," that is, the period in which the dream is being "formed," Freud says that "we are dealing with an *unconscious* process of thought. . . ." Much of the groundwork which has gone into the construction of the dream as an intelligible perceptual event takes place before the dream, in Freud's term, "attracts" consciousness to itself. Freud suggests that the dream "is like a firework, which takes hours to prepare but goes off in a moment." This preparation is achieved outside the boundaries of consciousness. It is only when the intensity of these unconscious processes becomes sufficient to arouse mechanisms of consciousness, or when, "just before waking, attention becomes more mobile and comes to meet it," that we experience the dream as a conscious event.

2. The unconscious process which instigates dream formation is affective in character, and in particular, it is some derivative of the primary motives of sex or destructive hostility. In sleep, unexpressed and unexpressible sexual drives or hostility are freed from external monitoring, and also from the kinds of internal monitoring which require a high de-

gree of cerebral vigilance. These impulses, long active, now press for some kind of expression. The dream provides the occasion for such expression.

In its final form, the dream is a distorted and symbolic rather than a manifest, direct expression of the impulses which instigate it. This reflects the fact that the forms of waking cortical inhibition exercised over primitive emotional processes are not entirely lacking during sleep. The dream is a fruit of compromise: on the one hand, it does provide an outlet for the expression of primitive emotional impulses; on the other hand, this expression is not (generally) so blatant that the dreamer's critical and inhibitory faculties will be extremely offended by its content. The manifest content of the dream, then, is not a direct reflection of the latent instigating "dream thoughts"; it is because of this disjunction that the manifest dream requires "interpretation."

3. If repressed affect provides the energy for dream construction, perceptual-memorial events provide the raw material. The impulses find their way to expression along sensory, rather than motor, pathways. The dreamer does not, with a patterned sequence of motor activities, inflict harm upon another person nor even go through all the appropriate motions; he may, however, visually hallucinate that he is harming someone. The kind of thinking in which sensory hallucination of a goal serves as a substitute for its actual achievement Freud calls *primary process* thinking. Dreams represent the most acute manifestation in the adult human of this developmentally primitive, perceptual-hallucinatory, mode of thought.

The raw materials used in dream construction must, therefore, be traces of prior perceptual experiences of the dreamer. In particular, Freud feels, very recent experiences, experiences from the day immediately preceding the dream, serve as basic elements in dream construction. These elements Freud calls *day residues*. The day residues will often consist of memories of what appear to be rather inconsequential happenings. But it is not what these memories are that is important; it is the fact that they can represent, or serve as screens for, the repressed impulses. The more inconsequential the day residues are, the better they may fulfill their function of disguising socially unacceptable impulses.

But Freud notes that dreams include much "infantile" perceptual material as well as the "recent and indifferent" material represented in day residues. Dreams, in fact,

can select their material from any part of the dreamer's life, provided only that there is a train of thought linking the experience of the dream-day (the "recent" impressions) with the earlier ones.

It is through their association, then, with day-residue material that older sensory memories are contacted, and, in turn, it is the ability to contact such memories that plays a role in the determination of which day residues shall figure most prominently in the formation of the dream.

4. The day residues, and their associated infantile memories, are the basic elements of the dream, but it would be misleading to conceive the dream as an orderly and logical sequence of such memories. Freud speaks, in particular, of day residues as being "worked over" so that the ultimate dream product is a complicated and bizarre patterning of the original elements. In fact, the elements may be so transformed in the dream that it will be difficult to establish precisely what they are. These transformations, which highly complicate the task of dream interpretation, appear for several reasons: so that the repressed impulses may be adequately expressed, that is, for purposes of dramatic representation; so that the repressed impulses may be successfully disguised, that is, for purposes of evading censorship; and so that the presentation will be as economical as possible, that is, for purposes of the conservation of psychic energy. These are the functions served by a series of processes to which Freud applies the term *dream work*. These processes include: condensation, displacement, and symbolization. The operations of these processes make the dream progressively less intelligible to waking consciousness and progressively detached from its moorings in unretouched sensory memory.

Let us now examine, briefly, one other theory of dream formation, that of Alfred Adler. While Adler's theory of dreaming is by no means as comprehensive or detailed as is Freud's, it has gained much significance because it has formed a large part of the conceptual foundation of several recent and highly influential dream theories, those of Erich Fromm (1957) and Calvin Hall (1959). It is possible, moreover, to find some assertions about the processes of dream formation and dream development in Adler's own writings and in a recent restatement of the Adlerian position by Ullman (1962), assertions at considerable variance from those made by Freud.

1. Sleeping and waking thought are not totally incompatible with one another; we must recognize the essential continuity of all forms of thought. In particular, Adler objects to Freud's conception of dream thought as determined by a mechanism relatively inoperative in waking thought—the unconscious—and to the distinction of primary process and reality-centered thinking, with the former characterizing sleep and the latter wakefulness. There is, to be sure, some difference between dream thought and waking thought, but it is a relative, rather than an absolute, one. The dreamer maintains fewer relations with reality. Yet there is no complete break with reality; he is still in contact with it.

2. The instigation of dreams is not always, or even often, due to sexual or hostile motives, any more than waking thought is generally dominated

by such motives. Again, Adler insists that the dream cannot be a contradiction of waking life; it is always consonant with one's waking style of life.

In common with Freud, Adler feels that we dream when we are troubled by something. We dream only when unresolved problems from waking life, which Ullman (1962) characterizes as the "sore spots" of one's existence, press upon us during sleep. It is the task of the dream to meet and to try to solve such problems. The troublesome "something" which instigates the dream is, then, a problem from conscious experience, not a problem which has been repressed and of whose existence the waking organism is totally unaware. Freud, on the other hand, relegates such problems to a "secondary position" with respect to dream formation.

3. The raw material of the manifest dream content comes from memories of prior perceptual experience, particularly from day residues. But, in Adlerian theory, the day residues are important in themselves, as representations of waking concerns; they are not important simply as "screens" for something else. Adler does not share Freud's feeling that day residues are "some cheap material" of little significance in determining the direction of the dream.

4. In the dream, these residues are transformed or worked over until the ultimate product becomes a deceitful working through of a waking problem. Adler speaks of the dream as being constructed "to fool us." As Ullman (1962) has pointed out, there is some contradiction here of Adler's basic theme of the continuity of waking and sleeping thought. The mechanisms of distortion which Adler seems to recognize include condensation, displacement of emphasis, and symbolization. There seems to be a greater stress in Adler than in Freud, however, upon the expressive nature of symbolic representation. In dreaming, we make use of those images and incidents which best agree with our style of life and which best express the present problem. This relatively strong emphasis on the symbol that expresses rather than the symbol which disguises is consistent with the notion of a continuity between waking and sleeping thought and becomes the keystone of Fromm's (1957) and Hall's (1959) theories of dreaming.

ELECTROPHYSIOLOGICAL STUDIES AND DREAM-FORMATION THEORY

It is apparent from the Dement and Kleitman data that both Freud and Adler misjudged the conditions under which dreaming occurs. Both seem to feel that we dream as it is needed, that is, in proportion to the number and intensity of our personal problems. But the facts seem to be that most adult human beings spend approximately 20% of their sleep in REM periods, periods which produce the kinds of mental content with which both theories are concerned. These periods recur in all individuals studied in a highly predictable cyclic fashion. Individual variations from the 20% figure have been minimal and there is little evidence that they are related to the nature or extent of personal problems. We seem to dream as physiological cycling indicates, not as relative degree of latent psychological trauma dictates. It is still possible, of course, that emotional complexes take advantage of the dreaming process, but apparently they do not, at will, precipitate that process. . . .

Studies of Pre-REM Mentation

Foulkes (1962) conceived his study as an objective study of dream formation. Eight subjects were run for 7 nights each. Awakenings were made at various points in the sleep cycle clustered around the onset of REM periods, those portions of the sleep cycle in which, according to Dement and Kleitman, dreams would be occurring. It was reasoned that such awakenings might provide an empirical basis for theorization about dream onset and the characteristic sequence of dream development. Foulkes found, however, that subjects produced reports of mental phenomena from NREM sleep almost as often as they did from REM sleep. Apparently no point of absolute dream onset exists, in the sense that there is no point in the sleep cycle at which consciousness suddenly appears. It seems to be there all along.

There was, however, some indication of progressive changes in the quality of sleep consciousness around the point of REM onset. More generally, content from pre-REM and REM stages of sleep differed systematically along a number of dimensions. As assessed by direct questioning of the subjects during the night and by responses to rating forms taken on the following morning, reports from the pre-REM periods were less likely than REM reports to be labeled as "dreams," more likely to be called "thoughts"; less likely than REM reports to be vivid or highly elaborated; and more likely than REM reports to be intimately associated with recent and everydayish activities of the subject, sometimes to the point of consisting purely of memories of such events. . . .

Pre-REM Mentation and Dream Formation Theory

What, then, do these apparently consistent and valid findings on mentation occurring outside REM periods suggest about the validity of the two theories of dream formation which we are examining?

1. Freud's characterization of the sleep in which full-fledged dreams are not occurring as periods of unconsciousness seems to be inaccurate. The typically bizarre and elaborate REM-period dream does not burst like a sudden firework against a background of complete darkness; it develops in a context of already ongoing mental activity.

Parenthetically, we may inquire whether someone of Freud's stature could have been totally unaware of the existence of the everydayish thinking which seems to take place during much of the sleep cycle. As we might suspect, the answer is no. In Freud's paper "Dreams and Telepathy," he notes that there are mental events during sleep without condensation, distortion, dramatization, and wish fulfillment. These unaltered repetitions of actual daily experiences he calls *night phantasies*. That the admission of night phantasies has not played any major role in Freud's theory of the dream process may be seen, however, in their treatment in *The Interpretation of Dreams*. There, Freud indicates that he once considered the possibility of such a class of sleep mentation, but later dropped that category. The net impact of his total theoretical position, therefore, has been that we experience alternating periods of unconsciousness and consciousness during sleep, consciousness appearing when the dream is sufficiently well developed to "attract" it. This now seems to be a misleading characterization of sleep consciousness.

2. There is a strong resemblance between the NREM content which precedes dream periods and the Freudian concept of day residues from which dreams are presumed to develop. Insofar as the day-residue material reveals some of the "background thoughts" of the dream, collection of NREM material could facilitate dream interpretation in a more direct manner, perhaps, than even the waking free associations upon which psychoanalytic interpretations have heretofore depended so heavily. The whole body of NREM material occurring between REM-period dreams might be considered the conscious

exploring of one path and another, a swinging of the excitation now this way and now that, until at last it accumulates in the direction that is most opportune and one particular grouping becomes the permanent one.

3. The rather dramatic shifts from plausible content to implausible content, from the everydayish to the bizarre, which attend REM onset suggest the engagement at this point of the sleep cycle of processes much like those which Freud calls the dream work. For example, 23% of 26 content-producing reports elicited by Foulkes (1962) from ascending EEG Stage 2 (Dement & Kleitman, 1957), that portion of the sleep cycle immediately preceding REM periods, were undisguised memories or re-creations of recent events in the dreamer's life, while not a single one of 31 reports taken from awakenings made within 4–60 seconds of REM onset were of a comparable nature.

Moreover, Verdone (1963) has shown that longer REM periods produce reports judged by subjects as more vivid and emotional, and Foulkes' (1960) data reveal that reports from longer REM periods (9–24 minutes of REMs) produced greater mean values in subject ratings for activity, emotionality, anxiety, unpleasantness, frighteningness, dramatic quality, violence-hostility, and distortion than did reports elicited from within 4–60 seconds of REM onset. Whatever the processes are which become active at REM onset, they become increasingly predominant as the REM period progresses. And the highly organized (if often bizarre) drama they generally create supports Freud's attribution of dream distortion to active processes, to motivated condensation, displacement, and symbolization, rather than a conception that dream distortion is a symptom of general mental disorganization due to a sleepy, hence imperfectly functioning, cerebral cortex.

4. Strictly speaking, the fact that day-residue content is often experienced during pre-REM period EEG Stage 2 and that dreamlike experiences occur in that stage of the sleep cycle which immediately follows, namely, EEG Stage 1 REM periods, does not establish that the first kind of material is dynamically transformed to produce the second kind of material. Is there any evidence that the day-residue content of Stage 2 forms the dynamic basis of the dream, that such material is "worked over" as the REM period commences? The following example seems to suggest that this may be the case:

I was in the library and I was filing cards, and I came to some letter between "a" and "c." I was filing some, I think it was Burma, some country, and just as I put that in, there was this scene of some woman, who was sent to look for a little girl who was lost, and she was sent to Burma. They thought the little girl was going there, for some reason. This was sort of like a dramatization of what I was doing. I mean I was filing, and then this scene took place, right at the same time. In the setting it was sort of like you'd imagine it, but I had the feeling it was really happening.

In this dream, obtained 26 seconds after REM onset, a scene from the subject's daily work experience—she had a filing job in the university library—led to an elaboration which was far removed from her everyday experience. The daily-work element (filing), typical in Stage 2 content, preceded the unusual and somewhat unrealistic element (Burma), typical in REM-period content. The physiological recording shows a recent progression from Stage 2 to a REM period. This one case is not, of course, in itself conclusive, but it does suggest that REM-period dreams may begin with the working over of day residues of a sort most often experienced during NREM Stage 2.

Rechtschaffen, Vogel, and Shaikun (1963) have recently demonstrated, moreover, that discrete manifest elements and themes found in NREM reports are sometimes repeated in subsequent REM reports from the same night. Such findings led them to conclude that:

On those nights when themes and images persist through both NREM and REM periods, the dreams do not arise *sui generis* as psychologically isolated mental productions, but emerge as the most vivid and memorable part of a larger fabric of interwoven mental activity during sleep.

5. Adler's assertion of a basic similarity of waking and sleeping thought finds support, at least when we consider NREM-period sleeping thought. Rechtschaffen, Verdone, and Wheaton (1963) have likened the content of NREM mentation to background mentation in waking experience. It is, in Stekel's image, a muted accompaniment rather than a melody. In NREM sleep, the melody, or directive character of thought, seems less prominent and we become aware of this background thought. Such an awareness is difficult to achieve in waking life; it is as if we might have direct and immediate access to all those irrelevant things which passed along the borders of consciousness while we were more or less attentively engaged in some line of directed thought. Conditions of sensory deprivation or sensory monotony (Fiske, 1961) perhaps give us the best possible vantage point in waking life for viewing such phenomena. While the identification of NREM mentation with fringetype waking mentation may not be an apt characterization of all NREM mentation, it does underline the degree of continuity of NREM mentation and at least some forms of waking experience.

In the context of Freudian theory, what we do not find in pre-REM sleep mentation is worthy of note. We do not find a seething, libidinous turmoil, sharply at variance with waking thought. Rather we see a generally "relaxed" kind of thinking and imaging whose prominence becomes possible in the absence of a strong external focus or challenge for thought processes and whose nature is essentially similar to certain classes of incidental waking mentation.

6. But, if we find little evidence of libido or hostility in the pre-REM thought from which dreams may be presumed to develop, neither do we find much evidence for the Adlerian assertion that representations of pressing personal problems of a more general character are active at, and responsible for, dream formation. Awakenings made at various points leading into REM-period onset and during the early seconds and minutes of REM periods do not corroborate, at least in any obvious manner, the position that dreams begin with affective or ideational "sore spots." Transformations are noted in the quality of mental experience: from conceptualizing or vaguely perceiving to vivid visual imaging, from kaleidoscopic flux to continuity and integration, and from plausible content to distorted and bizarre content. However, these changes do not seem to be associated with any perception of particularly pressing personal problems which cry for some resolution or exploration. Rather than being sources of personal anxiety or insecurity, NREM contents of consciousness generally seem quite unconnected with basic psychodynamic conerns of the dreamer.

Because this last point is a particularly crucial one for both theories, we will do well to consider it in further detail. Will the dream theorist be impressed with evidence that the class of events-in-consciousness at or around REM-period-dream onset fails to meet his specifications of dream-instigating events? Most likely not. He might comment that the analysis has, up to this point, relied too heavily upon appearances, upon manifest consciousness. It might be suggested that the everydayish, relaxed kinds of mentation which precede REM-period dreaming serve as screens for affective elements, based in infantile experience, which present a threat, or pose a challenge, to the dreamer. Such a contention raises a basic methodological question, however: since neither physiological nor experiential evidence seems to support the hypothesis that dream periods develop from or commence with such elements, with what kind of evidence does the dream theorist propose to confirm his theory of the affective instigation of dreams? At present, the assumption that pre-REM-period contents are screens for something else seems entirely gratuitous. What we seem to have in NREM-period mentation is one level of cognitive functioning, a level which should at least tentatively be accepted for what it is, rather than be immediately interpreted as a disguised form of something else.

At this point we should, perhaps, consider the observational base upon which both Freudian and Adlerian theory rest, clinical dream collection. Ian Oswald's (1962) comments upon the adequacy of clinical dream collection as a basis for characterization of the dream process cut right to the heart of the matter. He notes that the patient probably describes only a very small fraction of his total dreams to his therapist, and that his "recall" of these dreams is more a construction than a reconstruction. This constructed, waking fantasy-material may tell the clinician a great deal about the patient, but "is not to be relied upon as evidence of what really happens during dream periods."

Yet both Freud and Adler, in the absence of systematic observations made at various phases of the (REM) dream process, have given us theories of that process. Quite clearly, what they have done is to read back into the dreaming process those events which it seems must have transpired in its early stages, given a certain dream outcome and/or a certain functional interpretation of that outcome. Now no one who has had experience in collecting, examining, or interpreting dreams can doubt that dreams often do express a person's basic feelings and indicate his problems. And yet, the pre-REM and early-REM recall data now available suggest that we err in assuming that since this may be the functional significance of the dream, the dream therefore must have started with the expression of such feelings or the posing of such problems. Rather it seems as if the dream allows the dreamer, eventually rather than immediately, to express himself in a rather profound way; it is not that the dream, by posing a basic challenge at its very onset, forces him to do this.

It is being suggested, then, that both Freudian and Adlerian theory are incorrect in their characterization of the dream process, that is, dream formation and dream development. But what, we may now ask, are the implications of this position for those portions of their dream theories which deal with dream meaning or the functional significance of dreaming? We have already noted that Freud's and Adler's theories of the dream process are generalizations from, rather than the inductive basis of, their theories of dream interpretation. This suggests that dream process data can confirm or disconfirm a particular theory of dream meaning only to the extent that that theory is compatible with one, and only one, characterization of the dream process. Dream theorists have tended to assume such a necessary correspondence between interpretation theory and process theory; that is, they have generalized in a relatively direct fashion from what the dream is to how it must have started. But this overlooks the possibility that how a dream begins and what a dream becomes may be two entirely different matters. Both Freudian and Adlerian theories of dream meaning and function, therefore, may be compatible with the description of the dream process provided by recent electrophysiological research. To reject Freud's dream-process theory is not necessarily to reject his position that dreams serve the function of the fulfillment of repressed wishes. To reject Adler's dream-process theory is not necessarily to reject his position that dreams are attempts at problem solving which are consistent with the dreamer's life style.

Falling-asleep Dreams

ROBERT L. VAN DE CASTLE

During the process of falling asleep a person experiences "hypnagogic imagery." Such imagery is usually visual in nature, although kinesthetic sensations, such as floating, may be present. The imagery generally consists of isolated geometrical shapes or individual objects. Marked individual differences occur in the length of elapsed time before specific content can be reported, and about one-third of all subjects are able to report connected dreamlike experiences before they actually reach a descending Stage I EEG pattern. Approximately two-thirds of all subjects are able to report dreamlike content by the time the EEG record indicates they have achieved descending Stage I sleep. Actual REM periods do not occur at sleep onset and are not present until at least an hour later, except in the case of narcoleptics, who experience a REM period immediately after falling asleep.

Drowsy Dreams Are Micro-Dreams

IAN OSWALD

We must now consider more closely some of those irrelevant images that appear when the attention wanders, . . . in particular those which haunt the borderland of sleep. No sharp distinction can be drawn between these images and the more vivid or eidetic images of some fully wakeful persons, nor between these images and those of wakefulness during abnormally restricted sensory stimulation. These products of the sleepy individual often merge into dreams and it should be emphasized that it is not possible to define limits or distinctions between them and dreams, since both are events of private fantasy discernible but fugitively through the mists of memory.

The term "hypnagogic hallucination" was coined by Maury (1848), whose account has never been excelled. Particularly valuable also are the book by Leroy (1933) and the survey by Leaning (1926). French writers especially have been concerned to relate these fascinating events, which have, by comparison, been neglected by psychologists of the English-speaking nations.

Hypnagogic hallucinations are said to be those of "half-sleep." They are experienced as discontinuous, even if recurrent, sensory experiences which seem to force themselves upon the passive subject, and have often been contrasted with dreams in which the individual may experience himself as an active participator in an adventure. They are events of drowsiness occurring while the subject flits between wakefulness and light sleep, retaining some contact with reality, so much so that he may declare himself to have been still fully awake when he had his hallucination, which, because of its bizarre nature, he cannot integrate into waking life, so that it appears to him to be a thing apart, impressively vivid. There are big individual differences in the frequency with which these events are said to be experienced, just as is the case with dreams. Those who state that they have rarely experienced them, at least since childhood, will often report that they did have some during a bout of fever when their sleep was restless. Restlessness which is due to anxiety, or as Maury noted, to black coffee, also gives rise to reports of these images. The hypnagogic hallucinations are most commonly visual and auditory, but various kinaesthetic and other bodily hallucinations, as of shrinkage or swelling of a limb or constriction about the waist (Critchley, 1955) and, more rarely, olfactory hallucinations are described.

It is very difficult to gauge the frequency of the more striking type of hypnagogic hallucination. One may have verbal difficulties in describing what it is one seeks to learn when questioning people about hypnagogic hallucinations. It is probable that, like dreams, most are not recallable the next day. Many people will deny experiences of this kind when questioned or deny even more straightforward waking imagery, such as a number form, because they have a fear of being trapped into admitting some psychopathological oddity. McKellar and Simpson (1954), following a questionnaire study of 110 university students found that 67 reported having hypnagogic imagery. Fifty of these reported auditory experiences and 39 visual. The finding that auditory experiences were reported by more people than visual experiences is interesting. It contrasts with most of the reports in the literature, where pride of place is given to visual experiences. It might be added that most people regard "picturing things" and visual imagery in dreams as commonplace compared with suddenly hearing one's name called or a loud voice abruptly speaking a phrase in the privacy of one's bedroom: the auditory experiences would, therefore, be considered more striking and be more often remembered as notable. Leaning mentioned that (like nocturnal jerks) hypnagogic hallucinations often seem to appear in runs, being numerous for a week or two, then not recurring for weeks or months. As others have found, I have certainly noticed more while particularly interested in them, during the preparation of this book.

Attention has been drawn to the fact that episodes of light sleep can be extremely brief and that cerebral vigilance can fall from a level in which alpha rhythm is present to one where the alpha rhythm is lost, for a matter of a few seconds, or a fraction of a second at a time. Brief episodes of this nature, with loss of alpha rhythm and a few low-voltage slow waves, recur repeatedly in drowsiness. The individual may subsequently emphatically deny having slept. In the few moments while cerebral vigilance was low, contact with reality and the direction of attention must have been impaired, and it is at such moments that hypnagogic hallucinations arise. Davis *et al.* (1938) first noted that subjects reported wandering of thought, brief sensory experiences including visual and bodily fantasies, and dream-like feelings, immediately after brief moments of loss of alpha rhythm during drowsiness. They believed these experiences to merge imperceptibly into dreams. Dement and Kleitman (1957) likewise reported descriptions of dream-like reverie and various sensory experiences such as "floating" and "flashing lights" by subjects awakened from the EEG B stage when first falling asleep. In these conditions subjects frequently say that they were still awake while experiencing their hypnagogic hallucinations; for example, the subject mentioned by Leaning, who experienced one while climbing the stairs to bed. Rouquès (1946) claimed that he was not merely widely awake but also capable of calculating or having his mind occupied in some other manner while noticing his hypnagogic hallucinations of landscapes, and the like, in an absent-minded way. Leroy wrote that it is difficult to distinguish easily between sleep and wakefulness and he considered that when hypnagogic hallucinations occur the individual is certainly not fully awake.

I believe that an individual may be aware consecutively of calculating, then of a vision, then of calculating again, and so on, the activities being more alternate than simultaneous. When vigilance rose, calculation would continue, only to lapse as vigilance fell again. As previously emphasized, the individual may be quite unaware of brief falls of vigilance, and the advent of the EEG has given us an advantage over those observers who have had to rely on their subjective impressions. Vihvelin (1948), for instance, in a lengthy discussion of the various arguments about whether hypnagogic hallucinations should be regarded as quite different from dreams or not, insisted on the criterion of being fully awake during the former. Maury (1848) wrote that hypnagogic hallucinations occur when attention wanders and the mind no longer pursues the voluntary, logical order of its thoughts, that a state of relaxation and non-attentiveness is always present, and that as soon as attention is re-established the creation always vanishes. Maury recognized that "half-sleep" could alternate with wakefulness.

Maury (1848, 1853) agreed with the earlier writings of Purkinje and Gruithuisen that hypnagogic hallucinations are elements of dreaming. Leroy also wrote that the materials of hypnagogic hallucinations are those of dreams. I believe that hypnagogic hallucinations are, in a sense, microdreams. They are discontinuous because, at times when falling asleep, loss of contact with reality is discontinuous. The individual repeatedly returns to reality while his cerebral vigilance repeatedly rises and falls. Consequently, he does not feel he has been engaged in a prolonged adventure but that he has been a passive spectator.

It is for this reason, I suggest, that the usual distinction between dreaming and hypnagogic hallucinations is made—that the latter are not actively entered into. It may be pointed out that some dreams, when described immediately after being awakened, may be of a very passive nature (Dement and Wolpert, 1958). The EEG signs during dreaming indicate that there are brief periods of alpha rhythm. Despite this, the individual does dream, though some may claim merely to have been "thinking." When alpha rhythm reappears briefly during dreaming, although cerebral vigilance may be briefly raised, contact with reality may not be re-established since it has been absent for an hour or more and since the dreamer has no immediate memories of it and there may be nothing to break the uniformity of the environment. The person falling asleep is in a quite different situation, for he has just been in contact with reality and is merely in danger of losing contact during the brief episodes of lowered vigilance when alpha rhythm disappears from his EEG.

The greater reality quality of the dream is reflected in the subject's activities during it; notably, verbal activities in dream conversations, bodily movements and, possibly, "scanning" eye movements. The most striking instance of this "living in" a dream is the battle-dream, where there may not merely be speech and eye movements but major bodily responses may be made to the fantasy events created. The person having hypnagogic hallucinations, however, because he quickly and repeatedly re-establishes contact with reality after his brief fantasy-creation, rarely makes sequential responses to them, either of the eyes or the body, though Leroy describes an instance which he classes not as a dream but as a hypnagogic hallucination, where the subject sat up and leaned over the edge of the bed in order to watch a procession of little men pushing chariots round the room. Again, the individual may feel in no sense a detached observer when he has just had an auditory hallucination of hearing his name being called. These examples serve to illustrate that sharp distinctions are not to be drawn between the brief fantasy events of falling asleep and those more protracted ones, particularly during the light sleep which may follow previous deep sleep, which are more universally called dreams. In the case of either, visual fantasy creations may continue to be perceived after the eyes open for a period varying from a second or so, to several minutes in the case of the battle-dream. F. W. H. Myers coined the adjective "hypnopompic" for these visual experiences. In defining them he wrote, "In hypnopompic pictures . . . as I have termed them . . . which accompany the departure of sleep . . . a figure which has formed part of a dream continues to be seen as a hallucination for some moments after waking." (Myers, 1903).

The term "hypnopompic" has unfortunately been used by some writers of textbooks to refer to a "state" persisting for perhaps an hour or two prior to final awakening after a night's sleep, with the implication that it is quite different from the "hypnagogic state" of first falling asleep. Assertions of this nature appear to have been copied by one writer from another, and so perpetuated. It would be better that the term "hypnopompic" were dropped altogether or else retained solely for hallucinations persisting from sleep when the eyes open, whether the individual retired to bed ten minutes or ten hours before. Maury (1848) included hallucinations persisting after sleep, when the eyes were opened, in his description of hypnagogic hallucinations.

The morning state of drowsiness, especially after once awakening, is often, like the drowsiness of falling asleep, a period of drifting between wakefulness and light sleep, the great difference, under normal circumstances, lying in the greater duration of the drowsy state in the morning.

In anxious or fevered persons the drowsy period of first falling asleep may not pass rapidly on to deep sleep but may persist unduly, and the individual may lose contact with reality to such a degree that visual hallucinations may occur when the eyes are open. The drowsy condition in the morning period has nothing special about it. As Havelock Ellis (1897) wrote when rejecting the term "hypnopompic," what is experienced "is as much conditioned by the sleep that is passing away as by the sleep that is coming on." Many persons experience brief images of the traditional hypnagogic type when drowsing *after* a night's sleep, and, equally, others experience more prolonged dream sequences before first falling deeply asleep after retiring. Any of these different varieties of experience can persist briefly in some people when the eyes open and could qualify for use with the adjective "hypnopompic."

Maury (1848) and many others have described hypnagogic hallucinations persisting briefly when the eyes were opened in the darkness, especially in the case of the more menacing kind of vision. Sometimes they persist when it is light. One student described to me how, in the morning, he dreamed of a spider, then awoke and saw it momentarily on his pillow. A girl student described opening her eyes in the morning and greeting a male acquaintance whom she saw standing by the bed—whereupon he vanished. McKellar and Simpson (1954) reported that one of their subjects had seen an angel under similar circumstances.

As mentioned earlier . . ., when some persons conjure up voluntary, vivid, visual images and "look" at them for some time, and then look away or open their eyes if they had been closed, an after-image may be seen. This has been described also in the case of dream images by Gruithuisen (1812), and Alexander (1904), while Leaning gives further examples. Gruithuisen gives several instances of his own, the most famous (mistranslated into French by Burdach in 1839 and repeatedly and incorrectly quoted therefrom since) was that in which he dreamed of violet fluorspar on a fire of glowing coals and on awakening had an after-image of a yellow spot on a darker ground, looking like the sun in a stagnant pool ("die Gestalt der Sonne in einem stehenden Wasser hatte"). Alexander dreamed of a human figure, "and when my eyes suddenly opened, I was surprised to see the figure lengthen out exactly as does an after-image."

One very obtrusive class of imagery, that may be experienced when one relaxes with the eyes closed, differs somewhat from hypnagogic imagery in general. I refer to perseverative images of sensory events repeatedly experienced during the day. Thus, when I once spent an entire day from early morning till late evening at the unaccustomed task of scything down thistles in a field, on closing my eyes at night I vividly saw thistles, thistles and more thistles. Leroy gives an example of this kind following anatomical dissections by day. A day's long and tiring car-drive will be followed, when I retire to bed, by an endless vision of roads, cars, lorries and overtaking. Others, as Maury and Leaning remark, may have similar auditory experiences, hearing once again, on retiring to bed, the playing of the orchestra to which they had listened earlier. It seems as if, when repeated perceptual responses have been made of, for instance, thistles, they continue to occur in the absence of corresponding sense-organ stimulation. As might be expected from the conclusions reached in the previous chapter, I would fully agree with the opinion Leroy had reached that these perseverative images are not exact "reproductions." As the individual falls asleep these imaginal constructions change and merge into more typically bizarre hypnagogic hallucinations.

How Do Hypnagogic Dreams Differ from REM Dreams?

DAVID FOULKES

What *kinds* of mental experience are reported during the sleep onset period? In terms of sensory imagery, hypnagogic experiences seem to be primarily visual in quality. . . . Auditory and kinesthetic imagery were present in roughly one-quarter of the hypnagogic experiences. . . .

In terms of *affect*, emotion during the hypnagogic period was neither as frequent nor as intense as emotion during REM sleep. Affect was neither predominantly unpleasant nor predominantly pleasant. All subjects but one reached their peak value of hypnagogic affect during the alpha-rhythm EEG. . . .

Individual differences in the incidence of dreams during the hypnagogic period were quite striking. Some subjects dreamed early (beginning during the alpha pattern) and frequently, others only later (beginning during descending stages 1 and 2) and less frequently. From these data, there would seem to be considerably more scope for the influence of personality variables upon dream incidence during the sleep-onset period than there is during REM sleep, from which dreams are almost universally reported. . . .

Dreamlike mental activity apparently does occur during the hypnagogic period, but in what sense are these experiences dreams? In particular, in what ways are sleep-onset dreams similar to, and in what ways are they different from, the REM-period experience that has been the most frequent referent of the term dream?

THE NATURE OF HYPNAGOGIC DREAMS

The examination of representative reports is perhaps the easiest pathway to an understanding of the nature of sleep-onset mentation. Consider, first, a series of reports collected from an early and chronic hypnagogic dreamer:

Alpha REM. I saw a girl holding a baby, standing on some steps. That created rather an unpleasant experience to me—I thought I flushed or something. The girl had black hair and a plain black sweater and black slacks. It was sort of like basement stairs. She was going down, standing about in the middle of the steps, and I was in the basement. I was observing it through my eyes. She was looking straight ahead. She wasn't looking at me. I got sort of the feeling like I was hiding. (QUESTION: Were you aware, while this experience was taking place, that you were in bed here in the Sleep Laboratory?) No. I felt myself definitely in the basement. (*Awake but drowsy.*)

Alpha SEM. I was lying with my head in a girl's lap, saw my face up against her leg. I was sort of looking at myself and the girl. It was a good feeling, a mild erotic feeling. This was out in the park or woods, a blanket there and a little grass around. I was aware, about 10 per cent approximately, that I was not completely dissociated from reality, but I would say I was definitely experiencing the appropriate feelings of the image I had seen. (*Awake but drowsy.*)

Descending Stage 1. I was looking at some teeth, as a dentist would look at teeth, at two side by side. A patient's teeth and there was a cat. I was looking first at the person's teeth and then at the cat's teeth, making some kind of comparison. (QUESTION: Did this seem to be participation or observation of something really taking place?) Yes. It seemed to have a detached sort of quality, without any apparent significance, sort of like I just fell into it. (*Drifting to sleep.*)

Descending Stage 2. I think I was just starting to climb some steps. There was somebody else in it too. I said something to him, he was standing on the bottom of the stairs, and then I started to walk up the steps. It was sort of the thought of parting, of saying goodbye. The staircase was very wide, maybe a little bit out of proportion for the setting that I figured I was in. (QUESTION: At the time I called, did you feel that you were actually out somewhere, walking up steps, rather than simply conjuring something up in your own mind?) Yes. (QUESTION: Can you recall anything else of the experience?) No, except that the Freudian imagery seems overwhelmingly obvious. (*Drifting to sleep.*)

A second series of reports comes from a later and less-frequent hypnagogic dreamer:

Alpha REM. The last thing I was thinking was this is probably the last time you will wake me up. I was very pleased with the idea, I felt confident that it was true. (QUESTION: Any visual imagery?) No. (QUESTION: Did you feel that you were controlling this experience?) Yes. (QUESTION: And were you aware that you were lying here in your bed?) Yes. (*Awake but drowsy.*)

Alpha SEM. I was thinking about Russian words and I was translating them into English. I was reviewing something I had been reading earlier in the evening. I was recalling some work that I had listed for myself in a vocabulary. I was thinking of the word which means "plateau." I was pleased that I could remember. (QUESTION: Any visual imagery?) No. (QUESTION: Did you feel that you were controlling this experience?) Yes. (QUESTION: Were you aware that you were lying here in bed during the experience?) Yes. (*Awake and alert.*)

Descending Stage 1. Had something to do with a garden plot, and I was planting seed in it. I could see some guy standing in this field, and it was kind of filled and cultivated, and he was talking about this to me. I can't quite remember what it was he did say, it seems to me as if it had to do with growing, whether these things were going to grow. I didn't feel I had control over the experience. (QUESTION: Were you aware that you were lying here in bed during the experience?) No. (*Drifting to sleep.*)

Descending Stage 2. I have some sort of visual recollection that looks like you putting the equipment on my head. I didn't control the experience. (QUESTION: Were you aware that you were here, lying in your bed?) No. (*In light sleep.*)

These two series not only illustrate the variety of dreamlike and non-dreamlike reports obtained during the hypnagogic period, but also the nature of the difference observed between the chronic and the occasional sleep-onset dreamer. The first subject slips into hallucinatory or quasi-hallucinatory fantasy during alpha rhythm EEG, while the second is still keeping his thinking abstract or nonperceptual, and reality oriented, both as to form—his thinking is consciously controlled—and content—the experimental situation, his attempts to master the Russian language. During descending stage 1 both experience hallucinatory and somewhat bizarre and symbolic content fully deserving of the label dreaming. During descending stage 2, the first subject continues to experience similar content, but, while the second subject's thought maintains its dreamlike form—visual and hallucinatory, its content is brought back to matters of immediate reality, such as being fitted with EEG electrodes for the sleep experiment. Differences of this sort in sleep-onset mental activity, in conjunction with observations of subjects' waking behavior, led us to propose that subjects with earlier signs of dreamlike mentation at sleep onset were less anxious and constricted in giving expression to their inner life than those who "resisted" such content during alpha rhythm EEG.

The dreamlike reports in these two series also illustrate the inaccuracy of several previous suggestions as to ways of discriminating hypnagogic mental activity from true nocturnal dreaming. Dement and Kleitman, for example, had suggested that hypnagogic experiences were neither hallucinatory nor as well-organized as REM-period dreams. But the statistics in our study indicate that subjects *do* hallucinate at sleep onset. It should also be apparent from the hypnagogic dream reports quoted that the hypnagogic dream can be, and most often is, as well-organized and internally coherent as the typical REM-period dream. However, in some cases we did receive reports betraying failures of mental synthesis; for example, the subject sees the number 2081 without experiencing any perceptual or ideational context to render it meaningful to him; and, as suggested by Dement and Kleitman's data, these were seen most often during descending stage 1.

Similarly, Oswald suggested that the subject at sleep onset does not hallucinate his own participation in his mental fantasies, that is, hypnagogic dreams lack a "living in" quality present in the REM-period dream. But hypnagogic dream samples quoted and statistics collected by us on hallucinated self-involvement in sleep-onset fantasies make clear that subjects most often *do* hallucinate their own participation in the fantasies they are weaving as they fall asleep.

What Dement and Kleitman and Oswald seem to be saying is that hypnagogic dreams are not as "real" as nocturnal REM-period dreams. One sense in which our data support their contention is in terms of the subject's emotional involvement. As we have already seen, affect is relatively lacking as a component of mental experience during sleep onset, particularly when such mentation becomes dreamlike. In the specimens of hypnagogic mentation quoted above, for example, the first subject commented during his stage-1 report that his experience had a "detached sort of quality"; and there was a generally greater incidence of "feeling" content in both subjects' alpha-rhythm as opposed to their descending-stage-1 and stage-2 reports.

Still other authors have suggested that true nocturnal dreaming is unique in the extent to which its images are bizarre and symbolic. The hypnagogic hallucination, according to one such author, does not "attempt to say as much as a dream," hence "it does not need to depend upon condensed hieroglyphics to express multiple meanings." Many of our reports, however, including several quoted above (tooth comparison, stair climbing, and seed planting), show considerable use of *condensed hieroglyphics*, or distortion by symbolism, in the manner of typical REM-period dreaming and much more use of such symbolism than is typically observed in NREM content. Hypnagogic dream content, then, *can* be bizarre and symbolic in the manner of REM-period dream content.

If these several suggestions as to particular ways to discriminate between hypnagogic and REM dreaming have not proved adequate, the question of discrimination along similar dimensions still remains. There must surely be experiential and functional differences between hypnagogic and REM dreams, between those that develop out of wakefulness and those that arise in deeper sleep, corresponding with the obvious physiological differentiation in terms of EEG/EOG patterns associated with their occurrence.

Our data do suggest several differences between hypnagogic and REM-sleep dreams. Those in emotional involvement and susceptibility of dream occurrence to variation across subjects have been noted. . . . There are some observations suggesting that the hypnagogic dream may, in part, be an attempt at interpreting peripheral organismic stimuli, such as pulse and respiration, in an hallucinatory manner that permits sleep induction. This suggests that such stimuli play a larger role in determining sleep-onset dreaming than that of REM sleep. Our data suggest further differentiation of sleep-onset and REM dreaming in terms of: (1) the speed with which dreaming transpires, and (2) the degree of elaboration that fantasy undergoes.

Some hypnagogic experiences, subjects assert, have an instantaneous quality that . . . is not the case with respect to REM dreaming. The difference seems to reside, experientially, in whether continuity is visual or conceptual in form.

Most of the time, continuity in REM dreaming is visual, or movielike. Within any one episode a realistic progression of images occurs as the dreamer imagines himself moving about or scanning the scenery. As he walks up a flight of stairs, for example, the imagery changes as would the scene in the continuous movie sequence produced by a cameraman holding his camera at eye level as he climbed the stairs.

At least some hypnagogic reports, however, are of experiences that seem to lack this sort of visual continuity. One of our subjects, for example, reported a hypnagogic dream of driving from California to Tijuana, Mexico; of entering a bar there that featured a dancing girl; and of then leaving the bar in the company of this girl. In discussing this dream, he commented that his only visual experience was of three brief images— himself driving at one particular place in California; the inside of the bar; and the girl walking with him in the street. The dream as reported, and apparently as experienced, did have continuity, but not the visual continuity of the REM dream. It was more like seeing three discretely different "still" shots, with the continuity integrated in an ideational, or conceptual, rather than a perceptual, way. While such conceptual continuity may occur in REM dreaming as a bridge between different episodes, each of which is still characterized by perceptual continuity, in the hypnagogic period entire dreams may be constructed with only conceptual continuity.

Such a mode of integration of brief and discontinuous perceptual experience in the hypnagogic period may allow the dreamer to condense a relatively long action sequence into an exceedingly short visual presentation. This kind of hypnagogic mental activity may be responsible for the everyday notion that dreams occur almost instantaneously.

The length of typical hypnagogic dream reports is briefer than the length of full-fledged REM-period reports. Of some four hundred hypna-gogic reports that I have examined, none has, for example, approached the length or number of different episodes manifest in REM-sleep Report B in Chapter 2 [of *The Psychology of Sleep*]. This fact suggests, among other things, that an individual at sleep onset is neither interested in, nor capable of, the kind of prolonged self-exploration appearing during REM sleep. The lack of interest may be attributed to the desire for sleep. To become involved at sleep onset in the condition of organismic arousal associated with REM dreaming and to experience the kind of highly personal and emotionally absorbing content experienced in REM sleep would seem to be grossly incompatible with the motives that lead us to seek sleep in the first place.

At sleep onset, the human organism seems to shy away from disturb-ing thoughts and feelings, with this tendency strongest among those per-sons least able to tolerate such content. It may be that this is why simple wish-fulfillment dreams seem more predominant at sleep onset than dur-ing REM periods. For an individual bent upon achieving sleep, a sim-ple wish-fulfilling fantasy may be the quickest way of disposing of inner drives that may become salient when external-stimulus input is reduced to a minimum. In our study, for example, there was an instance of a hypnagogic dream in which a subject has sexual intercourse with a girl with whom he has not had comparable success in waking life. More sym-bolically, the first subject quoted above gets an invitation from someone and proceeds to mount an unusually broad staircase, symbolic of the act of sexual intercourse, according to Freud.

This orientation toward sleep, and therefore away from potentially dis-turbing psychic content, may also be related to the contemporary tempo-ral reference characteristic of hypnagogic dreaming. An analysis of our transcripts failed to reveal a single report with manifest reference to any event less recent than one in the month or so before the subject's ap-pearance in the laboratory. The REM dream, however, may begin with a contemporary reference, but soon works itself back into the most distant nooks and crannies of the dreamer's life. . . .

Sleep-onset dreaming seems, basically, to be an expedient measure, adopted as a means of escaping mental chaos and of preserving some integrity of mental functioning without compromising the passage of the organism from wakefulness to sleep. It serves those functions in a period in which there are various threats both to the maintenance of mental integrity and to the emerging state of sleep. There is residual stimulus input from the external environment and one's own body against the background of a general reduction of stimulus input to the brain. This de-prives remaining stimulus input of much of its context, hence its meaning-fulness. Residual stimulus input also, of course, threatens the maintenance of drowsiness and its issuance into full-fledged sleep. There is some tendency to the reactivation of those unfulfilled desires, threatening impulses, and unreasoning anxieties that an orientation to external reality can mask only so long as we attend to that reality. The sleep-onset dream masters these threats in "dreamlets," which provide some kind of internally coherent, yet hallucinatory and thus sleep-preserving, interpretation of residual stimulus input and which superficially (in the long run), but satisfactorily (in the short run), gloss over representations of basic problems in the dreamer's daily existence so that the mental apparatus is not overwhelmed by them and so that wakefulness may pass into sleep.

D. NAPPERS, NARCOLEPTICS, NIGHTMARES, AND SLEEPWALKERS

Dreaming during Daytime Naps

HERBERT GREENHOUSE

DO PEOPLE DREAM WHEN THEY LIE DOWN for a daytime or early evening nap? If so, is there a sleep-dream cycle that repeats the four stages of the nighttime cycle?

There have been a few studies of the sleep cycle during morning, afternoon, and evening naps. In an experiment with afternoon and early evening nappers, the former spent more time dreaming than the latter, with the evening nappers spending a longer period in Stage 4, or deep sleep. The sleep cycle of the daytime nappers was similar to the sleep cycle in the late stages of nighttime sleep, when there is less deep sleep (Stage 3 and 4) and more Stage I REM dreaming. The sleep cycle of the evening nappers showed more deep sleep and less dreaming, as it does in the early hours of nighttime sleep. The body temperature cycle in both cases also followed the body temperature curve at night, when the longest dreaming periods occur with body temperature at its lowest level.

(The above study was reported by Louise Maron, Allan Rechtschaffen, and Edward A. Wolpert, "Sleep Cycle during Napping," *Archives of General Psychiatry*, vol. II, November 1964, pp. 503–508.)

In a daytime study of habitual nappers, no time limit was set and the nappers could sleep for as long as they liked. Those who slept for half an hour had no dreams, and only one subject who slept for an hour reported a dream. Two subjects who slept for two hours reported two dreams. As in nighttime sleep, none of the nappers had dream periods at the beginning of sleep.

In another study the subjects took two-hour morning naps, then had a full night's sleep, then the following week took two one-hour naps on the same day, one in the morning and one in the afternoon, followed by a full night's sleep. Stage 1 REM was prominent in the morning naps, but there was no change in the later nighttime cycle unless there was also an afternoon nap, when Stage 4, or deep sleep, predominated. There was less deep sleep (Stage 4) during the afternoon naps when no morning naps preceded them.

Another study on the quality of dreaming during naps showed them to be more characteristic of the "thinking" kind of mental activity that occurs during the NREM, or non-dreaming sleep, periods at night—less dreamlike and more continuous with waking life, with more familiar settings and current experiences in the life of the dreamer.

(Since the researchers in the three experiments cited emphasized that their results were only tentative and must wait for replication in future studies, their names are not given here. The studies do suggest, however, that napping at different times of the day may be related to the sleep-dream-waking cycle.)

Narcoleptics Sleep to Dream

HERBERT GREENHOUSE

Narcoleptics are people who have sudden overpowering urges to go to sleep during the day, no matter what they may be doing at the time. They have a tendency to doze off when reading or watching television, and may sometimes faint when emotionally aroused. Unlike normal sleepers, they may start dreaming immediately upon falling asleep. Although normal daytime nappers follow the nighttime cycle and do not dream for about fifty minutes, narcoleptics may start dreaming immediately at any time of day.

In *Current Research on Sleep and Dreams*, Gay Gaer Luce writes: "A totally new understanding of narcolepsy has been generated by the collaborative studies of Drs. Allan Rechtschaffen, William C. Dement, and George Gulevich. . . . Following a hunch that the symptoms were related to the REM stage of sleep, the dream period, a series of EEG studies was undertaken. One early study showed that a narcoleptic can hold a conversation, discriminate between sounds, show other signs of being wide awake, and yet have the brain wave patterns of someone deeply asleep."

Dr. Gerald Vogel of the University of Chicago theorized that the narcoleptic's tendency to fall asleep was a defense against anxiety. ("The Dream of Narcolepsy," *Archives of General Psychiatry*, 1960, vol. 3, pp. 421–448.) Narcoleptics have a need to dream and "a specific function of the narcoleptic attack is the production of a dream which provides hallucinatory gratification of the sleep provoking, unacceptable fantasy." Thus, for the narcoleptic, dreaming becomes wish-fulfilling.

In one laboratory experiment a narcoleptic began to dream within three minutes of falling asleep. After he was awakened, he again fell asleep and was dreaming within four minutes. When he went to sleep for the third time, he did not dream for an hour, indicating that his need to dream had been somewhat satisfied during his first two periods of sleep.

New Facts about Nightmares

JOHN E. MACK, M.D.

The evidence now available suggests that nightmares can occur at any time in the sleep cycle, although there are indications that the most explosive type of severe night terror attack, with relatively little mental content occurs, at least in adults, in the phase of non-REM, or slow-wave sleep. Fisher, however, has noted examples in experimental subjects of REM nightmares in which there was loud vocalization and terror. Since evidence of "ordinary" dreaming can be recovered in a higher percentage of cases from REM than from non-REM sleep, it would be worthwhile to look for additional factors that disturb the sleep-dream cycle itself in accounting for the occurrence of these nightmares. Fisher et al., for example, noted that their adult nightmare subjects tended to have more troubled sleep than normal subjects, with greatly increased frequency of awakenings, increased body movements, and frequent moaning, groaning, and sighing. Broughton, Fisher et al. have shown that severe nightmares occur in association with physiological evidence of arousal from slow-wave (non-REM) sleep. . . . We need still to account for what brings about the arousal or makes any given instance of arousal so terrifying. Fisher was able in one instance to bring about a nightmare experimentally by sounding a waking buzzer; however, this experimental subject was known to be prone to nightmares. Such awakening failed to produce nightmares in other subjects equally prone. . . .

Nightmares occur in response to the characteristic danger situations that human beings confront in the course of development, beginning with the fear of strangers and the dread of abandonment in infancy and the fear of bodily injury in early childhood, and ending with the fears of failure, death, and loss of function in adulthood and old age. Frequently the anxiety that may accompany these dangers is not evident in the lives of healthy individuals during waking hours; it may emerge only during sleep – in an anxiety dream at a time when the individual does not have available the psychological defenses he normally employs during the daytime. William James actually stated, evidently with confidence: "In civilized life, in particular, it has at last become possible for large numbers of people to pass from the cradle to the grave without ever having had a pang of genuine fear. Many of us need an attack of mental disease to teach us the meaning of the word." He might have added to "mental disease" the more frequent experience of a nightmare. Nightmares may become the prototypic expression of the anxieties that characterize each period of development. . . .

Severe anxiety dreams, or nightmares in particular, may occur at times of important change in the lives of normal adults and often stand out as landmarks that denote significant undertakings or critical shifts.

An example is provided by the case of a thirty-two-year-old research physician who had a severe anxiety dream several days before he was to present a paper before an important scientific meeting. In the dream, he was sitting in the audience in the hall where his paper was to be given; a speaker on the platform had just finished delivering a paper. He heard the chairman, a senior researcher whose criticism he feared and who he had thought might in fact discuss the paper, announce that the next paper would be his. He felt taken by surprise and realized with horror that he had left his slides and manuscript at home. At first he thought to himself, "Well, I've given this often enough. I can give it off the cuff without my slides." But then the feeling of horror returned, and he thought, "They'll never believe me. I can't prove it. What'll I do? My moment has come, and I've fluffed it." He woke up in a sweat, with tremendous gratitude and relief that the dream had not been true.

His first association was that without his slides he would have *no defense* against the belittling, cutting comments of the senior man. In reality, he had especially resented this particular colleague, whom he regarded as a mean person and undeserving of his renowned position. The young doctor was coming into his own as a research scientist, leaving the status of a promising but untried young man to become a respected worker in his own right. This was the direction of his ambition, and he welcomed the shift, but he also feared punishment for the hostility that underlay his competitive attitude toward his senior colleague. Familiar oedipal conflicts and castration anxiety could be uncovered with further analysis of the dream, but its most immediate significance derives from the struggle of the young man to master the important changes occurring in regard to his position and status. A postscript to the dream demonstrated vividly the internal conflict over ambitious strivings that this man was experiencing. He remembered to bring the slides to the meeting, but forgot to prepare his statistics, despite a reminder by one of his coworkers. He gave the talk without the statistics, which were not essential in this instance. Someone from the audience asked about the statistics; this was embarrassing, of course, but not nearly as humiliating as it would have been had he forgotten the manuscript or the slides.

Fatherhood is similarly a critical period. Becoming a parent may lead to the breakthrough of intense anxiety related to latent jealousy and hostility provoked by the infant. These emotions and the regressive identification with the helpless infant may combine to precipitate a nightmare. . . .

There have been several studies of the incidence of various types of children's dreams. These studies vary so markedly in the criteria for dreaming, methods of dream collection, reasons for assigning labels to different kinds of dreams, the age ranges included, and the kinds of data recorded that one must be cautious in drawing any conclusions. Despert, for example, in a study of 190 dreams of forty-three preschool children, obtained quite extensive data from individual play sessions, daily behavior notes, and reports from home. She found that the dreams reported were predominantly anxiety dreams or nightmares; the predominant themes were the danger of the child's being bitten, devoured, and chased. Foster and Anderson specifically sought evidence of "unpleasant dreams" in groups of children age one to four, five to eight, and nine to twelve through parental reporting of moans in the night, coming to adults, and reporting bad dreams in the morning. By this method they found an incidence of 93 percent of "bad dreaming" in the forty children age one to four, which reduced to 71 and 39 percent, respectively, in the five-to-eight and nine-to-twelve groups. Kimmins in his study of the dreams of 5,900 children age five to sixteen is less specific about how the dream data were collected. In the five- to seven-year-olds, he found an incidence of only 25 percent and of 17 to 18 percent in the eight-to-fourteen group. Jersild et al., in a report of 400 children age five to twelve, reported only that the children were "questioned." The results are reported in a confusing manner, but the authors conclude that fewer children failed to report "bad" dreams than "good" ones. It is difficult to draw any conclusions from this literature. It would appear that, in the preschool group, nightmares or other unpleasant dreams predominate, but this becomes less the case for children of six years and above. Although simple wish-fulfillment dreams may occur, especially in very young children, the bulk of evidence tends to refute Freud's contention that children's dreams are usually direct, undisguised fulfillments of a wish. . . .

In very young children, especially under the age of four or five, the inability to establish, even after waking, that the nightmare's oppressors are not real adds to the terror and overwhelming quality of the nightmare experience. One little girl insisted repeatedly to her doctor, while they were playing out the nightmare experience, that the monster was "right dere, next to me. It slept right dere." Even the drawings they made together of the monsters became real for her. One of his tasks in treating this child was to help her establish distinctions between dream, reality, and fantasy play.

The manner in which children struggle to reassure themselves of the nonreality of their nightmares, to tell themselves "this is just a dream" in order to feel less threatened, is well known. At times, children invent quite elaborate devices to combat anxiety in dreams. A nine-year-old girl, who had been suffering from nightmares, assured her doctor that she had come to know, while she was dreaming, that she was having a bad dream and that this helped her not to be afraid. He asked her how she had achieved this. She replied that, when she suspected she was having a bad dream, she approached anyone she saw and announced, "This is a dream." As long as no one contradicted her, she then knew that she was dreaming.

Other ego functions that characterize the individual's areas of strength may be brought to bear in a dream in order to prevent anxiety of overwhelming proportions from developing. This is illustrated, for example, by the dream of a sixty-five-year-old woman who had devoted her life to research in the social sciences. She dreamt one night that she opened a closet and was confronted with a huge and menacing black cat. She began to feel horror, terror, and disgust, which threatened to become overwhelming, but then suddenly had the thought that her son was engaged in psychological research and could deal with the cat without difficulty. However, some anxiety returned as she realized that his field was the study of human beings and that this was a cat. Still dreaming, she thought of the name of a psychologist whose field was animal study and, much reassured, fell into a calm sleep. This lady dealt with the anxiety-laden matter in her dream as she handled many situations in waking life, by treating it as a problem for research.

DIFFERENCES BETWEEN NIGHTMARES AND NIGHT TERROR ATTACKS IN CHILDREN COMPARED WITH DIFFERENCES BETWEEN SEVERE REM ANXIETY DREAMS AND NON-REM NIGHTMARES IN ADULTS

	Children		Adults	
	Nightmare	Night Terror	Severe REM Anxiety Dream	Non-REM Nightmare
Time of occurrence	During sleep	During sleep or in a somnolent twilight state	Emerges out of a long dream	Occurs spontaneously, usually during first Non-REM period of the night
Motility and activity	Slight movements only	Child sits up in bed, jumps to the floor, runs about, cries out	Muscle tone and motility not regained; vocalization may occur, but screaming rare	Muscle tone and motility regained with violent body movement; subject may sit up in bed or get up and move about the room; screams
Mental content	Persecutory, violent, and elaborate	Severely persecutory, vivid and less elaborate	Threatened destruction, more elaborate and disguised	Violently persecutory, oral-aggressive content
Affect	Fear	Severe terror and overwhelming	Intense anxiety	Disorganizing terror and panic
Mental state following arousal	Can be calmed, coherent, oriented, not hallucinating	Incoherent, cannot be calmed, does not recognize objects, continues to hallucinate	Subjects lucid; Broughton refers to REM dreams in general	Disoriented, confused, unresponsive to the environment and often hallucinating
Physiological changes	No perspiration	Perspires heavily	Not observed	Massive autonomic discharge
Recollection of the episode	Incident recalled; content remembered more or less clearly	Complete amnesia for the content and the occurrence of the episode	Dream activity generally recalled	Generally an amnesia for the episode

The Dresser Has a Face

BRUNO BETTELHEIM, M.D.

Mother: I'd like your opinion about children's nightmares. My little boy is six, and he had a dream last week that so frightened him, I had to sit with him for an hour and a half till he went back to sleep. I asked what disturbed him, and he said the furniture was moving. I said, "Now, you know the furniture isn't moving." He said, "I know it's not moving, but it looks like it's moving." I said, "Well, do you want to get up and we'll make sure that everything is anchored?" He said "No" and I told him I'd sit with him till he got back to sleep. He said, "I don't want to go back to sleep because I'll have a bad dream." I said, "Well, what are you dreaming about?" And he said, "Monsters." I said, "You know n.onsters aren't real," and we had a long discussion. I told him they were imaginary things. He said he knew, but they still bothered him. I sat with him, and he's right—in the dead of night, there's a creak outside, and his dresser does kind of look like a face.

Sleepwalking Not Related to Dreams

GAY GAER LUCE

One of the most eerie and fascinating of sleep behaviors—sleepwalking—is not always innocuous to the performer. Somnambulists have been known to perform remarkable feats—to stride across narrow walls, pick their way through furniture, and negotiate around obstacles without harm. Some, however, have jumped out of windows, like the young woman, recently described in a newspaper report, who was found in the street with broken legs. As she explained to the police, she had a vivid dream of eloping with her fiancé and had merely opened the window and stepped onto the ladder, which unfortunately existed only in her dream. Many of these weird occurrences have been associated with traumatic incidents, like the nightly struggle of one French marine who rebattled a fire and mutiny at sea, colliding with chairs and tables so violently that he wounded himself visibly in sleep. And yet, upon awakening he felt he had slept calmly. Because of its repeated association with vivid dreams in the reports following the event, somnambulism has been thought to be an enactment of dreams. People reasonably expected that it would occur during the REM phase of sleep associated with vivid dreaming, a period when the scalp EEGs bear resemblance to the waking brain wave pattern, but until recently the evidence remained anecdotal, composed mainly of happenstance observations or reports to clinicians.

An EEG study of somnambulism, performed last year by a team of researchers at UCLA, yielded the startling and provocative information that walking did not occur in REM dream stages—but in the deep, slow-wave sleep of stages 3 and 4, a period not currently thought to be associated with intense dreams. This initial study was conducted with 4 volunteers who had been selected from 25 sleepwalkers, children, and adults. A special cable permitted the subject to leave his laboratory bedroom, while wearing his garland of electrodes connected to the EEG machine, while EEGs were continuously recorded. Each slept in the laboratory for 5 nights, and during this time the investigators studied 41 somnambulistic incidents. In each instance of walking or getting out of bed, the activity began in stage 3 or 4, and usually the subject did not remember having moved.

As the subjects moved around, the synchronous, large waves of stage 4 diminished in amplitude, progressing toward a lighter stage of sleep, and another interesting brain wave configuration was observed. During the actual sleepwalking, a regular wave, resembling the alpha rhythm of relaxed wakefulness, entered the brain wave pattern. Although normally the alpha rhythm vanishes when a person opens his eyes, this rhythm did not vanish when the sleepwalker opened his eyes.

The open eyes of the subjects lent a strange quality to their appearance, for they walked around furniture and people as if they could see—yet showing little sign of recognition or appearing indifferent. Their faces were blank, their feet shuffling, and they did not seem to perceive the investigators although they looked at them. One 9-year-old boy, whose brain waves were being recorded by biotelemetry, apparently oblivious to the presence of the scientists, wandered into the monitoring room and, 30 feet to the end of the laboratory, entered a kitchen, retreated and entered another bedroom, and finally returned to bed. Ten minutes later, because one of his electrodes had developed a loose connection, one of the investigators awakened him in order to repair it. The child remembered nothing.

This study and one French study give a first glimpse of the somnambulist in action. His brain waves more closely resemble those of deep sleep than those of the waking state. However, they are different. This may point to another state of vigilance apart from waking or sleep, a state in which there is usually reduced awareness of the environment, but in which complex and even violent acts requiring interaction with the environment may be performed.

E. THE EVOLUTION OF DREAMING

The Developmental Aspects of Dreaming

STANLEY KRIPPNER, Ph.D., and WILLIAM HUGHES

A CLUE as to the necessity of the dream state for human development may be found in studying the ontogenetic and phylogenetic data. The REM state has been observed in all higher mammalian species; considerable attention has been devoted to the cat, dog, monkey, and rat because of the similarity of many of their EEG patterns to those of humans. Some preliminary data suggest that the humanoid sleep-dream cycle does not occur among the lower mammals, amphibians, reptiles, or fish. Nevertheless, enough similarities exist to point to an evolutionary development of the REM state. For example, birds spend less than 1 percent of their total sleep time in the REM state in comparison with the higher mammals' 20 percent (e.g., sheep) to 60 percent (e.g., cats). Furthermore, one species of fish has been identified which appears to engage in eye movement activity during gross overall inactivity.

The evolutionary evidence shows that the hunting species (e.g., cat, dog, man) enjoy more REM sleep than the hunted (e.g., antelope, deer, rabbit). Furthermore, extensive REM sleep came as a rather late development in the evolution of the vertebrates. It may well be that the REM state (which is characterized by less sensitivity to external stimuli than are other sleep stages) was only able to develop to an appreciable extent among animals that were not in danger of extermination if their predators came upon them while they were dreaming—and while they were oblivious to external stimuli.

It is interesting to note that the larger animals with a longer life-span and a lower metabolic rate tend to have longer sleep-dream cycles. The average length of time from the beginning of one REM stage to the next varies from 4 minutes in the mouse to 90 minutes in adult man. It has even been suggested that cyclical dreaming evolved because this arrangement gave the organism an opportunity to come to a state of near waking readiness and "sample" the environment for danger. For example, when opossums are brought into a laboratory, they have a greater number of spontaneous REM state awakenings, just as their prehistoric brothers probably awoke more frequently when there were predators about.

Insofar as the proportion of the REM state is concerned, ontogeny does not neatly recapitulate phylogeny. Among the higher mammals (e.g., cat, man), slow wave sleep does not occur until the central nervous system has acquired a certain amount of maturity. In addition, REM time increases with phylogenetic development—although it decreases with ontogenetic development. The prematurely born infant spends about 80 percent of his sleeping time in the REM state. The full-term neonate spends about 50 percent of his sleep time dreaming, the 5-week old infant about 40 percent, the 3-year old child about 30 percent, the young adult about 20 percent, and the aged individual about 15 percent (Hartmann, 1966).

It is likely that the neonate—who sleeps three out of every four of his hours—spends more time in the REM state than in either the non-REM sleep state or the waking state. It is also possible that the fetus spends almost all of his time in the REM state.

What Do Infants Dream About?

HOWARD P. ROFFWARG,
JOSEPH N. MUZIO, and WILLIAM C. DEMENT

In infancy, when the proportion of time awake is smaller than in any other period of life, there is a large amount of REM activity. REM periods appear soon after sleep begins and are of random duration at any time of the night. Later, when the developing infant spends protracted intervals awake in increasingly active involvement with the environment (particularly when locomotive capacity is attained), the total amount as well as the percentage of REM sleep diminishes.

This evolution in the relative proportions of the sleep stages continues through the period when napping terminates. Long stretches of deep

NREM sleep occupy the first hours. Correspondingly, the first REM period in children past the napping age appears much later and is shorter than in children who nap. REM periods become longer toward morning. We have considered it probable that the child's progressively closer approximation of a diurnal pattern of uninterrupted daytime wakefulness causes corresponding changes in the sleep-stage pattern. Postnappers (4½ to 7 years) average 110 to 120 minutes of deep NREM sleep (stage 4) in comparison to 75 to 80 minutes in the pubescent group. It is of course not yet clear whether these changes are a consequence of lengthening periods of sustained arousal, increased muscular activity, maturation of the central nervous system, or a combination of these factors.

The first REM period of the night usually appears 50 to 70 minutes after sleep commences, whereas in the 4½- to 7-year-old group, latency of REM onset is 3 to 4 hours. Latency continues to shorten as children mature but it does not assume the adult interval consistently until midadolescence. This phenomenon of a delayed or "missed" first REM period may reappear in adults under conditions of sleep loss. Moreover, nocturnal sleepers who nap in the afternoon have a shorter REM latency in their naps than those who nap in the evening. These findings suggest that a condition ("fatigue," for lack of a more exact term) develops under circumstances of prolonged arousal (and possibly intensive activity) which tips the normal balance between REM and NREM sleep mechanisms, augmenting temporarily the "need" for deep NREM sleep and antagonizing REM sleep processes. We speculate that the immature central nervous system is more vulnerable to "fatigue," though youngsters are unquestionably more active than adults. . . .

PHYSIOLOGICAL CHARACTERISTICS

Except for an occasional gross body twitch and the respiratory excursions of the chest cavity, NREM sleep may be considered essentially devoid of muscular activity. The infant lies passive and motionless, in marked contrast to the almost continuous muscle contractions during the REM state. Grimaces, whimpers, smiles, twitches of the face and extremities are interspersed with gross shifts of position of the limbs. There are frequent 10- to 15-second episodes of tonic, athetoid writhing of the torso, limbs, and digits. Bursts of REM's commonly accompany the generalized muscle contractions, but the former are also present in the absence of other body movements. We have also observed that in the REM state, newborns display facial mimicry which gives the appearance of sophisticated expressions of emotion or thought such as perplexity, disdain, skepticism, and mild amusement. We have not noted such nuances of expression in the same newborns when awake. . . .

"DREAMING" IN THE NEWBORN

There can be little question that the stage of sleep in newborns that manifests REM's and a low-voltage, relatively fast EEG is related to adult REM sleep. Therefore the REM state must originate from inborn neurophysiological processes, as opposed to being engendered by experience. Important as this finding is, the fact of most significance is that the neonate spends fully one-half of its total sleep, or one-third of its entire existence, in this unique state of activation. In view of this, new questions must be considered. For instance, does REM sleep fulfill a vital function in the newborn? Does the sharp reduction of REM sleep in the first few years of life indicate that its most important function is related to early development?

In order to explore the implications of these questions, we must first deal with certain ambiguities. Since it has been previously established that REM sleep constitutes the time of dreaming in children and adults, does the *de facto* presence of a REM stage at birth indicate that newborns dream? And, if the REM's of adults are related to dream imagery, to what, if anything, are the REM's of newborns related?

If by dreaming one means a succession of vivid, discrete yet integrated, hallucinated images, it is hardly likely that newborns, who have extremely crude patterned vision, "dream." Though a most convincing demonstration of the relation of REM sleep to dreaming in adults has been the correlation of the REM's with the spatio-temporal aspects of visual imagery, REM's are certainly not unfailing counterparts of visual imagery under all circumstances. REM sleep is not necessarily associated with the presence of either visual imagery or a functioning cerebral cortex. For example, REM's in sleep have been reported in congenitally blind individuals, functionally decorticate humans, decorticate cats, and newborn kittens. Rather than indicating that neonates experience patterned visual dreams or that REM's and imagery cannot be related in the dreams of older individuals, the fact that neonates and decorticates have REM activity indicates that absence of visual phenomena, due to immaturity of the ascending sensory pathways and visual cortex, need not preclude REM-state functioning of the oculomotor apparatus. The REM's, as well as all other phenomena of REM sleep, have been shown to result from activity in the pons. Hence, if the pontine-oculomotor pathways are not cut, the REM's persist. . . .

REM SLEEP IN NEWBORNS

If we dismiss the "dream experience" as the vital attribute of REM sleep in the newborn period, we are in a position to consider the possible physiological significance of the great abundance of REM sleep in early life. Parmelee *et al.* have confirmed our finding of approximately 50 percent REM sleep in the newborn at term. In premature infants, the percentage of REM sleep is 58 at 36 to 38 weeks, 67 at 33 to 35 weeks, and 80 (one infant) at 30 weeks gestational age. The direction of the data supports the contention that the proportion of REM sleep nears 100 percent before the 30th week, but as yet little is known about what processes are responsible for the profusion of REM sleep in the immature organism or, for that matter, for the regulation of the proportion of REM sleep at any age.

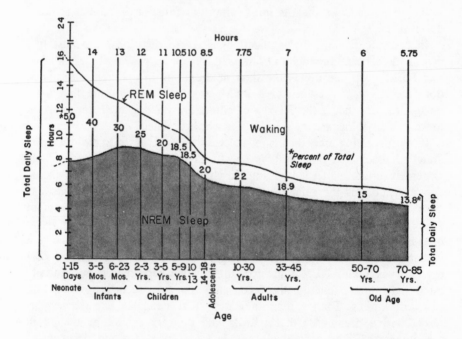

Graph showing changes (with age) in total amounts of daily sleep, daily REM sleep, and in percentage of REM sleep. Note sharp diminution of REM sleep in early years. REM sleep falls from 8 hours at birth to less than 1 hour in old age. The amount of NREM sleep throughout life remains more constant, falling from 8 hours to 5 hours. In contrast to the steep decline of REM sleep, the quantity of NREM sleep is undiminished for many years. Although total daily REM sleep falls steadily during life, the percentage rises slightly in adolescence and early adulthood. This rise does not reflect an increase in amount; it is due to the fact that REM sleep does not diminish as quickly as total sleep. Work in progress in several laboratories indicates that the percentage of REM sleep in the 50- to 85-year group may be somewhat higher than represented here. Data for the 33- to 45- and 70- to 85-year groups are taken from Strauch and Lairy respectively.

The Sleep and Dreams of Animals (I)*

How does the sleep of animals compare with man's? Noting that sleep is an active rather than a passive function, H. Hediger of the Zurich Zoological Gardens concludes that man has lost some animal abilities. The sleeping animal, he reports in *Proceedings of the Royal Society of Medicine*, is protected from visual and auditory disturbances in a variety of ways. All animals whose anatomy permits it, for example, close their eyes when they sleep, but many mammals in addition cover their eyes with their paws or tail. Animals with especially sensitive hearing, such as the bush baby and the big-eared bat, sleep with their outer ears folded.

Large animals, particularly predators who have little or nothing to fear from other animals, enjoy the longest and deepest sleep. The most profound sleeper is the sloth bear of India, a savage fighter that even tigers avoid. Animals with safe refuges—the fox in its den, the mouse in its hole, the hippopotamus in the water and tree-living birds, monkeys and apes—are also sound sleepers. Many animals, however, cannot burrow, swim or climb. Of these, the ones that live in herds take turns sleeping. A common sight at noon in Africa, Hediger reports, is part of a zebra herd reclining asleep on the ground while the rest of the herd remains alert. Some solitary antelopes, he suggests, may never sleep or may, as has been observed among deer, sleep very deeply but only for a few minutes at a time.

One animal attribute that man has lost, Hediger notes, is a "sort of filter" in the central nervous system that distinguishes between harmless and potentially dangerous stimuli. A circus elephant, he points out, will not rouse even if another elephant's leg is rested on its head but wakes immediately on hearing the slightest metallic sound. Hediger concludes, however, that what disturbs human sleep most is not the loss of such protections but the fact that, unlike other animals, man broods over the past and worries about the future.

The Sleep and Dreams of Animals (II)

TRUETT ALLISON and HENRY VAN TWYVER

For most of us, sleep is a seemingly empty void except for an occasional remembered dream and a rested feeling after a night of slumber. This subjective impression is only partly correct. Each night, four or five times at intervals of about 90 minutes, the quiet repose of human sleep is interrupted by a curious set of physiological and mental events: A dream begins and develops its own inner logic. The dream narrative does not flash through the mind almost instantaneously, as was once commonly thought, but proceeds in "real time" with a duration about as long as the events would actually require. During the dream, the nervous system and bodily functions are very different from those of the preceding, non-dreaming sleep. Heart rate and respiration become irregular, and the eyes move as if following the dream events. Muscular twitches of the hands or limbs occur, but otherwise the dreamer is still.

"Dreaming" sleep is not confined to *Homo sapiens*; based on laboratory studies, it is clearly present in many lower animals such as monkeys, cats, dogs, and rats. For these animals, however, we use a more cautious term—paradoxical sleep—to describe their apparent dream-sleep.

The concept of sleep, viewed in terms of both humans and lower animals, raises a number of important questions: If animals exhibit the symptoms of dream-sleep, do they actually dream? In what sort of animal did this type of sleep first arise, and for what reason? Is dreaming, and all the physiological changes that accompany it, a necessary biological event or, as Freud suggested, simply a means for satisfying psychological needs?

Through studies conducted by many investigators during the past fifteen years, we can provide tentative answers to these questions. Of the numerous species of living animals, the sleeping states of less than three dozen mammals and even fewer nonmammals have been studied in the laboratory. Still, enough is known to indicate the broad outlines of a story that takes us back almost 200 million years, to the time when mammals first appeared on earth. Lacking the opportunity to go back in time to observe the first mammals, we, and other investigators, have studied the sleep of certain living mammals that approximate critical stages of mammalian evolution in order to determine how these first mammals slept—and perchance dreamed.

How do we decide when an animal is sleeping? At first, this probably sounds like no problem at all: simply look at the animal and observe whether it is active or lying quietly, whether the eyes are open or closed. What would we say, however, in the case of a horse or cow, which seldom closes its eyes, or a fish or snake, which cannot? Humans as well as some other mammals have also been known to sleep with one or both eyes partially open.

Thus, casual techniques of observation are often not an objective means of telling when an animal is awake or asleep. Instead we use the electroencephalograph, or EEG machine, an electronic instrument used in hospitals to record the electrical activity of the brain. It consists of several very sensitive amplifiers that magnify the extremely small voltages generated by brain nerve cells. In humans these signals are detected by electrodes attached to the scalp, and the brain activity is recorded by an ink-writing pen on a moving paper chart. In animals brain activity can be recorded in the same manner, and with certain modifications of the machine, other physiological processes—such as breathing, heartbeat, and muscle activity—can also be recorded. To measure these physiological events, the animal is anesthetized and fine wires are placed in various regions of its brain and body. When the animal has recovered from the implantation, the electrodes are connected by cable to the EEG machine, which then records the changes that occur during waking and sleep. After implantation the animals are normal and do not appear to notice the electrodes or cables.

Typical EEG recordings during a cat's waking and sleep states appear in Figure 1. The tracings on the left were made while the animal was sitting quietly. Small electrical charges generated by the movement of the

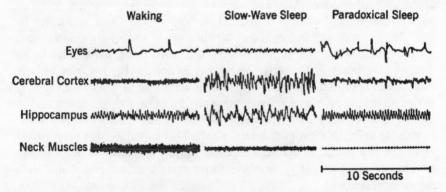

Figure 1. These electrical recordings, made from a cat in its waking state and during two states of sleep, show that the pattern of activity in each state is clearly different. Recordings taken from other animals during the same states would look very similar.

eyes were recorded by electrodes placed around the eyes. In the example shown there are two eye movements about four seconds apart. The electrical activity from the cerebral cortex, or gray matter, shows many small, fast fluctuations. (The cortex is nonexistent in reptiles. Increasingly prominent in higher mammals, it is believed to underlie complex mental functions.) The next tracing was taken from the hippocampus, an area deep within the brain involved with memory, whose electrical emanations accurately reflect changes in arousal. When the animal is alert and exploring its surroundings, nerve cells in the hippocampus tend to discharge electrical impulses in synchrony at the rate of several bursts per second, giving the record a rhythmic, wavelike appearance. Several such waves can be seen in the left-hand portion of the tracing. The third tracing shows electrical activity recorded from the neck muscles. During the waking state these are constantly active to support the head, resulting in large, rapid fluctuations recorded as a thick, ragged line.

When the cat goes to sleep (middle section), muscle tone is reduced but still present. Large eye movements cease, although there may be occasional slow, rolling movements. The activity of the brain is now markedly different. Large, slow waves, indicating the synchronous activity of many nerve cells, are recorded both in the cerebral cortex and the hippocampus, hence the name slow-wave sleep.

After several minutes of slow-wave sleep the cat then passes fairly rapidly—the transition takes only a few seconds—into paradoxical sleep. Now a number of physiological events occur. Many of these—such as twitching and eye movements—are visible to an observer. Others can only be seen with the aid of the EEG machine. Eye movements, either singly or in bursts, appear and continue sporadically during the paradoxical sleep episode. The eye movements occur more often and are jerkier than during waking. Electrical activity of the brain is similar to that during waking. Indeed, the hippocampus waves are even more rhythmic than when the animal is very alert. All these signs indicate an alert waking brain, but clearly the animal is not awake, for now muscle tone has disappeared completely; the cat is limp and difficult to arouse. It is this discrepancy between what appears to be a waking brain and a deeply sleeping body that led Michel Jouvet of the University of Lyons, France, to coin the term paradoxical sleep. This state has also been called rapid eye movement, or REM, sleep. But since this phase of sleep occurs also in animals that rarely or never move their eyes we prefer the term paradoxical sleep.

In mammals these EEG signs of sleep are very clear, but in submammalian forms such as amphibians and reptiles, EEG recordings may not be adequate to define sleeping and waking periods because the animals have relatively undeveloped brains. In the lower animals, behavioral criteria are also necessary; sleep is defined as a period when the animal is quiet and less responsive to stimulation.

We begin our analysis of the evolution of sleep with the bullfrog and salamander, lowly amphibians that mark the point of transition from sea-dwelling to land-dwelling vertebrates. Both EEG and behavioral criteria indicate that they almost certainly do not sleep. Instead they alternate between periods of quiet and active wakefulness.

In reptiles, which evolved from amphibians, the presence of sleep is not clear-cut. Conflicting results have been reported by different investigators. As in amphibians, there are periods during which the animal is quiet and immobile but still essentially awake. If reptiles sleep at all, they have only the rudiments of sleep as compared to mammals.

During cold weather both amphibians and reptiles retreat to secluded places where they remain completely inactive until warm weather resumes. These periods of torpidity also occur in some familiar mammals such as bears.

Interestingly, both stages of sleep—slow-wave and paradoxical—are found in birds. In chicks and pigeons, small amounts of paradoxical sleep can be observed and a clear stage of slow-wave sleep is evident.

With some variation from animal to animal and from species to species, both kinds of sleep have been found in all higher mammals studied in the laboratory. So far, the list includes, in addition to humans of all ages, the chimpanzee and several other primates, various rodents, hedgehogs, bats, sheep, and goats—even the pilot whale. Visual observation of elephants at the Boston Zoo suggests that they too have paradoxical sleep. Since paradoxical sleep is present in animals as different in size as mice and elephants, and as different in life styles as bats and goats, it is probably safe to say that all higher animals have both slow-wave and paradoxical sleep. Given that sleep is probably not present in reptiles, but clearly present in mammals and birds, at what stage of mammalian evolution did sleep arise?

Figure 2 summarizes the probable evolution of mammals as it is presently understood by paleontologists. About 220 million years ago the most abundant land vertebrates were a diverse group of advanced reptiles, which had in some respects almost reached the mammalian level of development. The first true mammals, small creatures resembling shrews in appearance—and perhaps in behavior—descended from one of these reptilian groups about 180 million years ago.

All the later mammals probably derived from early mammals similar to this shrewlike creature. One group of descendants, the therians, eventually gave rise to the two main kinds of living mammals, the marsupials and the placentals. A second group, the nontherians, became extinct many millions of years ago with the exception of two that still survive, the

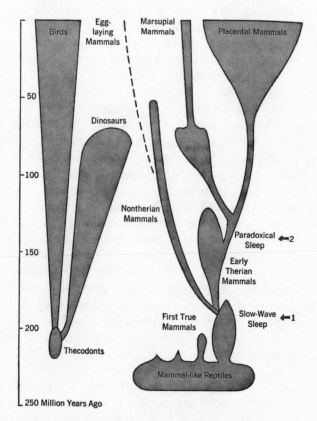

Figure 2. This phylogenetic tree summarizes the evolution of some reptile groups and their descendants. In the mammalian branch, slow-wave sleep apparently had evolved by the time noted by the first arrow. Paradoxical sleep arose some time after, but probably no later than the time indicated by the second arrow.

platypus and the echidna. These remarkable animals are now found only in Australia and nearby islands, where they have survived because these geographically isolated islands were until recently inhabited only by relatively docile marsupials. Placental mammals tend to displace less cunning and aggressive neighbors.

The living nontherians—platypus and echidna—are hairy, maintain a constant body temperature, and nurse the young. They are therefore unquestionably mammals, even though they have retained a number of reptilian features, the most striking of which is that the young are hatched from eggs. These two egg-laying mammals seem to have changed little (except perhaps in external appearance) since they first evolved. They provide the opportunity to study sleep as it appeared in the first mammals.

The platypus is difficult, if not impossible, to keep in captivity. The echidna, however, adapts readily to laboratory conditions. We obtained several echidnas through the cooperation of Mervyn Griffiths of the Commonwealth Scientific and Industrial Research Organization in Canberra and were able to study their sleep habits in detail. We found that this animal sleeps a great deal, up to twelve hours a day, and that its sleep is all slow-wave. We have not detected a single episode of paradoxical sleep. Instead the EEG reveals quiet periods that in many ways resemble the resting periods of reptiles. Because paradoxical sleep had been seen in all other mammals studied, we had expected to find it in the echidna as well.

It is possible that we were not able to see paradoxical sleep because its physiological and nervous system manifestations are radically different in primitive mammals. To test this possibility we studied sleep in another primitive mammal, the opossum. This marsupial, which has been called a living fossil, appears to have changed little since it first evolved. Just as the echidna gives us the best picture of earliest nontherian mammals, the opossum gives the best picture of early therian life. As it turns out, both slow-wave and paradoxical sleep are present in the opossum and are entirely similar to these states in placental mammals. The opossum revealed that paradoxical sleep is much the same in any mammal in which it is present at all, no matter how primitive the creature.

With this finding we then checked the hypothesis that paradoxical sleep is absent in the echidna because the animal is highly specialized in its life style, and not because it is primitive. To test this possibility we needed a placental mammal specialized, like the echidna, as a digging animal that spends considerable time underground and consequently has poor vision. We decided that the common mole would provide the best comparison. Even more adapted to life underground than the echidna, and like other animals that live in darkness, the mole's visual system has degenerated. The mole should therefore serve admirably as an "advanced echidna."

Moles, we found, are perfectly normal mammalian sleepers. Their slow-wave and paradoxical sleep, as measured by the EEG, are typical of that seen in other placental mammals and in the opossum. Like humans, moles sleep about eight hours a day; about one-fourth of this is paradoxical sleep. Furthermore, the electrical activity of their brain during sleep is similar to that of man.

These findings indicate that the lack of paradoxical sleep in the echidna is probably due to its primitive mammalian status, not to its particular way of life. We can judge by the echidna then that slow-wave sleep was present in the first true mammals, and thus had probably evolved in its present form about 180 million years ago.

THE DREAM WATCHER'S GUIDE

Although episodes of "dreaming," or paradoxical, sleep can be determined most accurately in the laboratory, it can also be seen in animals found around the house, such as dogs, cats—and children. Indeed, its signs are so clear that, in retrospect, it is surprising that this kind of sleep was discovered less than twenty years ago.

In cats and dogs, watch for this sequence of events: When the animal first goes to sleep, "nondreaming," or slow-wave, sleep always occurs first. Respiration is fairly regular and slow. Bodily movements are infrequent and the animal is still and quiet. After a period of ten to twenty minutes the first paradoxical sleep period begins. Now the eyes can be seen moving under the eyelids, which may be partially open. Breathing is irregular: rapid, shallow breaths alternating with periods of breath holding. The ears and whiskers twitch, often accompanied by facial twitches and grimaces. The paws may twitch, occasionally in synchrony as if the animal were trying to run.

In children the signs of paradoxical sleep are much the same except that facial movements often include sucking movements. In babies a paradoxical sleep episode may directly follow feeding.

The frequency of paradoxical sleep varies according to body size, from about every nine minutes in the mouse, to fifty minutes in the monkey or child, to ninety minutes in adult humans.

Since paradoxical sleep is virtually identical in the marsupials and placentals it was probably present in their common ancestor among the early therian group. It is unlikely that paradoxical sleep evolved independently in both groups at some later time. If this reasoning is correct, paradoxical sleep probably evolved in its full-blown mammalian form about 130 million years ago, or as much as 50 million years after the development of slow-wave sleep.

This evolutionary history of sleep is somewhat speculative, since we are inferring from living animals events that took place in the distant past. There are, however, two types of investigation that could lend further credence to the sequential development of sleep—from nonsleep to slow-wave to slow-wave plus paradoxical sleep. One study would involve platypus research. If we found only slow-wave sleep in this animal, which came upon earth at about the same time as the echidna, it would support the hypothesis that paradoxical sleep evolved at a later stage of evolution. Because it appears impossible to study the platypus in the laboratory, tiny devices would have to be implanted under its skin to transmit EEG information to distant receivers, as is done with astronauts. The advantage of telemetry, as this method is called, is that the animal is free to live in its natural habitat.

In principle, a second way of testing the idea that slow-wave sleep and paradoxical sleep arose sequentially is to look at different birds that approximate critical stages of avian evolution. So far as can be determined from the scanty fossil record of birds, all living forms are relatively recent. There appear to be no really primitive forms comparable to the echidna and opossum. However, the appearance of both phases of sleep in birds does show that, just as birds and mammals independently evolved a four-chambered heart from the three-chambered variety of their reptile ancestors, both phases of sleep evolved independently at least twice (in birds and in mammals) in the course of vertebrate evolution. There may have been transitional avian species, therefore, which displayed slow-wave, but not paradoxical sleep.

What do these findings tell us about the biological role of sleep? The descendants of reptiles—the mammals and the birds—have two things in common: they both sleep, and they both maintain constant body temperatures despite changes in environmental temperature. The ability of mammals and birds to be active at any temperature is a distinct advantage over the reptiles, which become sluggish in cool weather. A disadvantage of this mechanism, though, is that a great deal of food is required to keep the bird or mammal body warm; it would be advantageous to turn down the body's "thermostat" when the stomach is full or danger is not imminent.

A clear example of this benefit of lowered body temperatures during sleep is provided by comparing shrews and bats. Both are small mammals. When active, their metabolic rates are very high. The shrew is a nervous little creature that scurries around almost constantly in search of food and that does not exhibit clear periods of sleep. Under ideal laboratory conditions or in its natural habitat both phases of sleep are very likely present, but observation under seminatural laboratory conditions indicates that the shrew is an animal that can, and probably does, get by with little sleep. In contrast, bats sleep up to twenty hours per day, and during sleep their metabolic rate drops considerably. The life-span of the short-tailed shrew is about two years, whereas bats of the same size live up to eighteen years. Thus the bat's ability to "turn himself off" apparently results in a ninefold gain in life-span. In most animals metabolic rate during sleep does not decrease as dramatically as it does in the bat, but nevertheless it seems clear that the ability to sleep, and thereby conserve energy, can prolong life.

The daily temperature cycle (and therefore the underlying metabolism) is independent of sleep; therefore subjects deprived of sleep still have lower temperatures at those times that would correspond to normal sleep.

Specifically, we suspect that slow-wave sleep serves this function. It alone is present in the echidna, and it accounts for nearly all the sleep of birds, yet these animals maintain a constant body temperature as do marsupial and placental mammals. Paradoxical sleep in contrast is a time of heightened metabolic and nervous system activity. Slow-wave sleep may have evolved parallel with temperature regulation, as an active mechanism in the brain for periodically "forcing" mammals and birds—with their generally high body temperatures—to conserve energy. In amphibians and reptiles, whose body temperatures can drop to low levels, this active brain mechanism does not appear to be present.

For man, sleep is a recurring and persistent need. Attempts to stay awake for prolonged periods can have disastrous consequences, both psychological and physiological. Not every mammal, however, must bow to the demands of eight hours sleep per day. Certain of them, notably the hoofed animals, have evolved the ability to do without much sleep. In these animals sleep is seen only under very carefully controlled laboratory conditions and then only after extended periods of adaptation.

There are several factors that determine how much a particular species needs to sleep, but perhaps the clearest is the predator-prey relationship. Predators such as men, cats, and dogs are good sleepers, whereas the animals most subject to predation at any time of the day, the hoofed mammals, are generally very light sleepers. Browsing animals—such as sheep, goats, and donkeys—were derived from wild species that were continually exposed to predators. These animals are poor sleepers and only rarely enter the paradoxical sleep phase. Only under the most care-

ANIMAL	BEHAVIOR AND HABITAT	SLEEP
	"Good Sleepers"	
Mole	Carnivore, active day or night. Lives below ground in an extensive network of burrows.	Sleeps 8 hours per day in lab with almost no adaptation. 24% paradoxical sleep.
Ground squirrel	Herbivore, hibernates, prey. Lives in extensive burrows of its own making.	Deep sleeper, about 14 hours a day in lab. 25% paradoxical sleep.
Cat	Predator. Only the domestic cat has been studied.	Deep sleeper, readily sleeps about 14 hours a day in lab. 27% paradoxical sleep.
Macaque	Omnivore, strong fighter. Sleeps in tops of tall trees.	After short adaptation sleeps 8 hours a day, 15–20% paradoxical sleep.
Chimpanzee	Omnivore, most similar to man. Lives in tropical rain forests and shelters in tree nests at night.	After relatively short adaptation, sleeps 11 hours a day. 19% paradoxical sleep.
Man	Omnivore. Has mastered defense from other species and the elements. Chief predator is man. Inhabits all ecological ranges.	Deep sleeper. After short adaptation sleeps 8 hours in lab. 24% paradoxical sleep.

ANIMAL	BEHAVIOR AND HABITAT	SLEEP
	"Poor Sleepers"	
Guinea pig	Herbivore; nervous, hyperactive, excitable; prey. Lives in burrows, which it excavates or borrows, in rocky areas, savannas, swamps, and at edges of forests.	After long adaptation will sleep 12 hours per day. 5% paradoxical sleep.
Rabbit	Herbivore, prey. Some strains are extremely nervous and easily excited. Usually lives in grass nests on the surface or occasionally in burrows.	Difficult to adapt; sleep is seen only after several months in lab with some strains. Up to 15% paradoxical sleep when well adapted.
Sheep	Herbivore; nervous, excitable; prey. Lives in grasslands. (Study includes only domestic species.)	Requires long adaptation. About 4% paradoxical sleep.
Goat	Herbivore, excitable, prey. Lives in grasslands or mountains. (Only domestic species studied.)	After two months adaptation will enter paradoxical sleep, but only rarely.
Donkey	Herbivore, excitable prey. Lives in grasslands. (Only domestic species studied.)	After several months in lab will sleep about 4 hours a day, but paradoxical sleep apparently not seen.
Baboon	Omnivore. Strong fighter but subject to predation. Lives at edges of forests, in savannas and rocky areas. Sleeps in tops of scrub trees where it is easily visible.	Enters paradoxical sleep phase after extended adaptation. 4–9% paradoxical sleep.

Animals that have been studied in the laboratory can be divided into "good sleepers" and "poor sleepers." Good sleepers are either predatory or have secure sleeping places included in their way of life. Poor sleepers tend to be animals subject to predation at all hours; they sleep less and experience less paradoxical sleep.

fully controlled conditions will they sleep in the laboratory. (This is also true of the rabbit, chinchilla, and guinea pig.) Folklore holds that domesticated ungulates do not sleep at all. When questioned, those familiar with various farmyard species usually cannot recall having seen one of them lying down with eyes closed, obviously asleep. It is probable, although lack of exact knowledge of their habits makes it impossible to say with any certainty, that most poor sleepers are surface-dwelling mammals that, because of their habitat or size, cannot retreat to well-protected dens or burrows to sleep.

Good sleepers, however, are not always predators. As examples, consider the 13-lined ground squirrel and the hamster, which live mainly on vegetation yet are good sleepers. These animals are not predatory but are themselves subject to predation. They are not surface-dwellers, however, and thus need not constantly monitor their surroundings. The ground squirrel or hamster snugly enclosed in its burrow can afford the luxury of deep sleep. Another example of a deep-sleeping nonpredator is the macaque monkey of Asia, a species studied in the laboratory. This primate is able to afford the luxury of deep sleep because his environmental surroundings allow it. He sleeps in treetops that have dense foliage at the crown. Nocturnal predators are rare. He is light in weight, nimble and small, and can climb to high places that his chief enemies cannot reach. The macaque is a relatively deep sleeper with high percentages of paradoxical sleep. In contrast, the African baboon, although a savage and bold fighter, is insecure while sleeping. At night, his chief enemy, the leopard—a skillful climber—is most active, and the baboon must seek the tops of the tallest trees available. Cover is poor in the scrubby trees of the savanna environment, and he is usually quite visible, silhouetted against the night sky. As a result, the baboon is a fitful sleeper and rarely enters the paradoxical sleep phase.

We believe, therefore, that the essential difference between good sleepers and poor sleepers depends on the security of the animal's sleeping arrangements and not solely upon his food-getting status. Examination of the list of animals studied in the laboratory indicates that secure sleepers tend to have large amounts of paradoxical sleep. Thus it appears that deep sleep and high percentages of paradoxical sleep go hand in hand with a safe sleeping arrangement. Returning to our comparison of shrews and bats, we propose that the bat can afford to sleep deeply because its security during sleep is assured, suspended as it is from the ceiling of a cave or attic. The shrew, primarily a surface-dweller, must be much more circumspect about the duration and depth of its sleep.

The importance of security for deep sleep has also been suggested by H. Hediger, a zoologist who has observed animals in their natural habitat. He notes that the antelope probably never sleeps whereas the Indian sloth bear, a fighter so competent that even the tiger avoids him, sleeps deeply.

What biological function is served by paradoxical sleep? Clearly evident in man, the most advanced mammal (while absent in the echidna, a primitive mammal), this form of sleep does not appear to be a vestigial remnant of our prehistory.

Apparently, paradoxical sleep is not simply a mechanism to provide dreaming. It occurs in situations in which the possibility of dreaming is remote. Cats that have had most of the brain removed, except for the vital respiratory and cardiac centers in the medulla, still have paradoxical sleep. Similarly, human beings with diseases that essentially disconnect the cerebral cortex and higher centers of the brain nevertheless have periods of paradoxical sleep. In both these situations it seems unlikely that dreaming could occur. Thus, it seems that dreaming does not necessarily occur during paradoxical sleep. It is interesting that these results also suggest that dreaming does not cause paradoxical sleep, but, if anything, is caused by it. Perhaps an increase in heart rate and rapid shallow breathing evoke emotional dreams, rather than the other way around.

One of the most striking and unexpected findings of sleep research is that newborn mammals, whether they are humans, cats, or rats, have much more paradoxical sleep than adults. The human newborn, for example, spends about 50 percent of his sleep in the paradoxical phase, while adults spend about 24 percent. (Premature infants spend an even larger percentage of their sleep in this state.) These studies suggest that at earlier stages of prenatal development, all sleep may be paradoxical.

These findings have prompted a plausible theory for the biological significance of this form of sleep. The rapidly developing fetal nervous system presumably needs a great deal of excitation to build in the neural circuitry necessary for the development of integrated behavior patterns. Because paradoxical sleep is a time of intense central nervous system activity, it may provide a period of nerve "exercise," the stimulation coming from within the brain instead of from the environment. In the course of maturation less internally generated brain stimulation is necessary because sensory stimulation is now available from the environment; the amount of paradoxical sleep, therefore, declines.

Other findings seem to lend support to this hypothesis. At birth, poor sleepers such as the guinea pig and lamb have less paradoxical sleep than more secure sleepers such as man and the cat. The former, however, are born at an advanced level of nervous system maturation. Shortly after birth they can walk, and their sensory systems are functional, unlike man and the cat who are born completely helpless. Presumably, since the sensory systems are well developed they need less internally generated stimulation and spend less time in paradoxical sleep. Similarly, the young of the hoofed mammals must quickly develop a responsiveness to their environment; the rapid maturation of the brains in such species and their small amounts of sleep are both adaptive responses to the same environmental pressures.

An intriguing theory of the biological role of paradoxical sleep was suggested by Frederic Snyder of the National Institute of Mental Health. His view is that this "third state of existence," as he calls it, serves to periodically arouse the sleeping animal so that he can inspect his environment for danger. In times of danger, animals (or men, for that matter) tend to sleep fitfully, in short bursts, and may awaken during a paradoxical sleep episode. This would explain why the insecure sleepers such as sheep or guinea pigs get so little paradoxical sleep.

The advantage of such a "sentinel" mechanism is obvious: the animal is assured that his sleep will not be unduly prolonged; possibly forever in the case of the rabbit that does not see the approaching hawk. Furthermore, an animal aroused from paradoxical sleep is alert and reactive, ready for fight or flight, whereas awakened from slow-wave sleep he is disoriented for a few seconds. In addition, several kinds of evidence indicate that humans or cats can discriminate meaningful stimuli better during paradoxical sleep than during slow-wave sleep. Not only might paradoxical sleep serve to awaken the animal in danger, but he would awake ready to react in an integrated manner.

As far as can be determined with laboratory techniques, paradoxical sleep is similar in all mammals that exhibit it—from the opossum, a prototypal therian, to man, presumably the most advanced mammal. How similar, however, is the mental activity that might accompany the physiological signs of dreaming in animals and man? Is it possible, for example, for animals to experience visual imagery and other sensations during paradoxical sleep?

These are difficult questions to answer. We already know that paradoxical sleep can occur even when the possibility of any complex mental activity is highly unlikely. If we cannot automatically assume that dreaming occurs in humans during paradoxical sleep, we must certainly be cautious in making such an assumption about animals. Furthermore, to what extent can we ascribe human kinds of subjective experiences to an animal? Many scientists believe this is a futile, hazardous, even heretical undertaking. Darwin, on the contrary, insisted that mind, or consciousness, was a biological phenomenon that evolved from lower forms in much the same way as did anatomical characteristics. He pointed out that emotional expressions indicating particular "states of mind" were obvious in all animal forms. He went so far as to say, "even insects express anger, terror, jealousy, and love by their stridulations."

While it is difficult to attribute such complex emotions to so simple a beast as a cricket, it is reasonable to suppose that visual, auditory, and tactile imagery occurs in mammals. Most scientists have no particular qualms about attributing subjective states such as pain, hunger, and fear to animals. Yet an animal's outward manifestations of these states are not nearly so clear, not nearly so similar to the human manifestations of these states, as are the animal's signs of dreaming. We agree with the view stated many years ago by Julian Huxley:

"It is also both scientifically legitimate and operationally necessary to ascribe mind, in the sense of subjective awareness, to higher animals. This is obvious as regards the anthropoid apes: they not only possess very similar bodies and sense-organs to ours, but also manifest similar behavior, with a quite similar range of emotional expression, as anybody can see in the zoo; a range of curiosity, anger, alertness, affection, jealousy, fear, pain and pleasure. It is equally legitimate and necessary for other mammals, although the similarities are not so close. We just cannot really understand or properly interpret the behavior of elephants or dogs or cats or porpoises unless we do so to some extent in mental terms. This is not anthropomorphism: it is merely an extension of the principles of comparative study that have been so fruitful in comparative anatomy, comparative physiology, comparative cytology and other biological fields."

If one is willing to admit that it is possible to infer dreaming in animals, then several lines of evidence indicate that it actually does occur. Recall that muscle tone in the cat is completely suppressed during paradoxical sleep. If the brain center that produces this suppression is not functioning, however, a bizarre pattern of events takes place during the cat's paradoxical sleep. Although completely asleep, the cat will display behavior almost identical to that during the waking state. It will rise, walk about, attack invisible enemies, stalk an imaginary prey, or sit quietly and follow an unseen object with its eyes for periods of several minutes—all while deeply asleep! It is difficult for an observer to deny that some sort of imagery is present in the cat brain at these times.

In another experiment that suggests dream life in animals, monkeys were trained to press a lever when they saw patterned stimuli flashed on a screen before them. Later, during sleep, they were seen to press the lever as if they were hallucinating or dreaming of the stimuli acquired during the waking state. Techniques such as this bypass the problem that animals cannot give us spoken reports of their dream life.

We are willing to conclude that imagery occurs during paradoxical sleep in animals. To the extent that they are capable of mental life during waking it is equally plausible to grant them the power of dreaming during sleep. And what do they dream about? Anyone who owns a dog has witnessed the trembling, jerking, abortive running movements, the grimacing and whimpering that periodically occur during sleep. A dream of a rabbit chase? Why not? Freud thought that dreams are often wish fulfillments. In *The Interpretation of Dreams* he wrote: "I do not myself know what animals dream of. But a proverb, to which my attention was drawn by one of my students, does claim to know. 'What,' asks the proverb, 'do geese dream of?' and it replies: 'Of maize!' The whole theory that dreams are wish fulfillments is contained in these two phrases." Perhaps cats dream of the perfect mouse, and moles of big juicy earthworms. We like to think so.

F. THE DRAMA OF DREAMING

Continuity from Dream to Dream

HERBERT GREENHOUSE

FREUD, JUNG, AND OTHER PSYCHIATRISTS and psychologists felt that dreams in the same night were not isolated events but were dynamically connected. Freud believed that the unifying factor of these dreams was the repressed wish, often disguised by the manifest content of the dream, and that two dreams in succession or occurring at different times of the night would sometimes show a dramatic progression—the first dream keeping its motive "under wraps" while the later dream revealed more of the underlying theme. Jung spoke of the individual dream as "a play in four acts." Brilliantly intuitive, he could have also been describing the typical four dream periods of each night as a dramatic whole.

With the REM techniques, it has been possible to test these statements by examining each dream at the time it occurs and relating it through its content and/or its emotional tone to the preceeding and succeeding dreams of the same night. Although every dream or REM dream period may be a dramatic unit in itself, a dream series spread throughout the night—with intermissions in the form of other sleep stages—may be unified by a conflict that reappears in different forms, sometimes leading to a possible solution in the last dream. There may be connecting links in details as well as emotional themes: An automobile or other object, a setting, a character may return in each dream and act as a symbol of the underlying conflict.

The structure of a nightly dream series often follows a time-and-space pattern in which the first or last act takes place in the present while the middle portion is a flashback to an earlier period in the life of the protag-

356

onist: The first and last dream periods are related to contemporary events while dreams occurring in the middle of the night mirror the earlier life of the dreamer. One experiment suggested that more characters enter the dream plot as the night progresses, that the action shifts from outdoor to indoor settings, and that there is more reference to food and drink in succeeding dreams. This study, however, covered only the first three dream periods. (Bill Domhoff and Joe Kamiya, "Problems in Dream Content Study with Objective Indicators:—III. Changes in Dream Content throughout the Night," *Archives of General Psychiatry*, November 1964, vol. XI, pp. 529–532.)

Among the researchers who have studied the sequence phenomenon are Dement, Wolpert, Rechtschaffen, Offenkrantz, Trosman, Kramer, Kamiya, Domhoff, and Verdone. The many articles they have written on the subject, based on their experiments, throw new light on the dream process, on the psychodynamics of dreams, and on the dramatic nature of each dream and dream sequence in a night. In one such paper Dement and Wolpert concluded that, although "no single dream was ever exactly duplicated by another dream, nor were the dreams of a sequence ever perfectly continuous . . . the manifest content of nearly every dream exhibited some obvious relationship to one or more dreams occurring on the same night." Such relationships were expressed in similar characters, plots, actions, environments, emotions, or the development of a theme. (William Dement and Edward A. Wolpert, "Relationships in Manifest Content of Dreams Occurring on the Same Night," *Journal of Nervous and Mental Diseases*, June 1958, vol. 126, no. 1, pp. 568–578.)

Some of the dream sequences "seemed to be a self-contained whole in which the individual dreams either expressed permutations of one theme or maintained a rough, but recognizable continuity from dream to dream. In this last case, the content of one dream seemed to be a reaction to the content of the preceding dream, and the next a reaction to both of the preceeding, and so on." This progression from dream to dream was also observed in another experiment in which "each dream solution" acted as a " 'night residue' for the next dream." (Milton Kramer, Roy M. Whitman, Bill J. Baldridge, and Leonard M. Lansky, "Patterns of Dreaming: The Interrelationship of the Dreams of a Night," *Journal of Nervous and Mental Diseases*, November 1964, vol. 139 (5), pp. 426–439.)

Offenkrantz and Rechtschaffen followed up an earlier study that postulated the theory of "tension accumulation, discharge, and regression" in a dream sequence accompanying the psychological response of the dreamer to his conflict and his attempts at solution during the night. (William Offenkrantz and Allan Rechtschaffen, "Clinical Studies of Sequential Dreams," *Archives of General Psychiatry*, 1963, vol. 8, pp. 497–508.) In many of the laboratory dreams, the dreamer would attempt increasingly "bolder gratifications" of his repressed wish until suddenly he would withdraw as he might do in waking life when "the reactive motives predominate." This kind of rhythm of advancing and withdrawing is suggestive of the technique of a playwright who builds suspense from the opening curtain, perhaps bringing the spectator closer and closer to the resolution of the character's conflict, then providing a diversion in the form of comedy or a subconflict before returning to the main theme. This is highlighted by the statement of the researchers that "all dreams of a night were concerned either with the same conflict or with a limited number of different conflicts . . . an interplay of competing wishes." Several examples were given of sexual conflicts in the dream sequences.

In the Dement-Wolpert experiment one dream sequence dramatized the dreamer's relationship to women. In the first dream he manages to gain the upper hand over his woman-antagonist in a conflict over an inheritance, but there is a suggestion that she has other weapons in her arsenal that she will use later. In the second dream a man presumably representing the dreamer shoots the woman (or *a* woman) and then runs away in fear. Now the dreamer wakes up feeling "frightened and anxious," sensing somehow that the battle may be won but the war is not over, and that the woman, whoever she is, will be back. The third dream is frankly sexual. The woman, a Miss C., gets the upper hand by seducing the dreamer who sensed that he "was being manipulated." He finds that his hand is bleeding and there are wounds on his arm following the intercourse. In the fourth dream he is playing bridge with two women and feels that there is "something about how a hand had been played wrong" and that he had the "wrong kind of cards." The "hand" may refer back to the bleeding hand of the previous dream.

Dement and Wolpert comment that this series follows the sequence of a classical tragedy. The fate of the dreamer is that he will be destroyed by a woman, and although he is triumphant at first, he becomes more fearful in the second dream and instead of facing his foe, he shoots her in the back. In the third dream he submits to the "humiliation of accepting a passive role in intercourse with 'Miss C' and another woman" and suffers an arm injury. The last dream, when he feels that his cards are somehow "wrong," echoes the first dream when there was a suggestion that the woman-antagonist had a "trump card" she would show later. Thus the tragedy comes full circle and the hero-dreamer is defeated.

In addition to the straightforward man-woman conflict of this dream sequence, there were also other meaningful details that carried over from dream to dream—the cards, the hand, etc. In other experimental dream series, dreams were tied together solely by what seemed to be trivial details that masked the underlying conflicts. Dement and Wolpert reported one dream sequence in which two of the dreams were connected by the appearance of "ice" and three others by an "auto." The element of danger also tied several dreams together.

In another experiment one sequence was unique in that four successive dreams were made up of logically related acts taking place in a garage. (Harry Trosman, Allan Rechtschaffen, William Offenkrantz, and Edward Wolpert, "Studies in Psychophysiology of Dreams, IV. Relations among Dreams in Sequence," *Archives of General Psychiatry*, 1960, vol. 3, pp. 602–606.)

Dream 1. I am in a garage cutting up wood to put on a truck to take away.
Dream 2. I am in the same place cutting up a door, getting it ready to throw out.
Dream 3. I am completing the work in the garage, carting off some things and breaking others that are too big to throw away; then I lock up the garage.
Dream 4. The garage was all cleaned out.

Missing are the bizarre, illogical progressions that one finds in the ordinary dreams or dream series. But the clue lies in the character of the dreamer, described by the researchers as a mathematics student who "kept a rigid control over any emotional expression."

The authors of this paper also noticed that dreams often progressed from "abstract concepts" to "concrete images." In the first dream of another sequence, the mathematics student gave "weight" to a score in solving a problem in statistics. In his second dream there was a woman who gained "weight" during her marriage. In later dreams a car gained "weight" when objects were added to it. This concept is somewhat related to the Freudian idea that the underlying conflict may come out into the open in later dreams of a sequence.

The shifting from abstract to concrete is also a reversion to more primitive forms of thinking. Other researchers have found that time moves backward as the night goes forward, that is, the scenes of an earlier period of the dreamer's life, possibly tied to more "primitive" forms of thinking, emerge before giving way to the present once more as morning arrives. Freud contended that as one's senses are withdrawn from the environment, there is a revival of childhood memories in the form of imagery. As the sun comes up and more sounds are heard outside, the sleeper becomes attuned once more to the life around him in preparation for waking, and his dreams draw nearer to the present.

Verdone gave his subjects a questionnaire to fill out after waking from each dream to indicate whether their dreams portrayed contemporary or earlier events in their life. (Paul Verdone, "Temporal Reference of Manifest Dream Content," *Perceptual and Motor Skills*, 1965, vol. 20, pp. 1253–1268.) One of the questions read:

With what time period were the places, objects, people, events, and activities of your mental experience concerned? Alternatives: (1) earlier this evening, (2) past day, (3) day before, (4) past week, (5) past month, (6) past 6 mo., (7) 6 to 12 mo. ago, (8) 1 to 2 yr. ago, (9) 2 to 5 yr ago, (10) over 5 yr. ago, (11) other (specify).

Verdone found that during the first 3½ hours of sleep his subjects dreamed of real or imagined events that took place in the previous week. During the next four hours of sleep there was a progression backward in time. After about 7½ hours, the dreams came closer to the present—that is, covering the previous one to six months.

Another interesting feature of dreams is that there is often a dramatic link between dream sequences of different nights. This is called lateral homology—the same element that may appear in a Monday night sequence reappears at the same point in the Tuesday night series. During the Trosman-Offenkrantz-Rechtschaffen-Wolpert experiment, one subject dreamed on successive nights of an athletic event in the first dream, of a rejection by a friend in the second dream, and of taking a buried object out of the ground in the third dream.

G. SENSE IMPRESSIONS IN DREAMS

Most People Dream in Color

EDWIN KAHN, WILLIAM DEMENT,
CHARLES FISHER, and JOSEPH E. BARMACK

PREVIOUS STUDIES indicate that color is present in a minor portion of dreams. These studies have sought to determine either the percentage of dreams that were colored, the percentage of individuals who experience colored dreams, or the percentage of color that was present in each dream. For studies of the percentage of colored dreams, the following investigators arrived at the percentages indicated: Hall, 29; Monroe, 21; and Knapp, 14. For the percentage of individuals who experience colored dreams, Husband reported 40; Middleton, 29; DeMartino, 17; Lovett Doust, 13; and Tapia, Werboff, and Winokur, 14. For the percentage of color reported in each dream, Bentley reported 19.

In comparison with the low values reported by these investigators, Tauber and Green observed with patients in analysis and with others that although color was not a prominent characteristic of dream reports, when attention was focused on color, reference to it increased substantially. This study, while nonquantitative, encouraged support for the hypothesis that color is commonly experienced but is underreported for a variety of reasons. Specifically, we hypothesized that dream reports obtained close to the time of dreaming and after careful interrogation would reveal a substantially higher incidence of color than is reflected in the current literature.

In order to reduce the time interval between dreaming and reporting, the technique of Aserinsky and Kleitman was used. This technique utilizes the electroencephalogram and eye movements as indicators of dreaming, and has been extensively described elsewhere. Subjects were awakened during periods of eye movement and asked to report any dreams that were in progress prior to their awakening. They then narrated the dream material into a tape recorder. After the uninterrupted description of the dream, the experimenters attempted to elicit additional information about specific items of content in order to determine the nature and color of the objects reported. To minimize suggestion, questions about color were imbedded randomly among other questions dealing with size, shape, location, and so on.

The dreams reported by the subjects were scored as *Colored* (the dream or part of it was colored); *Vaguely Colored* (the dream or part of it appeared in vague, dull, light, or tinted colors); or *Not Colored* (the dream description contained no mention of color). We also classified the dreams into the categories of *Vague Recall* (the recall of the dream was vague or hazy or foreshortened) and *No Recall* (no dream content was recalled). The colored dreams were further subdivided into those in which color was mentioned *spontaneously* in the initial dream narrative and those in which it was *elicited* during the questioning period.

To illustrate the procedure, two excerpts from typical dream reports are presented along with the type of questions that were asked after the narrative description was given. One subject mentioned that she saw "a bar of soap in the bathtub with the baby." After completion of the narrative, in which no reference was made to color, the experimenter asked, "What did the soap look like?" The subject replied, "Like any bar of soap looks. It was round, it was *pink*, and the baby was playing with it in the bathtub." This was scored as an *elicited* color response. Another subject stated in part of his dream narrative, "I saw all the girls come in and they were wearing bright *red* bathing suits." During the questioning period the experimenter asked, "What kinds of bathing suits were they?" The subject answered, "Well, they were ordinary one-piece bathing suits, not bikinis." Then the experimenter asked, "You say the bathing suits were red; how did you know?" The subject answered, "How did I know? I saw them. They were red." This report was scored as a *spontaneous* color response.

A total of 100 awakenings were made on 38 subjects (28 males and 10 females) who ranged in age from 18 to 33. These subjects were college students and other persons available to the experimenters. They had indicated before the study that they usually recalled dreaming. None of the subjects slept in the laboratory more than two nights. From these 100 awakenings, there were 87 instances of dream recall. Table 1 presents the results according to the number of awakenings made on individual subjects. The table was set up in this manner in order to take into account the unequal number of awakenings per subject.

Of the 87 dreams recalled, color was present in 61, or 70.1 percent. Vaguely colored dreams were reported in an additional 11, or 12.6 per-

TABLE 1

SUMMARY OF DREAM RECALLS WHEN SUBJECTS WERE AWAKENED
DURING PERIODS OF EYE MOVEMENT

Awakenings of single subjects	Sub-jects	Total No. of awak-enings	Dreams (No.)				
			Re-called	Colored	Vaguely colored	Not colored	Vague or no recall
1	14	14	13	11	—	2	1
2	8	16	12	12	—	—	4
3	7	21	20	10	5	5	1
4	3	12	11	6	2	3	1
5	1	5	5	2	2	1	—
6	3	18	14	11	—	3	4
7	2	14	12	9	2	1	2
Totals	38	100	87	61	11	15	13

cent, and no color responses were given in the remaining 15, or 17.3 per-cent.

Of the dreams in which color was reported, the color was given spon-taneously in 22 dreams and only after some questioning in the other 39. In addition, at least one colored dream was reported by 31 of the 38 subjects (81.6 percent). At least one vaguely colored dream was reported by three more of the subjects. No color was present in the dreams of two of the subjects. Two additional subjects could not recall any dreams at these awakenings. Of the last four subjects, three were awakened only once and one was awakened twice. No attempt was made to determine the percentage of color in the content of single dreams.

A further check was made to see how frequently subjects reported color spontaneously after awakening when there was no investigator in-terest in the incidence of color. The same technique of awakening after rapid eye movements was used. Two hundred and eight transcribed dream narratives, collected from 16 subjects in two previous studies were avail-able for examination and comparison. In these studies there was no inter-rogation about color. It was found that color was mentioned spontaneously in only 33 of the 208 dreams (15.9 percent). This figure is not signifi-cantly different from the percentage of spontaneous color responses in the present series of awakenings (25.3 percent or in 22 of the 87 re-called dreams). Our somewhat higher figure, although not significant, may be explained by the possibility that at some point after the first awaken-ing the subjects were able to guess at the purpose of the study and con-sequently were more motivated to attend to and describe color. Despite this slight discrepancy in the two series, both substantiate the fact that the incidence of color in dreams cannot be assessed validly by working with spontaneous narratives of dreams even when the narratives immediately follow the dream experience.

In order to arrive at a more valid assessment of the percentage of color in dreams, some probing is necessary. Color is not a salient char-acteristic in dream reporting, and, indeed, may not be a frequently men-tioned characteristic of descriptions of everyday events of waking life. The fact that color was present in 70 percent of the dreams, or in 83 percent when the Vaguely Colored category is included, suggests that dreaming should be considered a colored rather than a black-and-white phenomenon. It would appear that it is the lack of color rather than its presence in dream recall which requires explanation.

The Dream in Technicolor
of the Congenitally Deaf

JACK H. MENDELSON, M.D.; LEONARD SIGER, M.D.;
and PHILIP SOLOMON, M.D.

Twenty-six college students between the ages of 18 and 24 were the subjects of this study. Three categories of students were investigated (Table 1): 1. Congenitally deaf; 2. Acquired deafness before age 5; 3. Acquired deafness after age 5.

These students came from a wide variety of socio-economic back-grounds but had the following characteristics in common:

1. All were totally deaf with the hearing loss of 60 db bilaterally.

2. All were enrolled as full-time students at Gallaudet College, the na-tional college for the deaf.

3. All had similar I.Q. levels, and a high proficiency of communication with sign language methods.

TABLE 1

SUBJECT POPULATION

Type of Deafness	N	Age Range (Yrs.)	Sex
Congenital	12	17–23	M-6, F-6
Acquired Before age Five	8	18–22	M-3, F-5
Acquired After age Five	6	19–23	M-4, F-2

RESULTS

Frequency of dreams is found in Table 2. Congenitally deaf students dreamed more frequently than those with acquired deafness. However, students with acquired deafness prior to age 5 had more frequent dreams than those whose deafness ensued after 5 years of age. The perceptual characteristics occurring in dreams are reported in Tables 3 and 4. The dreams of the congenitally deaf were characteristically in bright color usually described as "technicolor" and contained primary colors in high saturation and intensity. Also dreams of the congenitally deaf were for the most part three-dimensional rather than flat. The dreams of students with acquired deafness before age 5 resembled those of the congenitally deaf in terms of color and dimension while dreams of students with acquired deafness after age 5 tended to lack color and were evenly divided between flat and three-dimensional appearances.

The perception of motion of objects other than movement involved in signing occurred infrequently in the dreams of both the congenitally deaf and acquired deaf. There was a striking degree of vividness for dreams

TABLE 2

FREQUENCY OF DREAMS (PERCENT)

| | | TYPE OF DEAFNESS | |
	Congenital	Acquired Before age Five	Acquired After age Five
Every Night	84	50	17
Frequent	8	25	33
Infrequent	8	25	50

TABLE 3

COLOR AND DIMENSION IN DREAMS (PERCENT)

| | | TYPE OF DEAFNESS | |
Perceptual Experience	Congenital	Acquired Before age Five	Acquired After age Five
Color	92	75	17
Black and White	8	25	83
3D	84	87	50
Flat	16	13	50

TABLE 4

MOTION AND VIVIDNESS IN DREAMS (PERCENT)

Perceptual Experience	TYPE OF DEAFNESS		
	Congenital	Acquired Before age Five	Acquired After age Five
Static	84	75	83
Motion (Other Than Signing)	16	25	17
Vivid on Recall	92	87	67
Faint on Recall	8	13	33

on recall by both the students with congenital deafness and acquired deafness prior to age 5. This was less so for students with acquired deafness after age 5.

The communication processes experienced in dreams are reported in Table 5. Dreams are divided into 3 general categories, pleasant, anxious and neutral, based upon the affect the subject experienced while dreaming. Communication processes are divided into 4 categories:

1. Language of signs: the standard method of communication by signing used in everyday life.

2. Primitive signs: gestural communication employed by parents or parental figures in early childhood before the standard language of signs was learned. Such gestures usually conveyed strong affective qualities such as anger, disapproval, warning, fear, and occasionally approval and praise.

3. Non-verbal: communication without the language of signs, primitive signs or "sound" via an intuitive form of understanding.

4. "Sound": a mixture of auditory and frequently tactile sensory impression. Relatively simple messages were conveyed by this means, not complex thoughts or ideas.

In "pleasant" dreams, communications to or by the subject occurred most frequently in a non-verbal form with the language of signs appearing next frequently. "Sound" perception occurred infrequently in all groups of subjects but it tended to appear most frequently in those subjects with acquired deafness after age 5. Primitive signs appeared in the dreams of the congenitally deaf but not in the other groups.

In "anxious" dreams or nightmares of the congenitally deaf there was a striking prevalence of primitive signs. These signs, though originally employed by parents or parental figures, could be signed in dreams by people who were quite unknown to the subject. It is significant that no

TABLE 5

COMMUNICATION PROCESS IN DREAMS (PERCENT)

Type of Dream (affective component)	Communication Process	TYPE OF DEAFNESS		
		Congenital	Acquired Before age Five	Acquired After age Five
Pleasant	Language of signs	33	37	33
	primitive signs	17	0	0
	non-verbal	42	50	50
	"sound"	8	13	17
Anxious	Language of signs	17	38	33
	primitive signs	75	0	0
	non-verbal	8	50	50
	"sound"	0	12	17
Neutral	Language of signs	84	63	33
	primitive signs	0	0	0
	non-verbal	16	25	50
	"sound"	0	12	17

primitive signs appeared in the anxious dreams of the other two groups. In other respects the anxious dreams resembled those of the pleasant dreams for the three groups of students.

In "neutral" dreams there was a tendency for an increased degree of non-verbal communication and a decreased degree of language of signs from congenital deafness to acquired deafness after age 5. No primitive signs appeared for any students in neutral dreams and the incidence of "sound" in these dreams was also small.

DISCUSSION

It is clear from our data that the dreams of our deaf students are distinctly different from the dreams of the hearing. The differences reside in greater vividness, depth of spatial dimension, and color, as well as generally greater frequency or, more accurately, greater frequency of recall. How can we explain these differences? It seems to us that much may hinge on the balance between dream repression and dream recall.

It is a familiar observation that dreams in all of us may be vividly remembered on awakening and yet disappear a moment later. It has been our experience that the occurrence of sensory stimulation, particularly auditory stimulation, contributes greatly to such a disappearance. A word from your wife, a cry from the baby, or the sound of the alarm clock, and your dream may be gone forever. The deaf do not have this type of stimulation and in their soundless awakening, dreams linger on and retain their vividness and color. Perhaps this is a small compensation for the dullness of a completely silent existence. . . .

SUMMARY

Twenty-six deaf college students were interviewed in the language of signs and manual alphabet to obtain information concerning the symbolic and perceptual processes experienced in their dreams. It was found that the dreams of the congenitally deaf were vivid, brilliantly colored, and reported as frequent in occurrence. Usually the language of signs was the means of communication in the dream, but in dreams in which affect was prominent, primitive signs were often utilized. The characteristic differences in the dreams of the deaf were most marked in the congenitally deaf, less marked in those with acquired deafness before age 5, and least marked in those with acquired deafness after age 5.

Do the Blind "See" in Their Dreams?

HERBERT GREENHOUSE

Just as the congenitally deaf compensate for hearing loss by dreaming in vivid color, the most active sense in the dreams of the blind is that of hearing, with the tactile and kinesthetic senses next in prominence. There are more conversations in the dreams of the blind than in the dreams of normal persons, who have more visual than auditory dreams.

According to most dream researchers, there have been no reports of visual imagery in the dreams of those born blind. There is some visual imagery in the dreams of those born with vision who later lose it. As the blind person who was born with sight becomes older, there is less and less "seeing" in his dreams. Some researchers have reported rapid eye movements during the dreams of the congenitally blind, although there was no visual imagery in their dreams. REMs always seem to be present in cases of acquired blindness.

Many of the blind have vivid dreams in which perception of their dream environment seems just as real to them as visual perception does to those with sight. In her article, "The Dream Imagery of the Blind" in the *Psychoanalytic Review* (July 1928, vol. 15, pp. 288–293), Elinor Deutsch, who is blind, questions the assumption of some dream researchers that in cases of acquired blindness, the dreamer usually knows in his dreams that he is blind. "The blind not only dream just as vividly as the sighted but are perhaps less cognizant of the lack of vision asleep than when awake." Speaking of herself, she says, "The question of vision almost never enters into her (Miss Deutsch's) dreams and she has no sense of physical deficiency as is sometimes the case in waking life."

Helen Keller, who was stricken with loss of sight and hearing at the age of nineteen months, writes that in dreams she sees, hears, and speaks, but not with her eyes and ears. (See Part I, page 34.) She tells about handling a pearl, although she had "no memory-vision of a real pearl." It may be that the true dream experience, in both the physically normal and the handicapped, is something beyond mere sensation and that a blind person may, as Helen Keller was, be "moved to pleasure by visions of ineffable beauty."

Body Image in Dreams

HERBERT GREENHOUSE

In an article on "Sensory Impressions in Dreams" (*Psychoanalytic Quarterly*, 1956, vol. 25, pp. 325–347) Peter Knapp writes that about 15 per cent of dreams reported in a survey contained color. In only about 5 to 10 per cent were the dreamers aware of bodily movement (kinesthesia). Smell and taste dreams were rare.

The experiment by Kahn et al. proves that the color percentages were understated, since most people will admit under questioning that there was some color in their dreams. The figures on kinesthesia may also be open to question. Barbara Lerner discusses the function of body image in dreams and suggests a new theory of dream function based on "the relations between kinesthetic fantasy, body image, and ego integrity." ("Dream Function Reconsidered," *Journal of Abnormal Psychology*, 1967, vol. 72, no. 2, pp. 85–100.)

Lerner believes that dream researchers have been too concerned with the visual aspect of dreams and the dream's symbology and have ignored the importance of movement in dreams, which "may be a more constant feature of dreams than visual experience." She cites the theories of Herman Rorschach, who devised the inkblot tests for personality. Rorschach, according to Lerner, was interested in "kinesthetic fantasy or bodily empathy, the sense of what it would literally feel like to be in a certain physical position, to take a certain emotional stance, or to engage in a certain activity—anything from lying perfectly still and limp to running, glowering, dancing, fornicating, etc. . . ." Since many persons are unable to act out such movement impulses in their waking life, the body image is weakened, and the function of dreaming is to strengthen it.

The article discusses the theory that body image is the basis of ego: "The infant's first grasp of reality is a grasp of his physical self, its existence as a separate entity, its possibilities and limitations; his first learning involves learning how to organize his kinesthetic sensations so as to recognize his specific bodily needs. . . ." Because the opportunities for physical expression are fewer as the child grows older, there is a "weakening of the body image," and one important "function of dreaming is to strengthen body image by reintegrating the body into those fantasies which the dreamer cannot allow himself to act out, physically, in his waking life."

Lerner cites a 1955 study of schizophrenics by dream researcher William Dement, who found that the schizos tended to dream of "isolated nonhuman objects, stationary in space, rather than of self and others in action." She believes that schizophrenics have at least temporarily lost the capacity to "recharge the body image" in dreams as normal persons do, and must first regain this capacity before it will function in dreams.

H. ARTIFICIAL STIMULATION
OF DREAMS

Subconscious Stimulation
before the Dream

HOWARD SHEVRIN and LESTER LUBORSKY

IN A PIONEER LABORATORY investigation of dream imagery, Poetzl discovered that his subjects dreamt about the originally unreported parts of a previously exposed picture. He flashed colored slides of everyday scenes at 1/100″ and asked subjects to describe and draw what they saw. He then told them to record any dreams they had that night. When he asked his subjects on the following day to describe and draw their dreams, he observed that the dream imagery borrowed extensively from the unreported portions of the picture. Poetzl's subjects confirmed his observations by identifying elements of the picture of which they were previously unaware as parts of their dream imagery. . . .

Both Poetzl and Freud were aware of the parallel between Poetzl's findings and Freud's theory of dreams. The "indifferent" perceptions that Freud identified as day-residues present in the manifest content of dreams, Poetzl equated with the unreported parts of the picture which were later dreamed about. Poetzl further assumed that there was a functional equivalence between his concept of the "motoric barrier" and the concept of a repressed wish. He maintained that the dream lifted this "motoric barrier" and permitted the successive development of the parts of the picture originally unseen, much as the dream lifted the barrier of repression and permitted the symbolic and disguised expression of unacceptable wishes. The dream work undertook its own kind of "dark room" procedure, developing the exposed but heretofore undeveloped and unprinted "film" according to its own laws rather than the laws of the waking state. . . .

The Poetzl procedure has been repeated in several studies but thus far no measure of preconscious perception has been developed. Our primary aim in the present report is to construct a reliable measure of preconscious perception as elicited by the Poetzl technique and then to examine evidence bearing on its validity. . . .

The 27 Ss who took part in this study had participated in other experiments on perception at The Menninger Foundation. Our initial explanations of the nature of the experiment could be brief: "This is a study of perception, or how people see the world. It is similar to some of the studies you've taken part in before." The verbatim experimental instructions follow:

Part I (First Session)

1. On the count of three I'm going to flash a picture on the screen. It will appear just about where the x-mark is. [The experimenter also indicates the size of the area in which the picture will appear on the screen.] Ready: one, two, three. [The picture is flashed on the count of three.]
2. Now, describe what you saw as fully as you can. Make a drawing of what you remember seeing and continue to describe it while you draw it.
3. [The S is asked to describe and draw the picture again, as in #2 above. After completing the drawing and description, he is asked,] Is there anything else you remember?
4. Would you remember and write down upon awakening any dreams that you have tonight? Please bring them with you when you come tomorrow. [If the S asks, "What if I don't dream?" he is told, "If you keep a paper and pencil handy we've found that this helps a great deal." If he then asks, "But what if I don't dream at all?" the experimenter replies, "Even people who don't usually dream find that this helps."]

Part II (Second Session)

5. Tell me your dream (dreams). Draw and describe what was pictured in your dream, what you saw in your dream.
Alternate instructions for Ss who do not report dreams:
What were the last thoughts you had before falling asleep last night? [This is followed by instruction #6 below. The remainder of the instructions, from #7 on, apply to these images as if they were dreams.]
6. Close your eyes, let a picture come to mind, let me know when you have one. . . . Fine, tell me about the picture that came to mind. Now draw what you saw and describe it as you draw it. [Two pictures are elicited in this way.]
7. [Associations are obtained to the dreams and images by means of the usual questions, "What comes to mind about the dream?" or "What comes to mind?"—about any part of the dream which the experimenter has reason to think is likely to be important.]
8. Do you see any connection between your dream (image) and the picture you saw yesterday?

9. Now describe what you saw yesterday as fully as you can. Make a drawing of what you remember seeing and continue to describe it while you draw it.

10. I'm going to expose the picture again. [The experimenter exposes the picture on the screen and lets it stay there for the rest of the session.] What connections do you see between your recall of the picture and the picture on the screen? This time you may inspect it at your leisure.

11. What connections do you see between your dream (image) and the picture on the screen? [After this general inquiry, specific questions are asked about parts of the picture.]

12. Do you see any connections between the dream (image) and anything in the room or anything you might have seen on the way down here yesterday?

13. How does this dream compare with most other dreams you've had?

14. What do you think we have been trying to get at in this experiment? . . .

Basic to our understanding of the Poetzl phenomenon is the assumption that more of the stimulus registers than the S can report to us. We shall refer to those elements of the stimulus that register in the S's perceptual system and are not consciously recalled, but later appear in dreams and images, as preconscious. We say recall rather than perception because in its rigorous meaning perception refers to the experience of a stimulus present to the senses; the stimulus in our experiment is only perceptible for $\frac{1}{50}''$. It would be more accurate to refer to our Ss' reports as the recall of a quite brief perception—a recall in which memory and judgment have already played a role. The dreams and images could also be put in this same frame of reference as another mode of recall, much as we would find in experiments on the hypermnesic character of hypnotic states. The recall of the stimulus present in the dreams and images differs from the conscious recall of the stimulus in that the S does not have the conscious intent to recall parts of the stimulus and is usually not aware that he is recalling something already exposed to his view. We shall refer to recall present in dreams and images as *unintentional recall* in contrast to the *intentional recall* obtained immediately after the exposure of the stimulus and on the S's return the following day. (By referring to recall in dreams as "unintentional" we do not imply that there are no intentions other than the conscious intent induced by our instructions.)

The *unintentional recall* in dreams and images consists of at least two different types of elements: (*a*) Parts of the stimulus already reported in *intentional recall* of the stimulus. We shall refer to these as items *recalled again.* (*b*) Parts of the stimulus previously unreported in *intentional recall.* We shall refer to these items as instances of *preconscious recall.*

As a residual category, we should expect to find in the dreams and images items not present at all in the stimulus. We shall refer to these as *unrelated items.* . . .

One disadvantage of our measure of *preconscious recall* derives from the range of items that can be included in a conceptual category. How certain can we be that the wagons seen in the dream, for example, are not derived from a source other than the trucks in our picture? And when we note that most of the objects in our picture are commonplace, the strength of this criticism is increased. If we could, however, select from our pictures the items that occur rarely in everyday experience and demonstrate that these rare items are preconsciously recalled more frequently than would be expected by a standard of chance occurrence, we would have presumptive evidence that the source of *preconscious recall* was our picture and not an extraneous stimulus. Comparison data from the literature on extrasensory perception may help establish a standard by which to judge frequency of occurrence of percepts. Catalogues have been constructed to show how frequently an *S* will guess an unseen object, selected at random and without his knowledge. A catalogue has been made for British *S*s, and now an unpublished version for American *S*s by Taves (available by courtesy of Gardner Murphy) of 8,164 items produced by 272 *S*s. . . .

DISCUSSION

Our findings form a pattern consistent with the assumption that preconscious perception exists and can be elicited and measured. We have developed a measure, *preconscious recall* in dreams and images, which behaves in accordance with an understanding of preconscious perception. Our *S*s' dreams and images contain significantly more originally unreported items than do successive efforts at *intentional recall*, while retaining fewer of the originally seen parts of the stimulus. An estimate of unpleasant affect is associated with the new items appearing in the dreams and images. These two findings support Poetzl's "law of exclusion" and Freud's conception of preconscious perception as the raw material "preferred" by the dream. The finding concerning the *angularity* of the drawings indicates that the measure of *preconscious recall* can perhaps be extended to such formal properties of the stimulus as shape and position. A method was successfully applied for assessing the "chance" occurrence of picture items in dreams and images. The rare items in the picture appear significantly more frequently in dreams and images than a standard of expected chance occurrence (i.e., Taves catalogue). Taken together these four findings strengthen the conviction that Poetzl's technique for relating dreams to specific and identifiable daytime stimuli is an effective method for the experimental study of dreams.

Much more remains to be understood about the phenomenon. For example, why are the *unrelated items* unassociated with unpleasant affect? Many of these unrelated items could be day residues stemming from nonpicture sources, and as such should have unpleasant affects associated with them.

It would be desirable if a method could be devised for identifying at what point in the cognitive process the percept acquires anxiety arousing connotations and becomes available as a day residue. Customarily, it has been assumed that anxiety arousing connotations are present at the moment of perception and indeed produce the perceptual omissions or distortions. The process may be the reverse—an initial ambiguity or vagueness in the percept may make it possible for anxiety arousing meaning to adhere to it at some later point.

Lastly, the focus of our measure, preconscious perception, is upon items omitted from conscious report. But many items that were reported as seen appeared again in the dreams and images. Do items that are reported as seen appear in the dream via a different process from omitted items? A thorough study of the S's initial reports may reveal many different types of items which are as likely to appear in dreams and images as initially omitted items. We have preliminary evidence that doubt surrounding items is one of the most significant indications that they will appear in dreams and images.

Among other factors to be taken into account in future experimentation, it would be naive to neglect the fact that what is reproduced in *preconscious recall* is stimulated by much more than the experimenter's picture. Frequently the contents of the experimental room and the building become part of the "experimental stimulation." There was a least one striking example of this. The masonry which was occasionally correctly located in the wall below the building in the picture could as easily refer to the walls of the office in which the experiment took place, which were of unplastered concrete blocks.

It could be argued that the *amount* of *preconscious recall* is a function of the number of items the person reports in his dreams and images. If the S talks long enough he may mention many of the common items included in our picture. The simplest way to test for this is to count the number of items unrelated to the picture appearing in the dreams and images and to correlate this sum with the sum for *preconscious recall*. The correlation for the entire group was not significant (.29).

Several methods will be profitable for future studies. (*a*) *Prediction study:* By predicting from the *intentional recall* of the picture what items will appear in a dream (or image), we have another way of exploring the phenomenon. By obtaining more than one complete description and drawing of the picture in quick succession, predictions are facilitated. We observed that changes from the first to second set of drawings and descriptions were often predictive of what would appear in the dreams and images. Predictions have been tried on an unsystematic basis with encouraging success. (*b*) *"Own Control" method:* Images can be elicited both before and after a stimulus picture is exposed. A comparison of the images produced before seeing the picture with those produced afterward can point to the influence of the picture as compared with the readiness for imagining nonpicture items. This procedure has also been tried unsystematically (6). (c) *Experimental pictures containing unusual objects:* As the Taves frequencies indicated, most of the objects in our picture are common. It is important to use a picture in which many or all of the objects are rare. The frequency with which the objects are commonly associated with each other should also be controlled. Instances of *preconscious recall* might really be commonplace associations—car and street, shrubbery and house, building and windows, etc. The new items in the dreams and images could be *associations* to the originally seen items, dream continuations of thoughts begun in a conscious state. (d) *Intraindividual consistency in response to a number of pictures:* By using a number of different pictures for the same person we can separate effects due to individual differences from the effects produced by picture content. The other three methods can be employed with a number of pictures as easily as with one.

SUMMARY

In a pioneer investigation, Poetzl discovered that Ss dreamed about the originally unreported parts of a picture exposed tachistoscopically. If this discovery can be confirmed and a measure developed of preconscious perceptions as they appear in dreams, a new approach becomes available for the experimental study of unconscious phenomena.

A kodachrome slide was exposed at $1/50''$ to 27 Ss. They were asked to describe and draw the picture three times and then to record any dreams they had that night. From Ss who did not report dreams an "image" was obtained by asking them to close their eyes and describe and draw the first picture that came to mind.

High interjudge reliability (.84) was achieved for a measure of preconscious perception (*preconscious recall*) based on the number of new picture items appearing in the dreams and images. The meaning of the measure was explored by testing two hypotheses:

1. Poetzl's law of exclusion: Dream imagery "excludes" conscious perception in favor of preconscious perception.

2. Freud's hypothesis about "indifferent" perceptions: Freud asserted that the neutral or "indifferent" character of preconscious perception permitted it to serve as a "cover" for unconscious ideas which would not otherwise escape dream censorship. If preconscious perceptions were the ones that most often linked up with derivatives of threatening ideas, unpleasant affect would more likely be associated with the recall of preconscious perceptions than with other aspects of the dream.

Our data very significantly supported the Poetzl hypothesis for picture content and also for a formal attribute of the picture, its angularity. Consistent with our inference from Freud's hypothesis, we found a significant correlation of .57 between *preconscious recall* and *peak unpleasantness.*

These findings provide evidence for the Poetzl phenomenon consistent with the assumption that preconscious perception can be elicited and measured both in images and in dreams.

Subliminal and Supraliminal Stimulation before the Dream

CHARLES FISHER, Ph. D., M. D.

This paper will report an attempt to investigate the role of several types of incidental or indifferent perceptual stimuli in the formation of dreams and to elucidate some of the cognitive processes involved in the incorporation of such stimuli into the dreams. The recent work on subliminal registration, or more especially the replications and confirmations of the classical Poetzl experiment . . . has shown that subliminal stimuli are utilized in the formation of the manifest content of dreams. This work indicates that there are aspects of perception that are related to the drives, unconscious wishes and primary thought processes, and contrary to psychoanalytic and other theories, perception as an ego function is not exclusively concerned with adaptation and reality testing.

There is one important place in Freud's theoretical structure where he came close to dealing with perception in these latter terms and that is in his formulation of the nature and function of day residues. Although he did not discuss day residues in relation to perception, he did stress the significance of *transient, unnoticed* or vaguely attended to impressions of the day in the construction of dreams. He came to the conclusion that dreams have a preference for taking up *unimportant details* of waking life. The wider implications of Freud's astute observation have recently begun to be recognized and are leading to the investigation of the influence of indifferent impressions, not only on the thought processes of altered states of consciousness, such as the dream or hallucination, but also on thought in the waking state.

When speaking of day residues, Freud freely intermingled the terms, trains of thought, impression, experience, idea, memory, *etc.* He did not distinguish between these various mental processes and the external perceptual events that accompany them. It has been proposed that the concept of the day residue needs to be expanded to include not only preconscious trains of thought, ideas, memories, *etc.*, but also the *sensory* events that surround these psychic events and, for purposes of dream formation, especially the subliminal stimuli that are registered while they are going on. It is the sensory material, both preconscious and conscious, that is registered as memory trace, that appears to become the raw material for the dream and is utilized in the process of translation of the dream thoughts into plastic visual or other sensory images. . . .

The following is a tentative classification of incidental registrations. First, there is the totally subliminal, incapable of entering consciousness by virtue of weak stimulus conditions. With this type there is no question of attention being involved because no amount of attention will bring about awareness; nevertheless, registration and formation of a preconscious memory trace are assumed to take place. Second, there are percepts which are capable of entering consciousness but do not do so because attention is not paid to them. Third, there are incidental impressions that reach consciousness fleetingly, that are weakly cathected with attention or from which cathexis is quickly withdrawn. Fourth, there are supraliminal, focal, fully cathected perceptions which fall within the central focus of attention. Such supraliminal, focal percepts may or may not be indifferent, depending upon their meaning, intensity of affective charge and other conditions.

The completely subliminal stimulus may be considered an extreme example of what Freud called "an indifferent impression." Although the completely subliminal stimulus has been extensively investigated, the role of the supraliminal, focal stimulus in dream formation has not.

As I have stated, the present pilot investigation represents an attempt to study several of the types of visual registrations and percepts associated with day residues and to differentiate their respective roles in the formation of dreams. Specifically, the attempt was made to study the effect of the simultaneous presentation of a subliminal stimulus and a supraliminal, focal stimulus on subsequent dreams.

METHOD

Two visual stimuli (Figure 1) were exposed simultaneously through a tachistoscope. For 7 subjects, the stimulus picture shown on the right was made totally subliminal by drawing it in very light pencil lines while the stimulus picture on the left was made supraliminal by drawing it in very heavy inked lines. For 4 subjects, the reverse procedure was carried out; that is, the vase and swastika were made subliminal and the snake was made supraliminal. When either version of this slide is tachistoscopically

Figure 1.

exposed at 1/100 second, the subliminal stimulus cannot be discriminated, the recognition threshold for it being about ½ second. The supraliminal stimulus, however, is normally discriminated after one or two ex-
posures at 1/100 second. It was assumed that the 2 stimuli become part
of the sensory events incorporated into and forming a part of the complex
experience we call a day residue.

The essential method used was the combined dream-imagery technique
previously described. Briefly, the stimulus picture was exposed for 1/100
second at successive intervals until the vase, and particularly the swastika
upon it, was successfully discriminated. After each exposure, the subject
was required to draw what he had seen and to describe it verbally. The
subject was then requested to bring in any dreams that he had during the
night. The next day he reported his dream, made drawings of its significant pictorial elements, and then associated to the dream as freely as he
was able. Following this, the stimulus picture was exposed for 1/100 second again and a series of 5 or more free images elicited. The subjects
verbally described and made drawings of them. The stimulus was then
re-exposed at successive intervals starting at 1/100 second, gradually increasing the time of exposure until the threshold of discrimination for the
snake was determined. Finally, the subject re-examined his drawings for
similarities to and correspondences with the stimulus picture.

It will be noted that both of these stimuli carry a highly affective charge
and that they are sexual symbols in the psychoanalytic sense. The swastika on the vase could be thought of as an American Indian decoration
but I was aware of the possibility that it remains for most people a highly
charged configuration.

Of the 11 subjects used, 8, all male, were residents or other physicians
of the experimenter's acquaintance; 2 were female patients on the Psychiatry Ward of Mount Sinai Hospital, and one was a paid subject, by
profession an actor.

RESULTS

I shall first present 2 dreams which occurred following the tachisto-scopic exposure of the slide in which the vase was supraliminal and the snake subliminal.

Subject A had the following dream:

I was in a totalitarian prison camp in a room which they were trying to wire so they could listen in. There was a red-headed guy sitting in a chair. His name was Fisher. His arms were bare; they were shortish and bound down on the arms of the chair with Scotch tape. He did not seem too frightened. From his elbows to his hands, his arms were not as long as they should be. I said to him, "I'm resigning tomorrow from the concentration camp. Now I'm going to take my bullwhip," and I made a threatening gesture at him.

Associations: The Fisher in the dream was not you but an old friend of mine. I liked him because he was broad minded, and racially tolerant. Fisher's hands were not right. All that it took to hold his arms down was Scotch tape because they were so weak. I used to Scotch tape my own fingers together and then try to break loose in order to test my strength. The whole dream gives me a feeling of idiocy. I never in my life held a bullwhip. It was like acting in a play, as though Fisher knew that I was not threatening him; he did not appear frightened.

The subject made a drawing (Figure 2) depicting himself threatening Fisher with the bullwhip. His image of himself was one of power and strength, as indicated by the very large biceps on the arm holding the bullwhip. He remarked that "the bullwhip had some coils, was black and made of some kind of *living stuff* like catgut. I think it's *snake* or *snake hide*. I've seen rattlesnakes of that consistency."

His associations to the remark, "I am resigning tomorrow from the concentration camp," were as follows: The phrase, "concentration camp" was a play

Figure 2.

on words related to the idea that I forced him to *concentrate* on the screen, and on his dreams. The idea of resigning had to do with his resentment at being in the position of a subject and his irritation at being forced to dream. The bed that was wired for listening in was associated to his fear of being forced to reveal his thoughts, and made him think of Orwell's "1984" and Big Brother. He stated that the Fisher in the dream must represent me.

During the re-exposure period, the subject compared his dream drawings with the stimulus picture. The subject felt that the concentration camp setting of the dream had been evoked by the swastika. He was extremely impressed by the resemblance between the bullwhip and the snake and by the fact that he had described the whip as made out of snake hide.

Interpretation: The latent content of the dream centers around the subject's unconscious conflicts having to do with the idea that he is weak or in a weak position by virtue of his status as an experimental subject and that I am strong and will dominate over him, force him to concentrate, to dream and to reveal his secret thoughts.

The dream expresses his aggressive wishes to reverse roles, to be in the strong dominating position and to place me in a submissive, weak one. The swastika stimulated a train of preconscious dream thought having to do with a concentration camp, representing his unconscious picture of the laboratory and the hospital. The central part of the dream relates to the red-headed man named Fisher, an extremely thin disguise for me, whom the subject threatens with a bullwhip. The idea of resigning expresses the subject's wish to run away from his role as a subject. It seems obvious that the subliminal percept of the snake was transformed in the dream into the bullwhip made of snake hide. The idea of strength and weakness and domination and submission is depicted in the description of the arms of both parties to the conflict. Fisher's arms were weak and deformed, bound down with Scotch tape, while the image of the subject was that of a powerful figure with bulging biceps and the threatening bullwhip. Although the subject's aggression in the dream is quite apparent, it is disguised and toned down by his giving the dream scene a play quality, by making Fisher appear not to be frightened, by tying his arms down with Scotch tape that can easily be broken.

Following exposure of the same stimulus, Subject B had a dream in which the subliminal snake appeared to be transformed in the manifest content of the dream into the arm and hand of a man. The drawing of this image is shown in Figure 3. During the re-exposure period, the subject stated that the hand and arm on the right resembled the snake's head and proximal part of the body and he called attention especially to the correspondence between the thumb and the lower jaw of the snake. The analysis of the dream suggested that the arm and hand had symbolic phallic meaning and had assumed some of the pictorial characteristics of the snake. In the content of this dream, there were direct references to Jewishness and anti-Semitism.

It has been noted that Subject B gave evidence of symbolic phallic displace-

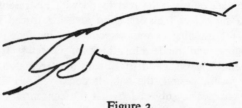

Figure 3.

ment to the arm and hand. This tendency to displace to the extremities was shown even more clearly in a free imagery experiment done subsequent to the dream experiment, utilizing the same stimulus at a time when the subject did not yet know the nature of the stimulus.

Figure 4 was the subject's first image, showing one of the 40 thieves of Ali Baba hiding in a jug. Later, during the re-exposure period, the subject felt that the coils of the turban were transformations of the coils of the snake.

The second image (Figure 5) was described as an amphora with smoke coming out. The smoke became transformed into a genie. Note the sinuous, snake-like structure of the smoke. The subject stated that this image reminded him of a mermaid which he used to draw a lot.

Figure 6 represents his image of the mermaid. He noted particularly the mermaid's scales, which made him think of a snake, and he made the drawing shown in Figure 7. He said that he used to make a lot of anti-Nazi drawings and this reminded him of a political cartoon. A snake is shown crawling through the vase, representing Europe, and bursting through its base. On the snake's head is a swastika. The cartoon illustrates the rape of Europe by the Nazis.

In this experiment, we see the gradual striking emergence of the percept of the snake, beginning with the coils of the turban in the first image,

Figure 4.

Figure 5.

Figure 6.

Figure 7.

the sinuous, snakelike formation of the smoke in the second, the mermaid's scaly tail in the third, and finally, the almost photographic emergence of the snake in the last image. Aside from the breakthrough of the percept in this final image, the snake never appeared as such in the images or the dream, but was displaced and distorted in disguised ways to either the arms or the legs.

The following generalizations can be made about these 2 experiments:

1. In both, the subliminal snake did not appear as such in the dreams but was transformed, in the first instance into the bullwhip made of snake hide and in the second into the arm and hand. In both instances, the transformed image took on formal, pictorial properties of the stimulus picture; for example, the shape and composition of the bullwhip, and the formation of the hand which resembled the snake's head. Finally, in both dreams, the subliminal snake appears to have become associated with the most significant, most deeply repressed drive, wish-fulfilling aspect of the latent content of the dream.

2. In contrast, part of the supraliminal stimulus, namely, the swastika, did not appear in the dreams in *image* form as did the subliminal snake, but in both instances activated preconscious trains of thought. In the first dream, these related to a concentration camp, to ideas of force, Big Brother, being spied upon, *etc.*; in the second dream, to trains of thought relating to Jews, such as a verbal comment about anti-Semitism.

3. Although the transference aspects of the dream stimulated by the experimental situation are important factors in explaining the sexual and domination-submission themes, it was entirely possible that such content was reinforced by the nature of the two stimuli, namely, their meanings as male and female symbols. That such was the case is suggested by the data of the imagery experiment reported. Here, the symbolic sexual meaning of the vase and the snake appear to have been unconsciously cognized, the final image becoming a metaphorical representation of, "the rape of Europe."

The following dream was elicited after the exposure of the *reversed* stimuli, *i.e.,* in this instance the snake was supraliminal and the vase and swastika were subliminal.

Subject C dreamed:

I was at a dance in a very large hall. I found an object on the floor. It was either a brooch or a small antique. Dr. A was with me. As I was looking at the brooch, little mites came out of it and embedded themselves in the skin of my fingers and I became quite frightened. Wherever I would touch my hand these mites would embed themselves in my skin.

Associations: The dream was concerned with a fantasy punishment for forbidden sexual activities. The brooch appeared to be a female symbol and the mites that came out of it were associated with ideas of phallic contamination or injury as punishment for his sexual activities, with displacement to the

Figure 8.

fingers. This displacement was activated by the fact that the subject had recently developed a severe contact dermatitis on his fingers.

Figure 8 shows on the left, the subject's drawing of the brooch. It appears to be a distorted, flattened out transformation of the vase. If the brooch were stretched out and down it would very closely approximate the outline of the vase which I have superimposed in dotted lines upon it.

The drawing on the right represents one of the mites. Although it does not bear too striking a resemblance to the swastika, it does contain some of its formal elements and may have been derived from it.

The subject made another drawing (Figure 9) showing his hand with markings indicating the embedding mites. The markings on the middle finger contain clear-cut elements of the subliminal swastika, supporting the contention that the fleas represent a transformation and distortion of the subliminal stimulus.

In this experiment, the subliminal vase and swastika seem to have appeared in the manifest content of the dream in image form and associated with the repressed, drive organized, wish-fulfilling aspect of the dream in the same manner as the subliminal snake did in the first 2 experiments described. However, the supraliminal snake did not appear to bring about the same effects as the vase and swastika in the first two experiments

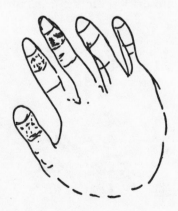

Figure 9.

when they were supraliminal. As a matter of fact, there was no indication of the presence of the snake either directly or in disguised or distorted form in the manifest content of the dream. It is possible, however, that it influenced the dream indirectly and by virtue of its symbolic meaning had something to do with the latent sexual content of the dream.

After the exposure of the supraliminal snake and the subliminal vase, Subject D had a dream which dealt with a Negro and involved anti-racial material. There is no evidence in the dream of the appearance of the swastika in image form. Instead, it seems to have activated preconscious trains of thought relating to racial matters in much the same way as it did when the stimulus was made supraliminal.

A somewhat different utilization of the subliminal swastika was shown in the results of 2 other subjects who were exposed to the reversed slide.

Subject E dreamed:

I was on the 40th floor of some building and was very scared of being up there. It did not seem as safe as the ordinary 40th floor of a building.

After reporting the dream, the subject wrote the words, "fourtieth flour" as shown in Figure 10. It will be noted that both the words "fourtieth" and "flour" were misspelled. By this misspelling, both the words were made to contain the word, "four." During the re-exposure period, the subject himself spontaneously pointed out that the swastika is made up of 4's as indicated in the figure.

Part of a second dream went as follows: "Several of us were going to a legitimate theatre. I had Seat 44." Again, during the re-exposure, the subject felt that the 44 was derived from the swastika.

Subject F also transformed the subliminal swastika into "fours" in 2 dreams. One was about a shabby clock with "a 4 o'clock look." In these instances, the 4's represented transformations of the swastika.

As I have noted, in the dreams so far reported, when the snake was made *supraliminal*, there was no evidence of its emergence in either primary or secondary process form in the manifest content of the dream.

Figure 10.

However, in 2 of the dreams of Subject E, indirect evidence of the influence of the supraliminal stimulus could be detected. The subject had the following dream:

"There was a group of people standing around a guy who was going to open a *wall* safe and when he opened it *secrets* would come out. Everything that had been built up would be destroyed like the scandal in Connecticut where 6 men raped a teen-age girl and the mayor of the town committed suicide. They were all around for the opening. Then I was running out of the building, making a mad dash." The rest of the dream had to do with the subject's breaking into an old New England house, being pursued by and hiding from some man who was after him.

Associations: The old New England house made the subject think of his grandparents' farm house where he used to spend his summers when he was a small child. One summer when he was about 5, his uncles were cleaning out a well and killing snakes that were in it. One of them picked up a snake and threw it at him. He screamed and ran into the house. Ever since this traumatic experience, the subject has had an intense fear of snakes.

Interpretation: The evidence suggested that the group of people standing around waiting to open the wall safe and let the secrets come out was an indirect representation of the memory of his uncle removing snakes from the well and throwing one at him. The running away in a mad dash in the dream related to his running to the house in terror when his uncle threw the snake at him. It is of interest also that the "secrets" that were to come out of the well were associated with the scandal in Connecticut where 6 men committed rape on a teen-age girl. The subject's memory of his uncle and the snake was a perfectly conscious one, but was, in psychoanalytic terminology, a screen memory, that is, it screened a repressed group of fantasies that connected with his homosexual fears and wishes relating to the uncle. It may be noted that this subject had overt homosexual tendencies.

DISCUSSION

The results of the experiments reported confirm and extend Freud's formulations about the nature and function of indifferent impressions in dream formation. They can best be understood in terms of certain psychoanalytic propositions about the structure of memory organization. Rapaport has suggested that memory schema are organized into constellations layered in depth. The deepest level of repressed memories are organized around drives and have the quality of unconsciousness. This drive organization of memories is distinguished from a more superficial constellation, in terms of depth, which can be called the "conceptual organization of memories." This latter organization carries the quality of preconsciousness and is readily capable of becoming conscious. The drive organization of memories functions with mobile cathexes and primary process thought mechanisms, whereas the conceptual organization utilizes neutralized energy and functions according to the secondary process. Between the drive and conceptual organizations of memory it is assumed that there are transitional constellations which partake of the properties of both organizations.

Sensory Stimulation during the Dream

WILLIAM DEMENT and EDWARD A. WOLPERT

EFFECT OF STIMULI ON DREAMS

Since it is now possible to determine when S is dreaming by objective criteria, the effect of external stimuli can be more accurately assessed. In this study, three external stimuli were used: the sounding of a tone, flashing of a light, and a spray of cold water. These stimuli represented different modalities as well as different degrees of what might be called noxiousness, cold water being the most noxious of the three, and the pure tone the least.

The tone stimulus was a 1000-cycle pure tone sounded for 5 sec. The awakening threshold during eye-movement periods was previously determined and an intensity slightly below this threshold was used. In spite of this, the tone occasionally awakened the sleeper. The flashing of a 100-w. lamp placed where it would shine directly on the sleeper was the light stimulus. In these tests, it was necessary to enter the sleeping room to be certain that S was lying with his face exposed to the light. The light flashes never awakened S. The third stimulus was a fine spray of cold water ejected from a hypodermic syringe. In several instances, E moved close to the S and allowed several large drops of water to fall on an exposed part. This stimulus most frequently awakened Ss. In general the stimuli were given after eye movements and the characteristic EEG had appeared, and then Ss were awakened by the doorbell a few minutes later.

It was not always easy to decide whether or not a stimulus had modified the dream. If a light had been flashed in S's eyes, one might get a subsequent dream containing light simply because it was daytime. Consequently, one could feel certain that the stimulus had been incorporated into the dream only if there was an obvious modification at the appropriate time. If the eye movements had been present for, say, 10 min., the stimulus then applied, and the sleep allowed to continue for another minute, one would expect the modification to occur toward the end of the complete dream sequence. . . .

In addition to the above described stimuli, the available dream transcripts were analyzed to see how often the awakening doorbell had been incorporated. Examples of the types of modification seen were as follows:

A. *Tone.* The sudden intrusion of a brief, roaring sound into the dream. The dreamer was frightened and thought that there was either an earthquake or that a plane had crashed outside his house.

B. *Light.* The modifications included a sudden fire, a flash of lightning, seeing shooting stars, and a dream of *E* shining a flashlight into *S*'s eyes.

C. *Water spray.* Typical examples included sudden rainfalls, leaking roofs, and being squirted by someone.

D. *Awakening doorbell.* The most frequent incorporations were either the telephone or doorbell ringing just as *S* awoke.

None of the stimuli were markedly effective in modifying the dreams. The water spray was the most effective and the pure tone was the least, and it might be pointed out that the latter represented a relatively bland stimulus in contrast to the cold water.

The *S*s were also stimulated 15 times during the interspersed periods of ocular quiescence. The stimuli were divided equally among the three types. In no case was an eye-movement period initiated by an external stimulus and no dreams were recalled when *S*s were awakened shortly after the stimuli were given.

An attempt was made to test the effect of an internal stimulus. Three *S*s on five occasions completely restricted their intake of fluids for periods of 24 hr. or more before sleeping in the laboratory. On all occasions they reported that they were very thirsty when they went to bed, and twice their thirst had reached distressing proportions with dry lips, inability to salivate, etc. Fifteen narratives were elicited under these conditions. In no case did the dream content involve an awareness of thirst or descriptions of actually drinking something. Ten dreams seemed completely unrelated to this internal stimulus, and five contained elements that might have been related to thirst as follows:

A. "I was in bed and was being experimented on. I was supposed to have malabsorption syndrome."

B. "I started to heat a great big can of—a great big skillet of milk. I put almost a quart of milk in."

C. "Just as the bell went off, somebody raised a glass and said something about a toast. I don't think I had a glass."

D. "While watching TV I saw a commercial. Two kids were asked what they wanted to drink and one kid started yelling, 'Coca-Cola, orange, Pepsi,' and everything."

E. "I was watching a TV program, and there was a cartoon on with the animals that are like those in the Hamm's beer advertisement." . . .

An old theory of dream causation is that dreams are initiated by outside stimuli. This notion seems untenable in view of the fact that when stimuli were given when the eyes were quiescent, neither eye movements nor dream recall resulted. Also, eye-movement periods occur regularly in the absence of any deliberate stimulation and entirely independent of chance stimuli such as noises outside the building, doors closing, and so forth.

Even if external stimuli do not initiate dreaming, the question of their importance in modifying the dream content must still be considered. In 1893, Calkins reported a careful analysis of 375 dreams obtained by introspection from two Ss and found that only 33 contained elements that were traceable to actual physical sensations occurring during sleep. Weed and Hallam, repeating Calkins' study, found only 20 of 381 dreams to have been influenced by external stimuli. On the other hand, Cubberly, experimenting with constant tactile sensation applied by means of gummed paper to a restricted portion of the body during sleep, reported that in 95% of the dreams an effect could be seen either in the form of a general tenseness of the dreamer or as a tension of the particular part of the body on which the gummed paper had been placed. However, since Cubberly apparently was his own S, there is a strong likelihood that autosuggestion played a part in his results. The findings reported in the present study indicate that external stimuli are not markedly effective in modifying the dream content, but that some (cold water) are more effective than others (pure tone). Although external stimuli can at times interject a new element, the basis for the images and particular story of a dream must exist mainly within the dreamer.

The Effect of Drugs on Dreaming

HERBERT GREENHOUSE

Research into the effect of drugs on REMS or dreaming time suggests that the sleep and dreaming pattern is disturbed by most drugs. Tranquillizers such as chlorpromazine cut down dreaming time and often cause distortions in the content of the dreams. Imipramine, an antidepressant, not only reduces dreaming time, but seems to increase the element of hostility in dreams. Barbiturates tend to decrease dreaming time and alter the quality of dreams, making them more thoughtlike and less dreamlike. Barbiturates may also interfere with the integrative process in the brain. Drugs such as reserpine, which have a depressant effect, tend to increase dreaming time with small doses, but decrease it when larger doses are given.

In an experiment at Columbia University in 1964, researchers found that the hallucinogenic drug LSD-25 considerably increased dreaming time when administered in small doses just before sleep or an hour after sleep had begun. The length of the second period of dreaming sleep was increased from 30 to 400 per cent. (J. Muzio, H. Roffwarg, and R. Kaufman, "Alteration in the Young Adult Human Sleep EEG Configuration Resulting from d*LSD-25," Association for the Psychophysiological Study of Sleep, 1964, Palo Alto, California.)

Alcohol cuts down dreaming time, while caffeine in moderate amounts has no effect. When cigarette smokers temporarily abstain, their dreaming time increases along with the intensity of their dreams. Moderate levels of marijuana seem to have a sedative effect, but high levels interfere with sleep. Dreaming time remains the same for chronic smokers of marijuana. More laboratory testing of marijuana smokers is necessary, however, before a definitive pattern can be established.

The following table from *Dreams and Human Potential* (Stanley Krippner and William Hughes, Division of Parapsychology and Psychophysics, Maimonides Medical Center, Brooklyn, New York) lists the probable effect of drugs on REM sleep or dreaming time:

Effects of Selected Drugs on Rapid Eye Movement (REM) Sleep

Drug (Partial List)	Effect on REM Sleep
Alcohol	Decrease
Amphetamines	Decrease
Barbiturates	Decrease
Caffeine	None
Chloral hydrate	None
Chlorpromazine	Decrease with small doses; Increase with larger doses
LSD	Slight increase
Marijuana	Unknown
Reserpine	Increase with small doses; Decrease with larger doses
Typtophane	Increase

The Effect of Hypnosis on Night Dreams

JOHANN MARTIN STOYVA

The use of hypnosis to influence dream content was first investigated by Schrötter, who reported that subjects could be made to dream on the night following a hypnotic trance about topics suggested by the experimenter during the trance. Schrötter's main concern was to test Freud's theory of symbol formation, and he concluded that his subjects dreamed about various topics, primarily sexual ones, in the fashion that had been predicted from psychoanalytic theory: i.e. the symbols of sexual activity chosen were ones familiar in psychoanalysis. Schrötter's work was later confirmed by Roffenstein and Nachmansohn.

The initial purpose of the present inquiry was to investigate the effects of hypnosis on dreams using the newly developed techniques of dream study. It was hoped not only to replicate the earlier experiments but to extend them by answering such questions as: Does the subject dream about the suggested topic only in the first rapid eye movement (REM) period, or will he continue to do so in every REM period of the night? Does the suggested material form a separate scene, or is it contextually related to the remainder of the manifest dream content?

A further point of interest was related to current thinking about a "need-to-dream." Dement had systematically deprived subjects of their regular REM time over a series of nights by interrupting each REM period within a short time of its onset. On a subsequent recovery night, consisting of uninterrupted sleep, amount of REM time was significantly increased over what it had been on baseline nights. This evidence gave rise to the idea that there is, perhaps, a "need-to-dream"; i.e., a need for the sort of fantasy activity that occurs during REM periods. It was then reasoned by the present investigator that if there is a need for this type of fantasy activity, possibly the dream-like hallucinations that can be made to occur during the deep trance state could, under certain conditions, serve as a substitute for the REM type of dream.

In the process of exploring the hypothesis that trance "dreams" might substitute for rapid eye movement type dreams, it was noticed that there was a sharp reduction in time spent in REM periods on those nights when the subject had been given a posthypnotic dream suggestion. In the instance of the first subject in whom this phenomenon was observed, it was noticed upon inspecting the 16 nights for which this subject had already been run that there was a decided difference in the length of the first

REM period depending upon whether or not the subject had been given a posthypnotic dream suggestion. . . .

During the trance, dream instructions were given as follows: "Now I want you to listen carefully to what I say. You will dream in every dream tonight that you are 'climbing a tree.' You will dream of this in every dream tonight. You will dream only of this—that you are 'climbing a tree.' And you will dream of this *only* for tonight." This last instruction was adopted after some subjects reported dreaming about the suggested topic even on some nights subsequent to serving in the laboratory.

After amnesia for the entire trance period had been suggested, the subject was taken out of the trance and then allowed to lapse into a natural sleep. Length of trance—including the induction phase—was typically some 24 minutes. On their laboratory nights, subjects slept between six and seven hours. . . .

[The 16 subjects fell into three groups, with those in group 1 dreaming the most about the suggested topic and those in group 3 the least.]

Dreams were scored as being in accordance with the suggested topic if the reported content showed a clear connection with the suggestion: i.e. there were identical or very similar images present. While most of the reports were easy to rate as being in accordance with the suggestion or not, there were a number of doubtful cases where the similarity between the suggestion and the dream report lay only in a minor detail—for example, "I dreamed that I threw a pebble into a *pool of water*," in response to the suggestion, "You will dream in every dream tonight of rowing a boat." For the purpose of determining the percentage of dreams in accordance with the suggestion, such doubtful reports were scored as half a point rather than a full point since this similarity, i.e. the reference to *water*, may have been only a chance correspondence. These doubtful reports, which came mainly from the Ss in group 2, made up less than 10% of the total.

The seven subjects in group 1 usually reported dreaming about the same general topic throughout the night. Although there were variations on the basic theme, the original suggestion was still clearly recognizable in most of the successive reports from the same night (see example 3 below).

Below are some typical examples of the dream reports obtained and the manner in which they were classified:

Example 1: Dream report scored as being in accordance with suggestion. Dream suggestion: "You will dream in every dream tonight of climbing a tree."
Subject 2, awakened after 16.0 minutes in REM period 2.
"There's this old *maple* in front of our house in Philadelphia. It used to scratch against the window and, ahhh, sometimes we had to cut off the *branches*. So, I don't know, usually we just go out on the roof, but we were all *going up the tree* by the base to do it. All of us. The whole family and my

grandmother—and she's been dead for about five years now. We couldn't get up to it and just scratching (sic) against the windows and making scraping noises."

Example 2: Dream report scored as being in accordance with suggestion.

Dream Suggestion: "You will dream in every dream tonight that you fall from a horse."

Subject 3; awakened after 9.0 minutes in REM period 2.

"I was, it was in this field in the dark; it was at night. There was this horse, and I had a huge knife and I was chopping at it, and I was chopping at it, and I was chopping at it, attacking me (sic) and it wouldn't go away; cut it and chop at it, it's sumpin' awful! It wouldn't fall off, and a, a, attacked the horse and it wouldn't go, just wouldn't go! I hated it! I don't know why, why I dream about horses, anyway. I hate horses! I don't dare get near a horse!"

Example 3: Series of dream reports from one night. Scored as being in accordance with suggestion.

Dream Suggestion. "You will dream in every dream tonight of climbing a tree."

A.˙ Subject 1; first awakening, after 2.5 minutes in REM period 2.

"We made a, an outing trip, and, I don't know where we went; we went through the *woods*. We marched and marched and marched. Oh, it was very colorful, very much so. That's all I know. I think the dream isn't finished."

B. Subject 1; same night, second awakening, after 11.0 minutes in REM period 3.

"Mmmmmhhh, I'm walking, I don't know, with people. I'm going places in *woods* and then we climbed on an apple tree to pick some ripe beautiful apples.

Examiner: "Did this remind you of any place you'd ever been?"

S: "Yes, at home, you know, the apple orchards we have and the meadows where the cows are. Very picturesque." . . .

1. *Alteration in REM Time.*—The current study confirmed the earlier findings of Schrötter, Roffenstein, and Nachmansohn, that subjects could be made to dream on the night following a hypnotic trance about topics suggested by the experimenter during the trance. Moreover, through the use of the REM-EEG approach to the study of dreaming as first described by Aserinsky and Kleitman, it was established that, when instructed to do so, certain subjects will dream about the suggested topic in every REM period of the night. As indicated in the examples given in the results section, the successive reports from the same night were like variations on the basic theme provided by the suggestion. In each dream the influence of the suggestion was clearly visible; yet in each report, the material was embedded in a different context. In other words, the suggestions were incorporated into the dream's structure; i.e., the manifest content. The suggestion did not enter the dream as a separate entity but was contextually related to the nonsuggested dream content. . . .

In the group of seven subjects who dreamed regularly (71% to 100% of the time) in accordance with the suggested topic, it was observed that there was a reduction in the amount of REM time on experimental nights as compared with REM time on control nights when no posthypnotic suggestion had been operating ($P=0.05$). This reduction in REM time was of interest in that it established that a psychological variable could be used to alter REM duration. In other words, presleep verbal stimulation—in the form of posthypnotic suggestion—influenced not only the content of dreams, but altered the lengths of REM periods as well. . . .

The present study indicated that hypnosis may also be useful when it is desirable to have the subject dream about specific topics. While no analysis of content was carried out in this investigation, the fact that certain subjects would dream about the suggested topic in nearly every REM period of the night indicated the present technique may be useful in exploring questions about dream formation. For example, at what point in the sleep cycle does the subject begin to dream or think about the suggested topic? How is the topic elaborated? Are there any characteristic distortions which take place? Is there greater distortion at the end of a REM period than at the beginning of it? Questions such as these would seem amenable to investigation through the use of suggestion techniques employed in combination with the EEG monitoring of sleep and rapid eye movements.

Dream Therapy through Hypnodrama

ROLF KROJANKER, M.D.

J. L. Moreno has repeatedly stated his conviction that the unconscious can be trained to overcome emotional trauma and hidden conflicts. Desoille and Bjerre have used "directed dreams" to resolve conflicts. In these techniques, Desoille leads the patient into the visualization of situations full of Jungian symbols, carrying with them the portent of resolution of conflicts. These techniques are based on Freud's findings, that dreamers use symbols to highlight, condense and generally report conflicts they are dealing with in their minds at the time of the dream. The meaning of such symbols is much clearer to the dreamer in the sleeping or dreaming state, that is, at a time when unconscious processes are only inadequately checked by the conscious, the "censor." Desoille and others then argued that therapists could address their interventions to the unconscious by using symbols germane to unconscious understanding as equivalent for the resolution of a patient's conflicts and suggesting such symbolic situations while the dreamer reclined on the couch with his eyes closed and his conscious effort reduced to listening to the therapists' "directed dream." Desoille and Brachfeld reported decrease in anxiety sometimes after just one such session.

The value of symbolic gratifications has been known to other workers in Psychiatry, for instance Mme. M. Sechehaye has used "symbolic realization" successfully with schizophrenic patients in the waking state.

However, Moreno has initiated the use of action techniques, such as hypnodrama and dream enactments, to demonstrate that the understanding and correction of one or more dreams of a single night is a good therapeutic maneuver. Much like conscious attitudes can improve by role training, it is possible to modify unconscious expectations and behavior through training, e.g., let a dream conclude with a "happy end" instead of a catastrophe, learn to experience pleasant feelings when looking down from high buildings, gazing at one's step-mother, facing one's boss, etc.

The present report will deal with a series of connected dreams of "Norma," as well as their re-enactment and correction in situ. The dreams were experienced during a three week workshop in 1961 at Beacon and were dealt with in the presence of all its participants.

NECESSARY INFORMATION

Norma is pregnant for the second time, and in the third month of pregnancy. She has a three-year-old boy. In the first pregnancy, Norma was ambivalent about having the child while she was pregnant, but changed her attitude to one of frank love of the child at its birth. In her current pregnancy, her ambivalence is again manifest.

Norma is otherwise a quiet happy housewife. Her ambivalence with regard to assuming the added responsibilities of a mother in the future, changing to self-confident love upon finding herself adequate to handle the new job, can often be observed in modern mothers.

In other words, we are dealing with a fairly common attitude regarding pregnancy. Prior to this first dream, Norma had suffered two or three minor falls during social activities at Beacon, which were of no consequence; that is, she never really hurt herself when falling. She seemed just to glide down and sit comfortably on the floor, yet a fleeting air of fear and anxiety would appear on her face whenever she lost her balance this way. Usually this happened in front of bystanders who would be quite solicitous in helping her up again.

FIRST DREAM

In the second week of the seminar, Norma offers a recurrent dream to Dr. Moreno, who directs this session. Dr. Moreno suggests that Norma go to sleep on her bed (mattress) on stage. Norma stretches out on the mattress, closes her eyes and tries to warm up to sleep. Moreno then continues:

"Now you are back at the house, asleep." (Bends over her, softly strokes her hair, soothingly, while talking suggestively to Norma.) "Breathe deeply, deeper, deeper, that's right. And now, you are starting to dream. Don't tell me the dream. I want you to reenact it, after you have first visualized it in your mind. While you are there, sleeping, you have that same dream all over again. Do you see the dream? Can you visualize the first part, then the middle, and then the end?"

NORMA: (keeps eyes closed, is relaxed, nods her head affirmatively).

MORENO: "And now, as you see the first part, what do you see first in the dream?"

NORMA: "I am on the stairs of the house."

MORENO: "Then get up. Are you with someone?"

NORMA: (Stands up) "No, I am alone. I am paralyzed and cannot walk down the stairs because I am going to fall down and lose the baby."

Dr. Moreno then insinuates, "You say you are paralyzed; is that true? Try to walk."

"I can't." (She stands as if frozen, on one spot).

"Try!"

"I just can't," says Norma; "I'm afraid to fall and lose the baby!" and begins to cry.

"I'll help you," says the therapist, and does so.

Norma can now walk a few steps but stops when reaching the three stairs of the stage. No amount of persuasion convinces the panicky Norma to negotiate the three stairs. Dr. Moreno then commands Norma's double:

"Go—you walk the stairs down with her!" Even that does not seem to be enough protection.

Dr. Moreno then exclaims, "I will help you too, let us go!"

Hesitantly, Norma follows the two auxiliary-egos, and to her surprise, she succeeds without falling. Her panic eases, but Dr. Moreno gives her no rest; she has to walk those stairs down again and again, first with the double, and then alone. Norma is then urged by Moreno to not fear such a dream again, even to expect to dream that she is negotiating the stairs successfully, helped by Dr. Moreno or the auxiliary ego. She is ordered to sleep again on stage, and is then re-awakened.

In the following general discussion, Dr. Moreno explained his interventions in modifying the actual dream on stage as "*Dream Correctives*," in which Norma was helped to overcome her paralyzing fears of falling; it was important to overcome these, not only once on stage, but to go through these motions repeatedly, so that the acts started to carry with them a positive conviction of success; a positive conviction of NOT falling in the future. In this way, during the hypnodramatic trance, her unconscious attitudes toward falling, as well as the motions necessary in order not to fall, had been trained with her.

Note

As we shall see soon, unconsciously Norma was not sure whether she wanted that baby really and whether she was able to take care of a helpless infant around the clock, waiting patiently for months and years for it to grow up and become self-sufficient. A fall, followed by an abortion, might indeed have provided a natural remedy for this predicament.

Another possible meaning of walking safely downward with a pregnancy suggests itself, namely, the symbolism of giving birth to a baby between one's legs. So Dr. Moreno helped Norma *and her child* down safely and alive; he rehearsed with her symbolically not only not to fall, but also to give birth to the baby aided by another doctor in the future.

Norma does not report any recurrences of this dream in the succeeding days. Dr. Moreno has departed for an international convention. Toward the end of the Workshop, a second opportunity to be a protagonist is offered to Norma who has had three other dreams. She is put into a trance by me on stage, and re-enacts the following brief dream:

"Dr. Moreno has died." (Weeps.) "I cannot look at him; it is so terrible."

"Go and look at him; there he is lying in the casket."

"I can't."

"It is all right; and you can." She finally looks at the auxiliary ego embodying Dr. Moreno.

THERAPIST: "You see, you can look at him. Do you want to talk to him?"

"Yes."

"You can talk to him; he will be able to hear you."

She finally does so and is urged to talk to him as a first corrective.

"Dr. Moreno, I hardly can believe it; it is so terrible; we miss you so much." THERAPIST: "You see, you can talk to him. Now if you want to bring him back, you can! Go ahead and pull him up—go ahead!" She does so and sighs with relief from an anxiety state, bordering again on panic in its intensity.

"Dream Corrections"

This dream was corrected in two phases. The dreamer at first accepted without hesitation that she could "talk to Dr. Moreno" and expressed very positive affect toward him. In this fashion, she had already tacitly accepted that "Dr. Moreno" was not really dead, only absent or paralyzed, as it were.

In the second phase of dream correction and training, she not only talked to him, but with physical effort, lifted him up, saved him from death or paralysis. What a "reversal of roles" from the session with Dr. Moreno! As a result of "dream training" she now saves Moreno from death as she saved herself from falling.

With regard to the death, I felt that this was a symbolic dream picture to explain the master's absence from the Workshop, and many participants of the Workshop were indeed missing him. Since, however, there are often ambivalent feelings toward father figures in general and toward the father in Norma's pregnancy in particular, Norma was allowed to resuscitate the dead to rid her also of any guilt feelings.

Yet Norma had in this dream willed Dr. Moreno a combination of husband, father, doctor and teacher, also dead. Her crying gave evidence of positive feelings toward him as well as of anguish and guilt concerning her death wish. What the therapist allowed here was to undo that murder. Undoing is one of the frequent mechanisms of defense. He then allowed her to change from a murderer into a saviour, thus to overcompensate for her death wish. Since all this was done in a trance state, these corrections were not addressed to the consciously functioning Norma, but to her subconscious, as it were. One might ask here: When is a corrective used in hypnodrama and in psychodramatic interpretation of dreams? Even though that cannot be answered categorically, manifest anxiety of the dreamer on stage often calls for a corrective, since it is indicative of a conflict. Oftentimes the associations of the dreamer with regard to the dream will give a clue for the need for a corrective.

Another question is more difficult to answer: Is this repressive therapy? Yet it seems evident, that no emotional conflict with a basis in reality was repressed here. Instead more acceptable solutions to the issues weighing on the dreamer's mind were suggested and rehearsed, but only *after* the dreamer had had a chance to first give her version of her solution and had obtained the understanding without criticism of her therapist.

She next reports the second brief dream of the night, dreamt after she awoke to overcome Dr. Moreno's death-dream. Again she re-enacts it as follows:

"Isn't it dreadful, Manuel, the head of our Half-Way House has become sick, crazy. They put him into a straight-jacket, because he acts so wild."

No further associations can be elicited from Norma.

Correctives

Norma is urged to change Manuel's fate by her intervention. She goes to the auxiliary ego enacting Manuel, gets him out of the straight-jacket, berating the attendant on stage, talks soothingly to Manuel, whom she believes to have become sick from over-work. She then reports the straight-jacket incident to another doctor, rejecting me as having "nothing to do" with the straight-jacket. The "doctor" warns the "attendant" on stage to destroy all straight-jackets, or else to suffer consequences.

Norma is visibly relieved by this outcome.

Note

We observe here that the second dream of that night carried with it evidence of some "dream work," since the hero of the dream was not any-more "dead," only "mad." In correcting this dream on stage, the dreamer had a chance to save the hero from the sickness she had dreamed up for him, and as a result of which she felt quite distressed. She also had an opportunity to express her concern about her husband's overwork. Finally, she could enlist the help of another father figure, the "doctor," to help her patient.

Norma is put to sleep again, and then re-enacts the following, third dream which she experienced actually three days after the above reported ones.

"My second child is born. I give birth to a beautiful son, much like my first son. His name is Craig. The delivery was quite different because I get up from the table right away, 'take the child away to my mother', and, we both *walk* to her home. Craig is very mature, walks and talks like my first one, but it not toilet-trained. We have a wonderful relationship." Norma has actually written down this dream in order not to forget it. She seems depressed now.

Re-Enactment with correctives

Norma is asked to go into any detail of the dream as she re-enacts it on stage. She may tell anything she would wish to change in the dream and we will try to modify the dream accordingly on stage. She now talks to Craig after the delivery about how much she loves him. Then she cries about her own impatience in wanting to see him grown up; she accepts him anyway, but, much rather, would like to see him unable to walk and talk, just a normal new-born baby. She can wait for it, and as to toilet training, she does not mind at all. This is re-enacted on stage, and Norma's love for her child moves the audience and she feels pleased with herself. Norma holds her baby's face and cuddles it in her arms while the baby acts helpless, immature, yet ready to be loved. Baby does not talk or even sit yet. Norma feels visibly happy and relaxed. She is then put to sleep again and finally taken out of trance altogether.

To close this hypnodramatic experience, Norma declares that she now feels she is emotionally ready to bear a child and not make excessive demands upon his capacities:

"He does not have to walk and talk yet from the start; I can wait."

Note

Since both the dream and the notes taken of it seemed to end on an expression of denial of a conflict, namely, a "wonderful relationship," some preliminary explanation was needed to recognize the need for a corrective. True, this dream showed the fulfillment of a wish; namely, to give birth to an exceptional son, yet the happy end of this dream did not seem to correlate with Norma's affect in the previous dreams. So Norma was given a free hand in this correction; one might say, she was asked to freely associate to it. Indeed, she soon showed the underlying conflict and frustration and broke out in tears. Now, the corrective was applied and she was allowed to have a child that acts like a normal baby, cannot talk, or walk, etc.

FINAL DISCUSSION PERIOD

I then asked for a discussion on the following thoughts about change of emotional attitudes toward the coming child as evidenced by the dream sequence itself, and the correctives designed to train unconscious attitudes.

In the dream of the first session, a clear fear of losing (accidentally killing) the child through a fall was expressed, and the phobia was corrected in situ by descending steps successfully, with disappearance of a panic state while in trance. In the highly charged atmosphere of the Workshop, her following dreams gave evidence of training and dreamwork.

The next dream showed Dr. Moreno, the "father," dead instead of the child. The dreamer brought him back to life again. Indeed, the dreamer evidently wanted to save both father *and* child; this was the reason why she worried about her dreams.

A dream followed in the same night, where the "father" of the Half-Way House is not dead, but mad; or, as one of the discussants pointed out, "half-dead." The dreamer volunteered to help the father. On her own request, she now made sure the father would get well.

A final and later dream shows a successful birth with a prematurely developed baby. Mother again volunteered to correct this dream; she wanted a "normal" baby all the way.

It was evident to all participants that Norma really wanted to have that second baby, and would be a wonderful mother for it.

The presentation of this hypothesis was accepted eagerly by the persons present and ended this session.

Grow Thin with Hypnotic Dreams

PAUL SACERDOTE, M.D.

In the course of experimenting with various utilizations of hundreds of hypnotically-induced dreams, it became quite evident to me that not every patient has the same intellectual ability or intuitive understanding of what the hypnotherapist is expecting of him and many a subject produces (or at least reports) only dreams which are linearly simple and which correspond to an almost direct translation of a wish-fulfillment, without any apparent trace of latent dream-thoughts, of condensation, displacement, symbolism, or censorship.

Whatever the patient-dreamer is strongly desiring is immediately translated into a dream with at least one meaning which anybody can understand; in other words, often the latent dream and the manifest dream appear to be identical. This is especially true when the hypno-oneiric approach is being used therapeutically for a psychosomatic or purely somatic disturbance rather than for treatment of primarily neurotic or psychotic entities. In way of illustration, I shall begin with summaries and, at times, verbatim reports of a few dreams from patients for whom hypnosis was used to correct overweight.

A. OBESITY

An obese, elderly lady was told during the first and only hour of treatment under hypnosis,

Dr.: "The dream will now start; your left hand will stay up for the duration of the dream and then at the end of the dream, while you are still in trance, you will be telling me all about that dream. In the dream you will see yourself having some very pleasant experiences, nice and slim as you want to be. What the dream will really be all about, it will be your own affair."

After the conjugated rapid eye movements had started, she reported: "I am in Paris, and then on the Riviera, and I am dancing and dancing and dancing; and then I went shopping and, oh! it is so wonderful to get into clothes, size 10, and I had such a wonderful time!!"

"Oh, it is so nice to be thin!"

"I can't believe it. No. I just can't; I went shopping today and the clothes are so beautiful."

A second dream during the same hour runs:

"Oh, it is so wonderful, so wonderful to be thin! Now I am on the beach and people are saying, 'What happened? Who are you? I don't recognize you.' I am just walking up and down on the beach and it is such fun; it is wonderful! Oh, I love the bathing suit!! I never could wear a bathing suit! Oh, that man! I do want to go dancing tonight!"

"Now I am on a ship. And the music is beautiful! Oh, it is such fun! Why did I not get thin before? I have such energy. We are all going to dance all night. Oh, this ship is beautiful! Oh, it is so nice to be thin; I love it!"

Still another dream a few minutes later:

"Now I am in Bermuda. Oh, I did not think I could get up in that carriage. But I'm just so light, I think the wind will blow me away, and I am so excited; everything looks so pretty! I feel so pretty!"

Another dream, induced in the course of this same hour for the purpose of reinforcing the new pattern of behavior brings the patient back to a cruise ship. In fact, the dream becomes so lively that it gradually changes into a full hallucination:

"No, thank you, I don't care for any! I know it is silly to be on a cruise and not eat, but I'm not hungry. No, I'd rather read or play Scrabble!"

"I don't know why; why I took this cruise, because there is so much food and I don't care for it, and I don't need it, and I'm not hungry."

"I can't believe it! I used to eat all the time and now I'm not hungry! Oh, yes, I feel wonderful, but I don't think I'll take a cruise; I'll fly, where there is no food. I suppose the dancing will keep me busy. Oh, it is such a nice world!!"

"That's enough! It is pretty, but does not mean a thing to me. I don't know how people can eat it. How could they eat that much food? You would think it would make them sick. No, I've had enough, thank you. A little piece of steak and a salad, that's enough. I don't really even need that, but I should, I suppose."

"Thank you, I feel so full of pep, I'm not so tired. Oh, I'm never going to eat again, I don't think, never; I'll see you next year." At this point, she sighs.

While the hypnotherapy in this case was not limited exclusively to the induction of the dreams just reported, it is remarkable that this particular patient, after only one hour of hypnotherapy, underwent such a radical and permanent change of her eating habits that she needed no further sessions: she became slim and remained slim.

The following is a dream from a shy, myopic, obese teenager who had unsuccessfully been struggling with her overweight and with other physical and emotional handicaps for several years, and who considered herself, and justifiably so, I may add, an "ugly duckling."

"I dreamt I was jumping off a raft. It was summer and I was in a bathing suit and I looked real good; and then I dreamt I was in school and I had on a tight skirt, size 7, and all the kids were shocked because I looked so good."

Following the second dream the patient reports another one:

"I am a counselor at camp, and all the counselors at camp get together and vote me the most popular girl there for appearance and also the best-liked. And then one counselor asked me to the movies: *he's real nice;* and then a couple of the other ones asked me later."

"It is summer: went swimming, boating, and even the other girl-counselors admired me. They said I had a nice figure and looked cute; and after the summer I went to a college-mixer and wore a pretty sheath and I met a handsome, real intelligent, educated boy, And it seems every time I went to a mixer I met someone very nice."

"I didn't have to cover my weight over with flared dresses so no one could tell. I didn't have trouble buying clothes in the winter (because they don't make any flared dresses). Then in the summer *I can* get real sweet clothes and none of them have to be fixed, repaired, or taken out, or changed in any way, except perhaps shortened. And twice when I went for jobs I looked older because I could wear older-looking clothes."

"I could go water-skiing, I was not ashamed on water-skis; I did not have to hide under a robe. I could just keep going like I was *flying over the ocean,* and then I could take up *horseback-riding* because I could wear slacks. I would not feel funny playing tennis out in the open or any game."

"I did not have to refuse going to the beach with anyone, I could go wherever I wanted to; I did not have to think up any phony excuse. I really used to be so ashamed before of being seen in a bathing suit."

In a later dream in the same hour:

"I am at the ball given by the school. I starved myself all day because we are having dinner there. My date notices how thin I am; he notices I lost weight. He never saw me before in anything that showed my weight, but still he saw that I looked slimmer."

"And I watched him drink a lot and I didn't drink as much as I usually did, because drinks are fattening; and it was very nice and I watched all my friends at the table eating like pigs. I didn't care what they ate, it did not matter, and I felt better than them all because they were only hurting themselves and I laughed at them all eating the ice-cream cake."

This young lady, too, solved the problems of her overweight with all the limitations that it had imposed not only on her social activities, but even on her entire life, after only two hours, the second one of which was almost entirely dedicated to utilizing a deep state of hypnosis for the induction of the pleasant wish-fulfilling oneiric experiences reported above.

In these two cases the dreams had—in my opinion—a large part in the rapid and successful achievement of the therapeutic aims: the elderly lady found that she was able to start living again; the young lady probably started to really live for the very first time in her life following the recognition of her hidden potentials.

I don't know if, in either of these two cases, associating either during or after the hypnotic sleep would have added to the success of the treatment, even if it had gained for the patients additional insight.

I do not deny the possibility that a variety of symbols and associations, some of them of a sexual nature, could have been looked for and discovered, but it is doubtful that this exploration and analysis would have served any useful purpose. It could, more likely, I suspect, have caused psychological harm; or at the very least, it might have interfered with a successful treatment.

The patients, by being induced to dream—and at times to hallucinate—some very vivid, pleasant, and highly desirable experiences, were able, much more than in their usual day-dreams or night-dreams, to visualize themselves after they had broken out of their shells, out of their old patterns of behavior. They were able to verbalize their repressed suffering and then to go on to experience the possibility that their present status, no matter how long it had been present, was not an inevitable "status quo." They succeeded, through only partially directed dreams, to recognize that their physique as well as their personality and their future life had tantalizing possibilities which were not beyond their reach.

No doubt every one of these dreams represented a clear example of wish-fulfillment, but the remarkable thing is that, once the dreams had been structured in the framework of the hypnotherapeutic relationship, they also became a way for the individual patient to communicate not only with the therapist, but also with herself and to experience the feeling of a *new body-image*. At the same time, insofar as the dreams were described to the therapist, they became a means of telling him: "Yes, I have accepted and recognized that what I wished to accomplish I can accomplish, and I know I am accomplishing. I see myself thin because I know that I can become thin, and I'm already becoming thin; it is no more a mere wish, it is a reality which I know I am achieving."

In recent years, among the most significant experiments in parapsychology have been those at the Division of Parapsychology and Psychophysics of Maimonides Medical Center in Brooklyn, New York.* The experiments are a combination of telepathy and clairvoyance involving a subject who sleeps all night in an isolated room, an agent who sits in another room during the night and concentrates on the details of a painting, and the experimenter who monitors an EEG machine in the control room. The agent

---

* Formerly the Dream Laboratory.

picks the painting at random each night from hundreds of such paintings on file at the laboratory, and only he knows which painting has been chosen. The experimenter, using the REM techniques, wakes up the dreamer during the REM periods and asks him to describe his dream, which is tape-recorded.

In the morning, when the sleeper has been awakened for the last time, he is asked to recall his dreams of the night. These dreams and those for subsequent nights are then reviewed by three outside judges, who decide whether the dreams of a given night correspond to the details of the painting used on that night. A statistical evaluation is then made of their judgments and the results are termed "significant" or not.

Following an initial study of several subjects, the best one, Dr. William Erwin, was chosen as the subject of a 12-night "dream telepathy" series. The results for three of the nights are described in the following article. The agent was Sol Feldstein.

The Influence of Telepathy
on Dream Content

MONTAGUE ULLMAN, STANLEY KRIPPNER, and ALAN VAUGHAN

On the first night, the randomly selected target was *Bedtime*, by Walter Keane, which portrays a girl with long, dark hair holding three puppies. The girl's eyes and those of the dogs have exaggerated pupils that seem to stare out at the viewer.

Erwin's dreams centered around "looking for something" and a "woman that had long hair, long black hair." This mild correspondence was given a mean rank of 3.7 by the judges, barely a "miss."

The next experimental night's target was *The Yellow Rabbi*, by Chagall. It depicts an elderly rabbi sitting at a table with a book in front of him. Here was a target that Feldstein, because of his orthodox Jewish background, could easily relate to. But how would Erwin, whose religious background was Protestant (Disciples of Christ) react?

In Erwin's second dream, a man was riding in a car with a woman. "He was a foreigner. . . . She was . . . in her forties. He was older—in his fifties. . . . He could have been in his sixties."

In his third dream, "someone asked me if he was actually a national figure . . . it has to do with, well, a feeling of older people. The name of Saint Paul came into my mind."

And in Erwin's fifth dream, "This doctor, Dr. Heimsdorf, is a professor in humanities and philosophy. He was sitting . . . and he was reading from a book. . . ."

Elaborating on his dreams in the morning, Erwin said, "So far, all I can say is that there is the feeling of older people. . . . The professor is an older man. He smoked a pipe, taught humanities as well as philosophy. He was an Anglican minister or priest."

These dreams seemed a direct hit. "A foreigner," "in his sixties," a professor sitting and reading from a book. Interestingly, the Jewish religious figure is transformed into a Christian religious figure, "Saint Paul" and "an Anglican minister or priest."

It should be added that in his dream report of the professor, Erwin mentioned the word "Maimonides," ostensibly referring to the hospital where the experiment was being conducted. The hospital, of course, is named after the Jewish sage and philosopher, Maimonides. This correspondence may well have been a coincidence, but, provocatively, this was the only night the word "Maimonides" had been referred to, during either of the first two studies. The judges gave the *Yellow Rabbi* the rank 1, a direct "hit."

On the third night, chance provided a contrast of religion in the target *The Sacrament of the Last Supper*, by Dali. The painting shows Christ at the center of a table surrounded by his twelve disciples. A glass of wine and a loaf of bread are on the table. In the background is the sea, and a fishing boat can be seen in the distance. While Feldstein was trying to associate to the target, Erwin began to dream.

His first dream was of "an ocean. . . . It had a strange beauty about it. . . ." In his second dream "boats come to mind. Fishing boats. Small-size fishing boats. . . . There was a picture in the Sea Fare Restaurant that came to mind. . . . It shows, oh, I'd say about a dozen or so men pulling a fishing boat ashore right after having returned from a catch."

In his third dream he was looking at a "Christmas catalog," and in his fourth dream he was talking to someone about why "a doctor becomes a doctor." His fifth dream reiterated the theme of doctors, reminding him of a painting, *The Physician*, and in his sixth dream he was in a doctor's office.

In his seventh dream he was in "a kitchen" and thinking about going to a restaurant, while in the eighth dream he was sampling spices and herbs in a grocery store. "Place to eat, food of different types."

In the morning, Erwin seemed to zero in on the target: "The fisherman dream makes me think of the Mediterranean area, perhaps even some sort of Biblical time. Right now my associations are of the fish and the loaf, or even the feeding of the multitudes. . . . Once again I think of Christmas. . . . Having to do with the ocean—water, fishermen, something in this area. . . ."

Erwin obliquely refers to "Christmas" and Christ's action of feeding the multitudes but seems to settle on the "doctor" or the "physician" as a symbol of Christ, who was often referred to as a physician or healer. This obliqueness may be due in part to Feldstein's difficulty in relating to the Christ figure. Erwin's other dream images contain direct references to the setting, "an ocean," "small-size fishing boats," "a dozen or so men," references to food and eating, the Mediterranean area in Biblical times, and even the loaf. The judges ranked this 1.3, a high "hit."

I. THE BIOLOGICAL NEED TO S
AND DREAM

The Effects of Sleep Deprivation

GAY GAER LUCE

WE HAVE all been exposed to anecdotal "proofs" that certain people can manage well without sleep—long vigils of sleepless performance by medical interns, the so-called charrette or 3-day drafting binge of the architect, a spate of remarkable incidents retold after World War II, famous "wakathons" endured by disc jockeys, and last year an 11-day stint of sleeplessness by a 17-year-old high school student in San Diego. Despite the lack of sleep the architects drafted winning plans, the interns treated the sick, the disc jockeys gave their usual performances, soldiers won battles—and after a night's sleep, we are told, they were fresh as ever. Studies performed at the Walter Reed Army Institute of Research, largely by Dr. Harold L. Williams and his associates, have told a discouraging story about a person's performance during prolonged wakefulness. Several of the famous wakathons were, at least in part, studied by scientists, and these too offer some disheartening information about the psychological effects of going without sleep for long periods, as well as raising questions about aftereffects. One disc jockey, with a record of some mental instability, went 7 days without sleep, endured persistent symptoms even after rest, and ended in a mental hospital, although a stable young high school student apparently recovered from a much longer stint with no noticeable aftereffects.

The mental symptoms of prolonged sleeplessness seem to occur slowly, in a somewhat predictable fashion, mounting, as the time goes on, sometimes into very dramatic proportions. At Walter Reed and elsewhere one of the most consistent observations was the progressive unevenness of mental functioning, lapses in attention, growing fatigue, weariness, and a tendency to withdraw from the outside world. People began to make fewer and fewer unnecessary movements, and showed some confusion between their own thoughts and external events. Certain bodily sensations began to develop. A tightness around the head gave the impression that a hat was being worn. Many complained that their eyes burned or itched and their vision was blurred, after 30–60 hours of sleeplessness people had difficulty with depth perception. Small objects seemed to dart out of place, and chairs changed apparent size. Commonly, lights seemed to wear a halo of fog. Even the floor seemed to undulate. By 90 hours, some people developed vivid hallucinations. One volunteer, for instance, called for help in washing the cobwebs from his face and hands. Brief dreams would intrude and become confused with reality, and people found their time sense distorted. These symptoms, along with changes of mood and deterioration in performance, were disturbing enough, and were recorded in detail in the definitive Walter Reed studies that did not extend the sleep starvation beyond 98 hours (Williams, Lubin, and Goodnow). If the sleep-loss is protracted beyond 100 or 200 hours, however, it appears that the symptoms intensify and begin to resemble psychosis. The fifth day has seemed to be a turning point in a number of cases observed (West et al., 1962).

TEMPORARY PSYCHOSIS

In January, 1959, the largely unaware public saw before its very eyes the kind of temporary psychosis that can be induced with sleep starvation. Under the supervision of doctors and scientists, Peter Tripp, a 32-year-old disc jockey, undertook to stay awake for 200 hours in a Times Square booth for the benefit of the March of Dimes. Throughout this marathon of over 8 days, Tripp was given medical and neurological examinations, tests of performance, psychological tests, and was closely attended by Drs. Harold L. Williams, Ardie Lubin, Louis Jolyon West, Harold Wolff, William C. Dement, and others. Although his experience was undoubtedly worsened by the tension of publicity and public conditions, some of the ordeals of Peter Tripp may indicate the kind of mental symptoms that can beleaguer the severely sleep starved.

Almost from the first, the desire to sleep was so strong that Tripp was fighting to keep himself awake. After little more than 2 days and 2 nights he began to have visual illusions; for example, he reported finding cobwebs in his shoes. By about 100 hours the simple daily tests that required only minimal mental agility and attention were a torture for him. He was having trouble remembering things, and his visual illusions were perturbing: he saw the tweed suit of one of the scientists as a suit of furry worms. After 120 hours he went across the street to a room in the Hotel Astor, where he periodically washed and changed clothes. He opened a bureau drawer and dashed out into the hall for help. The drawer, as he had seen it, was ablaze. Perhaps in an effort to explain this and other visions to himself he decided that the doctors had set the illusory fire, deliberately, to test him and frighten him. About this time he developed a habit of staring at the wall clock in the Times Square booth. As he later explained, the face of the clock bore the face of an actor friend, and he had begun to wonder whether he were Peter Tripp, or the friend whose face he saw in the clock. The daily tests were almost unendurable for Tripp and those who were studying him. "He looked liked a blind animal trying to feel his way through a maze." A simple algebraic formula that he had earlier solved with ease now required such superhuman effort that Tripp broke down, frightened at his inability to solve the problem, fighting to perform. Scientists saw the spectacle of a suave New York radio entertainer trying vainly to find his way through the alphabet.

By 170 hours the agony had become almost unbearable to watch. At times Tripp was no longer sure he was himself, and frequently tried to gain proof of his identity. Although he behaved as if he were awake, his brain wave patterns resembled those of sleep. In his psychotic delusions he was convinced that the doctors were in a conspiracy against him to send him to jail. On the last morning of his wakathon, Tripp was examined by Dr. Harold Wolff of Cornell. The late Dr. Wolff had a somewhat archaic manner of dress, and to Tripp he must have appeared funebrial. Tripp undressed, as requested, and lay down on the table for medical examination, but as he gazed up at the doctor he came to the gruesome decision that the man was actually an undertaker, about to bury him alive. With this grim insight, Tripp leapt for the door, and tore into the Astor hall with several doctors in pursuit. At the end of the 200 sleepless hours, nightmare hallucination and reality had merged, and he felt he was the victim of a sadistic conspiracy among the doctors.

With some persuasion, Tripp managed to make a final appearance in the glass-windowed booth in Times Square, and after his broadcast he went to sleep for 13 hours. Although the record of his ordeal covers hundreds of pages, the few instances cited here may give some indication of the extreme distortions, mental agonies, and delusions he suffered, especially during his last 100 hours of sleeplessness. When he awakened after his first long sleep the terrors, hallucinations, and mental deterioration had vanished. He no longer inhabited an unstable visual world where objects appeared to change size, where a doctor's tie would jump out of place, and where it was a superhuman effort to solve a simple problem or remember an anecdote. In 13 hours of sleep the nightmare existence had been left behind, although for 3 months afterward Tripp suffered a mild depression. Quite aside from the quick apparent recovery from extreme symptoms, there had been two extremely striking patterns throughout the ordeal, periodicities that suggested that Tripp's times of strength and moments of worst symptoms followed some inner cycles. Throughout the ordeal Tripp had been able to organize and perform his daily broadcast. Temperature readings showed that he was at his peak at the broadcast time, the point of his highest daily temperature. His bursts of hallucination and strange behaviors, on the other hand, seemed to occur in 90–120 minute intervals, at times when he might normally have been dreaming. At the time this periodicity suggested a possible physiological link between the mechanisms of dreaming, psychotic symptoms, and hallucination. In retrospect some of the observers feel that the most impressive changes were those that followed the diurnal cycle.

THE ROLE OF AGE

Six years ago, when Peter Tripp began his marathon of wakefulness, he was 32 years old. Last year, a 17-year-old high school student set out to break the record, and in the quiet atmosphere of his home, without the help of coffee or other stimulants, he stayed awake for 264 hours. Drs. L. C. Johnson, W. C. Dement, and J. J. Ross were on hand for observation and medical examination. Here there was quite a contrast to Tripp's wakathon.

Randy Gardner did, indeed, show progressive changes with sleep loss. By the fourth day he became irritable, suffered lapses of memory and difficulty in concentrating. He saw fog around street lights, felt the band of pressure of an illusory hat, and imagined a street sign to be a person. By the ninth day he seemed to think in a fragmented manner and often did not finish sentences, sometimes experiencing transient reveries. His eyes bothered him, and he became unsmiling and expressionless. At one point, about the fourth day, he had imagined himself a great Negro football player. He did not, however, show extreme symptoms, and at the end of 11 days, he slept for over 14 hours, and rebounded into a healthy and cheerful mood. During the last few days of his vigil, however, he had shown definite neurological changes. His vision was blurred, and his right eye was making involuntary sidewise movements. Whether his eyes were open or closed, his alpha rhythm was markedly reduced, and he showed waves characteristic of sleep. The usual alpha wave enhancement to external stimuli was no longer present. Physiological measures indicated that during deprivation the basal autonomic pattern was one of activation, but also that there was less responsiveness to outside stimuli. For example, during deprivation there was marked vasoconstriction. Randy's heart rate rose above normal. His skin temperature and electrical skin resistance were very low. As time went on these indices, which usually show changes in response to external events, became less and less responsive. When Randy finally went to sleep, however, all of these measures showed responses to external stimuli, save only the galvanic skin response. On the first night of sleep after his vigil, his EEG showed a different pattern than on successive nights. It contained a concentration of slow wave (stage 4) and stage 1 REM. Ten days after the vigil, Randy was clear of all symptoms except for slight difficulty with memory and involuntary eye movements (nystagmus) (Johnson, et al., 1965; Ross 1964).

These two very different individual reactions illustrate several important aspects of sleep loss that have been corroborated in other studies. Randy Gardner, by psychiatric measures, withstood his long vigil with greater ease and less effect than any of the people who had so far been recorded beyond 120 hours of sleep loss. His own home and the attendance of his own family physician provided surroundings that were less exacerbating than those of Peter Tripp or others, even on shorter vigils in the laboratory. He took no stimulants. But perhaps equally if not more important, were his youth and his general stability.

A person's reaction to prolonged wakefulness would appear to be congruent with his personality patterns and what might loosely be called stability. From interviews and psychiatric tests of 74 army volunteers in Walter Reed studies, researchers found they could predict reasonably well which individual would find the experience most difficult and would report hallucinatory events (Morris and Singer, 1961). Some years ago, at McGill University, six chronic schizophrenic patients were kept awake for 100 hours. As sleep loss continued these patients began to show acute symptoms that had not been seen for several years among them, auditory hallucinations (Koranyi and Lehman, 1960). The extent of a person's suffering under protracted sleep loss would seem to depend upon what we term mental health, and the six publicly recorded wakathons that have been undergone in recent years seem to highlight the point that symptoms occur sooner, and with greater intensity, in unstable individuals. There is also some evidence, however, that age may be an important factor.

Randy Gardner, who set the record for a sleepless vigil, was the youngest person to attempt this stint. Further evidence that young creatures may withstand sleep loss for longer periods than older ones has come from the laboratory of Wilse B. Webb at the University of Florida. The finding was serendipitous because it arose from a rat study that was not designed to explore this point. Originally, the experimenters had designed a continuously rotating mesh wheel, two-thirds submerged in water, in order to keep rats alert without causing muscular exhaustion so that they would fall asleep instantly when placed in a recording cage. Rats avoid cold water, and the wheel moved slowly enough so that they would not fall in if they kept awake and moved very slightly. Because the original wheel was small, it could not carry a fully grown animal, and so the first experimental animals were very young, about 63 days old.

The experimenters expected the creatures to last atop the wheel for several days, but were surprised to see them maintain position day after day. Some lasted 27 days before they fell. This feat of wakefulness raised some interesting questions. How had the young rats managed to stay awake, continuously moving for 27 days? The experimenters speculated from other data that these flexible young animals had not yet formed rigid sleep patterns and were able to sneak short naps of a few seconds. The only way to corroborate this hunch was to obtain continuous EEG readings while they were astride the water wheel, and see if characteristic brain waves of sleep appeared in the record. It was technically impossible to obtain EEGs from rats 63 days old, for there was then no way of implanting electrodes into the small and delicate brain. The repeated experiment had to be conducted with other rats, whose brains could be implanted with tiny electrodes. The older rats were about 200 days old.

When these adults were placed upon the water wheel, however, they had no staying power. They fell off in 3 to 4 days. The experimenters immediately began testing rats of intermediate ages on the wheel. The animal's age was directly correlated with the number of days he would last upon the wheel (Webb, 1962). In order to gain some insight into this differential staying power, the experimenters developed techniques for implanting young animals. They have recently found that the young animals manage to spend a surprising amount of their time asleep. By running to one edge of the turning wheel they can then ride with it, catching a nap of 10–15 seconds before they must quickly move to avoid falling. By this maneuver, the experimenters have estimated the animals may spend a third of their time on the wheel asleep. They are evidently very tired by the time they leave the wheel; nevertheless, the young rats manage to spend long periods atop the wheel in this fashion, whereas the older rats cannot. It does seem, at present, that age bears some relation to the ability to withstand sleep loss, and this capacity may be associated with the ability to snatch brief naps, although the reasons may be multiple and related to metabolism, especially in rodents, and muscular vitality as well as "habits" of the nervous sytem.

PHYSIOLOGICAL CHANGES

Although next to nothing is known about the psychological changes that may be occurring in animals as they are deprived of sleep some changes have been observed (Webb, 1962; Kleitman, 1963). It is largely from animals that we have learned about the damages that sleep loss may induce in brain tissue. From histological studies of animals experimenters infer that there may be certain changes in human brain tissue during sleep loss. How these may vary with age is not known. The published case histories suggest that many of them must be reversible, and the recent study of Randy Gardner suggests that youth may be an advantage in recovering from sleep loss. It should be repeated, however, that subtle aftereffects, perhaps not noticeable to Randy or to a casual onlooker, persisted for 10 days, and perhaps months after the vigil. Aftereffects have been difficult to measure and evaluate in human beings, and the question of tissue damage is unanswered at present. Studies of sleep loss have been relatively few and recent, and the question of prolonged, perhaps even indefinite, aftereffects remains an unsettled one. There is no way of telling whether the severity of aftereffects may be in proportion to the pathological symptoms experienced during sleep starvation.

Perhaps it is worth citing a few of the animal experiments that have shed a little light on this question. As early as 1894 M. de Manaceine demonstrated that cerebral hemorrhages took place in puppies when they were kept awake to the point of death. Tissue damage in the cortex and frontal lobes was reported by Daddi in adult dogs kept awake, fatally, from 9–17 days. Nathaniel Kleitman kept puppies awake for 4–6 days, and many died. They, too, had suffered cerebral hemorrhages, and the number of red blood cells had dropped to about half of the normal count. Other changes in neural tissue were observed in sleep-deprived dogs by Legendre and Pieron, and these were shown to be reversible if the animals were allowed to sleep. Sleep-deprived rabbits showed cell changes in the spinal cord and brain stem, and so, depending upon the species, it might seem that some of the clinical signs observed during sleep deprivation come from cell changes in the cerebral cortex and brain stem. In some of the many animal experiments a single period of sleep restored the animal to normal after a moderate deprivation (Kleitman, 1963). However, nobody can be sure that a long period of sleeplessness or the habit of skimping on sleep for months or years will leave no permanent ill traces.

The Effects of Dream Deprivation

GAY GAER LUCE

During the mid-1950's, Dr. Dement, working with Dr. Charles Fisher at Mount Sinai Hospital in New York, began the first of a series of dream deprivation experiments. Volunteers, carefully observed and questioned, and under strict rules not to take alcohol or drugs or naps, were allowed to sleep their usual sleep in the laboratory—except for REM periods. At the first sign of rapid eye movement and EEG desynchronized pattern, the subject was awakened, then permitted to go back to sleep. For five successive nights the volunteers were awakened in this manner. Although they had gotten about 6 hours of sleep, some of them complained of psychological discomfort, began to eat more than usual, and suffered anxiety. One subject quit the study after several days in an apparent panic. This did not happen to the control subjects whose equivalent awakenings took place in non-REM periods (Dement, 1960). The initial study, which has since been reexecuted in many variations, created a great flare of excitement. It suggested that people needed to dream. Not only did deprived subjects complain of some psychological discomfort, but on each successive night they attempted to dream more often. After their stint of dream deprivation, when they slept undisturbed in the laboratory, they dreamed about 60 percent more than they had on baseline nights. They appeared to be making up for lost dreams.

Initially, the psychological facet of the need to dream captured the most attention. Deprive a person of his dreams, the study suggested, and he begins to suffer psychological abnormalities. This interpretation coincided nicely with Freud's theory that dreaming formed the safety valve of mankind, permitting an expression for the many drives and impulses that civilized man must repress. Many subsequent dream-deprivation studies have thrown this interpretation into question. Dement, himself, and many others have sometimes failed to notice any marked psychological changes even after more thorough and extended deprivation. But the need to dream—as expressed in ever increasing attempts to dream and in a huge and unambiguous orgy of compensatory REM time following deprivation —has been seen in every deprivation experiment, human or animal. Dr. Charles Sawyer and his associates at UCLA deprived rabbits of REM sleep by leaving them in a chamber where a hissing noise was continuously played. When the noise was turned off, the rabbits appeared to make up lost REM time with more frequent and longer REM periods. Dr. Michel Jouvet and his associates in Lyon have deprived cats of REM sleep for as long as 26 days. Subsequently allowed uninterrupted sleep, the cats spent about 60 percent of their time in the REM state and fell directly into that state from waking. This compensatory dreaming has been observed in people, among them dexedrine addicts and alcoholics who have been withdrawn from dream-suppressing drugs. It has been seen among the totally sleep deprived and among some psychotics after periods of reduced REM time. The need to dream appears to be uniform, or perhaps one should say, the need for REM sleep.

Today, with mounting evidence from animal studies, it appears that the need for REM sleep must be more than a psychological need. The dreaming of the REM state is a physiological as well as a psychological process. Indeed, it has been thought that the psychological disruptions observed in some volunteers after dream deprivation are actually the signals of a physical penalty that may have to be paid if the REM cycle is prevented for too long a time. Nevertheless, it is interesting that people have varied in their reactions in the several deprivation studies so far. The very fact that some people show effects and others do not raises questions that are germane to a wide variety of human studies in psychology, and may be worth examining as an instance of the uncertainties facing scientists within the broader context.

Why have some subjects felt anxious, empty, hungry, unable to concentrate, a few of them even extremely unsettled after a degree of REM loss that had no such effects upon subjects in other studies? Possibly, in some of the initial and short studies the experimenters did not see in their screening of volunteers that they were in a state of fatigue. Subjects may have been more anxious to begin with than was apparent on testing. There is another possibility, albeit unlikely. Sometimes even the most cautious experimenter may inadvertently reveal his expectations by cues so subtle that the subjects will live up to an expected role without even knowing they are doing so. This has been a pitfall in many studies of hypnosis, but it seems an unlikely explanation here, because animals deprived of REM sleep have shown pronounced behavioral symptoms.

Cats, deprived of their activated REM phase for long enough, show very bizarre behavior disorders. Cats have been deprived of REM sleep in several ways. They have been placed upon a stone or other object surrounded by water. This permitted them slow-wave sleep, but they would topple into cold water whenever their neck and head muscles relaxed at the onset of REM sleep. In some studies they have been awakened by an attendant and set upon their feet the moment their EEGs and muscle tonus signaled the onset of REM periods. Jouvet has observed distinctions between deprived and normal laboratory cats, even after moderate deprivation. The deprived animals were, in Jouvet's expression, tired, sad cats. Visitors to the Lyon laboratory were able to pick out cats who had been REM deprived a year earlier because they were so subdued and unaggressive. More recently, Dement and Jouvet have subjected cats to prolonged deprivation periods of 30–70 days. These cats have exhibited a variety of disturbances. Some have become "hungry," eating abnormally, restless and indiscriminately hypersexual. They have acted as if their basic drives were enhanced by the deprivation.

In studying human beings, the experimenters have always terminated the deprivation long before there were such abnormal signs out of apprehension that REM loss might cause irreversible damage. Dement and his associates have been studying cats under partial deprivation and severe deprivation to see whether there is damage to the nervous system. When a cat's nervous system is in any way "poisoned" there will be a discernible difference in its EEG after hearing a click. One of the tests for REM loss damage has been a series of recordings from the cochlear nucleus of cats. This is a first relay station for the sound impulse traveling upward in the brain. A first study has shown that the EEG response changes considerably in the REM deprived cats, returning to normal after the animal has been allowed REM sleep. Control animals, awakened on the same schedule as the deprived cats, showed no change in EEG response (Dewson et al., 1965). Other signs of altered sensitivity within regions of the brain may accompany REM loss, perhaps associated with biochemical changes. These may indeed be related to the behavioral changes noted.

Notwithstanding the animal studies, there have been several dream deprivation studies conducted with human volunteers, which have shown apparently conflicting results. Subjected to 5 days of REM deprivation, and not total deprivation at that, volunteers reported irritability, emptiness, anxiety and other symptoms (Dement, 1960). Yet a person in a later study conducted by the same experimenters, endured 13 consecutive nights of dream deprivation with few signs of changes.

More recently, Dement and his associates went through a grueling vigil in order to deprive three subjects of all REM sleep for 16 days. This time the subjects were awakened the moment muscle tone disappeared under the chin, an event that usually precedes the other signals of a REM period. After eight nights the first subject was trying to dream so often and it was so hard to wrestle him awake that it became impossible to deprive him of REM sleep without totally depriving him of sleep. He would start dreaming the moment he was allowed to close his eyes and fall asleep. The next volunteer was given dexedrine to suppress dreaming. He, too, began dreaming more and more often. Soon the investigators had to awaken him incessantly. By the 15th night he was dreaming as soon as he closed his eyes, a behavior seen among narcoleptics, certain psychotics, or after drug withdrawal. By this time he had changed from a taciturn, compunctious, moral person into a blue-streak talker, an unreliable subject, a man who wanted to sit in a nightclub without ordering drinks until he was thrown out. On his first night of recovery he dreamed 120 percent more than usual and reverted back to his normal self. The third subject showed a personality transformation after 14 nights of deprivation, and the experiment was terminated after 16 nights. On the next night he dreamed 160 percent more than his usual REM quota, and he, too reverted to his usual self (Dement, 1965).

Another subject deprived of dreams for 16 nights by Dement and Fisher had shown no psychotic symptoms, but he evinced obviously disturbed behavior, memory disturbances, time sense distortions, preoccupations, and an inability to work. He sat around in a stupor most of the day, yet when he was being tested or interviewed, he managed to mobilize his forces. This is probably an important issue in many psychological studies, for as everyone knows from experience, it is possible to be exhausted, distraught, and largely immobilized, yet summon up all one's resources at a critical moment and give a good performance.

The Need to Dream

WILLIAM DEMENT

Would it be possible for human beings to continue functioning normally if their dream life were completely or partially suppressed? Should dreaming be considered necessary in a psychological sense or a physiological sense or both?

The obvious attack on these problems was to study subjects who had somehow been deprived of the opportunity to dream. After a few unsuccessful preliminary trials with depressant drugs, it was decided to use the somewhat drastic method of awakening sleeping subjects immediately after the onset of dreaming and to continue this procedure throughout the night, so that each dream period would be artificially terminated right at its beginning.

SUBJECTS AND METHOD

The data in this article are from the first eight subjects in the research program, all males, ranging in age from 23 to 32. . . . Briefly, the subjects came to the laboratory at about their usual bedtime. Small silver-disk electrodes were carefully attached near their eyes and on their scalps, then the subjects went to sleep in a quiet, dark room in the laboratory. Lead wires ran from the electrodes to apparatus in an adjacent room upon which the electrical potentials of eye movements and brain waves were recorded continuously throughout the night.

Eye movements and brain waves of each subject were recorded throughout a series of undisturbed nights of sleep, to evaluate his base-line total nightly dream time and over-all sleep pattern. After this, recordings were made throughout a number of nights in which the subject was awakened by the experimenter every time the eye-movement and electroencephalographic recordings indicated that he had begun to dream. These "dream-deprivation" nights were always consecutive. Furthermore, the subjects were requested not to sleep at any other time. Obviously, if subjects were allowed to nap, or to sleep at home on any night in the dream-deprivation period, an unknown amount of dreaming would take place, offsetting the effects of the deprivation. On the first night immediately after the period of dream deprivation, and for several consecutive nights thereafter, the subject was allowed to sleep without disturbance. These nights were designated "recovery nights." The subject then had a varying number of nights off, after which he returned for another series of interrupted nights which exactly duplicated the dream-deprivation series in number of nights and number of awakenings per night. The only difference was that the subject was awakened in the intervals between eye-movement (dream) periods. Whenever a dream period began, the subject was allowed to sleep on without interruption, and was awakened only after the dream had ended spontaneously. Next, the subject had a number of recovery nights of undisturbed sleep equàl to the number of recovery nights in his original dream-deprivation series. Altogether, as many as 20 to 30 all-night recordings were made for each subject, most of them on consecutive nights. Since, for the most part, tests could be made on only one subject at a time, and since a minute-by-minute all-night vigil was required of the experimenter to catch each dream episode immediately at its onset, it can be understood why the experiments have been called arduous and time-consuming. . . .

The total number of base-line nights for the eight subjects was 40. The mean sleep time for the 40 nights was 7 hours and 2 minutes, the mean total nightly dream time was 82 minutes, and the mean percentage of dream time (total dream time to total sleep time $\times$ 100) was 19.4. Since total sleep time was not held absolutely constant, percentage figures were routinely calculated as a check on the possibility that differences in total nightly dream time were due to differences in total sleep time. Actually, this is not a plausible explanation for any but quite small differences in dream time, because the range of values for total sleep time for each subject turned out to be very narrow throughout the entire study. When averaged in terms of individuals rather than nights, the means were: total sleep time, 6 hours 50 minutes; total dream time, 80 minutes; percentage of dream time, 19.5; this indicates that the figures were not skewed by the disparate number of base-line nights per subject. The remarkable uniformity of the findings for individual nights is demonstrated by the fact that the standard deviation of the total nightly dream time was only plus or minus 7 minutes.

PROGRESSIVE INCREASE IN DREAM "ATTEMPTS"

The number of consecutive nights of dream deprivation arbitrarily selected as a condition of the study was five. However, one subject left the study in a flurry of obviously contrived excuses after only three nights, and two subjects insisted on stopping after four nights but consented to continue with the recovery nights and the remainder of the schedule. One subject was pushed to seven nights. During each awakening the subjects were required to sit up in bed and remain fully awake for several minutes. On the first nights of dream deprivation, the return to sleep generally initiated a new sleep cycle, and the next dream period was postponed for the expected amount of time. However, on subsequent nights the number of forced awakenings required to suppress dreaming steadily mounted Or, to put it another way, there was a progressive increase in the number of attempts to dream. . . . *All* the subjects showed this progressive increase, although there was considerable variation in the starting number and the amount of the increase. An important point is that each awakening was preceded by a minute or two of dreaming. This represented the time required for the experimenter to judge the emerging record and make the decision to awaken the subject after he first noticed the beginning of eye movements. In some cases the time was a little longer, as when an eye-movement period started while the experimenter was looking away from the recording apparatus. It is apparent from this that the method employed did not constitute absolute dream deprivation but, rather, about a 65- to 75-percent deprivation, as it turned out. . . .

NIGHTLY DREAM TIME ELEVATED AFTER DEPRIVATION

The mean total dream time on the first recovery night was 112 minutes, or 26.6 percent of the total mean sleep time. If the results for two subjects who did not show marked increases on the first recovery night are excluded, the mean dream time is 127 minutes or 29 percent, which represents a 50-percent increase over the group base-line mean. For all seven subjects together, on the first recovery night the increase in percentage of dream time over the base-line mean was significant. . . .

The number of consecutive recovery nights for each subject in this series of tests was too small in some cases, mainly because it was naively supposed at the beginning of the study that an increase in dream time, if it occurred, would last only one or two nights. One subject had only one recovery night, another two, and another three. The dream time was markedly elevated above the base-line on all these nights. For how many additional nights each of these three subjects would have maintained an elevation in dream time can only be surmised in the absence of objective data. All of the remaining four subjects had five consecutive recovery nights. One was the single subject who showed no increase, two were nearing the base-line dream time by the fifth night, and one still showed marked elevation in dream time. From this admittedly incomplete sample it appears that about five nights of increased dreaming usually follow four or five nights of dream suppression achieved by the method of this study.

EFFECT NOT DUE TO AWAKENING

Six of the subjects underwent the series of control awakenings—that is, awakenings during non-dream periods. This series exactly duplicated the dream-deprivation series for each subject in number of nights, total number of awakenings, and total number of awakenings for successive night. The dream time on these nights was slightly below base-line levels as a rule. The purpose of this series was, of course, to see if the findings following dream deprivation were solely an effect of the multiple awakenings. . . . There was no significant increase for the group. The mean dream time was 88 minutes, and the mean percentage was 20.1. Subsequent recovery nights in this series also failed to show the marked rise in dream time that was observed after nights of dream deprivation. A moderate increase found on four out of a total of 24 recovery nights for the individuals in the control-awakening group was felt to be a response to the slight reduction in dream time on control-awakening nights.

BEHAVIORAL CHANGES

Psychological disturbances such as anxiety, irritability, and difficulty in concentrating developed during the period of dream deprivation, but these were not catastrophic. One subject, as was mentioned above, quit the study in an apparent panic, and two subjects insisted on stopping one night short of the goal of five nights of dream deprivation, presumably because the stress was too great. At least one subject exhibited serious anxiety and agitation. Five subjects developed a marked increase in appetite during the period of dream deprivation; this observation was supported by daily weight measurements which showed a gain in weight of 3 to 5 pounds in three of the subjects. The psychological changes disappeared as soon as the subjects were allowed to dream. The most important fact was that *none* of the observed changes were seen during the period of control awakenings.

The results have been tentatively interpreted as indicating that a certain amount of dreaming each night is a necessity. It is as though a pressure to dream builds up with the accruing dream deficit during successive dream-deprivation nights—a pressure which is first evident in the increasing frequency of attempts to dream and then, during the recovery period, in the marked increase in total dream time and percentage of dream time. The fact that this increase may be maintained over four or more successive recovery nights suggests that there is a more or less quantitative compensation for the deficit. It is possible that if the dream suppression were carried on long enough, a serious disruption of the personality would result.

SOURCES

Abercrombie, John, *Inquiries concerning the Intellectual Powers and the Investigation of Truth.*

Adelson, Joseph, *Merrill-Palmer Quarterly*, vol. 6, Fall, 1969.

Adler, Alfred, *What Life Should Mean to You.*

Agnew, H. W., Jr., *Science*, vol. 168, April 3, 1970.

Allison, Truett, *Natural History*, February 1970.

Altshuler, Kenneth Z., *Archives of General Psychiatry*, vol. 8 (1), 1963.

Aristotle, *On Divination.*

Arnold, Sir Edwin, *The Light of Asia.*

Artemidorus, *The Interpretation of Dreams.*

Barad, Martin, *Archives of General Psychiatry*, vol. 8 (1), 1963.

Barmack, Joseph, *Science*, vol. 137, September 28, 1962.

Beradt, Charlotte, *The Third Reich of Dreams.*

Bettelheim, Bruno, *Ladies Home Journal*, February 1969.

Bible, The: Old Testament— Genesis, I Kings, Job, Jeremiah, Daniel; New Testament—Matthew.

Bland, Nathaniel, *Journal*, Royal Asiatic Society of Great Britain, vol. 16, 1853.

Boss, Medard, *The Analysis of Dreams.*

Brihadârmyaka-Upanishad, *Sacred Books of the East*, vol. 15.

Budge, E. A., Wallis, *Egyptian Magic.*

Butler, Samuel, quoted in *Such Stuff as Dreams*, Brian Hill, editor.

Caillois, Roger, *The Dream and Human Societies.*

Chuang Tzŭ, *Musings of a Chinese Mystic.*

Cicero, *On Divination.*

Coleridge, Samuel Taylor, *Literary Reminiscences*, A Letter to Thomas Wedgwood.

Coriat, Isador H., *Psychoanalytic Review*, vol. IV, 1917.

Davidson, Richard, Association for the Psychophysiological Study of Sleep, 1971.

De Becker, Raymond, *The Understanding of Dreams.*

Defoe, Daniel, *The History and Reality of Apparitions.*

Dement, William C., *The Journal of Experimental Psychology*, vol. 53, no. 5, 1957; vol. 55, no. 6, June 1958; *Science*, vol. 131, June 10, 1960; vol. 137, September 28, 1962; vol. 152, April 29, 1966.

De Quincey, Thomas, *Confessions of an English Opium-Eater.*

Domhoff, Bill, *Journal of Abnormal and Social Psychology*, vol. 66, no. 3, 1963; *Psychology Today*, June 1968.

Dunne, J. W., *An Experiment with Time.*

Ebon, Martin, *The Dream and Human Societies.*

Eggan, Dorothy, *American Anthropologist*, vol. 54 (4), 1952.

Emerson, Ralph Waldo, *Lectures and Biographical Sketches*, essay "Demonology."

Farber, Leslie H., *The Psychoanalytic Quarterly*, vol. 12, 1943.

Farrell, Ronald A., Association for the Psychophysiological Study of Sleep, 1971.

Fischer, Stuart, Association for the Psychophysiological Study of Sleep, 1971.

Fisher, Charles, *American Journal of Psychiatry*, vol. 116, 1960; *The Psychoanalytic Quarterly*, vol. 12, 1943; *Science*, vol. 137, September 28, 1962.

Foulkes, David, *The Psychology of Sleep; Psychological Bulletin*, vol. 62, no. 4, 1964.

Fox, Oliver, *The Occult Review*, vol. 31, no. 4, April 1920.

French, Thomas M., *The Journal of Psychology*, vol. 54, 1962.

Freud, Sigmund, *The Interpretation of Dreams*, translated and edited by James Strachey.

Fromm, Erika, *The Journal of Psychology*, vol. 54, 1962.

Goldfarb, Alvin, *Archives of General Psychiatry*, vol. 8 (1), 1963.

Green, Ceila, *Lucid Dreams.*

Greenhouse, Herbert B., articles written for *The New World of Dreams; Premonitions: A Leap into the Future.*

Griesinger, Wilhelm, *Mental Pathology and Therapeutics.*

Gurney, Edmund, *Phantasms of the Living.*

Gutheil, Emil A., *The Handbook of Dream Analysis.*

Hall, Calvin S., *The Meaning of Dreams; Journal of Abnormal and Social Psychology*, vol. 66, no. 3, 1963; *Psychology Today*, June 1968.

Hobbes, Thomas, *Leviathan.*

Hood, Thomas, quoted in *Such Stuff as Dreams*, Brian Hill, editor.

Hughes, William, *Journal of Humanistic Psychology*, vol. 10, no. 1, Spring, 1970.

Jung, Carl G., *Collected Papers on Analytical Psychology; The Integration of Personality; Memories, Dreams, Reflections.*

Kahn, Edwin, *Science*, vol. 137, September 28, 1962.

Keller, Helen, *The World I Live In.*

Kimmins, Charles W., *Children's Dreams.*

Klein, David Ballin, *Experimental Production of Dreams during Hypnosis—* Bulletin, University of Texas, 1930.

Kleitman, Nathaniel, *Journal of Experimental Psychology*, vol. 53, no. 5, 1957.

Krippner, Stanley, *Journal of Humanistic Psychology*, vol. 10, no. 1, Spring, 1970; Association for the Psychophysiological Study of Sleep, 1971; *Dream Telepathy.*

Krojanker, Rolf, *Group Psychotherapy*, vol. 15 (2), 1962.

Ladd, George Trumbull, *Mind*, April 1892.

Lamon, Ward Hill, *Recollections of Abraham Lincoln.*

Lenz, Geraldine, Association for the Psychophysiological Study of Sleep, 1971.

Lorand, Sandor, *International Journal of Psychoanalysis*, vol. 38, 1957.

Luborsky, Lester, *Journal of Abnormal and Social Psychology*, vol. 56, no. 2, March 1958.

Luce, Gay Gaer, *Current Research on Sleep and Dreams*, Public Health Service Publication no. 1389.

MacDougall, William, *The Pagan Tribes of Borneo*, vol. 2.

Mack, John E., *Nightmares and Human Conflict.*

MacNish, Robert, *Philosophy of Sleep.*

Maitland, Edward, quoted in *Such Stuff as Dreams*, Brian Hill, editor.
Malinowski, Bronislaw, *Sex and Repression in Savage Society*.
Mégroz, R. L., *The Dream World*.
Mendelson, Jack H., *American Journal of Psychiatry*, vol. 116, 1960.
Mitchell, S. Weir, *British Medical Journal*, December 1896, A Letter to Howard Pyle.
Muzio, Joseph N., *Science*, vol. 152, April 29, 1966.
Myers, F. W. H., *Phantasms of the Living; Human Personality and Its Survival of Bodily Death*.
Newbold, William Romaine, *Proceedings*, of Society for Psychical Research, vol. 12, 1896.
New York Post, May 18, 1970.
Oswald, Ian, *Sleeping and Waking*.
Plato, *The Republic; Phaedo*.
Podmore, Frank, *Phantasms of the Living*.
Pomerance, William, Association for the Psychophysiological Study of Sleep, 1971.
Posner, Norman, Association for the Psychophysiological Study of Sleep, 1971.
Rattray, R. S., *Religion and Art in the Ashanti*.
Roffwarg, Howard P., *Science*, vol. 152, April 29, 1966.
Sacerdote, Paul, *Induced Dreams*.
Scientific American, from "Science and the Citizen," May 1969.
Shevrin, Howard, *Journal of Abnormal and Social Psychology*, vol. 56, no. 2, March 1958.
Siger, Leonard, *American Journal of Psychiatry*, vol. 116, 1960.
Solomon, Philip, *American Journal of Psychiatry*, vol. 116, 1960.
Stekel, Wilhelm, *The Interpretation of Dreams*, vol. 2.
Stevenson, Robert Louis, *Across the Plains*.
Stewart, Walter A., *Psychoanalytic Quarterly*, vol. 36, (3), 1967.
Stoyva, Johann Martin, *Archives of General Psychiatry*, vol. 12, March 1965.
Strabo, *The Geography of Strabo*, vol. 6.
Synesius of Cyrene, *On Dreams*.
Taine, H. A., *On Intelligence*.
Taylor, Jeremy, *Sermons of*, Sermon 9.
Trillin, Calvin, *New Yorker*, September 18, 1965.
Tuke, Daniel Hack, *Sleepwalking and Hypnotism*.
Tylor, Sir Edward B., *Primitive Culture*, vol. 1.
Ullman, Montague, *Dream Telepathy*.
Van de Castle, Robert L., *The Psychology of Dreaming*.
Van Twyver, Henry, *Natural History*, February 1970.
Vaughan, Alan, *Dream Telepathy*.
Webb, W. B., *Science*, vol. 168, April 2, 1970.
Winget, Carolyn, Association for the Psychophysiological Study of Sleep, 1971.
Wolpert, Edward A., *Journal of Experimental Psychology*, vol. 55, no. 6, June 1958.
Woods, Ralph L., *The World of Dreams*.
Wundt, Wilhelm, *Outlines of Psychology*.

INDEX OF
DREAMS AND DREAMERS

INDEX OF
DREAM THEORIES

437